Praise for *When a Billion Chinese Jump*

"This is the book on China and climate change that the West has been waiting for. Watts uses his long experience of China to track the country's environmental calamity up close, uncovering its causes, its contradictions and its shocking human toll. Then he poses perhaps the most seminal question of all—can it save itself and, by extension, the planet?"

—James Kynge, author of *China Shakes the World*

"The world's chance of avoiding catastrophic climate change rests in large part with decisions being made today in Beijing. If China raises its standard of living to Western standards without controlling the emissions from industry and power plants, it will wreak havoc with the world's climate—with unforeseeable and irreversible consequences. If it takes the road now opening up to a low-carbon economy and leads the world in developing and deploying clean energy technologies, it can show the way to a sustainable future for the planet. Jonathan Watts turns a keen eye on China's choices—previously made and yet to come—that will affect us all."

—Timothy E. Wirth, president, United Nations Foundation and Better World Fund

"Jonathan Watts brings us up to date on China's economic miracle and the environmental consequences not only for China but for the entire world. With wonderful travelogue-like writing, Watts takes us on an incredible journey through today's China—and our tomorrow."

—Lester R. Brown, president of Earth Policy Institute and author of *Plan B 4.0: Mobilizing to Save Civilization*

"This is the environmental book that I am most looking forward to for 2010. I admire Jonathan Watts for his rigorous approach to journalism and his devotion to human stories at the grass roots."

—Ma Jun, founder of the Institute of Public and Environmental Affairs and author of *China's Water Crisis*

When a Billion Chinese Jump

How China Will Save Mankind—Or Destroy It

Jonathan Watts

Scribner

New York   London   Toronto   Sydney

SCRIBNER

A Division of Simon & Schuster, Inc.
1230 Avenue of the Americas
New York, NY 10020

For information about special discounts for bulk purchases, please contact Simon &
Schuster Special Sales at 1-866-506-1949 or business@simonandschuster.com.

The Simon & Schuster Speakers Bureau can bring authors to your live event. For more
information or to book an event contact the Simon & Schuster Speakers Bureau at
1-866-248-3049 or visit our website at www.simonspeakers.com.

Designed by Carla Jayne Jones

Manufactured in the United States of America

1   3   5   7   9   10   8   6   4   2

Library of Congress Control Number: 2010029901

ISBN 978-1-4165-8076-8
ISBN 978-1-4391-4193-9 (ebook)

To Aimee, Emma, and Murray

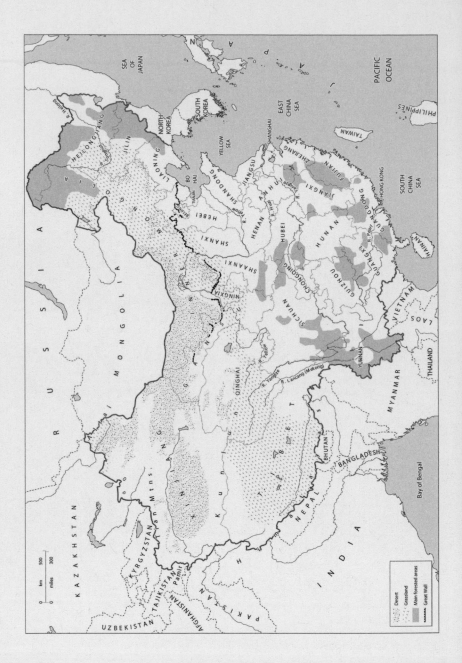

Contents

Contents

Beijing

As a child, I used to pray for China. It was a profoundly selfish prayer. Lying in bed, fingers clasped together, I would reel off the same wish list every night: "Dear Father, thank you for all the good things in my life. Please look after Mum and Dad, Lisa (my sister), Nana, and Papa, Toby (my dog), my friends (and here I would list whoever I was mates with at the time), and me." After this roll call, the sign-off was usually the same. "And please make the world peaceful. Please help all the poor and hungry people, and please make sure everyone in China doesn't jump at the same time."

That last wish was tagged on after I realized the enormousness of the country on the other side of the world. For a small British boy growing up in a suburb of an island nation in the 1970s, it was not easy to grasp the scale of China. I was fascinated that the country would soon be home to a billion people.[1] I loved numbers, especially big ones. But what did a billion mean? An adult explained with a terrifying illustration I have never forgotten. "If everyone in China jumps at exactly the same time, it will shake the earth off its axis and kill us all."[2]

I was a born worrier and this made me more anxious than anything I had heard before. For the first time, my young mind came to grips with the possibility of being killed by people I had never seen, who didn't know I existed, and who didn't even need a gun. I was powerless to do anything about it. This seemed both unfair and dangerous. It was an accident waiting to happen. Somebody had to do something!

Life suddenly seemed more precarious than I had ever imagined. In variations of my prayer, I asked God to make sure that if Chinese people had to jump, they only did it alone or in small groups. But in time, my anxieties faded. With all the extra maturity that comes from turning six years old, I realized it was childish nonsense.

I did not think about the apocalyptic jump again for almost thirty years. Then, in 2003, I moved to Beijing, where I discovered it is not only foolish little oiks who fear China leaping and the world shaking. In the interim, the poverty-stricken nation had transformed into an economic heavyweight and added an extra 400 million citizens. China was undergoing one of the greatest bursts of development in history and I arrived in the midst of it as Beijing prepared for the 2008 Olympics.

The city's transformation was vast and fast. Down went old *hutong* alleyways, courtyard houses, and the ancient city walls. Up rose futuristic stadiums, TV towers, airport terminals, and other monuments to modernization. Restaurants and bars one day were piles of rubble the next. Tens of thousands of old walls were daubed with the Chinese character *chai* (demolish). The hoardings around a nearby development site were decorated with giant pictures of the old city and a half-mocking, half-mournful slogan: "Our old town: Gone with the wind."

Living amid such a rapidly shifting landscape, it was hard to know whether to celebrate, commiserate, or simply gaze in awe. The scale and speed of change pushed everything to extremes. On one day, China looked to be emerging as a new superpower. The next, it appeared to be the blasted center of an environmental apocalypse. Most of the time, it was simply enshrouded in smog.

Soon after arriving, I walked home before dawn one morning in a haze so thick I felt completely alone in a city of 17 million people. The milky white air was strangely comforting. Skyscrapers had turned into thirty-story ghosts. The world seemed to have vanished. Yet it was also being remade. Overhead, cranes loomed out of the mist like skeletal giants.

Over the following years, the crane and the smog were to become synonymous in my mind with the two biggest challenges facing humanity: the rise of China and the damage being wrought on the global environment. The builders were constructing the most spectacular Olympic city in history. The chimney emissions and car exhausts were destroying the health of millions and helping to warm the planet as never before.

The year after my arrival, China's GDP overtook those of France and Italy. Another year of growth took it past that of Britain—the goal that

Mao Zedong had so disastrously set during the Great Leap Forward fifty years earlier. From 2003 to 2008, China stopped receiving aid from the World Food Programme and overtook the World Bank as the biggest investor in Africa. Its foreign-exchange reserves surpassed those of Japan as the largest in the world. The former basket-case nation completed the world's highest railway, the most powerful hydroelectric dam, launched a first manned space mission, and sent a probe to the moon.

This was a period in which the population increased at the rate of more than 7 million people per year, when more than 70 million people moved into cities, when GDP, industrial output, and production of cars doubled, when energy consumption and coal production jumped 50 percent, water use surged by 500 billion tons, and China became the biggest emitter of carbon in the world.[3]

As a parent, I worried for my two daughters' health when the air became so bad that their school would not let pupils out at break times. I feared too for my lungs. A regular jogger since my teens, I found myself wheezing and puffing after even a short run. When the coal fires started burning each winter, I suffered a dry, rasping cough that sometimes left me doubled up. In Beijing I was to suffer two bouts of pneumonia and, for the first time in my life, I was prescribed a steroid inhaler. The city was choking and so was I.

To be in early twenty-first-century China was to witness the climax of two hundred years of industrialization and urbanization, in close-up, playing at fast-forward on a continentwide screen. It soon became clear to me that China was the focal point of the world's environmental crisis. The decisions taken in Beijing, more than anywhere else, would determine whether humanity thrived or perished. After I arrived in Beijing, I was first horrified at the chaos and then excited. No other country was in such a mess. None had a greater incentive to change.

The environment had become a national security issue and the government started to respond. The leadership—the hydroengineer Hu Jintao and the geologist Wen Jiabao, or President Water and Premier Earth, as I came to think of them—started to shift the communist rhetoric from red to green. They wanted science to save nature. Instead of untrammeled economic expansion, they pledged sustainability. If their goals were achieved, China could emerge as the world's first green superpower. Alternatively, if they failed and the world's most populous nation continued to leap recklessly onward, our entire species could tip over the environmental precipice.

These were the extremes. The truth was probably somewhere in between—but where? That became the biggest question of my time in China. For the first five years as a news correspondent for the *Guardian,* the environment was my primary concern. After that it became such an obsession that I took six months off for private research trips and then returned to a new post as Asia environment specialist. Traveling more than 100,000 miles from the mountains of Tibet to the deserts of Inner Mongolia, I witnessed environmental tragedies, consumer excess, and inspiring dedication. I went to Shangri-La and Xanadu, along the Silk Road, down coal mines, through dump sites, and into numerous cancer villages. I saw the richest community, the most polluted city, and the foulest sea. On the way I talked to leading conservationists, politicians, lawyers, authors, and China's top experts on energy, glaciers, deserts, oceans, and the climate. Most compelling were the stories of ordinary people affected in extraordinary ways by a burst of human development and climate change the like of which the world had never seen before.

This, then, is a travelogue through a land obscured by smog and transformed by cranes; one that examines how rural environments are being affected by mass urban consumption. What are we losing and how? Where are the consequences? Can we fix them? It projects mankind's modern development on a Chinese screen.

Though the chapters progress through regions and themes, the structure is polemical rather than geographic. When I had to choose between a strong case study and a line on the map, I opted for the former even if that occasionally meant leapfrogging provinces, returning to some places twice, and cutting across boundaries. Lest anyone fear that I am asserting a new territorial claim by Dongbei on Inner Mongolia, or by the southeast on Chongqing, I should state their place in these pages is determined by the powerful trends they illustrate. Similarly, my apologies to anyone who feels slighted or frustrated by my selective approach. Omission of a province is not intended to dismiss its importance any more than inclusion is meant to indicate a paradigm case.

The choice of location and topics in these pages is determined purely by my own experience. Even over many years and miles, that is limited. China is simply too vast and changing too fast to capture in its entirety. Starting from the world's high, wild places and descending into the crowded polluted plains, the book tracks mankind's modern development and my own growing realization: now China has jumped, we must all rebalance our lives.

Southwest
Nature

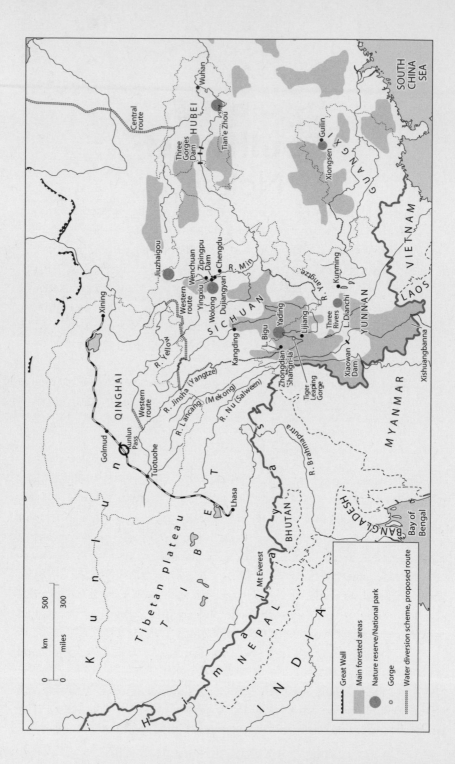

SOUTH CHINA SEA

Central route

Wuhan

HUBEI

Three Gorges Dam

Tian'e Zhou

Guilin

G U A N G X I

Xiongsen

Jiuzhaigou

Wenchuan

Zipingpu Dam

Chengdu

R. Min

Western route

Yingxiu

Wolong

Dujiangyan

Kunming

YUNNAN

Kangding

L. Dianchi

Three Rivers

Xining

Yading

Lijiang

L. Bigu

Zhongdian 'Shangri-la'

SICHUAN

R. Yellow

Tiger Leaping Gorge

Xiaowan Dam

R. Jinsha (Yangtze)

R. Lancang (Mekong)

R. Nu (Salween)

R. Yangtze

Xishuangbanna

Q I N G H A I

Golmud

Western route

Kunlun Pass

Tuotuohe

K u n l u n

VIETNAM

LAOS

M Y A N M A R

Lhasa

T   I   B   E   T

Mt Everest

R. Brahmaputra

BHUTAN

BANGLADESH

Bay of Bengal

Tibetan plateau

H i m a l a y a

N E P A L

I N D I A

km   500

miles   300

0

0

Great Wall

Main forested areas

Nature reserve/National park

Gorge

Water diversion scheme, proposed route

Useless Trees
Shangri-La

A man with a beard is respected. The same applies to mountains.
A person with a beard and hair is like a mountain covered with
forest and grass. In the same vein, a mountain sheltered in forest
and grass is like a person well clothed. A barren mountain is no
different from a naked person, exposing its flesh and bone. An
unsheltered mountain with poor soil painfully resembles a penniless
and rugged man.
—*Inscription on monument found in Yunnan, dated 1714*[1]

Paradise is no longer lost. According to the Chinese government, Shangri-La can be found at 28° north latitude, 99° east longitude, and an elevation of 3,300 meters at the foot of the Himalayas in northwest Yunnan Province. I started my journey at this self-proclaimed mountain idyll with the intention of working my way down and across China, tracking the progress of development on the way. Shangri-La seemed a fitting place to begin. Environmentalists considered it pristine, economists thought it backward. I planned to search here for natural and philosophical ideals, for untouched origins. But I may have arrived too late. Bumping along a dirt road through the mountains, I spied muddy hovels and forests spoiled by the blackened aftermath of logging teams. Gray drizzle doused a blaze of purple azaleas and white rhododendron shrubs. A track cut through a field of flowers to an alpine pool scarred on one side by the stumps of dozens of felled trees. The landscape, once one of the most stunning in China, had been violated.

For millennia, Bigu Lake in the heart of the region was protected by its remoteness. Although worshipped by local Tibetan communities, it was not mentioned in the extensive canons of Chinese literature. Government administrators and poetic wanderers rarely made it this far. It was too poor, too little known, too difficult to exploit.

All that changed in December 2001, when the Chinese authorities found a new way to sell northwest Yunnan's beauty: they renamed the region Shangri-La. As well as being a brilliant piece of marketing, the appropriation of a fictional Utopia dreamed up seventy years earlier on the other side of the world was a remarkable act of chutzpah for a government that was, in theory at least, communist, atheist, and scientifically oriented.

The tourist trickle quickly became a flood. Road builders, dam makers, and hotel operators added to the height of the swell. Beauty was marketed as fantasy, often with disastrous consequences. When the Oscar-nominated filmmaker Chen Kaige wanted a spectacular location for a new kung fu blockbuster, *The Promise,* he came to Bigu Lake and completely reconfigured the idyllic landscape. With the enthusiastic support of the local government, the director's team built a road through the field of azaleas, drove 100 piles into the lake for a bridge, and erected a five-story "Flower House" for the love scenes. Nobody took responsibility for the consequences.[2] After he ended shooting, the concrete-and-timber house was left dilapidated; the ground was strewn with plastic bags, polystyrene lunch boxes, and wine bottles. The lake was split in half by a bridge nobody needed. A temporary toilet and road besmirched the landscape, and locals demanded compensation for sheep that choked to death on the refuse.

I had come with one of the environmental activists who exposed the scandal and forced a cleanup. Zeren Pingcuo was a thickset Tibetan who worked as a nature photographer and conservationist. He was a man of few words, but what he said was usually to the point.

"Sacred places are no longer sacred," he said, showing me before-and-after pictures of development in which lakesides and pastureland quickly filled with tourists, cars, and hotels.

He showed me older pictures of his Himalayan home: breathtaking scenes of hillsides decked with azaleas in spring, lush green valleys in summer, a forest in glorious autumn reds and golds, and mountain snowscapes in winter. There were intimate portraits of Naxi children and Tibetan monks, and lively scenes from monasteries, markets, and festivals. That idyll had first been disturbed in the eighties and nineties by logging teams, then by tourism.

As our car climbed the steep mountain road, the destruction became more evident. Vast tracts of spruce forest were chopped and burned. The hillsides were filled with the blackened, stumpy corpses of trees and the withered brown saplings that were supposed to replace them but had failed to take.

"This all used to be virgin forest, but now it is an ecological war zone," said Zeren. "The timber companies came here and cleared the hillsides."

His home village of Jisha, which nestled in a high mountain valley, was suffering the results. He explained: "With less forest cover, there are fewer birds. With fewer birds there are more insects. And more insects means more damage to the crops."

Although many locals believed their home was Shambala—a form of heaven on earth—Zeren was no romantic about the past. Before development, life for locals was tough and often short. But, even among his own people, the long-term trends disturbed him.

"Tibetans have lived in harmony with nature for hundreds of years. But now we consume in a decade what we used to use in a century."

I too was here to get a taste of Shangri-La, albeit for work. I had come to look at beliefs. At the time, commentators in China complained their nation was mired in a grimy materialist mind-set that lacked an ideal of what a better world might look like. I wanted to see the alternatives. In such a diverse nation there were many: Taoism, Buddhism, Islam, Christianity, nature worship, romantic escapism, and political utopianism. Shangri-La seemed as good a place as any to start.

But as I soon came to realize, searching for paradise was a complicated business, particularly when there were furiously competing claims to be the "real" Shangri-La. The word first appeared in the 1933 fantasy *Lost Horizon* by the British novelist James Hilton. After a crash landing on the Tibetan Plateau, the Western survivors stumble across the idyll of Shangri-La:

> A strange and half-incredible sight . . . It was superb and exquisite. An austere emotion carried the eye upwards from milk-blue roofs to the gray rock bastion above . . . Beyond that, in a dazzling pyramid, soared the snow slopes of Karakal . . . the loveliest mountain on earth. (p. 66)

This resonated with visions of an earthly paradise found in other religions. The elements are remarkably consistent: fertility, diversity, color, tranquillity, and sparse, peaceful populations. These tropes form a baseline of sorts for man's ideal view of the world. In economic terms, paradise is a place where natural supply exceeds human demand, where there is plenty of everything.

Hilton's interwar fantasy was conceived not in southwest China but in northeast London, in Woodford Green, a Sunday afternoon's drive away from my home in Barnet. Hilton never revealed the source of his inspiration, but the closest the author ever got to the Himalayan or Kunlun ranges was Pakistan. His descriptions of the mountain Utopia were widely—though probably not accurately—believed to be based on scientific studies and *National Geographic* reports about Yunnan by the eccentric U.S. botanist-adventurer Joseph Rock.[3]

The Shangri-La myth of a land that could reseed human civilization after the planet was destroyed by war struck a chord in the 1930s, when development seemed geared only toward industrial destruction. After the award-winning Hollywood director Frank Capra released a film version in 1937, it became the ultimate escapist fantasy for a world on the brink of military conflict. Franklin D. Roosevelt named his newly converted presidential retreat in Maryland Shangri-La.[4]

Hilton's utopian dream was later transformed into a marketing gimmick. In 1992, Asia's biggest luxury hotel group was founded in Hong Kong with the Shangri-La name. Market research suggested that the majority of Western tourists to Tibet and Nepal came seeking a Shangri-La experience.[5] China's communist authorities started to take notice. Although the state had spent years dismissing Hilton's fantasies as romantic nonsense, local governments suddenly began competing with one another to be recognized as Shangri-La. The fiercer the rivalry, the more distorted the utopian ideal became.

I headed to Lijiang, Joseph Rock's base from 1922 to 1949. Like all of northwest Yunnan, the setting was idyllic. In the old town, traditional wood buildings sloped up the hillside, the Jade Dragon Snow Mountain towered in the distance, and the streets thronged with a colorful ethnic mix. The city was historically rich. Kublai Khan's troops crossed the river here. The Red Army passed through on their Long March. For decades, the spectacular setting, Naxi-minority architecture, and canal-lined streets attracted artists, writers, and adventurers. After 1996, when it was recognized as a UNESCO World Heritage Site, it became a fixture on the banana-pancake trail of foreign backpackers.[6] After the rebranding of northwest Yunnan as Shangri-La, this swelled into a wave of domestic travelers.[7]

Lijiang was a center of Dongba shamanistic culture. Its followers believed the overuse of natural resources would invite the wrath of heaven because man and nature were half brothers. This worship of nature was thought to have its roots in the ancient Bon spiritual tradition that was once the dominant belief system in the Himalayas and gave Tibetan Buddhism its animistic character, notably the worship of mountains and lakes. But those values had been marginalized by an influx of outsiders.

Wandering through the cobbled alleys in the afternoon, I saw flag-waving tour guides steer coachloads of Han—the ethnic majority in China—from trinket shop to trinket shop. In the evening I strolled along the raucous bar street by the canal. The picture-postcard scene of willow trees, limpid waters, and rough-hewn stone was illuminated by hundreds of red lanterns, neon signs, and the flashes of tourist cameras. The traditional wooden structures were packed to the rafters. Tourists joined girls in colorful Naxi costume in singing contests between balconies on either side of the stream. Some of the women claimed to be from the nearby Mosuo matriarchal community, where a tradition of "one-night marriages" has become synonymous with free love. Locals said they were really prostitutes from other parts of China who counterfeited the Mosuo image to lure customers. It was intellectual piracy, brand-name theft.

Sexual freedom was one of many fantasies on sale in Lijiang. The myth of Shangri-La was another. I went in search of the man who has done more than anyone to shape discussion of the lost paradise. Xuan Ke was not hard to find. Almost every night, he leads one of the planet's most remarkable orchestras. The Naxi Ancient Music Association plays to packed houses at every performance. With bright, flowing robes and wispy white beards, the orchestra members ambled slowly to their antique instruments like a council of wizards preparing to demonstrate their spells.

Xuan was their conductor. He was also a scholar, musician, raconteur, mission-school Christian, former political prisoner, and—according to his enemies—a self-promoting charlatan. He was a man with a story to tell. In 1957, during Mao Zedong's anti-rightist campaign, Xuan was put in prison along with his father, who was to die in jail. It was only after Mao's death that he was pardoned.

Since then, he has become a celebrity. The concert-hall audience lapped up his anecdotes about the hard times of the past. Between each piece, Xuan skillfully harangued Han Chinese and foreign tourists with criticism of contemporary politics sweetened by jokes about his orchestra's age and infirmity.

"I am seventy-seven years old. I have spent twenty-one of those years in jail. But I shouldn't talk about this for too long or our elder members might fall asleep at their instruments," he said, first in Putonghua and then in remarkably good English, to chuckles from the crowd.

After the performance, we waited for half an hour as he signed autographs and posed for photographs with a long line of fans. Over dinner, he told us how he was responsible for the "Shangrilazation" of northwest Yunnan.

Xuan's father was Rock's guide. Xuan remembered from childhood the eccentric U.S. botanist who traveled through the remotest areas with a full set of cutlery and a plastic bathtub. "Rock was a very hot-tempered man. He was short, with a loud voice and always shouting. I could hear his sopranolike voice at great distance. He used to quarrel about everything," Xuan recalled.

In 1995, when Xuan first made the link between Rock, Hilton, Shangri-La, and his mother's home in the neighboring county of Deqin, he was condemned by local officials, who said the idea of an otherworldly Oriental Utopia was a colonial concept. But when the Shangri-La myth started to draw in tourists and money, they quickly changed their tune.

Any community where Joseph Rock might conceivably have plonked his portable bathtub tried to cash in on the fantasy. In Yunnan, rival claims to be the inspiration for Shangri-La were made by Zhongdian and Lijiang. In Sichuan, the candidates were Daocheng, Jiuzhaigou, Xiangcheng, and Derong. In Gansu, it was Xiahe. A community in Pakistan's Hunza Valley claimed to have directly inspired Hilton on his visit there a few years before he wrote *Lost Horizon*. Others in Tibet, Bhutan, and Nepal claimed to be closer to the far older Buddhist concept of "Shambala," the Sanskrit word for spiritual Utopia, that some believe inspired the name of Hilton's hidden paradise.

In an ideal world, the competition could have been a test of which community was living in closest harmony with the environment. Reality was rather different. The contest in China was political, driven by greed and characterized by bribery, dubious academic research, and an overriding desire to attract millions of big-spending, high-consuming, paradise-seeking tourists. Zhongdian, the main town in Diqing prefecture, hosted a conference of journalists from all over the country. The reporters were lavishly wined and dined and, according to Xuan, each given two local beauties as company.[8]

"They used the trick of wine, women, and song to make the journalists write that this was Shangri-La, even though there was no such place. I taught them this strategy," he boasted proudly.

It got messy after 1997, when Zhongdian—which neither Hilton nor even Rock ever visited—unilaterally renamed itself Xianggelila, Shangri-La. The Xinhua News Agency wrote of "chaotic" battles between rival paradises. Xuan was inundated with demands and threats from mayors and governors, who wanted him to declare Zhongdian a fake.

"I was a little scared," he recalled. "Because I did not know the real Shangri-La. I had just read Hilton's book and watched the film."

With the contest starting to turn nasty, the central government stepped in. In December 2001, the State Council, the highest decision-making body in the government, declared the matter settled in a red-bannered document that ruled Zhongdian is Shangri-La.

Xuan laughed. "The stupid government changed the name into Shangri-La, even though it is only an ideal. It is not strictly speaking a village, or a county or even a place, but although it is not one hundred percent true, the renaming is still a good thing because it feeds people's ideals and dreams."

When I asked about the environmental impact, Xuan was less confident about the benefits of the renaming. He claimed logging was halted after Zhongdian became Shangri-La, but the water and air quality have deteriorated because of the influx of people.[9] The solution, he believed, was to raise the quality of the visitors. "If we can find such a place where many cultures and traditions can live harmoniously together, that should be enough. Why should we worry about water and air pollution?"

Such an attitude, I was beginning to realize, was a major challenge to conservation in China. In mainstream thought, Utopia was not about nature, it was about people.

Xuan was proud of his role. The benefits of Shangrilazation could be seen, he said, in the huge crowds that crushed through the city streets.[10] Business did well but he acknowledged that the town had become a less pleasant place to live. "It is so crowded and there are so many bars and cafes with loudspeakers playing music that I cannot sleep. So I made my old home into a hotel and moved my bed into the countryside."

Although the idea of a lost paradise echoes the biblical story of Eden, it's odd that the location of Shangri-La was so heavily influenced by three Christians: Rock, Hilton, and Xuan. Commentaries in the *People's Daily*, the Communist Party mouthpiece, routinely castigate Westerners for their dreamy view of Tibet.[11] But not only Westerners look to the Himalayas for ways of life that have been lost elsewhere. *Lost Horizon* became popular in the West during one of the most disruptive and frightening phases of industrialization. Even though he was writing on the other side of the world about a place he had never been, Hilton may have stumbled onto a yearning that is just as keenly felt in modern China as it was among the Western audience he wrote the novel for more than seventy years ago. Zhongdian initially adopted the name Shangri-La to attract wealthy foreigners, but most of the tourists in northwest Yunnan were Han Chinese. They came in search of a pristine environment and culture—an alternative to their homes in the modern megalopolises of Shanghai, Guangzhou, and Beijing. For some, it was a revelation. The Beijing-based activist Hu Jia told me he was inspired by the natural scenery and religious beliefs he found in these forests and mountains.[12] Others leave disappointed. "I spent six months meditating in a Tibetan monastery, but all I discovered was that the monks are as corrupt and lecherous as everybody else," lamented another Beijinger.

China had its own images of a lost paradise. The closest to Shangri-La is probably the myth of the Land of Peach Blossom. Set in the Eastern Jin dynasty (AD 317–420), this is the tale of a humble fisherman who wanders through a narrow cave to discover a hidden mountain-ringed Utopia. The inhabitants are descendants of war refugees from the Qin dynasty, who had lived undisturbed for hundreds of years in perfect harmony with each other and nature. The fisherman returns home to tell the story, but he is never again able to find the idyllic valley. The Land of Peach Blossom has become an ideal of beauty. Images of this land are painted in gorgeous colors on the Long Corridor of the Summer Palace in Beijing. It is also the inspiration for China's most innovative and influential landscape gardener,

Yu Kongjian, a young professor from Peking University who calls for his countrymen to seek the utility of nature, rather than repeating the mistakes made by emperors over thousands of years in trying to re-create its beauty artificially in decorative gardens.[13]

Ancient Chinese art and literature contains numerous other paeans to nature. As early as the Eastern Zhou period (700–256 BC), there was a saying: "People who are of ruling quality but are not able to respectfully preserve the forests, rivers, and marshes are not fit to become rulers."[14]

But more dominant philosophies have tended to stress the importance of ordering humanity and taming the wild. Under Confucianism, humanity's relationship was filial—man should honor nature as he respects a parent or a ruler. In this hierarchy, even the emperor was subservient and obliged to pay homage to the natural order at the temples of heaven, sun, moon, and earth. The fourth-century BC Confucian philosopher Mencius equated moral advancement with a better understanding of nature. But most Confucians emphasized society rather than the environment. Legalism, also known as Realism, took an even more hard-boiled approach. Its advocates believed the primary concern of a leader was to maximize the power of the state. The environment, like everything else, was sacrificed for this goal. Buddhism introduced the idea of reincarnation and respect for all living creatures. There is no duality between man and nature—they are one. But many believers also revere holy lakes and mountains, particularly in Tibet, where Buddhism is mixed with ancient Dongba traditions.

Taoists took an altogether more relaxed and anarchic approach that dismissed mankind's attempts to impose order on all-encompassing, endlessly mutable cosmos. The Tao is what changes rather than what man thinks it should be. Believers aim to get as close as possible to the natural world, to balance with it rather than to worship or rearrange it. Their closest term for nature was *ziran*, which conveys a sense of "spontaneous unfurling in which the earth is seen as a boundless generative organism"— a concept that has come to appeal in the modern age to the "deep green" eco-movement.[15] Its nonmaterialist outlook was best illustrated by the story of the Taoist sage Zhuangzi, who was dozing in the shade of a gnarled tree when a rival took the opportunity to pour scorn on his philosophy.

"Your teachings are as useless as this tree. None of its branches will produce a single straight plank. Nothing can be carved from its knotted grain," sneered the worldly critic.

Zhuangzi giggled. "Useless? Oh yes. I certainly hope so. You could plant this tree in a wasteland and still rest in its shadow, still eat its fruit. No axe will ever be sharpened to chop its trunk, no saw will ever trim its branches. If your teachings are more useful, you are the one who should worry."[16]

In ancient literature, Taoists envisaged a lost Utopia where everything had been in harmony. According to the Book of the Prince of Huainan, this cornucopia was made possible by the wisdom of the Three Emperors, who—according to myth—ruled 5,000 years ago at the dawn of Chinese civilization.[17] They were depicted as masters of restraint:

> The laws of the former kings did not permit the extermination of the whole herd or flock or the trapping of the young. They did not allow the draining of ponds to fish, the burning of woods to hunt, the spreading of nets in the wild prior to the autumn's wild dog sacrifice, the setting of nets in the water prior to the spring's otter sacrifice, the stretching of bird nets in valleys and river gorges before the autumn falconry, the logging of hill forests before the autumn shedding of leaves, the burning off of fields before the hibernating of the insects. They did not allow the killing of pregnant animals, the collecting of fledglings and bird eggs, the taking of fish less than a foot in length, or the consumption of piglets less than a year old. Thus grasses and trees billowed forth like rising steam, birds and animals rushed to their domains like a flowing spring, and birds of the air warmed to them like clouds of smoke because they had that which brought all this about.[18]

This expression of an ideal balance between man and nature was part of an ultimately unsuccessful polemic in a political battle. The Book of the Prince of Huainan was written at an intellectual turning point in China's history around 150 BC. The golden age of philosophy, which had produced Confucius, Mencius, Zhuangzi, and Lao-Tzu, had come to an end and the ideas of the greats were literally being fought over. The book, thought to have been compiled by the Taoist naturalist Liu An,[19] challenged many of the prevailing beliefs of the age. Liu advocated a rational, activist naturalism, a search for harmonious balance—or what we might today call sustainability. He redefined the central Taoist concept of *wuwei* from "no inteference" to "no interference contrary to nature."

But this led him into conflict with schools of Confucianism and Legalism, for whom the organization of human society took precedence.[20] Liu

An rose up in rebellion against his nephew, the Wu emperor, in 122 BC. When his army was crushed, so was the concept of Taoism he espoused.[21] This changed everything. If Liu An's rebellion had succeeded and he practiced as a ruler what he preached as a rebel, China might have had an ancient model of sustainability and a deeper reverence for nature. Instead, Confucianism, which is primarily a human-ordered view of society and nature, has dominated decision making ever since.

The tendency to control nature is pithily summed up by the environmental historian Mark Elvin, who writes: "Classical Chinese tradition is as hostile to forests as it is fond of trees."[22] In *Retreat of the Elephants*, Elvin traces how forests, wildlife, and ethnic minorities have been steadily pushed to mountain peripheries in China by what he calls 3,000 years of unsustainable development by the Han ethnic majority. In ancient times, he says, China had abundant forests and wildlife, including elephants as far north as Beijing, but relentless deforestation has followed the Han push to the south and west.[23]

Until the late 1990s, Yunnan contained many of nature's last great holdouts against human development. The province's name, which means South of the Clouds, encapsulates its remoteness. Historically, it has been a refuge. During the last ice age, the mountain gorges were among the few geological channels on earth where temperate animals and plants could survive, while most animals in Europe were wiped out.[24] Its remoteness kept it from the worst ravages of human development during the past two centuries. For novelists and filmmakers it became "The Land That Time Forgot." For conservationists and ethnologists it was, and still is, an ecological treasure house for species wiped out elsewhere.

The range of natural and human life in Yunnan is greater than anywhere else in China. The province covers 4 percent of the nation's land area, but it is home to more half of the country's vertebrates, higher plant species, and orchids as well as 72 percent of the country's endangered animals, many of which cannot be found anywhere else in the world.[25] Almost a third of the 42 million population are from ethnic minorities, including Tibetans, Naxi, Bai, and Miao. Ethnic and biological diversity were vital elements in any Shangri-La worthy of the name.

As the car carrying my assistant and me wound through the misty mountain road from Lijiang to Shangri-La, I saw why this area might be considered paradise on earth. Looking up, I could see the misty slopes of holy mountains that soar over 6,700 meters. Down below, I saw perilously deep ravines including the churning waters at Tiger Leaping Gorge. This was the gateway to the Three Parallel Rivers National Park, where three of Asia's great waterways—the Yangtze, Lancang (better known outside China as the Mekong), and the Nu (Salween)—run within fifty miles of each other. As they descend through mountains and foothills, these rivers had carved out spectacular canyons teeming with life. More than three-quarters of the area was carpeted with dense forest. Occasionally the wood gave way to precariously cultivated terraces, grassy plains, crystal streams or vast lakes. It was a spectacular land, sparsely peopled by farmers and monks.

I didn't need to be a botanist to see why conservationists get hot flashes about this place. A single gorge can be home to more varieties of life than are found in entire countries. The steep slopes that rise up from the Gangqu River are particularly abundant, ranging through six climatic zones from the subtropical in the moist, warm valley to the alpine in the cool and craggy peaks.

It is a living museum of biological history, a glorious reminder of what nature was capable of. Rhododendrons—ornamental garden shrubs else-where—grow here into gnarled Tolkienesque trees. Twelve percent of the animals, reptiles, and fish in Shangri-La are found nowhere else in the world. Thirty mammal species are "protected," including the musk deer, the Chinese screw mole, the black-necked crane, and the Yunnan Golden Monkey—until recently presumed extinct. Today, there are thought to be about 1,500 in the wild, roaming in a narrow strip of land between the Mekong and the Yangtze, mostly in Shangri-La. To satisfy tourists' hunger for novelty, locals reportedly drive these endangered animals from their mountain forest homes to the valley resorts below almost every day. So much for "protection."

The value of biodiversity is yet to be fully understood. There are at least 7,000 known plant species in this region, and many more as yet unidenti-fied. Yunnan's forests have proved to be a medicinal gold mine. The Hima-layan yew is important in the production of artemisinin, the drug identified by the World Health Organization as the best treatment for cerebral malaria, though Tibetans have known for centuries of the plant's healing power. Such "discoveries" were bad news for the forest. Two Himalayan yews had to be felled for each patient given a course of Taxol, one of the most effective treatments for breast and ovarian cancer. Villagers tried to stop the unsustainable plunder of their forest, but they were powerless against local businessmen and officials who worked on behalf of suppliers to the big pharmaceutical companies.

By the time we reached the Shangri-La tollbooth, dusk was already gathering in the mountain valley. My assistant was sleeping. I was groggy. We had been driving all day on Route 204 and the view was not always utopian, electricity pylons vying with the breathtaking gorges for dominance. I also spied a hydroelectric dam and the wreckage of three recent accidents, including a bus that had slipped into a ravine during the previous day's rains, killing the driver and more than a dozen passengers.

I had not expected paradise and tranquillity, but the first impression of Shangri-La was disappointing. No sooner had we passed through the giant red ornamental pillars of the tollbooth than we hit a construction site. A short drive on, Zhongdian was even less dreamlike. Like almost every other county town in China, it was filled with square buildings decorated with white tiles and tinted windows. The crowds and traffic seemed as far from nirvana as the signs for the Shangri-La branch of the Industrial and Commercial Bank of China and the Shangri-La headquarters of the Chinese Communist Party.

We checked into the Paradise Hotel, which was decorated with plastic azaleas. Its main feature was a pool that was rarely used because exercise is not recommended for visitors to an altitude of 3,300 meters. Nearby, an "old town" was being built almost from scratch. Carpenters were busy hewing timber beams and erecting curved roofs and tapering balustrades. Their work was part of a 300-million-yuan makeover aimed at making the town look less like Zhongdian and more like Shangri-La. The faux-antique decoration was the epitome of modernity. Some of the elegantly carved wooden buildings were already completed and full of trinket sellers offering fluffy yaks, prayer beads, and ceremonial daggers. On the new cobbled streets, black-market hawkers touted fake Rolex watches and Ray-Ban sunglasses.

We entered a Tibetan restaurant and ordered tsampa. Two beggars wandered from table to table asking for money. They got short shrift from the only other customers, a group of soldiers, who were reluctant to interrupt a drinking game that had one of them throwing up beside the table. "Don't bother us. Go and ask the foreigner for money," they said as they shooed the beggars away. Tired and grumpy after the long drive, I couldn't help feeling that the closer you got to Shangri-La, the farther away it seemed from Utopia.

I returned to the hotel dispirited, but other hotels guests were in a party mood. Next to my room, flashing red neon tubes illuminated the way to the Paradise karaoke bar, where hostesses were on offer for a fee: 100 yuan to sing together for an hour, 200 yuan for a shared dance, more for something extra. Shangri-La's attractions came in many forms.

At a hot-pot lunch the next day with A Wa, the chief of the local tourist bureau, I got a clear idea of the government's priorities: "We have two targets: promoting economic development and raising people's incomes, both of which we hope to achieve through tourism."

Between tasty bites of yak meat and mountain vegetables I had never seen before, A told me money and class would solve Zhongdian's environmental problems. The region aimed to attract more middle- and high-end tourists because they spend and consume more, yet waste and pollute less. This was the same environmental compromise sought by growth-obsessed governments across the world: it was the essence of the "pollute first, clear up later" outlook on development. But, I wondered aloud, didn't this still lead to the clearance of forests and grassland, the drawing of more water, and increased demand for timber, concrete, and other building materials? How could it be called a formula for sustainability? A answered that people's welfare was the priority.

Until recently, trees had taken the brunt of developmental stress. Yunnan's forest cover had halved since 1950.[26] Although the government introduced tight logging restrictions in 1998, just a few years later timber companies were felling 40 million square meters of forest, almost fifty times the permitted limit.[27] Since then, efforts to reverse the destruction had been compromised by Yunnan's shift toward cash crops. By the Burmese border, the ecologically rich tropical rain forests of Xishuangbanna— one of the last homes of elephants in China—were steadily being replaced by rubber and sugarcane plantations.[28] In Simao, ancient pines were felled for a project to convert 1.8 million hectares of land for fast-growing eucalyptus cultivation by Asia Pulp & Paper, the region's biggest tree chomper.

It was a poor long-term investment. Old forests were filled with life accumulated over thousands of years. Their biodiversity and vitality enabled them to cope with invasive species just as a body on a balanced diet is better able to withstand illness. The rows of new monoculture trees, however, were felled every ten years or so. Little life could be nourished beneath their temporary canopy and the trees often succumbed to the invading competitors. Not for nothing were these plantations called "green deserts."

Environmentalists believe we need to look back to move forward. Bob Moseley, an expert in alpine ecology who set up the Nature Conservancy's Yunnan programs, sees traditional beliefs and customs as the best hope for the sustainable management of the land and forests. This runs contrary to the prevailing wisdom in top-down, technocratic China, where poor, uneducated villagers are often blamed for gathering so much firewood that forests are depleted. Moseley has used repeat photography to back his counterargument. He collected more than a thousand old photographs of northwest Yunnan spanning 100 years and commissioned new pictures to be taken at the same spots. The comparisons suggest forest cover around indigenous communities has been constant—and in many cases increased—as a result of sensible limits on wood gathering and tree felling. In contrast, government-backed programs of old-growth cutting, clearance for rubber plantations, and forest conversion to monoculture have taken a heavy toll. His conclusion is that "millennia of accumulated ecological knowledge among local people has a lot to tell us about how to manage for biodiversity in the future."[29]

Chinese scholars recognize that indigenous groups have a better appreciation of "useless trees." Botanists and forestry experts at the Kunming Institute of Botany see the worship of holy mountains and trees as a means by which locals promote sustainability. From a study of Yunnan, they conclude that minorities take better care of nature than majorities.[30]

Historical documents show that the province had a system of elected forest guardians and logging quotas as far back as the Qing dynasty. The epigraph at the start of this chapter was inscribed on a monument in Yunnan from 1714. It appeals for the preservation of forest ecosystems in terms that sound very similar to those used by green activists today.[31]

> Everyone understands that only healthy green forests and fertile soil can nurture ever-flowing springs. None doubts the significance of those fundamental elements of nature, such as soil, water, and fire. Yet, do we know

it is the root of trees and forest that bring us water? It is for our benefit and fortune.

The mountains I saw in Yunnan were being stripped bare, but this time it was ice rather than forest cover that was disappearing. Glaciers were melting and retreating so fast that local monks blamed themselves for being insufficiently pious.[32] The forest and grasslands are also being overexploited for mushrooms. I had never imagined how huge this fungal industry was until I set out from Zhongdian to see another of the candidates that had fought the Shangri-La contest.

Yading, a few hundred kilometers north across the border with Sichuan Province, was the most remote yet. After we left the resort areas, the clouds lifted, the forest thickened, and the valley road climbed past brightly colored Tibetan farmhouses. People here were clearly making money. Many of the huge homes were newly built. Shafts of sunlight made the bare timber shine almost as brightly as the fresh paint.

They were paid for by the global mushroom economy. We saw our first roadside fungus hawkers an hour outside of Zhongdian. It was grueling work for the collectors: twelve hours a day scouring the hillsides for the slim, 2-centimeter stemlike protuberance that is all of the fruit that sticks out of the earth. On a good day, they said they could find five fungi that they could sell for about 15 yuan each.

Yunnan is home to 87 percent of all the fungi found in China.[33] With strong demand from overseas and more Chinese able to afford such exotica, northwest Yunnan and other Tibetan areas are in the midst of a fungal gold rush. The province's most lucrative agricultural export market was Matsutake pine mushrooms, prized in Japan for their fragrance and taste. Consumers in Tokyo and Kyoto were willing to pay up to 10,000 yen (US$110) for the best specimens.[34] Chinese consumers preferred the caterpillar fungus *Cordyceps sinensis,* which consumed its host, the ghost moth caterpillar, from inside out as it hibernated on the mountain grasslands. But rising demand and intense competition is driving foragers to collect earlier in the year, sometimes before the fungus has had time to release spores. This means it has no way to reproduce. Production has plummeted over the past twenty years, driving up the price of the fungus to almost twice the price of gold, gram for gram.[35] Many Chinese believe this ghoulish parasite, known in Tibetan as *yartsa gunbu,* or *bu,* is variously a cure for cancer, an aphrodisiac, and a tonic for long-distance runners.

During the two-month season in early summer, more than a million people comb the alpine hillsides for the "Himalayan Viagra," which could earn an adept picker more than most Chinese villagers earn in a year.[36] Mycologists warn that the fungus is threatened by massive, unsustainable harvesting. The grasslands are being trampled into dust. Scarcity has even led to gun battles and killings over prime fungal turf.[37] Parasite hunting is a hard and destructive way to make a living.

As the road climbed, the views became more spectacular, the people looked poorer, and the going got harder. Tarmac gave way to gravel, gravel to mud. The gradients got steeper and the roadside drops more perilous. Here and there we navigated the debris of recent landslides. Small puddles became extended stretches of mud. In most cars this would be the point to either turn back or get stuck. But our four-wheel drive ground onward and upward, skidding and squelching through the sludge.

Delays on these treacherous narrow roads sometimes lasted days when big vehicles broke down, causing backups for tens of miles. You could tell when a traffic jam was serious because drivers left their cabs and played cards at the side of the road. When it was really bad they gave up waiting altogether and returned to their cabs to sleep.

We stopped to try to help a bus that had been marooned all day on the steep, slippery mountain road. We towed and pushed and shoveled for more than an hour, but it would not budge. The passengers faced a night stuck on a hellish road while we headed off in search of another paradise. The rough going continued for several hours until the provincial boundary, where asphalt marked our transition from dirt-poor Yunnan to upwardly mobile Sichuan. Instead of bumping along at 15 kilometers per hour, we could cruise at 50.

The muzzy feeling in my temples told me we were picking up altitude as well as speed. We left the forests behind and the landscape grew bleaker and the air thinner. Just outside Sangdui Village we stopped to take in the view from a Tibetan stupa at a mountain pass. A sign said we had hit 4,500 meters. The wind blew hard and cold, the clouds looked close enough to touch, and the only sound was the tolling of yak bells. The desolate landscape of barren hills, rocky plains, and the odd patch of snow appeared unwelcoming, but it seemed closer than anywhere on our trip to Hilton's description of the Tibetan Plateau: "The loftiest and least hospitable part of the earth's surface . . . two miles high even in its lowest valleys, a vast, uninhabited and largely unexplored region of windswept upland."

After ten hours on the road, we hit Daocheng, a traditional Tibetan town. Monasteries and stupa dotted the bleak landscape, the words of a Buddhist incantation were written in giant stone characters on the hills, and every home had a shrine with a picture of the tenth Panchen Lama. The people here were obviously poor: their brightly colored clothes were ragged and many of the buildings looked as if they would provide little shelter against the cold of winter, when temperatures can plunge below minus 20°C.

We spent the night at the best hotel in town, which had no heating in the rooms and provided hot water only from 7 p.m. to midnight. The next morning my assistant greeted me with a wheeze and a raspy hello. She couldn't sleep well because of the thin air. The only vehicle we could hire was an old minivan. The suspension was so bad that we bumped and bounced even on good roads. On the dirt tracks, our teeth rattled and I had to grip a handle to stop my head from being jolted against the roof. At the first tollbooth, the battery died and I had to push-start the van.

Soon after, we neared our destination. The approach to this Shangri-La was similar to that described by Conway, the world-weary narrator of *Lost Horizon*:

> The mountain wall continued to drop nearly perpendicularly, into a cleft that could only have been the result of some cataclysm in the far past. The floor of the valley, hazily distant, welcomed the eye with greenness, sheltered from the winds and surveyed rather than dominated by the lamasery. It looked to Conway a delightfully favoured place.

The road plunged into a previously hidden gorge, and the landscape underwent a sudden, spectacular transformation. Bleak mountain slopes gave way to forest, fertile terracing, and a community of Tibetan homes and temples. Again, it was just as in the novel:

> The valley was nothing less than an enclosed paradise of amazing fertility, in which the vertical difference of a few thousand feet spanned the whole gulf between temperate and tropical.

Yading was not mentioned in any of my English guidebooks. Compared with Zhongdian and Lijiang, it was remote, spiritual, and—because of the altitude—disorienting. But this pilgrims' route was in the early stages of being harnessed to the tourist trail. New hotels were under construction. Women were arriving from faraway villages to work as waitresses, masseuses, and prostitutes. The local government planned to build a cable car up to one of the sacred sites. The party secretary of Yading, A Wangsiliang, a cheerful fellow with straggly, matted hair and a beaming smile, was optimistic. As well as being a communist, he was a Tibetan, a Buddhist, a caterpillar fungus collector, and a cautious convert to development.

"Our biggest source of happiness is the increase in tourists. Although their rubbish hurts the environment, they bring money," he said with an infectious grin. Even when I asked what the downside might be, he did not stop smiling. "Our main worry is that the authorities will seize our land to build hotels, just as they did in the other Shangri-La."

The town had just started a new pony-trekking business. We saddled up for a one-hour ride along the pilgrims' trail. It felt a little sacrilegious. This was a holy place. The trees were draped with scarves, the roadsides lined with cairns, and every few hundred meters there was a stack of slate etched with scriptures. Farther on we dismounted and climbed a steep slope to a jade-colored tarn. It was utterly tranquil. The only sound was the distant thunder of avalanches caused by melting snow on Xiannairi Mountain. Apart from a herder, who looked at me curiously as he passed by with a yak, and my interpreter, there was not a soul around. There was nothing to worry about, nothing to hurry toward. In this environment, even my Barnet cynicism seemed to fade. Shangri-La was not so daft after all. Imagining or chasing after a lost ideal was surely a positive human instinct. Hilton evoked the mood perfectly:

> There came over him, too, as he stared at that superb mountain, a glow of satisfaction that there were such places still left on earth, distant, inaccessible, as yet unhumanised.

I took a deep breath of the thin mountain air. I wanted to absorb the moment. It felt sublime, close to paradise. But my reverie was cut short when my assistant threw up. The altitude was taking its toll. She apologized, but I was the one who felt guilty. I had been too self-absorbed to notice the symptoms of mountain sickness. It was time to get back down to earth.

We drove down from the peaks as a thunderstorm ripped open the sky above the bleak Tibetan Plateau. After it passed, we hit Kangding, where work was under way on the world's second-highest airport, sited well above the snow line at 4,000 meters. This was not just south of the clouds, it was above them. Even on the runway, the planes would be halfway to their final cruising altitude. The airport was part of a huge new transport network that the Chinese government and neighboring states were putting in place to develop the entire Mekong region, encompassing Yunnan, Laos, Vietnam, Cambodia, and Burma. With the construction of roads and railways, asphalt and iron were piercing their way through mountains and forests. China's thirst for hydropower was driving developers into ever more remote areas of Yunnan.[38] The Mekong was being widened for container ships. With Yunnan's rivers marked out as a base for hydropower development, half a million people were due to be relocated over the following ten years, and ancient valley refuges for biodiversity were threatened with flooding.[39] Shangri-La was undergoing a transformation.

On our last day, we picked up a hitchhiker. Yezong Zuomu was a wrinkled, weatherbeaten Tibetan pilgrim who visited Yading each year to walk around the three sacred mountains in the hope that it would bring good fortune to her family. At sixty-seven, she had never talked to a foreigner before. I needed double interpretation—the driver from her Tibetan into Mandarin, and my assistant from Mandarin into English. Her story had to be repeated again and again because of the noise of the rattling van and the language problems, but it left me with a clear picture of the harshness of life at 3,500 meters, the old spirituality of the Tibetans, and the modern lure of material development.

Yezong's annual pilgrimage took weeks, but she carried no possessions apart from her prayer beads and a little food. The rest of the time she relied on the comfort of strangers. Every day, just before nightfall, she sought the charity of caterpillar fungus diggers, whose mountain shacks offered respite from the bitter winds that sliced across the Himalayan plains. Each dawn she set off again, chanting scriptures, fingering her prayer beads, and slowly trekking around the sacred mountain Xiannairi. The 6,032-meter peak was said to represent the closest Tibet had to a patron saint, Avalokiteshvara the Bodhisattva of Compassion. Buddhists believed a circuit of this mountain was worth chanting a hundred million scriptures.

For almost all of her life it had been thus for Yezong—living close to nature, close to the spiritual, and precariously close to starvation. Despite her poverty, such was the beauty of the landscape and the power of her belief that she, like many local people, felt she lived in Shambala, a spiritual paradise.

One of the fastest changes in world history had started to intrude. First came the new road, then the first cars. Homes were hooked up to the electricity grid. TV antennas were erected on the mountains, and the mobile phone network had expanded toward the peaks. Tourists began to appear in increasing numbers. The start of the commune's pony-trekking business gave Yezong's family an income for the first time in her life. Shambala had become Shangri-La. All within ten years.

It transformed her values. On her latest pilgrimage, Yezong said, she prayed as usual for a good harvest, her family's health, and peace. But when we set her down, Yezong revealed a new set of priorities as she bid us farewell.

"I will pray for all of you because you gave me a ride," she said. "And I will pray for more money. Money brings happiness."

I waved good-bye, grateful for the prayer and the company, but also wondering whether Yezong realized the impact that modernity would have on her, her community, and their way of life as development advanced into the world's formerly remote highlands. The protection of inaccessibility was disappearing. The baselines of beauty and diversity were shifting as migrants moved in and a young generation grew up unaware of the former wealth within the forests. Traditional values of sustainability were coming under new pressures. Man was crowding into almost every corner of the world. In ancient times, the poet Li Bai called the journey to the southwest "harder than the road to heaven." For me, the climb up to the world's roof had simply been a long, long drive. It would soon become even easier than that.

2

Foolish Old Men
The Tibetan Plateau

The strong moral conviction is growing up that in these days of
overcrowding the resources of the rich portions of the earth cannot
be allowed to run to waste in the hands of semi-civilised peoples
who will not develop them.
—*Francis Younghusband, British imperialist*[1]

There was once a foolish old man who could not bear the sight of two
mountains blocking the view outside his home. With the help of his
two sons, the old man started trying to move them. Every day, they took
rocks and pebbles from the slopes with the intention of dumping them in
the sea far away.

This astonishing sight caught the attention of a wise man, who laughed
scornfully, "You silly old fool! You are so decrepit that you can barely climb
to the peak, how do you imagine you can ever shift two huge mountains?"

Undaunted, the foolish old man replied, "After I die, my sons will carry
on. When they die, my grandchildren will keep up the work. My family
will grow and grow and the peak will get lower and lower. Why can't we
move the mountains?"

Having put the wise man in his place, the foolish old man returned to
his task, moving rocks through the hot summer and the cold winter with
his sons. God was so impressed by his determination that he sent two
angels down to carry away the mountains.

Every schoolchild in China is taught a version of this fable, known as

Yugong Yishan or "The Foolish Old Man Who Moved the Mountains." Written more than 400 years ago by the philosopher Li Yukou (also known as Liezi), the moral is that man can achieve anything with determination, time, and sufficient male offspring.

Mao Zedong loved the story and reinterpreted it to justify a war on nature and China's colonial enemies. For him, the two mountains were imperialism and feudalism:

> The Chinese Communist Party has long made up its mind to dig them up. We must persevere and work unceasingly, and we, too, will touch God's heart. Our God is none other than the masses of the Chinese people. If they stand up and dig together with us, why can't these two mountains be cleared away?[2]

For much of the past sixty years, the Chinese politburo has been trying to do just that. The ideological children and grandchildren of Mao are reengineering nature just as the Great Helmsman planned to build a stronger nation and liberate the population from supposedly backward traditions and foreign threats.

It required a very different way of thinking from that espoused by the philosopher dozing under a "useless tree" noted in the last chapter. But the mountain-moving mind-set has prevailed. I saw this on the Tibetan Plateau, where mankind's ambitions were pushed to the earth's limits.

"Aren't we Chinese great? They said it couldn't be done. And yet, we've not only done it, we've done it ahead of plan. No other country in the world could do this. Chinese people are so clever."

We were two hours, several beers, and half a roasted duck into a journey along the world's highest railway, the 1,900-kilometer line from Xining to Lhasa, the capital of Tibet. But my patriotic conversation partner, Wang Qiang, was just warming up on his favorite subject: China's engineering prowess.

"The new track follows the highway built by our soldiers in the 1950s. The terrain is so harsh that three of them died for every kilometer of road. You have to admire their spirit. But now, we've built the railway without the loss of a single life. Isn't China great?"

Wang, a stout and ruddy power-plant worker from Hunan, was in the bunk two below mine. He was as keen to demonstrate the conviviality of China as he was to wax lyrical about the country's strength. As well as cracking open a bottle of beer and sharing his food, he offered a packet of Dongfanghong cigarettes—"I smoke these because it was Mao's favorite brand"—and travel advice about the province we were passing through. "Actually there isn't much trouble in Qinghai. It's full of police and soldiers, but we have very good public order."

Wang was one of about sixty passengers squeezed into a "hard sleeper" carriage as our overnight train rattled toward the sunset, passing a half-visible rainbow, the world's largest saltwater lake, hillsides quilted with yellow rapeseed and the occasional white Tibetan yurt.

With a couple of hours left until lights out, my fellow travelers were looking for ways to kill time and forget the cramped and smoky conditions of our shared compartment. Some played cards, others sang with their children, a curious few chatted with a Tibetan monk. And when that entertainment ran out, several attempted to talk to me, the only Western face in the carriage.

They were engagingly friendly. A family from Xining poured a pot of instant noodles and offered sightseeing tips. A policeman who often traveled the route explained why the door to the "hard-seating-class carriage" was kept locked. Two young sightseers from Hong Kong shared their herbal remedies for altitude sickness and talked enviously about the pioneering character of the mainland.

"There is an amazing can-do spirit in China these days," said Susan Hong, a math teacher from the former British colony. "We used to have a bit of that in Hong Kong. But now we are so conservative compared to the mainland. Anything seems possible in China these days. It's very exciting."

But there was a dark side. As I got ready to turn in, Wang qualified the level of his friendliness. "I am happy to share food and drink with you. We are friends with all countries now, except Japan. If you were Japanese I would not share my food with you. And I would not let you sleep in the bunk above me."

A little drunk, he repeated the threat for the third time as I clambered up to my bed. It was almost the highest I had ever slept—both from the floor, which was about two meters below my third-tier bunk, and from sea level.

Perhaps it was the lack of oxygen or the frequent patrols by ticket inspectors, but I had trouble getting to sleep. My mind raced back across the contrasting impressions of the previous few hours: the warmth of my fellow passengers, the sometimes alarming nationalism of Wang, and the can-do spirit that had impressed the tourists from Hong Kong. Behind was Han China, the materialistic, modernizing, go-getting world of Wang. Ahead was Lhasa, the capital of what was once arguably the most spiritual, traditional, and remote land on the planet. In the former, nature was there to be conquered. In the latter, it was there to be worshipped. In my muzzy-headed state, the journey started to feel like something more than a simple ride along a track. It was a trip back in time, tracing human development in reverse. Or so it felt.

Brits should be cautious about high places. We are not used to them. Ben Nevis, at 1,433 meters the tallest mountain in Britain, would be a minor foothill in the Himalayas. Up on the roof of the world, it is all too easy to misjudge scale, to forget the sudden changes in the weather that occur that close to the clouds, and to be confused by the tricks that the mind and the body play when deprived of the usual amount of oxygen.

My background reading suggested that the rarefied air could go even further to a man's head when it was mixed with a desire for power. In 1903–4, Major Francis Younghusband, one of the most intriguing and ignominious figures in British imperial history, led a military mission into Tibet that turned into an invasion. Based in India, he was supposed to settle a border dispute near Sikkim. Instead, he marched 2,200 troops all the way to Lhasa, crushing any sign of opposition on the way. A museum in Gyantse depicts the massacre that took place there when Younghusband's Maxim guns and cavalry mowed down 700 monks in four minutes. The Tibetans, who were armed with nothing more than muskets and boulders, were cut down by bullets and swords even after they turned their backs and attempted to flee.[3] Even for imperial-era London, Younghusband's actions were considered excessive, as was the harsh indemnity that he imposed on the Dalai Lama. The terms were eased, but Britain maintained a presence in Tibet until 1947. Younghusband's "invasion" was to be Britain's last colonial adventure in Asia.

For the forty-year-old major, it was a turning point. The awe-inspiring sight of the Potala Palace, temples, and monasteries in Lhasa mixed with remorse in his oxygen-starved brain and set him suddenly on a spiritual quest. The experience, he wrote, "thrilled through me with overpowering intensity . . . Never again could I think evil, or ever be at enmity with any man. That single hour on leaving Lhasa was worth all the rest of a lifetime." After a period wandering the mountains and leading an ascetic life, he returned to Britain, helped found the World Council of Faiths, espoused the creation of a new religion, and advocated a doctrine of mystical beliefs and free love.[4]

Younghusband fascinated and appalled me. In conquering Tibet with a tiny army, he reached the peak of the British Empire and his own military career. On the way up, he was a hero; on the way down, a villain. Little wonder that he looked for an alternative direction with esoteric mysticism. The more I read about him, the more compelling was his story. A classically repressed Victorian with an imperial superiority complex as full as his walrus mustache, he was at various times a journalist, a guru, a war criminal, and a Great Game spy.

He was also a British version of the indomitable old man in Yugong Yishan. In his youth, Younghusband was the first European to travel overland from Beijing to India, en route crossing the Gobi Desert and the Himalayas. Toward the end of his life, he organized some of the first expeditions up Mount Everest. In between he attempted to explore the psychic realm, claimed there were extraterrestrial beings on a planet called Altair, and heretically called for a replacement religion for "puny and childish Christianity."

Judged by today's standards, Younghusband was an arrogant jingoist, who wrote in 1898 of "John Chinaman" failing to be a "perfect animal" and Indian Baltis as "a patient, docile, good-natured race whom one can hardly respect, but whom one cannot help liking in a compassionate, pitying way."[5]

His value system was based upon power: Superior races exploited nature. Inferior ones were condemned by their failure to do the same.

It was a common view at the height of the British Empire, where like all colonialists of the era and many Chinese today, the justification for conquest was civilization: the living standards of "less advanced" people would be raised slightly as partial compensation for stealing their natural resources. In Younghusband's philosophy this was an ethical imperative, as the epigraph to this chapter attests.

The self-righteousness of those who plunder resources continues today.

★

When it opened in 2006, the railway across the roof of the world was hailed by China as a means of improving the living standards of remote, undeveloped Tibet. Supporters of the Dalai Lama, the exiled spiritual leader of the region, condemned it as a political tool, a weapon of cultural genocide, and a means to suck natural resources from the Himalayas.[6]

The Sky Train is indisputably a triumph of engineering. At its maximum altitude in the Tanggula Pass, the track runs 5,072 meters above sea level, higher than Europe's greatest peak, Mont Blanc, and more than 200 meters above the Peruvian railway in the Andes, which was previously the world's most elevated track. Building a railway through this terrain required the blasting and building of seven tunnels and 286 bridges.

China's statistics are always mind-boggling and often unreliable, but they serve as the scripture of China's materialism, evidence of the powerful gospel of "Scientific Development." So was the speed at which the track was laid, three years ahead of the original seven-year schedule. For the disciples of the economic miracle, it was proof that China was overtaking the United States.

Like many other Chinese modern megaprojects, the Golmud-Lhasa railway is a realization of the dream of the ultimate mountain-moving man, Mao Zedong. As early as 1950, the chairman sent engineers to Tibet to look into the construction of a railway, and in 1973 he announced the project to the outside world.[7]

Construction began the following year on the first part of the route from Xining, the provincial capital of Qinghai Province, to Golmud, the garrison town in China's wild west. After it was completed in 1984, the engineers were stuck. For the next twenty years, this was the route to nowhere. Flanked by mountains, Golmud appeared as much of a dead end as the ocean.

It had been thought that no one could build a line any farther across the Tibetan Plateau, certainly not all the way to Tibet. It was too bleak, too cold, too high, too oxygen-starved. Even the best Swiss tunneling engineers concluded that it was impossible to bore through the rock and ice of the Kunlun mountain range. And if that was not impassable enough, even the flats were filled with perils. A meter or so below the surface was a layer of permafrost. Above that, a layer of ice that expanded or melted according to the season and time of day. How could tracks be laid on such an unstable surface? And how could a regular service be run in an area plagued by sandstorms in the summer and blizzards in the winter?

As the great train traveler and writer Paul Theroux notes in *Riding the Iron Rooster,* these obstacles protected the former Himalayan kingdom of Tibet from modernity:

> The main reason Tibet is so undeveloped and un-Chinese—and so thoroughly old-fangled and pleasant—is that it is the one great place in China that the railway has not reached. The Kunlun Range is a guarantee that the railway will never get to Lhasa. That is probably a good thing. I thought I liked railways until I saw Tibet, and then I realized that I liked wilderness much more.[8]

That was written in 1988. Less than two decades later those protective barriers were falling, though Tibet was still more inaccessible than almost anywhere else on earth. A World Bank study located the planet's most remote place in Tibet. The region was also home to much of the last 10 percent of the planet that was not within a 48-hour car, train, or speedboat ride of a city. The advent of the Sky Train will change that.[9]

The railway was a meeting of opposites. On one side was the heir of Mao's legacy, Hu Jintao, the engineer-president who preached a philosophy of "Scientific Development." When he opened the track, he celebrated it as a symbol of national progress and unity that would help to improve life in Tibet and draw it closer to the rest of China. On the other was the Dalai Lama, the political monk who advocated a philosophy of compassion and conservation. He warned that Tibet was threatened by cultural genocide as the railway brought more Han settlers, tourists, and businessmen. His support for development was tempered by his Buddhist concerns about the natural environment: "The world grows smaller and smaller, more and more interdependent . . . today more than ever before life must be characterised by a sense of universal responsibility, not only nation to nation and human to human, but also human to other forms of life."[10]

In the Western world, the train has been the subject of much hypocrisy. The British in India, the French in Africa, and the European settlers in North America built railway lines to subjugate indigenous populations, but when China did the same thing in Tibet, it was pilloried. This may be because of the strategic importance of the Himalayas. As early as 1889, another mustached British colonial, the writer Rudyard Kipling, noted with alarm: "What will happen when China really wakes up, runs a line from Shanghai to Lhasa . . . and really works and controls her own gun-factories and arsenals?"[11] The fact that Beijing has now done exactly that shows how global power has shifted.

Orientalist fantasies often reached absurd levels in Tibet. Adolf Hitler sent an expedition there in search of paranormal powers to strengthen the Third Reich and to make contact with the mythical kingdom of Shambala. More recently, a host of Hollywood stars have seen in Tibet the spiritual core missing from their homes in California. Steven Seagal was named a reincarnated lama, but he is far from alone in being mocked for an obsession with "Shangri-La-La Land."

Tibet has not always been associated with peace, spirituality, and remoteness. It once boasted an extensive empire that stretched through much of central Asia. At other times, it was invaded by Mongols, Manchus, Dzungars from Xinjiang, and Gurkhas from Nepal, and its leaders built alliances with Arabs, Turks, Indians, and Chinese. The first Europeans, a group of Portuguese missionaries, arrived in 1624. Buddhism was not native to the region; it was introduced either via China or Nepal or directly from India. Neither were monks necessarily peace-loving—the "Dobdobs" were the most famous of many bands of warriors based in monasteries that once fought for control of territory—nor are they necessarily any less tempted by money and power. Before 1959, 95 percent of the land was concentrated in the hands of 5 percent of the theocracy. Tibetan scholars have never claimed their land was Shangri-La.[12]

Chinese rule has brought very real economic and health benefits even as it has curtailed religious and political freedom.[13] The Xinhua News Agency, China Central TV, and the other organs of state propaganda insist Beijing's rule is not just benign, it is altruistic. Less often stated, but more crucial, is the strategic importance of the world's peaks and the mineral wealth they contain. Tibet covers an eighth of China's landmass and contains an abundance of valuable ores, including gold, lithium, copper, magnetite, uranium, borax, and lead. More important still, it is also the source of Asia's biggest rivers.

We were woken just before dawn as the train approached Golmud, from where we were to continue by car for a closer look at the plateau.

I was prepared for the worst. My Lonely Planet guidebook warned that this "forlorn outpost in the oblivion end of China" was set amid an eerie and inhospitable moonscape at 2,800 meters. Golmud did not disappoint. Desolate in the early morning gloom, this was clearly a frontier town for Han materialism. There were few signs of the indigenous Tibetan population and a high concentration of soldiers, miners, and police. Formerly a small trading post, this city of 200,000 had become a key supply point for the People's Liberation Army in Tibet. With the addition of potash production and oil drilling, Golmud had expanded rapidly to become the second-biggest city in Qinghai Province.

And with the railway, it was expected to grow further and faster. Development was evident everywhere. Many of the roads and buildings looked new, and there was a plethora of cranes and construction sites. The newest addition to the cityscape was a giant two-story TV screen blaring out advertisements for cosmetics and electrical goods. The city had become more hospitable too. Eight years ago when my guidebook was published, there had been only one hotel that would accept foreigners. Now there were several four-star inns, along with neon-lit streets of restaurants, pink-lit "massage parlors," and gaudy karaoke bars.

According to hotel staff, tourist numbers were rising, but most are en route to Tibet. With a few hours to kill, we went for breakfast with Zha Xi, a burly Tibetan and a member of the Wild Yak Brigade. This ragtag patrol of two dozen vigilantes had been formed to fight off poachers threatening the chiru (Tibetan antelope) and other endangered species. Their leader, a local government official named Sonam Dorjee, was killed in a gun battle with the hunters, becoming a martyr for the Chinese environmental movement. His exploits were mythologized by the award-winning film *Kekexili* (Mountain Patrol).

Over a bowl of noodles, Zha expressed mixed feelings about the pace of change on the plateau. "Overall, I think it is a good thing because this area is poor and isolated so people need more economic development. But it is bad for the environment. The railway is being built through the habitat of the chiru. They are very timid animals and they have been scared off by the construction work which goes on night and day."

Before setting off, we asked to be taken to the closest thing the city had to a museum, the former home of General Mu Shengzhong, who oversaw the construction of the road from Golmud to Lhasa in 1954.

He was the Younghusband of his day, an empire builder who believed in the duty of "advanced civilizations" to help more backward societies. He too led his country's first military intervention into Tibet in the guise of a diplomatic mission. In 1950, against a background of deadly fighting in other parts of the region, the general led 1,100 troops from the Eighteenth Army on a grueling overland march into Lhasa to reaffirm Chinese control. The fatalities are disputed. According to Tibetan accounts, 5,000 Tibetan soldiers were killed by the superior People's Liberation Army. The "peaceful liberation," as it is styled in Chinese history textbooks, resulted in envoys of the sixteen-year-old Dalai Lama signing a seventeen-point agreement affirming Chinese sovereignty in return for a promise of high autonomy.[14] The Tibetan leader later disavowed the arrangement completely.

To secure Beijing's control over the region, General Mu knew a road for his troops was more important than any document. In 1953, he was given 300,000 yuan, 1,500 kilograms of explosives, and 500 men to build the world's highest highway. He did it in a year. Tibet's remoteness had been breached. When the Dalai Lama led an uprising against Chinese rule in 1959, it was crushed by troops that flooded in on the road built by General Mu. Ever since, Tibetan policy has been determined in Beijing rather than Lhasa.

Almost as soon as I set out on the road that General Mu built, I saw a jarring sight: row upon row of freshly painted blue and gray single-story buildings in the middle of an otherwise empty and dusty plain outside Golmud. It was a new housing estate for thousands of Tibetan herders who had been resettled from the open spaces of the plateau, where their families had lived for generations, to a city built by Han soldiers. I asked some of the inhabitants what had happened.

Da Jie was the fifty-eight-year-old head of a family of eight. He had the weather-beaten face of a man who had spent his life roaming the plateau. He had been given a new home and a promise of 500 yuan a month for ten years in return for leaving the land. There was little choice or explanation. "Our leaders told us we must leave. They didn't tell us why. There is still plenty of grass on the plateau, but the land isn't ours—it belongs to the government," he told us. He and his family are coping, but the adjustment is huge. "I've herded animals all my life. I had more than a hundred sheep. Now I have no job."

They were environmental refugees, part of a nationwide resettlement of millions of people affected by climatic shifts, ecological stress, and politics. Most of the people in this housing estate formerly lived close to what was now the railway, which had led to forced relocation along other sections of the track, particularly near Lhasa. But it was not just the arrival of the train that forced the Tibetans in Golmud to give up their old way of life. Modernization, Sinicization, and climate change had also played a part in driving them off the land.

Nomads depended on grassland to feed their herds. But this fragile high-altitude ecosystem was degraded by China's and mankind's rush to develop. A moderate amount of grazing is good for grassland as it keeps the plants in check. But the balance between herd sizes and territory had been knocked out of synch by economic reforms and administrative policy set in distant Beijing. The deregulation of herd sizes in the early 1980s prompted nomads to buy as many goats, sheep, and yaks as they could afford. Subsequent policies that, for purposes of taxation, valued yaks four times as highly as sheep led to a surge in the numbers of the latter, which were far more damaging to the grasslands. The situation was not helped by a ban on polygamy that encouraged status-conscious Tibetan men to compensate for the loss of wives by increasing the size of their herds.[15]

As a result, wide areas of grassland were so overgrazed they turned to desert.[16] This was calamitous. Denuded of its thatch covering, the roof of the world was less able to absorb moisture and more likely to radiate heat. The result? The mountains of Tibet warmed more than any other part of China.

To make matters worse, the high Kunlun and Himalayan ranges acted as a chimney for water vapor to be convected high into the stratosphere instead of being trapped at a lower level and released as rain or snow. This was bad for several reasons: First, water vapor has a stronger greenhouse gas effect than carbon dioxide; second, its dispersal over a wider area potentially deprives arid areas of China of water; third, it contains pollution, dust, and black carbon, which create brown clouds that spread over the region.[17] Xiao Ziniu, the director general of the Beijing Climate Center, told me Tibet's climate was the most sensitive in Asia and impacted other parts of the globe. Changes in the soil here fed back rapidly into the atmosphere, affecting global air circulation just as rising ocean surface temperatures affected storm patterns.

Beijing's efforts to reverse these effects and restore grassland focused on resettling between 50 and 80 percent of the 2.25 million nomads on the Tibetan Plateau.[18] China's propaganda organs depicted the end of the nomadic way of life as a triumph. A Xinhua report claimed former Tibetan herders shed tears of joy on becoming the first generation of industrial workers. "Machines are now roaring on the pastureland where melodious pastorals used to be heard," the agency said.[19] Supporters of the Tibetan government in exile said the forced relocation of herders merely shifted the blame for grassland degradation and paved the way for exploitation of the region's mineral wealth.[20]

There was a checkpoint on the road ahead. A few days earlier, some foreign tourists had been turned back because they didn't have a special permit for Tibet. Neither did I. But on the advice of a friend familiar with the area, I had bought a long-peaked baseball cap before setting off. When the guards looked into the vehicle, I was napping in the back with the cap pulled far enough down to cover my big nose and Western face. It worked. There were no awkward questions about travel permits and we were allowed to drive on.

This was where engineers had started blasting and building the first of the seven tunnels and 286 bridges on the 1,110-kilometer stretch of the railway line. We climbed rapidly to the Kunlun Pass. At 4,776 meters, this was one of the great doorways to the top of the world. It was also the northern shore of a vast sea of permafrost that stretched more than 600 kilometers across the plateau toward Tibet and the Himalayas, prompting some to describe it as the third pole of the world. It was an apt term. The plateaus and the mountain ranges around it contained 37,000 glaciers, some of which were 700,000 years old.[21] Together they contained the largest body of ice outside of the Arctic and Antarctic.

This barrier had been considered impassable for a railway, but China's scientists believed they had overcome the challenge. Their big technological breakthrough was to insulate the track from the unstable surface above the permafrost. It was a huge challenge. Near the surface, the permafrost thawed every summer day and froze by night, dropping and lifting and turning the earth into mush and puddles. On a normal line this would buckle the rails, collapse bridges, and collapse tunnels. But for the new railway, engineers pumped cooling agents into the ground so the earth around the most vulnerable tunnels and pillars remained frozen and stable.

But there were doubts that even this ingenious and expensive solution would be enough to protect the track from the worst hazard affecting the plateau. Global warming was melting the permafrost faster than engineers had imagined. Temperatures on the Tibetan Plateau were rising three times faster than the global average.[22] If the trends continued, Chinese climatologists forecast a 3.4°C temperature rise by 2050, which would lead to a shrinking of the permafrost and a greater risk of the railway track buckling.[23]

There were other warnings that the thaw of the world's third ice cap was well under way. Yao Tandong, a professor of the China Academy of Sciences, told me glaciers in the region had been shrinking at the rate of four meters a year since he started monitoring them in 1989. The rate of retreat is accelerating.[24] A Greenpeace expedition found one of the world's most spectacular ice formations, a towering forest of seracs, some as tall as 20 meters, near Mount Everest base camp, had almost disappeared during the previous forty years.[25] The news horrified me. Though the seracs usually merited only a paragraph or two in the memoirs of explorers, the gnarled pillars of ice were one of the world's hidden treasures. Now they were almost gone.

I was to look more closely at the impact of climate change in Xinjiang (see chapter 12), but it was near the railway to Tibet that I first saw the problem up close. We took our 4 x 4 vehicle off the road to see one of the biggest glaciers on the route, the wall of ice wedged between two peaks near Dongdatan. It was a hard drive across broken rock and streams, then a short climb to the foot of the glacier. The bright sun had me sweating. The mountain also seemed to be perspiring. The heat had cut deep rivulets into the ice. As we drew closer, each crease in the ice proved to be a torrent of gushing water, some of which had probably been locked solid for hundreds, possibly thousands, of years.

There were signs of landslides too, both on the slopes and back on the road, where subsidence caused by melting foundations had brought down bridges and cracked and potted several stretches of the road. Global warming was not the only cause. Near Kunlun Pass was a monument marking the huge earthquake that struck the area in 2001. The temblor, which measured 8.1 on the Richter scale, ripped a 7,000-meter crack through the earth, part of which was still clearly visible.

To minimize the risk of a disaster, rail planners had placed seismic monitoring systems at several points along the tracks that were designed to give advance warning about earth and temperature movements. This railway was going to be even harder to maintain than it had been to build.

The farther we progressed alongside the track, the more obvious was the damage to the roof of the world. It was leaking. Overgrazing had stripped off its thin grassy cover, and global warming had burned through its liquid insulation. The road and the railway accelerated these trends by lifting temperatures and heaping man-made stress onto the already fragile surface vegetation. Between the rail and the road were puddles and pools of melted ice. Other areas were turning into mountain desert. On either side of the track, herds of cows and sheep munched on blotchy patches of grassland near man-made barriers erected to keep the encroaching sand dunes at bay. The loss of grass and topsoil was not just a threat to the beauty of the plateau and the grazing of the cattle; it also accelerated the speed at which the permafrost melted and raised the risk that billions of tons of methane hydrates contained inside the ice would be released into the atmosphere.[26] Methane's greenhouse gas effect is fifty times that of carbon dioxide.

Settlement and modernization had also brought the problem of nondegradable rubbish. Behind each cluster of buildings on the route, such as the small village-garrison of Wudaoliao, was a stinking pile of rotting bags, empty tins, plastic bottles, and gas cans. When I asked my driver how the refuse was disposed of, he laughed. "We leave that job to the wind and the rain and the dogs."

The rubbish was piling up elsewhere in the mountains along with improved transport links. The problem was notorious at Mount Everest, which is known locally as Chomolungma. Ahead of the Olympics, builders laid a tarmac road to within 20 kilometers of base camp for the torch relay leg up to the world's highest mountain. The greatest of man's expeditions in the 1950s was now just a car trip away and was starting to suffer the same problems of any other crowded sightseeing spot. Since Edmund Hillary and Tenzing Norgay first scaled the mountain on May 29, 1953, there had been more than 4,000 ascents and countless other visitors to the base camps in China and Nepal. Both countries are struggling to deal with the empty beer cans, discarded oxygen bottles, and other refuse left behind. With climate change also posing a threat in the form of meltwater floods, in 2005 Sir Edmund called for Everest to be added to the UN list of endangered heritage sites.

But, on the Chinese side of the mountain at least, economic development took priority. That was clear in the treatment of wildlife. The plateau is home to thousands of species of plants and more than 500 species of birds. The railway runs through three nature reserves: Hoh Xil, Chumarleb, and Soga. Nearby is another, Chang Tang, the second-largest reserve in the world and, at 334,000 square kilometers, more than 50 percent larger than Britain. About a third of Tibet's lands are protected. They are home to rare wild animals such as the black-necked crane, huge-horned argali sheep, wild yak, white-lipped deer, gazelle, snow leopards, and, of course, the chiru.

Selected as a mascot for the Beijing Olympics, the chiru, a talismanic creature that is actually more goat than antelope, is much in demand for its fine shahtoosh wool. At least three animals have to be killed to produce a single shawl. Despite being listed under the Convention on International Trade in Endangered Species of Wild Fauna and Flora since 1979, they are still shot for their fleece. No reliable data exist on their numbers, but there is widespread agreement among scientists that the population dropped precipitously in the 1990s from hundreds of thousands to tens of thousands. The wildlife zoologist Richard Harris says the poaching was as vital to the local economy as opium cultivation in Afghanistan or coca growing in Colombia.[27] Just as in those cases, the blame for the illegal trade ultimately rested with rich Western consumers who buy expensive shahtoosh shawls.

Chiru numbers have recovered somewhat in recent years thanks to strengthened government conservation efforts. But all too often the protected status of the animals is not backed with enforcement. Tibet has one of the lowest levels of nature reserve staff in China.[28] Poaching remains rampant. In 2008, one poacher was caught with 400 skins.[29] Many more killings go undetected.

Like everything else in Tibet, wildlife conservation is a political issue. One of the biggest acts of defiance in 2006 was the mass burning of animal pelts after the Dalai Lama said he felt ashamed that Tibetans wear clothes made from endangered species.[30] The burnings of otter, leopard, tiger, and fox skins became such a symbol of loyalty to the exiled leader that Chinese authorities reacted by ordering Tibetan TV presenters to wear fur during broadcasts.

Peering through a pair of binoculars, our driver saw a chiru far in the distance on the stony plain. He passed the glasses over so I could see the beautiful, funny-looking creature with snowy white hindquarters. It gazed curiously in our direction for a while, then bounded off as soon as we tried to approach.

The chiru is famously shy. Designers of the railway added underpasses to allow the beasts, as well as yaks and wild asses, to migrate without disturbance. The effectiveness of these measures was hotly contested. Tibetan overseas groups claimed the passages were too narrow and animals often panicked and stampeded with fatal results. Nonsense, retorted Chinese scientists, who claimed more than 95 percent of chiru used the passes.

The political sensitivity of the issue was demonstrated in 2006 by an award-winning photograph that appeared to show chiru bounding healthily below a passing train. The harmonious image of Tibetan nature and Chinese technology side by side was selected as one of the photographs of the year by the state broadcaster CCTV. But it was faked. The Xinhua photographer claimed he waited eight days and nights in a bunker for the shot, but it transpired it was knocked up in a few hours using Photoshop software. The harmonious ideal was a computer fabrication.[31]

Downstream from the glacier and far across an endlessly bleak plain was our destination, the station at Tuotuohe. The biggest town between Golmud and the Tibetan border was the archetypal frontier community, a narrow strip of grubby buildings populated by a few hundred railway workers, soldiers, truck drivers, and the providers of the services they sought: gas stations, restaurants, open-air pool tables, rough beds, and a brothel. The town was such a dot in the middle of nowhere that our government map located its position incorrectly. But that didn't stop an endless stream of trucks from roaring through on the road that General Mu built, which, until the railway, was the main channel for the manufactured goods flowing into Tibet and the minerals flowing out.

The natural wealth of Tibet was one reason that the region's Chinese name is Xizang, or "western treasure house." While road and air were the only forms of transport, it had not been economical to extract or develop these resources. But this would change with the Sky Train.

Minerals also became easier to exploit as the Sky Train cut freight charges by 75 percent, according to the railway ministry. With global commodity prices surging as a result of the growing demands of China's factories, miners could suddenly see the potential for profit in Tibet's mountains. A Gansu fluorite miner explained to me that Tibet and Mongolia were the future for his business because reserves elsewhere were fully exploited, while the train made it cheaper to mine on the plateau.

With the transport ministry planning six more lines on the plateau by 2020,[32] more of the mineral wealth of Tibet is likely to be freighted to the eastern seaboard. The story of Yugong Yishan is coming closer to being realized. Mountains are being moved, freight car by freight car.

Hydropower is another resource that will probably be developed. The Tibetan Plateau is the water tank of the continent, the source of the Yangtze, Mekong, Yellow, Salween, Brahmaputra, Indus, and Ganges, and other mighty rivers that slake the thirst of at least two billion people who live downstream.[33] Until recently it had relatively few dams, though some, such as the one at Yamdrok Tso, are major barriers. Tibetans considered them a defilement of sacred lakes and rivers. The prospect of local opposition and high cost of working in remote areas held back development of other areas. The railway weakens those barriers by making it cheaper and easier to move engineers, materials, and the troops to guard them. The government's plans for new dams, such as the giant 40,000-megawatt plant at the bend of the Yalong Zangbo (Brahmaputra) and water diversion projects threaten the environmental security of South Asia.[34]

We stayed overnight in a grimy truckers' lodge. Over dinner at the Chengdu First Class Restaurant, I was too tired by the journey and the 4,500-meter altitude even to chat. We had reached the place where China's can-do spirit, the essence of Peak Man, pushed people and the environment to the limit. But the population was swelling here too.

Close to the southern bank of the river, new homes had been built for Tibetan nomads relocated from the plains. There were also fresh residents at the local weather-monitoring station, where three recent graduates had just arrived from their urban homes on the coast. They had already noticed the impact of climate change in their measurements. The cold season in Tuotuohe now began in early October, instead of late September. The rise in temperature was prompting different avalanche patterns.

But the graduates' more immediate concern was how to pass three years in the middle of nowhere. "We play mah-jongg and I've started fishing," said one young scientist. "We'll have to be imaginative or we'll die of boredom here."

Many other migrants were having to adjust. Demographic changes follow railways.[35] The number of tourists visiting the Tibet Autonomous Region more than doubled to 4 million within two years of train services to Lhasa. The government was encouraging further migration. As part of its "Go West" policy to develop inland regions such as Tibet, the government encouraged college graduates to take jobs in target regions by refunding their tuition fees.[36] This was part of an influx that affected the environmental and social order. A major cause of the deadly ethnic riots in Lhasa of 2008 was anger among the local population at Han and Hui migrants who dominated business in the center of the city.

Beijing's politburo of engineers would never accept a challenge to their control over Tibet. The strategic value of this highest of high ground was simply too great. The unrest was quelled. Government spokesmen accused the Dalai Lama of being "a wolf in monk's clothing." The colonization of the mountains was once again portrayed in the state media as a benevolent act of development. I recalled Younghusband, who also believed he was bringing civilization to Tibet by making its resources exploitable. He left Lhasa "boiling over with love for the whole world" just weeks after ordering the slaughter of any Tibetan who stood in his way.[37] The Chinese government was less murderous but more effective in exercising control in the name of progress.

In Tuotuohe, my head was pounding. The altitude was taking its toll. I had thrown up once. A bag of oxygen offered only temporary respite. Ahead was another vast barren plain, then the towering peaks of the Tanggula range, which marked the border with Tibet. The railway stretched forward, but for me it was the end of the line. Thinking back over what I had seen on the roof of the world, and what I had read of imperial and industrial history, I jotted down a line in my notebook: "In the nineteenth century, Britain taught the world how to *produce*. In the twentieth, the US taught us how to *consume*. If China is to lead the world in the twenty-first century, it must teach us how to *sustain*."

But how could it do so when the foolish mountain movers prevailed over the useless-tree philosophers? Those who quested for power overcame even the wisest of those who were content to sustain.

Returning on the road we had come, our car passed a long convoy of military trucks heading toward Lhasa. The clouds, now dark and heavy with rain, sagged down almost to the plateau. A mass of brightly colored

Tibetan prayer flags fluttered on the banks of a small river that would swell downstream to become the mighty Yangtze.

We passed over it on Mu's concrete road beside Hu's iron rail. Generations after Mao, the old chairman's dream was being realized. Man was asserting its will over the mountains. As I was to learn farther downstream, the same was true of the rivers. Human ambition did not get much greater. Nor did the consequences.

3

Still Waters, Moving Earth
Sichuan

Walls of stone will stand upstream to the West
To hold back Wushan's clouds and rain
Till a smooth lake rises in the narrow gorges.
The mountain goddess if she is still there
Will be shocked at a world so changed.
—*Mao Zedong, anticipating the Three Gorges Dam
in his 1956 poem "Swim"*

The cracked and shaken dam was safe. That was what the engineers said. But I could not help feeling a twinge of anxiety riding on the back of a motorbike toward the 156-meter-high slab of concrete that was holding back the Min River.

Four days had passed since China's most devastating earthquake in more than thirty years struck just a short distance upstream, wobbling the earth, reshaping mountains, and tearing chunks off the dam's concrete skin. The repair work continued. So did the aftershocks. As I drew closer, a cascade of water thundered through the floodgates above my head, covering me in a fine mist. Pressure from the reservoir on the other side of the barrier was being hastily released.

Half as tall again as the better-known barrier at the Three Gorges, Zipingpu was one of the newest and biggest of China's 87,000 dams.[1] But it was not designed to withstand an almost direct hit by a magnitude 8 earthquake.[2]

Within seconds of that temblor, death and destruction rippled across an area the size of Belgium. More than ten million man-made structures came crashing down, landslides swallowed entire villages, 4 million people were instantly homeless, and tens of thousands of people were buried alive. The toll of dead and missing from that single minute of instability would eventually rise above 87,000.

In the chaotic aftermath of the quake, the government's biggest concern was that a major dam might give way.[3] Sichuan, a province of high mountains and mighty rivers next to the Tibetan Plateau, has more of these barriers than anywhere else in China.[4] But Zipingpu was in a fear category of its own. Perched above the densely populated city of Dujiangyan, the dam was all that stood between 110 million cubic meters of water high in the mountains and 600,000 dwellers on the plains below. The juddering had opened fissures at the top of the dam, distorted the base, and put two floodways out of action. The state-run Xinhua News Agency described the cracks as "extremely dangerous."[5] If the dam collapsed, the death toll from the earthquake could easily multiply severalfold.

Thousands of soldiers were dispatched to the area.[6] The vice minister of water resources flew in by helicopter to lead an emergency team charged with inspecting and repairing the dam. As they rushed to find out how much the quake had weakened the structure, the barrier was also tested by a rainstorm, which increased the volume of the reservoir and the pressure on the concrete wall. Fortunately, it held. The spillways were opened.[7] As the water ebbed away so did the danger. That night, a relieved inspection team confirmed the barrier was stable. What they did not reveal is that the dam may have triggered the quake. This was to be the biggest scientific aftershock.

Zipingpu had been built on a fault line that had been still for millions of years, but seismic activity had increased after the reservoir went into operation. Each time it filled and emptied, more than 300 million tons of water rose and fell. It was like a giant jumping up and down on a cracked surface. Several leading scientists speculated that the result was a reservoir-induced earthquake. By stilling the water, they said, the engineers may have moved the land.

No nation on earth has gone as far as China in trying to stabilize its hydrology. For more than 2,000 years dams and dikes have been at the heart of the country's politics and civilization. Under the principle of Tian-ming, or the "Mandate of Heaven," emperors were judged by their ability to control the environment as well as the people. Earthquakes, floods, and droughts indicated that the world was out of balance and a change of rule imminent. To avoid rebellion, emperors knew they had to find harmony or at least impose order on chaos. Controlling the rivers was central to ruling the population.

Though the Mandate of Heaven was introduced at the start of the Zhou dynasty (1100 BC), the concept is far from dead. If anything, efforts to tame the torrents have been ramped up to new levels under a politburo dominated by former engineers. Billions of tons of concrete have been poured into the Yangtze, Yellow, Pearl, Liao, Songhua, Han, Huai, Jinsha, and Min rivers for hydroelectric and flood-control projects. The country's waterways are now blocked by almost half of the world's 45,000 biggest dams[8] and many more smaller barriers for reservoirs, sediment control, and water diversion. China's president, Hu Jintao, is a trained hydroengineer. His view of the world has been shaped by his knowledge of water and how it can be controlled. This approach and its consequences are most apparent in Sichuan, the vast southwestern province named after its waterways.[9] The mightiest of them is the Yangtze, which, if its tributaries are included, accounts for 40 percent of the water volume in China and feeds a delta that produces 40 percent of the country's economic output.

Zipingpu Dam sits on the Min, one of the Yangtze's most spectacular tributaries. This 734-kilometer river starts high in the northern Sichuan mountains and flows down to the plains north of Chengdu, the provincial capital. The 10-kilometer stretch near the earthquake zone reveals how the philosophy and science of hydrology have changed since ancient times. At one end is Dujiangyan, a 2,200-year-old Taoist eco-engineering system that harvests water seasonally for irrigation. At the other sits Zipingpu, a concrete megadam that constipates the river to generate power. There are few sharper contrasts in China between the desire to find harmony and the instinct to impose order.

Dujiangyan is one of the oldest and most remarkable hydroengineering schemes on the planet. Built in 256 BC as an irrigation and flood-control system, it has been credited for providing prosperity for Sichuan and establishing a base of agricultural production that allowed Chinese civilization to endure for millennia. It is the antithesis of a dam. Instead of a permanent obstruction, the levees, weirs, and channels of Dujiangyan allow the Min to be harvested during the summer floods, when part of the river's waters are diverted toward the plains for agriculture. The rest of the year, the Min follows its own course. Unlike dams, the channels have almost no effect on the migration of fish and other species. Maintenance is minimal. The ancient system still functions today, irrigating more than 6,000 square kilometers of land. It was barely affected by the earthquake.

The United Nations has recognized the waterworks as a World Heritage Site. Chinese environmentalists describe it as a model of Taoist eco-engineering.[10] Historians believe this huge irrigation and flood-control project created the conditions for the unification of China by reducing floods and ensuring sufficient food surpluses to fund a strong army for the Qin emperor.[11] The subsequent political system in which subjects had to pay tributes to the emperor by boating them along tributaries (hence the name) is underpinned by the river-centered philosophy that partly originated here.[12]

Taoist temples in the area are dedicated to the third-century BC Qin-era administrator and engineer who designed Dujiangyan, Li Bing.[13] His project fit comfortably with the sages' understanding of water as an element associated with goodness, fecundity, and the principle of *wuwei,* or yielding power. Lao-tzu, the sixth-century BC Taoist philosopher, observed: "Water is good. It benefits all things and does not contend with them. It settles in lowly places that all disdain."

In the modern era, however, the prevailing approach to water is not to go with the flow but to block it. Higher upstream, the barrier at Zipingpu exemplifies the "Scientific Outlook on Development" of President Hu. The future leader of China entered the water business at the height of the Great Leap Forward, a period when the nation was rallying to Mao's call for a war on nature. From 1959, Hu spent six years studying hydraulics in the Department of Water Conservancy Engineering at Tsinghua University,[14] then moved to Gansu for his first job outside academia: overseeing the resettlement of people from the Liujia Gorge Dam. His old work unit, Sinohydro, has since expanded under his presidency to become the biggest dam-building company in the world, with operations in forty-two countries. Although growing awareness of the risks posed by dams has cooled enthusiasm in most developed nations, lobbying by the president has helped Sinohydro and other Chinese firms embark on a global building spree.[15] The company has already built 70 percent of the hydroelectric capacity in China, including the world's biggest dam in terms of generating power (Three Gorges), the world's tallest dam (Xiaowan), and many of the world's most controversial dams (including Merowe in Africa and Bakun in Asia). In 2006, Sinohydro built Zipingpu Dam. Two years later, its engineers were the first to be called to repair the damage done by the quake.

Each generation of communist leaders aims to leave an ideological legacy. "Mao Zedong Thought," "Deng Xiaoping Theory," and Jiang Zemin's "Three Represents" are the closest the ruling party has to a canon of beliefs. Hu's contribution is "Scientific Development," which attempts to balance economic progress and concern for the environment and social equity. The approach is vaguely defined: It aims at quality over quantity and harks back self-consciously to the Confucian harmony between man and nature, but in practice, it often proves to be more about engineering projects and new technology than scientific research or lifestyle changes. Nonetheless, it is—at least on a rhetorical level—a breakthrough for the environmental movement because millions of cadres across the country are now theoretically committed to putting the economy on a sustainable track.

If that sounds like qualified praise, it should. The huge Chinese ship does not change direction easily. Policy and thinking are still guided by the momentum from an earlier age and the selfish desires of the present. The dam at Zipingpu is a case in point. Like the railway to Tibet, the barrier is the realization of one of Mao's dreams. It was conceived in 1955 after the chairman expressed disappointment that he could not swim in the Min because its waters were too turbulent. The Sichuan party secretary was so embarrassed that he ordered local officials to build a reservoir.[16]

Swimming meant a lot more than exercise to Mao. He used it to demonstrate his mastery of the waters and political authority. One of the first things he did after taking power in 1949 was to have a pool built in his new residence, where he would later embarrass the Soviet leader Nikita Khrushchev, who could not swim.[17] Seven years later, after a dip in the Yangtze, the chairman wrote the poem "Swim," which declared that a dam would be built at the Three Gorges, and set the stage for a frenzy of hydroengineering projects during the Great Leap Forward. They were a disaster, but Mao returned from the political doldrums in 1966 with the most famous swim in Chinese political history. Mao's dip in the Yangtze at the age of seventy-three demonstrated his physical and political vigor. Scratchy propaganda footage of that event shows hundreds of adoring youths plunging into the waters behind Mao with red flags. The Cultural Revolution followed soon after. Mao had used water to change the direction of the country.

The political chaos of those years saved Dujiangyan. The ancient waterworks were due to be flooded under plans to build a series of dams on the Min. Work on Zipingpu and another barrier began in 1958 but had to be halted amid the famines and chaos of the 1960s. It was not until the 1990s that the plan was revived.

Despite warnings of seismic instability,[18] the government pressed ahead with a dam that could provide a stable supply of water and 3.4 kilowatt-hours of annual electricity-generating capacity for the provincial capital of Chengdu. With the backing of the politburo and Japanese finance for the $800 million project, Zipingpu was named one of the nation's "ten key projects" and put at the forefront of a massive plan to develop the poor western regions of China.[19]

Critics had little opportunity to express their concerns. There was no mention of the seismic risks in the domestic media. Most of the hearings were held behind closed doors. Construction started in 2001. Tens of thousands of people were relocated. Less than two years after the reservoir was filled, the earthquake struck.

My goal was to get to the epicenter. Looking down from the top of the dam into the shadow of Zipingpu, I saw the makeshift military camp that served as the doorway in and out of the central disaster zone. Tents, trucks, and high-speed dinghies clustered on the shore of the reservoir, which stretched back beyond Yingxiu, the town directly above the seismic rip. I scrambled down the steep slope to the river, passing evacuees who had just come off the boats at the jetty. They carried few belongings. Many left homes and loved ones buried under the rubble.

The camp thronged with soldiers and medics. They had little time for journalists. My first direct attempt to board a ferry was impatiently rebuffed. I switched my attention to a group of young soldiers gathered around the dinghies. I had come prepared for such a situation with a carton of Zhongnanhai cigarettes, which I took out of my backpack as a self-introduction. I am not a smoker, but I knew the soldiers would be more willing to chat over a cigarette while they waited for orders to move out.

There was no guarantee I could join them, but my best chance was to wait and hope and smoke. The time and tobacco paid off. Two hours and three packets of Zhongnanhai later, they finally got the word to go. I was thrown an orange life jacket and told to jump in a dinghy. I felt a sense of gratitude from deep in the bottom of my lungs.

At any other time, the hour-long ride along the river would have been a pleasure. But we were among the first to see the effects of the seismic face-lift. We passed newly exposed hillsides, where the slopes had slipped into the waters, and a missing section of a massive bridge that left me imagining cars below the water that must have plunged into the sudden void.

Our dinghy cut around eddies of debris and frequently reduced speed to pass through clusters of broken branches or to avoid large pieces of timber floating in the river.

I started chatting to the other civilian on the boat, who was carrying a large red-white-and-blue-striped plastic bag that suggested he was a migrant worker. Wang Fangbin was happy to talk. Worry and determination had driven him 2,000 kilometers over the previous four days almost without sleep. As soon as he heard the news of the earthquake, he had left his job as a construction worker in distant Xinjiang and headed back to his hometown for the first time in seven years.

"I have to see if my mother is OK. It looks as though everything was flattened," he said with impressive equanimity. "I don't know if my home will still be there. I want to see for myself."

Wang was part of the floating population of migrants that have built modern China. Estimated at between 100 and 200 million, this vast population of itinerant workers had provided the human fuel for the country's economic engine. They were a flood unleashed.

During the Mao era, migration was tightly restricted. Without permission, it was very difficult for people to leave the area of their *hukou* (family registration). But after the economic reforms of the late 1970s, controls were relaxed, allowing a huge pool of cheap rural labor to move to factory production lines and city construction sites. The spectacular economic development that followed is largely attributable to the opening of the migration floodgates.

But the surge of people away from their homes had brought with it a sense of restlessness, uncertainty, and social unease. This was particularly true when the relocation was forced, as was often the case for major construction projects, especially dams.[20] As familiar buildings were reduced to rubble, as neighbors moved on and values seemed to become as fluid as the waters of the Yangtze, early twenty-first-century China was a country where it was possible to feel lost simply by standing still.

Mutability inspired some of the best contemporary art and film in China. The most evocative was *Still Life,* a film about the Yangtze, released in 2005 by the director Jia Zhangke. At once stunningly beautiful and disturbingly bleak, it told the story of a Sichuanese migrant who, like Wang, returned after ten years to search for a family in a town reduced to rubble and soon to be swallowed by the elements. In this case it was not an earthquake that transformed the landscape, but demolition teams and the Three Gorges Dam. The scenes of devastation, however, were remarkably similar.

Close to 1.4 million people were relocated for the Three Gorges Dam, the most ambitious and controversial hydroelectric development ever undertaken. It took fifty years to plan, fifteen years to build, $24 billion to pay for, and 16 million tons of reinforced concrete to fill. The giant barrier has created a reservoir that stretches back along the Yangtze almost the length of England.[21] This mass of water drives twenty-six giant turbines to generate up to 18,000 megawatt-hours of electricity. There are few more fitting monuments to early twenty-first-century China.

Even more than Zipingpu, the Three Gorges Dam was driven forward over massive political opposition and scientific doubt. Three generations of strongmen pushed it through: Sun Yat-sen approved a plan for the dam in 1919 as a defense against floods; Mao Zedong took the idea a step further in the 1950s, when he commissioned Russian engineers to draw up blueprints; but construction could not begin until 1992 when the premier, Li Peng, forced the plan through despite unusually vocal domestic opposition.[22] As with Zipingpu, the rebalancing of people and water along the biggest river in China triggered far deeper social and environmental disturbance than anticipated.

I too failed to grasp the consequences the first time I traversed the chocolate brown waters of the Yangtze. It was 2003. The Three Gorges Dam was not yet finished, but I was upbeat. For an energy-hungry nation, the dam seemed a clean alternative to thirty conventional power stations. It would also reduce the risks of the deadly floods that killed thousands and ravaged croplands every few years.

At the time, I was, like many new arrivals, impressed to find a nation that was far more open, modern, and forward-thinking than I had believed before visiting. Outside China the dam was a symbol of the communist government's poor record on human rights and the environment. About 1.4 million people been forced from their homes by the rising waters, which inundated precious ecosystems, heritage sites, and some of the most stunning scenery on the planet, but I wanted to see if there was another side of the story.

I took a boat called the *China Universe*. Despite its grand name, the closest this scruffy multitiered tourist vessel came to the stars or the state was a hiccuping karaoke machine filled with patriotic songs about the Yangtze. Dirty water sloshed around on the floor of the cabin, and the galley was so dank that I was sick for a week afterward.

Up on deck, however, the view of the gorges lived up to the poems and legends. Imposingly steep and narrow at the water's edge, the slopes rose up hundreds of feet to fantastically shaped crags that seemed to sharpen against the sky as the sun set.

It was dark by the time we reached Xiling, the last of the Three Gorges. I went to the bridge, where the captain's face was illuminated by the sonar screen needed to negotiate this notoriously treacherous stretch of river. Crewmen illuminated the slopes on either side with searchlights that seemed to draw the jagged sides of the gorge nearer and make the river darker.

We hit the dam soon after. In the depths of the night, it was an awe-inspiring sight. Miles and miles of vast, silent darkness suddenly gave way to an enormous, noisy, frenetic building site. Everything was illuminated: the massive locks with orange fairground lights, the construction rigs with strings of colored lights, and the ground with the headlamps of cranes and tractors. The effect was that of a Spielberg science-fiction epic.

As the *China Universe* waited for its turn in the lock, I alighted with the other passengers to wander the site. Our guide declared the dam a "miracle for the whole world," and briefly, I almost believed it. Watching from a viewing gallery as thousands of tons of water thundered out from turbines the size of cliff faces and churned up the river far below, I was soaked, deafened, and awestruck. This was power, raw power. Mighty but tamed. A placid reservoir above, a seething torrent below. Humanity stood between the two, controlling, directing, milking the elements.

If there was ever a moment when I was ready to embrace the man-made glory of the new China, it was then. The developed world had asked the country to reduce greenhouse gases, and here was a massive alternative to carbon-fueled power. Westerners complained about mining accidents and air pollution from coal, and now here was a hydropower plant that generated the energy equivalent of 50 million tons of coal each year. Why, I wondered, were these benefits so rarely talked about overseas? If the dam had been designed by a modern-day Isambard Kingdom Brunel, rather than Chinese communists, wouldn't we be celebrating it as a work of genius?

But like so many aspects of China's brave new world, the dam looked very different in the cold light of the following day, when it resembled a gray scar on an otherwise stunning landscape.

Just how big an eyesore was apparent at the exhibition center, where the flood of superlatives from the guides were part boast, part self-indictment. The dam, they said, was not just the biggest hydropower plant in the world, it also contained more concrete and steel than any other structure, and necessitated the biggest resettlement program in engineering history. The guide insisted the relocations were a success and the environmental challenges were being overcome. But there was something missing from the official endorsement of the dam. On the walls were photographs of state leaders visiting the site and congratulating the engineers on their work. But there was no picture of Hu Jintao.

Neither he nor Premier Wen Jiabao, a trained geologist, attended the dam's completion ceremony in 2006. This raised suspicions that President Water and Premier Earth were distancing themselves from a project that was quickly proving a disaster for the river and the land.

As the water rose, the weight of the reservoir began triggering landslides and deadly waves.[23] Such was the concern that the government had to postpone plans to raise the level of the reservoir to its maximum height.[24] The water quality deteriorated as the river became less able to flush garbage and algae out of its system. Domestic newspapers said the pollution was "cancerous" and a threat to marine life and drinking supplies in 186 cities. The state news agency Xinhua warned that the Three Gorges could become an "environmental catastrophe" unless remedial action was taken. Alarm bells rang even louder when the State Council's point man on the project, Wang Xiaofeng, spoke of "hidden dangers" that could cause pollution, landslides, and "other geological disasters."[25]

This represented a volte-face by the establishment. Until then, such grim warnings had come only from academia and the NGO sector. Historically, the government's usual response to pollution and disaster was to cover up bad news and arrest the critics.

No one knew that better than Dai Qing, one of China's most indomitable environmentalists, who was imprisoned for ten months after publishing a searing criticism of the Three Gorges Dam in 1989. After her release, she continued to be an influential critic of the government's water-management policies and won the Goldman Environmental Prize in 1993.[26]

Dai told me China had a long history of building dangerous dams and then covering up the consequences. Construction surged in the 1950s. Initially, there was a debate between Taoist and Confucian dam builders. The Taoists preferred to use low levees and the natural flow of the water, as in Dujiangyan, while the Confucians wanted high dikes and other big projects to control the course of rivers.[27] Mao, as we have seen, threw his support behind the latter's megaprojects.

In a fury of dam building at the start of the Great Leap Forward, Dai said, 580 million cubic tons of earth was shifted for barriers and irrigation channels. In one insane year, 1958, that will come up again and again in this book, the amount of earth moved for hydro projects was more than double that in the whole of the previous decade.[28]

Scrappily built and inadequately checked, many collapsed with deadly consequences. The first big dam to go was the Fushan, which lasted just four months before bursting and drowning 10,000 people downstream. By 1980, 2,796 dams had failed with a combined death toll of 240,000. This was not made public until many years after.

But the problems caused by haste, vanity, and secrecy remain. "The crap from that era has not yet been cleaned up," the former chief engineer of the Water Resources Bureau of Henan Province, Ma Shoulong, told Dai. The year 1958 may have been exceptional, but China remains a country of massive and often reckless hydro ambitions.

The biggest of them is another megascheme approved by Mao, the South-North Water Diversion Project.[29] More than twice as expensive as the Three Gorges Dam and three times longer than the railway to Tibet, the fifty-year, 450-billion-yuan project aims to divert water along three channels—each nearly 1,000 kilometers long—from the moist Yangtze basin up to the dry lands north of the Yellow River. It is an emergency operation: a transfusion of water to an area dying of thirst. In European terms, it is like using the Rhône to save the Rhine. In America, imagine the Mississippi being tapped to rescue the Colorado.

The operation is staggeringly complex, expensive, politically difficult, and environmentally perilous.[30] There is no certainty it will save the Yellow River, which has been massively overexploited and polluted for decades. And there is every chance that it could hasten the decline of the Yangtze.

The scheme has been dogged by delays and cost overruns that set it back at least four years. What should have been the easiest section, the east leg, was supposed to have been on tap in Beijing in time for the 2008 Olympics. Planners originally hoped to use the 1,400-year-old Grand Canal that already ran from south to north, but its waters were too contaminated by toxins, urban waste, and chemical fertilizer. The designers earmarked more than half the budget for that section on water treatment. But the filthy green slime proved almost untreatable. In 2007, 300 hectares of wheat died in the fields after local farmers used the canal for irrigation.[31] More than a year after the Olympics, Beijing had yet to receive a drop of water from the east route and it was unsure when it ever would.

Instead, the government rushed ahead on the central route from the Han, another tributary of the Yangtze. Engineers from the 16th Bureau of the China Railway Construction Group were dispatched to start on the most complex section, a 4.1-kilometer tunnel under the Yellow River. From there, a long expanse of farmland was cleared for the channel that is one day expected to carry 9.5 billion cubic meters of water every year to slake the thirst of Beijing and nineteen other cities in the north. But this leg too has proved far more expensive than expected. As well as enormous pipes and aqueducts, northern plumbing systems are having to be adapted for the high levels of acidity in the southern water.

The social impact is likely to be felt most by the 300,000 people who will be forced to resettle, most of whom live in an area that will be flooded when the Danjiangkou Dam is completed at the southernmost point of the route. Even those who will remain in their homes fear the easing of the north's water shortage will worsen the south's problems of pollution, sedimentation, and drought.[32]

The challenges facing the western leg have proved more difficult still. Under the government's blueprint, 17 billion cubic meters of water were supposed to be pumped from the Jinsha, the headwater of the Yangtze, at an altitude of 4,100 meters on the Tibetan Plateau, down to the Yellow River. Crossing these highlands will require pumping stations and tunnels. It will be hugely expensive and politically difficult.[33]

Fears arose that it could prove a megaproject too far, even for China. The plans submitted by the Ministry of Water Resources were postponed indefinitely. Influential supporters of the scheme started to backtrack.[34] Downstream provinces, including the major industrial centers of Nanjing, Wuhan, and Shanghai, worried that they would end up dry because the Yangtze was already showing the strains of overuse, overdamming, climate change, and pollution. In 2006, several dozen scientists in Sichuan published a collection of memorandums that called into question the feasibility and desirability of the western leg.

The debate suggested the Maoist approach to development—"think big, move fast and worry about the consequences later"—was belatedly being called into question.[35] Even the most audacious Chinese engineering visionaries were discovering limits to what man could or should attempt in the campaign to conquer the natural world. The new big idea was "think small," or so it seemed. For the environment, that was good news. But for at least one member of the old guard, it was lamentable.

Guo Kai was one of the last survivors of the Yugong Yishan, mountain-moving generation of Maoists. While the rest of humanity looked on in awe at the grand hydroengineering schemes of modern China, the retired general told me he was frustrated by the nation's lack of ambition.

I met Guo in a tea shop. He looked very much the pensioner, dressed in thick layers of vests, shirts, and cardigans as he explained his world-transforming plan to me. Along with his chief collaborator, Li Ling, another retired officer from the second artillery division, we talked over glasses of green tea that were too hot to hold, much like their proposal has been since it was first mooted in 1976.

They wanted to redraw the hydrology of Asia. Pointing on a vividly colored map of Asia's river systems to the four thickest blue veins coursing through Tibet, Guo said only one, the Yangtze, ran east to China. The others flowed south to form the Brahmaputra in India.

"The rivers cross the border. It is a waste. The water is needed here. Look how dry China is." And with that his finger moved north to Xinjiang, Gansu, and Inner Mongolia, where the map was indeed marked with huge brown and yellow splodges of desert.

Fixing the problem, he said, was a simple matter of logic. India and Bangladesh get so much rainfall they often suffer from floods. If China, with a seventh of the precipitation, diverted a third of Tibet's rivers for its own use, he argued, all three nations could benefit.

Not surprisingly, politicians in Delhi and Dhaka are unwilling to donate even a drop from the Brahmaputra, which they consider vital for irrigation and drinking supplies. Indian newspapers have expressed outrage at Guo's idea. If Beijing was ever to formally adopt such a plan, there would be a high chance of a water war between Asia's two most populous nations.[36]

Fortunately, there is no sign of this happening any time soon. Despite the support of several old generals, Guo and Li have been politely shunted aside by the politburo. Fiercer critics dismiss them as eccentric has-beens.

Guo's hydrological training was not just old-school, it was no school. He taught himself about river systems while locked in a cellar by Red Guards during the Cultural Revolution. A hydrological study of western China was one of the only books in his makeshift cell. Criticized by the young ideologues and filled with self-doubt, he devoted his detention first to the book and then to drawing up a plan to solve China's water problems. It was to become a lifetime obsession.

But Guo's reputation was not helped by his association with a still bolder plan to use nuclear weapons to blast a 2-kilometer-wide air tunnel through the Himalayas that would allow warm, moist currents from the subcontinent to circulate north. The general calculated that 200 warheads, each with the power of the Hiroshima bomb, would be needed to clear the necessary 3 billion cubic meters of rock.

The proposal to shift the planet's most immovable object raised eyebrows even in mountain-moving China. Guo was ridiculed. One of his associates, Mu Qinzhong, ended up in prison. Guo distanced himself from that crazy scheme, but he has not completely given up on his revolutionary solution to China's water shortage.[37] Fortunately, more cautious heads have prevailed.

Guo's failure was revealing and, from an environmental perspective, encouraging. Although the old Maoist beliefs live on in grand nature-conquering schemes, they are now contending with rival ways of thinking that show more respect for the environment.

A new generation of scientists, journalists, and environmentalists are questioning the fundamental tenets of nation-building with the tacit support of senior leaders. They are a source of hope that the Scientific Outlook on Development might one day pioneer a more sustainable path between Taoism and Maoism.

The new generation is far better educated than their predecessors, many of whom secured posts through political contacts during the Cultural Revolution (when most universities were closed). Rather than battle nature, this new wave sought to understand man's place within it. Instead of expansionist megaprojects they focused on grassroots conservation work. Instead of using science to support political dogma, they saw it as a means to pursue truth and efficiency. Instead of secretive, top-down planning, they championed bottom-up accountability and transparency. And, most important, they had a different view of nature's limits because they were confronted on a daily basis with the foul consequences of pollution, depleted resources, and hard-to-maintain megaprojects. Even some of the old-timers agreed it was time for a rethink.[38]

There is reason to hope that Mao's view of nature will go the way of Mao's view of politics, but this has not happened yet. Momentum is a powerful force in a country the size of China. Once started, engineering schemes are difficult to stop. Once locked into a certain technology, more spending is often required to deal with the unforeseen consequences. Dams are a case in point.

Hydroelectric plants appear to be green, because they emit no carbon.[39] But the reality in Sichuan and Yunnan is often the opposite.[40] After many dams are built, dirty factories and coal mines soon follow them. Because hydroelectricity generated in remote mountain areas cannot be economically supplied to the national grid, local governments encourage chemical and smelting plants to move near to dams. Unfortunately, those energy-intensive industries require a constant supply of electricity, which dams are unable to provide in the dry season. The only way to avoid seasonal fluctuations is to open coal-fired power plants to provide supplementary energy. For that to be viable, mines have to be dug close by.[41] The result of this cycle is that clean energy turns dirty very quickly. The consequences are alarmingly apparent in southeast Sichuan, where I saw areas of verdant hillside speckled with black coal mines. Some of the world's dirtiest industries are moving into this spectacularly beautiful area. Panzihua and Zhaotong have become hubs of production for yellow phosphorus and other heavy-polluting, energy-intensive processes that have been phased out elsewhere in the world.[42] There are few more glaring examples of how rich countries outsource pollution to China. Hydro plants along the Jinsha (the Yangtze headwater) lead the way. Ironically, many of those same dams have qualified for carbon credits under the Clean Development Mechanism even as they help to foul an area not far from Shangri-La.[43]

Similarly, one dam often spawns others. A major reason for the cascade of hydroelectric dams on the Jinsha is to ease the buildup of silt at the Three Gorges. It is a similar story on the Yellow River.[44] As the dams expand, so does the influence of the power companies behind them. From 2000 to 2002, China experienced a rush for hydropower as five newly created utilities, Huaneng, Huadian, Zhongdiantou, Guodian, and Datang, divided up the major unexploited rivers of Sichuan and Yunnan.[45] These firms are extremely powerful. Their heads rank at vice-ministerial level in the political hierarchy, but they often also exert informal influence through family ties.[46] Though nominally under the jurisdiction of the most powerful body in government, the National Development and Reform Commission, the utilities can often evade the full societal and environmental costs of their operations.[47]

But they have occasionally been defeated. One of the greatest reversals for the hydropower lobby occurred at Dujiangyan. A dam that had been planned nearby at Yangliu Lake would have flooded the ancient waterworks. The local authorities and power companies knew this was controversial and started construction work in secret, but even with China's strict censorship controls, it is not easy to hide a dam. After the plan was exposed, a coalition of heritage officials, seismologists, environment groups, academics, and journalists mounted a successful media campaign to block the project. In 2006, the Sichuan governor backed down. This landmark victory was hailed as a sign that authoritarian China was becoming more politically pluralistic.[48] But it was not so much a defense of nature from man, or a triumph of Taoism over Maoism; rather it was a patriotic campaign to maintain a cornerstone of the nation's heritage. A similarly nationalistic motivation would be hard to drum up for other conservation projects.

Like the growing academic and journalistic criticism of megaprojects, the campaign to save Dujiangyan was encouraging but not yet a sign of a dominant new trend.

With the former Sinohydro employee Hu at the nation's helm, the influence of the dam builders has increased. "Scientific Development" has sidelined dangerous dreamers like Guo Kai, but it has given more influence to corporations that can pay for academic reports to justify commercially driven projects and use political ties to suppress critical coverage in the domestic media.

Hydroelectric energy is increasingly important for China's energy security and profitable for the utilities. Plans to develop the Nu and the Jinsha have been partially held up, but the pressures to build dams on every river are growing along with the risks to people and the environment.

Four days after the Sichuan quake and one hour after hitching a ride on the dinghy, I walked with the returning migrant Wang along a broken, muddy road to the epicenter at Yingxiu. There were small landslides on the slopes above us that sent pebbles and rocks bouncing down. Columns of soldiers, some bearing red regimental flags, marched alongside military trucks carrying supplies and equipment. We passed below the massive, fractured legs of a collapsed expressway and trucks knocked down like skittles by boulders the size of houses.

This was a road Wang had taken many times in his youth, but he did not slow for a second. Such was his hurry to return home that I could barely keep up. He stopped only when we reached Yingxiu, the nearest town to his village. The seismic ripple had wrought its greatest destruction here. The town was pulverized. In the worst-hit area, the primary school was no longer recognizable as a building. It was reduced to chunks of stone, pieces of twisted metal, and scattered intimate belongings. Rescue workers with dogs sniffed for bodies under the rubble while parents kept an ever more hopeless vigil.

Not a single building in this town would ever be used again. The structures had collapsed, been buried, or cracked and buckled beyond the point of being safely habitable. Concrete had never seemed so brittle and fragile. The residents were more yielding and resilient, but still in shock and pain. At least 3,000 had died, and thousands more, including countless unregistered migrants from the surrounding countryside, were missing under the rubble. Battalions of soldiers were camped out on the plain, as far as possible from the mountain slopes and possible landslides. Helicopters and boats evacuated anyone who could be persuaded to leave. Most of those who stayed did so because they were waiting for the bodies of loved ones to be found. Others, pragmatically, held corpseless funerals, burning clothes in place of the missing. Their pyres burned alongside the river as night fell.

Wang had not yet reached his mother's village, but soldiers warned him not to go any farther into the disaster zone. The path forward was narrower, the sides of the gorge steeper, and landslides made it almost impassable. "There is only death that way," said a soldier, forbidding us to continue.

Wang did not want to delay, but the soldier gave him no choice, at least for now. He went off to seek food at a refugee tent. I felt sure he would try again in the morning and wondered if I should try then to rejoin him.

I met up with an Australian Broadcasting Company TV crew, who had hiked across the mountains, risking landslides and aftershocks, to get to Yingxiu. We shared food, a satellite phone, and insect repellent. When rain started to fall, they offered me space in their tent on the edge of the army camp. The drizzle was refreshing at first, but then it started to pour. Soon, a full-blown mountain storm was trapped in our valley, the thunder rolling up and down almost without a break. Lightning tore across the sky above while—"Bloody hell, do you feel that?"—a series of powerful aftershocks jolted the earth below my sleeping bag. With death and destruction outside, soldiers everywhere, and water building up behind a landslide farther up the valley, the thought flashed through my mind that this was as close to the apocalypse as I ever wanted to get.

Suddenly, I felt thrilled to be alive, relishing every second of the experience. Feeling such elemental extremes was terrifying but also a privilege. It lasted a few hours. The tent leaked a little. There was another, smaller aftershock. Then the storm eased, the earth settled, and I drifted off to sleep.

There was no sign of Wang the next morning. I presumed he had slipped away before the soldiers woke. He faced a perilous journey. People were still being crushed by landslides and tumbling boulders. I felt guilty and worried, but also relieved that I wasn't with him. Not for the first time as a journalist I wished a person well as I left them to dangers I was unwilling to face. To this day, I wonder what became of Wang.[49]

The cause of the Sichuan quake remains contentious. While it is still classified as a natural disaster, some scientists believe the Zipingpu Dam may have been at least partly responsible.

Geologists noted the Yingxiu-Beichuan fault line had been relatively inactive for thousands of years before the dam was built. Fan Xiao, a chief engineer of the Sichuan Geology and Mineral Bureau, argued that the 320 million tons of water in the reservoir may have jigged it back into life.[50] His views won support from several foreign seismologists.

"The added weight [of the Zipingpu reservoir] both eased the squeeze on the fault, weakening it, and increased the stress tending to rupture the fault," wrote geophysical hazards researcher Christian Klose of Columbia University's Lamont-Doherty Earth Observatory. "The effect was 25 times that of a year's worth of natural stress loading from tectonic motions . . . When the fault did finally rupture, it moved just the way the reservoir loading had encouraged it to."[51]

Reservoir-induced seismicity is a known phenomenon. There have been several well-documented cases across the globe.[52] In the planning stage for the dam on the Min, Fan and other scientists had warned of the risk of a quake but they were ignored.[53]

The government rejected claims that Zipingpu caused the quake. Several senior Chinese geologists said seismic activity was unchanged after the reservoir filled and that, in any case, the 280-kilometer rupture in 2008 was far too great to have been caused by a dam. While evidence for a link is inconclusive, their views have prevailed. The power of the hydroengineering lobby is unshaken. A year after the disaster, the authorities announced plans for twenty new plants on the upper Yangtze and its tributaries, many of them close to fault lines.[54] These were not the only risks that development posed to Asia's greatest river, nor were humans the worst affected victims.

4

Fishing with Explosives
Hubei and Guangxi

Although the cranes have wild instincts and are free to leave the
royal park, the king's moral government makes them stay, their
captivity . . . being their reason for joy.
—*Early Han dynasty poet*[1]

had never heard of the baiji before coming to China. Even then, I did
not pay much attention at first. As far as I could tell, the Yangtze dolphin
was just another item on the endangered species list. Little news there.
So many creatures were at risk that I had grown almost numb to reports
about the loss of the wild. But then I was assigned to cover an international
search for the animal. No story has made more powerful impression on me.

It began with a shipful of high hopes and good intentions. The launch
party in Hubei on the misty banks of the Yangtze gathered together the
great and the good of the marine biology community.[2] On the deck of the
Kekao 1 survey ship, I clinked glasses with the world's leading zoologists
and sonar engineers. Local communist cadres chatted with executives
from the American beer company that was cosponsoring the project. The
Swiss philanthropist who helped to organize the mission was ebullient
that, after years of preparation, something was finally being done. Alcohol
foamed down a cascade of champagne glasses as the dignitaries posed for
the cameras. The speeches mentioned unprecedented international cooperation, state-of-the-art equipment, and determination not to give up on
the baiji. The dolphin was in danger, but if anyone could find and save the

animal, it was this group. I couldn't help thinking this would make a great start for a feel-good Hollywood movie. Indeed, we seemed to be on the set of a film. Our ship, decked out in bright bunting, red-bannered slogans, and a display of corporate donor logos, was an incongruous sight amid the empty gray farm fields and swirling brown waters of the river. To any passing farmer we must have made a peculiar spectacle.

At least something was being done. The expedition was a last-gasp effort to save a remarkable creature.[3] August Pfluger, the enthusiastic Swiss millionaire who helped to pull the team together, and Samuel Turvey of the Zoological Society of London explained the animal's significance and its decline as we embarked on our journey.

Between twenty and twenty-five million years ago, a pale, long-snouted dolphin left the Pacific Ocean and began navigating the muddy brown waters of the Yangtze. Over time, it became distinct from other cetaceans. Eyesight was of little use in the murky river and it became almost blind, developing instead a highly sophisticated sonar for navigation. With fish plentiful and predators few, the baiji flourished. Until a few thousand years ago they would have been a common sight, frolicking by sandbars as tapirs emerged from densely forested riverbanks to drink waters that sustained as rich a variety of life as the Amazon does today. In that golden age of ecological diversity elephants ranged from the Yangtze to Beijing, where they lived wild along with Bactrian camels and a cornucopia of other species in an area that was then densely forested.

Man was a latecomer. The earliest archaeological records of *Homo erectus* (upright man) date back about two million years to Africa. It was another million years before their descendants moved to Asia and probably several hundred thousand years more until they reached southern China. But certainly by 6500 BC our species—by then evolved to *Homo sapiens* (wise man)—had settled in the Yangtze delta and domesticated rice for the first time in human history.[4]

Early civilizations worshipped the baiji as a river goddess.[5] Capable of growing up to 2.5 meters in length, able to swim up to 60 kilometers per hour, and communicating in a series of clicks and whistles, the creature would have mystified our ancient ancestors. In one ancient romance, a baiji is transformed into a beautiful maiden who falls in love with a man.[6] In other writings, the dolphin is adored as the "Goddess of the Yangtze."

Over the years, the baiji has been known by many names, but the most prescient was given by the first Westerner to record its existence: *Lipotes vexillifer,* which is Latin for "left-behind flag bearer."[7] This proved appropriate, as the mammal, which preceded man in making a home in Asia by tens of millions of years, has effectively been abandoned for at least half a century. As humanity pressed into the Yangtze delta in ever-larger numbers, the dolphin was first neglected and then squeezed out of its habitat.

The Yangtze delta supports more than one in twenty of humanity and 40 percent of China's economy. There is barely any room left for other species or activities. Elephants and tapirs have long since been driven away. Other fantastic creatures such as the Yangtze crocodile are now on the brink of extinction. The baiji may already be over the edge. Far more so than the giant panda, its demise illustrates the sacrifices that nature has been forced to make to support and enrich the world's most populous country.

In the 1950s, there were 6,000 baiji in the Yangtze, their only home. From then on their numbers fell calamitously. By 1984, there were only 400 left, and since then their decline has followed an almost perfect inverse relationship to the nation's economic rise.[8] The last confirmed sighting was in 2002.

For many years, it was difficult for Chinese scientists to publicly acknowledge the damage done by economic development. Highlighting the decline of species was tantamount to criticizing government policy and causing a loss of national face. This began to change when the extent of the problems facing the baiji and other animals became more widely known.

Aboard the *Kekao 1,* Wang Ding, the country's leading baiji expert, was more than willing to talk. Having studied the mammal for more than twenty years, he clearly cared deeply about its fate. With sadness and frustration, he spoke about the impact of development, river traffic, and recklessly indiscriminate fishing.[9]

"The fishermen electrify large areas of water, then gather up all the dead fish. We haven't seen those tactics in this area in the last couple of days, but it is still common elsewhere. At Dongting Lake it is very bad."

I shook my head, but not in disbelief. I had seen small-scale electric fishing near Beijing, where workers from local restaurants wandered the streams and pools in rubber waders with giant batteries strapped to their backs connected to a pole in each hand that they dipped into the water, electrocuting everything in between. This was by no means the worst form of indiscriminate fishing in China. I had read and heard numerous reports of fishing with explosives. Not surprisingly, given such techniques, recorded catches on the Yangtze have halved over little more than a decade.

Wang tried to prevent the slaughter. As a senior government adviser, he recommended a complete halt to fishing on the Yangtze so stocks could recover. But the Yangtze Management Commission was reluctant to take a step that would hurt the livelihoods of millions of people. Instead it initiated a four-month halt during the spawning season in the lower and middle reaches of the Yangtze. For the baiji, it was not enough.

"When we started monitoring twenty years ago, we could be certain of seeing baiji on every trip. It would be better if we had tried to conserve them then. But the problem at the time was that China was very poor. The government was focused only on economic development. People didn't care about the environment at all. Now our country has more money and people are more aware. The baiji is a flagship. Its fate is connected to humanity's. If the Yangtze cannot support them, it cannot support us. Perhaps it is too late, but we have to do something."

China had implemented a capture-and-relocation scheme during much of the eighties and nineties. But it proved an expensive and difficult failure: just six animals were caught and taken to dolphinariums; all of them died, most after less than a year in captivity. Back then, China was too poor to organize such a complex conservation effort alone. Better facilities were needed, and more knowledgeable assistance from the international community.

Now, finally, everything seemed to be in place for a twenty-first-century rescue. Foreign conservationists and the Chinese authorities had agreed on a plan to capture the dolphins and start a breeding program. It was to be a major operation. To safely seize a single animal would require at least fifty fishermen, a kilometer-long net, a speedboat, a command ship, and two other vessels—at a cost in excess of 300 million yuan ($43 million).[10] Once caught, the animals were to be relocated into a haven where they could rebuild their population away from predators and pollution.

Our group was taken to visit a relocation site, the Baiji National Reserve in Tian-e-Zhou. Established in 1992, the 21-kilometer-long oxbow lake was one of three reserves set aside for the translocation of the baiji into a seminatural setting, protected from fishermen, factories, fertilizers, and river traffic.[11]

The scene was idyllic. On the roadside, villagers combed through thick white clouds of newly harvested cotton. A wrinkled farmer in a straw hat led his ox along a path striped by shafts of sunlight and shadow. Herons flapped lazily along the lush green riverbank.

There were signs of hope. Yangtze finless porpoises, fondly known as river pigs, arced out of the water. The porpoises, only recently added to the endangered species list, had been successfully relocated to the haven. More encouraging still was a nearby wetland, where our group saw herds of magnificent large-antlered milu, or Père David's deer. This animal, which was indigenous to China, showed how species could be pulled back from the brink of extinction. At the exhibition center artists' illustrations showed how the animal had almost been wiped out. They were already at risk in the nineteenth century, when the French missionary Father Armand David became the first Westerner to record their existence. The last known herd was in the emperor's hunting grounds. This stock was decimated by Western smugglers, who took the deer for exhibition to Europe, and by British and Japanese troops who ate most of the remaining animals around the time of the Boxer Rebellion. To save the species, the last eighteen specimens were taken to Woburn Abbey in Bedfordshire, where they were successfully bred and reintroduced to China. There were now 3,000 of the deer worldwide, including about 500 at Tian-e-Zhou. Despite fears of inbreeding, biologists said there were no signs of genetic problems.

The park's managers hoped the baiji could make a similar comeback. They showed us induction pens designed to hold the dolphins until they were proven healthy and ready for release into the lake. But the pens were empty. There were no dolphins. Not one. The alarming reality was that there were more baiji reserves than baiji. Until that changed, the park would serve as a monument to conservation failure.

Our expedition aimed to change that. But, I asked August, why wasn't the plan put into place twenty or even ten years earlier, when baiji numbers were less precarious?

He sighed: "Over the past twenty years the baiji has been the victim of politics and scientific disputes. The view in the West was that more should be done to conserve the dolphin in the river, its natural habitat. The view in China was that it should be moved to the oxbow lake. In the end, they couldn't decide, so the baiji is the victim."

These opposing outlooks were at the heart of the dispute about environmental protection in China. Western scientists and conservationists wanted to leave vast tracts of the country as an unspoiled and wild sanctuary. The Chinese authorities counterargued that economic development was a greater priority. They accused the West of hypocrisy in calling for protection of forests and species in other nations. After all, industrialized nations had already decimated their own woodlands. Chinese authorities tended to argue that species were best protected by fencing them off, penning them up, and helping them breed with artificial techniques.

The philosophies were different. As the American zoologist Richard Harris noted: "The root of the problem lies in Chinese failure to value wildness for its own sake . . . China currently lacks effective wildlife conservation because it has yet to acknowledge what wildlife really is and what conservation really means."[12]

The stakes could not be much higher. One of the strongest arguments for a different approach in China is that it has so much more to lose.[13] Half of the species in the northern hemisphere are found here. Sichuan alone contains a greater range of life than all of North America.[14] Nationwide, China is a treasure trove of biodiversity and home to some of the world's mightiest beasts, including the huge Himalayan griffin, wild yaks that weigh a ton and can outrun a jeep, and the world's largest amphibian, the 40-kilogram giant salamander.

Most have retreated to the peripheries of Han civilization: the high peaks, barren plains, dense jungles, and deep waters. But as human activity spreads even to these remote areas, many mammals are threatened. Other less well-known reptiles, insects, and varieties of moss are dying off completely. It is a similar story worldwide. The rate of species extinction in the first decade of the twenty-first century is many orders of magnitude higher than at any time in the history of the planet.[15] But the situation is particularly grim in China, where the die-off is reckoned to be taking place at twice the speed of the global average. According to the China Species Red List, it is accelerating.[16]

China came late to conservation. Although certain areas were nominally protected more than fifty years ago, it was only after the country opened up to the outside world in 1978 that any systematic attempt was made to track the populations of species and support those most at risk of extinction. After that, the central and provincial governments set aside 2,531 nature reserves.[17] These actions may have been delayed too long. When the United States began protecting nature around the turn of the twentieth century, its population density was ten people to a square kilometer. When China started, its population was squeezed 145 to the same area. There was not much room left for other forms of life.

Many environmentalists—foreign and domestic—believe Chinese culture is skewed against the wild. There, nature has traditionally been valued for its utility and scope for consumption. It was something to tame and control. Harris noted the deserts and mountains of the far west are often described in official writing as *elie,* which could be translated as "vile" or "of low quality." The word for wilderness, *huangdi,* also means "wasteland." The nation's scientists showed little interest in studying wildlife in the wild. Biology in China was traditionally taught in the laboratory rather than the field.[18]

Until the 1990s, the signs on cages in Beijing Zoo identified which parts of each animal could be eaten or used in Chinese traditional medicine. Among the very few wildlife books before then was *Economic Birds of Sichuan,* which listed species that were either medicinal or tasty.[19] After that, attitudes started to change as the impact of development—and the overutilization it brings—became better known.

History helps to explain the divergent viewpoints. In the West, the systematic study of nature did not hit full stride until industrialization. Then too, utility was a major motivation. Many researchers looked to the wild for new dyes, ingredients, chemicals, and other resources. In China, the most influential study of natural resources came far earlier. Li Shizhen (1518– 93) was the author of the premier pharmacopoeia for Chinese traditional medicine, the *Bencao Gangmu,* which listed more than 1,800 treatments. Along with other traditional medical guides, this led millions to believe that stewed turtle cures cancer, crocodile meat relieves asthma, pangolin scales regulate menstruation, and scorpion venom helps stroke victims.

More than four centuries after his death, Dr. Li's remedies continue to have ever more serious consequences for wildlife. Though well intentioned and respected for his scholarship, Li wrote in an age of abundant natural resources and low population density. Applied in the modern age, his prescriptions have become death warrants for many of the species he named. About 1,500 varieties of flora and fauna are close to being wiped out in the wild because of the demand for traditional medicine.[20] Other populations have increased, but only in captivity. Mixed with modern free-market principles and animal husbandry techniques, Li's teachings on traditional medicine have led to the establishment of commercial breeding centers for several rare animals. Though their owners often claim to be conservationists, most facilities are little more than battery farms.

"Our park is a salvation for wildlife," said the guide at the Xiongsen Bear and Tiger Mountain Village, in Guizhou Province, as he led me and the rest of the tour group around spacious pens and cages filled with tigers, lions, black swans, and black bears.

The more fortunate beasts shared a few football pitch–sized enclosures. Others provided entertainment for tourists. Inside the "Dream Theater"—an elevated gladiatorlike arena surrounded by nets—performers with whips and sticks prodded tigers to jump through flaming hoops and ride on the backs of horses. Outdoors, beasts paraded on a carnival float, along with monkeys riding camels and a bear cycling across a high wire without a safety net. One tiger was so placid—or doped—that he sat and posed for pictures beside tourists.

But the most compellingly gory spectacle was feeding time. From a viewing balcony, I watched alongside children, parents, and elderly tourists in fascinated horror as a water buffalo munched its last clumps of grass next to a pen in which a hungry tiger paced back and forth. As soon as the keepers lifted the gate, the predator bounded out and chased down its terrified prey. Within a minute, it sank its teeth and claws into the victim's back, raking at the skin as the buffalo cried and defecated in pain and fear. The bovine shook the tiger off and galloped away, but the respite was only temporary. The hunter jumped again and again at its neck, biting deep into the flesh until its jowls were scarlet with blood.

Squeamishness was apparently inappropriate and misplaced. The guide told us the hunt was an important training exercise for animals that would one day be released into the wild. It did not look like that would happen any time soon. The predator was too domesticated to finish off its prey. After fifteen minutes watching the bloody mauling, the crowd began to lose interest and wander away. The keepers shooed the tiger back to its cage, then dragged the wounded buffalo away on a cart for slaughter in the park's abattoir.

The real reason for the bloodfest was economic. The park desperately needed to attract tourists because it was losing a fortune on its farming business.

Xiongsen's animals were a commercial investment. The black bears were there for their bile, which was harvested through a hole punched into the side of their stomachs. The lions were raised so their meat and bones could be sold to restaurants and pharmacies. The black swans were an eco-stock holding. With only 300 left in the world, the guide told us each one was worth $20,000. But the most valuable of them all, the tiger, was proving a huge loss maker.

The park had staked its future on speed-breeding tigers, the most prized animal in Dr. Li's ancient pharmacopoeia. In terms of production it was ruthlessly efficient. The single breeding center, which was no bigger than Regent's Park, contained almost as many tigers as the entire wild population in India. Then, in 1993, the government banned the tiger trade. This was lauded by the Convention on International Trade in Endangered Species as an important step toward stabilizing the species. But for Xiongsen it proved a financial disaster.

Xiongsen's cub nursery was the start of a production line that churned out hundreds of tigers each year. They were far too genetically intermixed and tame to survive outside the farm. Most spent their lives lying around listlessly or pacing back and forth between the wire and concrete of tiny cages. Wandering away from the tourist areas, I saw that most of the animals were crammed together in thirteen rows of a dozen small cages, each containing up to four tigers. With the market blocked by the government ban, these assets ended up frozen, both economically and literally.

A keeper still with blood on his hands from dragging the wounded water buffalo to the butcher told me Xiongsen was desperate for the government to lift the ban. "Every part of the animal is valuable, but we can't sell them at the moment because it is forbidden by law. One or two tigers die every year. We put them in freezers, where they will stay until the government gives us permission to sell."

He said he has not been paid for three months. The park had filed for bankruptcy. Every day it had to pay hundreds of thousands of yuan to feed the growing population of animals. But the owner, Zhou Weisen, a former snake trapper, raised the stakes by accelerating the breeding of tigers. Conservationists accused him of using the animals to blackmail the government. "Either relax the ban or take responsibility for slaughtering more than a thousand tigers that no one can afford to feed" was the unspoken message.

Xiongsen was pushing at, and possibly beyond, the boundaries of the law. The park's restaurant, which overlooked the biggest of the animal enclosures, offered a dish called "conquering king"—the classical term for tiger—for 500 yuan, along with lion, crocodile, peacock, snake, bear, and civet cat in equally thin disguises. "Everything comes from our park," the waitress said proudly. "We don't list the ingredients. You must use your imagination."

Along with our food we got a full serving of the captive-breeding sales pitch. A poster next to the tables rhetorically asked: "Why does our country categorize the tiger as a class A protected species?" The answer it supplied had more to do with classical views of nature's utility than modern fears about declining numbers. "Because if you look at the 5,000-year history of Chinese medicine, the famous doctor Li Shizhen noted that every part of the tiger's body is a treasure."

On the black market, a single animal could be worth hundreds of thousands of dollars. The bones, used in tonics, were the most valuable part: the 25 kilograms yielded by the average tiger can fetch 2.4 million yuan ($343,000), about ten times the price of a pelt.[21] The park's "museum" was a showroom containing the skeleton of a sixteen-year-old tiger and six huge clay urns each filled with 2,000 liters of "bone-strengthening wine." Assistants encourage visitors to buy half-liter tiger-shaped bottles of the tonic for about $90. Each drop, they claimed, was distilled in vats containing the paws of tigers that died of natural causes.

They were either lying or lawbreaking. The State Forestry Administration allowed sales of the wine on condition that the only bones used in it were from lions. That was possible—Xiongsen has 200 captive-bred African lions—but in Chinese medicine these beasts were traditionally considered a poor substitute for tiger.

The park epitomized the utilitarian, nature-conquering approach to the environment and its consequences. At Xiongsen, the number of captive tigers had surged from twelve in 1992 to 1,300. But in the wild, the population had shrunk from several thousand in the 1950s to fewer than fifty. The trend was clear: the fearsome jungle predator had been subdued into a caged farm animal. The government had taken half a step away from these traditions by putting a ban in place. But it had not halted the industrial production of tigers even when the ancient tonic for health had become a drag on the economy.

Nor had there been an attempt to change the traditions behind the demand for tiger. At a pharmacy outside, the displays were filled with des-iccated sea horses for breast cancer, dog penises for virility, deer hooves for arthritis, baby snakes for sore throats, and ant lotions for beriberi. One rheumatism treatment had a picture of a tiger on the packet, but the only animal part listed among the ingredients was powdered leopard bone. Tibetan medicine, which was increasingly popular, placed just as much importance on acquiring ingredients from rare species, such as antelope horn, snake meat, and caterpillar fungus. Some potions proved useful, but there was not enough consideration of efficacy and rarity. In many cases endangered animals were being slaughtered for nothing. The saiga ante-lope, which once roamed the plains of China and Russia in huge herds, was hunted to the brink of extinction because its translucent pale pink horns were thought to have magical healing qualities in traditional medi-cine. Western science suggested, however, that consumers could get the same amount of nutrition by chewing their fingernails.[22]

The government protects China's traditions better than it protects the country's wildlife. Health ministry officials defend Dr. Li's ancient prescriptions as part of an almost blanket endorsement of traditional medicine. Rare animals are protected only selectively and usually inad-equately. The Wildlife Protection Law of 1988 epitomized the superfici-ality of much conservation work in China. On the surface, the law was progressive, prohibiting the killing of about 1,300 endangered species, encouraging forestry bureaus to set up nature reserves, and designat-ing all wild animals as the property of the state. But it made only vague mention of habitat protection.[23] Instead it established guidelines for the management of captive-breeding centers. In effect, the law encouraged the setting up of farms like Xiongsen that supplied restaurants and phar-macies.

In the decade that followed, 164 such centers were established. There are now farms of scorpions, salamanders, crocodiles, herons, musk deer, black bears, golden coin turtles, and cobras.[24] Though many are nominally listed as conservation centers, their true purpose is evident from their location. Half of the farms are sited not where the animals live in the wild but near the main two markets for traditional medicine and exotic food, Guangdong and Guangxi.

Wildlife has been caught in a pincer between traditional medicine and modern development. The government offers little protection from either. Bureaucratic efforts at conservation are stymied by weak laws, fragmented oversight, and the long-standing belief that nature needs to be managed.[25] Few people seem to accept that the best way to let animal populations recover is to leave both them and their habitats alone.

I saw just how intrusive the alternatives could be at the most celebrated conservation park in China. The Wolong Nature Reserve was a four-hour drive from Chengdu, mostly through dense mountain forests.[26] It was dark before I reached my hotel. On the approach I caught glimpses of steep river gorges and broad reservoirs in the moonlight, but it was only as I watched the sun rise the following morning that I appreciated the true beauty of the setting. It was early autumn, the hillsides were dappled with red and gold, and the crisp air was filled with birdsong.

The forests here extend hundreds of miles to the stunning opal rock-salt pools of Jiuzhaigou. In this beautiful, biorich area, the famous botanical explorer E. O. Wilson made seed collections between the wars that transformed British gardens with new varieties of azaleas, buddleia, peonies, hydrangea, magnolia, aster, and columbine. It is also home to black bear, takin, golden monkeys, musk deer, blood pheasants, minivets, rock squirrel, and black- and red-striped swallowtails.[27]

But by far its most famous resident is the giant panda. For most of the late twentieth century this epitome of bestial cuteness seemed doomed to extinction. Yet Wolong's scientists were boasting that they had brought Old Black Eyes back from the brink. I met the man who claimed to have saved the world's most famous endangered animal. It was a shocking introduction to the hard-core realities of modern animal husbandry.

Zhang Hemin was known as the "Father of Pandas," a nickname that revealed more about his paternalistic relationship with the animals than his formal title, director of Wolong Nature Reserve Administration. Bespectacled, moon-faced, and engagingly enthusiastic, he gave me a warm welcome as soon as I arrived at the research center. Zhang told me he had good news: the panda was no longer in danger because he had mastered a breeding technique with a near 100 percent success rate. As a result, the problem was no longer a shortage of pandas but of space.

To prove his point, he took me to the nursery, where there were too many newborns for the incubators, so three or four tiny cubs dozed on blankets on the floor. Next door, the pandagarten was similarly crowded with ten one-year-olds vying playfully for the top spot on a tree branch. More mature pandas had to be rotated between the spacious forested enclosures on the hillside and the narrow concrete pens close to the entrance. As we wandered among them, Zhang said his target was a captive population of 300 by 2016 (up from 120 in 2006), which would guarantee the survival of the species for at least a hundred years.

Zhang told me his breeding techniques had been developed after twenty years of trial and error. No experiment, it seemed, was too bizarre. Concerned that the captive-bred pandas might lack basic instincts, the keepers provided sex education in the form of wildlife videos showing the animals mating in the forests. When this panda porn failed to boost the beasts' sex drives, the scientists tried the remedy used by millions of humans: Viagra. "We'll never do that again," Zhang said with a wry smile. "The panda was excited for twenty-four hours. We had to beat his erect penis with a stick."

I laughed in sympathetic horror. Funnier and more pitiful still was the matchmaking deception used to minimize the risk of inbreeding. Male pandas were a discerning bunch. Left to their own devices, they would all mate with the sexiest females, which would shrink an already small genetic stock. To avoid this, researchers had to find a partner for even the least alluring females. How did they do that? "We tricked them," Zhang said with another mischievous grin. The ruse was to put a fertile and attractive female into a breeding pen, where she left scratch marks and droppings before being taken away. A male panda was then introduced. Sniffing around, he grew excited to the point of sexual incontinence. That was the point for the zookeepers to bring in the new, less attractive female scented with the urine of the animal she replaced. The "ugly panda" was introduced into the mating pen rear end first, so the male could not see the face of his partner until they finished copulating.

"Don't they get upset?" I asked, incredulously.

"Oh yes," Zhang replied. "When the males find out, they get very angry and start fighting the female. We have had to use firecrackers and a water hose to separate them."

I laughed louder and cringed more deeply, but we had not yet reached the bottom of this well of indignity for China's national symbol.

Artificial insemination is far more effective than a blind date as a means of taking advantage of the three-day fertility window of a female panda.[28] How, I wondered aloud, did the zookeepers harvest the semen? Since being shown, giant pandas have never seemed quite so cute and innocent.

Zhang took me to a lab, where researchers displayed a selection of large metal probes. These instruments were inserted into the anus of a sedated male, connected to an electricity supply, and then charged ever more powerfully until the panda ejaculated.[29] Animal husbandry was not a subject for the fainthearted.

Such practices are the consequence of viewing animals primarily as an economic resource. Pandas make money. They are rented out to overseas zoos or nature parks for up to a million dollars a year.[30] This generates suspicions that the breeding center was yet another rare-animal farm.[31] That may be a little unfair on Zhang, who seemed genuinely concerned for his subjects. But, at the very least, it is a diversion from the more important task of conserving the wild population in their natural habitat.

Such concerns prompted the World Wide Fund for Nature, which uses the giant panda as its logo, to quietly drop support for Wolong in the early 1990s. Within China too there was a debate about its usefulness. Many zoologists, including Pan Wenshi, a leading exponent of eco-civilization theory, and Professor Wang Song, the founder of the China Species Red List, have distanced themselves from the work done at Wolong and similar facilities.

Many zoologists criticize the central assumption used to justify the breeding program, namely that giant pandas are naturally inadequate mates because they have short penises, narrow vaginas, and a low sex drive.[32] Many studies suggest panda inadequacy is a myth, that the animals breed without difficulty in the wild,[33] and that the reproductive problems, which appear to occur mainly in zoos, are not surprising in an unnatural habitat under constant surveillance.

I asked Zhang whether he was commercially motivated. No, he insisted, the ultimate goal was to build up the captive population so it could one day replenish the low numbers in the wild. He proved far more sincere than the tiger farmers of Xiongsen, but no more successful. Zhang's team later released a captive-bred panda into the wild for the first time. Xiang Xiang was killed by rivals in less than a year.[34] But Zhang insists the release program will continue. As with breeding, he hopes trial-and-error experiments will eventually result in success.

But there is a danger that the reliance on money and science will distract efforts from the core conservation problems of development and consumption. The giant pandas at Wolong have had more money and attention lavished on them than the majority of the world's population. Cubs born there have a better chance of surviving than human babies in more than a dozen countries.[35] But outside captivity, where the animals could not generate rents of a million dollars a year, the situation is very different.

The wild panda population remains precariously small, despite efforts to protect its natural habitat. One of the most encouraging conservation developments of recent years was a government's pledge in 2005 to expand and connect the scattered nature reserves in the Min mountain range, which is home to Wolong and almost half of the world's 1,590 wild pandas.[36] More than the captive-breeding program, this could have improved the panda's long-term chances of survival. But the well-intentioned creation of reserves was compromised by economic development. Roads, bridges, and dams were still being built in the protected areas, cutting the panda communities off from each other.

The survival of the panda is crucial for other creatures that share the same ecosystem. Like the tiger, it is an "umbrella species." By protecting the habitats of such wide-ranging beasts, many smaller—and less attractive—creatures can be protected too. This is vital for species that taste better and look worse. Darwin never mentioned survival of the cutest, but it is a reality on a planet dominated by mankind. The public is willing to donate time and money to conserve big-eyed creatures but rarely considers amphibians, insects, or plant life.[37] Many snakes and turtles are being eaten into extinction.[38] The saddest example is that of the giant Yangtze softshell turtle. The last two in the world are at Suzhou Zoo. They are aged 80 and 100, but zookeepers have tried to mate them without success. Once they go, the earth will have lost another magnificent creature.

Conservation is failing in China. That is the view I have heard again and again in discussions with biodiversity experts, former officials, and environmental journalists. Captive breeding can prevent some threatened species used in traditional medicine from dying out completely, but overall wildlife is being decimated. The despondent view of John MacKinnon, one of the first foreign experts to work in China, is typical. "I've been doing biodiversity conservation for forty years," he told me. "It is a bit depressing. We are doing more things, in more sophisticated ways, and yet destruction has outpaced us. I have written so many technical reports, but I have preached to an audience that doesn't believe me."

Xie Yan, the head of the Wildlife Conservation Society of China, told me the problem was a lack of love for nature and animals, except in regard to how they could be consumed: "When I go out with people to watch wildlife, they often say, 'That looks very good to eat.' It is hard to change thousands of years of culture. Because Chinese people eat everything, they can kill anything."[39]

Despite this grim prognosis, neither of them have given up. There are reasons for hope. The government is doing more than in the past. Species such as the Tibetan chiru and the gray snub-nosed monkey have been brought back from the brink. Public awareness is growing, particularly among the young urban middle class. Bird-watching is becoming popular, and no longer just for economic or culinary reasons. Small groups of young activists are trying to change consumer attitudes and put pressure on restaurants and markets.[40] In academia, Zhao Qikun of the Kunming Institute of Zoology is among those calling for a more spiritual approach to nature. Peking University has set up the nation's first Ecological Civilization Research Center, headed by Professor Pan, reportedly an opponent of captive breeding. President Hu Jintao has made the creation of an "eco-civilization" a goal of his "Scientific Development" program.

The Communist Party takes a utilitarian view of nature. Its leaders are aware that the limit of exploitation is creeping closer. Cadres are told they should do more to protect "natural resources necessary for production." Western wildlife zoologists have also recognized that economic incentives are necessary for conservation, proposing the replacement of ineffective blanket bans with limited fee-generating hunting as a way for nature reserves to generate funds.[41] International cash has come pouring in and conservation groups have grown both larger and more influential. But wildlife remains under ever-increasing pressure from climate change and economic development.

★

Until the baiji expedition, I had hoped that the threat to China's wildlife could be averted by the use of money, intelligence, and technology. But after joining the world's smartest, best-funded scientists in the search for the Yangtze dolphin, I realized there came a point when it was too late to do anything.

On my last day with the expedition, we set off on the *Kekao 1* just after dawn. Sharp early morning sunlight cut through the mist and shattered into glittering shards on the water. On deck, Wang Ding, China's leading baiji expert, and Brent Stewart from the Hubbs-Seaworld Research Institute in San Diego were peering through the giant binoculars. Down below, Tomonori Akamatsu from Japan was listening for an audio trace with hydrophone omnidirectional equipment.

The baiji too relied on sonar. They navigated and communicated using a high- and low-frequency acoustic system. This sensitivity to sound was a handicap in the modern age. The increasing noise from ships' engines disrupted their perception of the world.

After the last of six captive baiji, Qi Qi, died in the Wuhan Institute of Hydrobiology in 2002, the only records of the animal left behind were photographs, skeletons, and a single "sound image" of the dolphin's 5,000-hertz whistle. When Akamatsu played it back on the boat, I told him it sounded mournful.

"No," he replied. "It sounds like an engine. That's the problem. In calm, quiet water, a baiji can communicate with other dolphins up to a kilometer away. But the noise from traffic makes it hard for them to do that."

Back on deck, I looked out at speedboats, giant container ships, fishing vessels, and barges heaped with coal, cement, and gravel. If there were any surviving baiji, they must find it difficult to locate one another amid the chugs and shrieks of the engines.

There was still life on the river. "Pied kingfisher off the starboard bow," cried a spotter. A few minutes later, another reported a small pod of porpoises. The sight briefly raised hopes. But the veteran Yangtze watcher Wang shook his head. "There are little more than a dozen. Last time we saw more than a hundred in this area. This also used to be where we saw the most baiji too. But now there are none."

We were passing along the stretch of the river where the baiji was formerly most plentiful. Everyone was on deck, peering through binoculars, eyes strained into a gray expanse. Blurred by the haze, the sky, mud banks, and river all merged into one. The loss of biodiversity and color appeared written on the landscape.

Near Chenglingji, acrid smoke billowed out of a coal-fired power plant, and a paper factory discharged an unceasing torrent of filthy water into the river. The smell was so pungent that the crew grimaced more than half a mile away. It marked the end of the stretch where hopes of finding a baiji alive were highest, but the world's best spotters and advanced technology had failed to detect the telltale whistle or sight a single pale dorsal fin.

The mood on board darkened. Some began to ask angrily why mankind killed off the baiji. The rescue mission had become a whodunnit.

"Why does nobody pay attention to a species until there are almost none left? What's wrong with human nature?" said Samuel Turvey, of the Zoological Society of London. The baiji, he said, was a mammal family that diverged twenty million years ago from other ancient types of dolphin. "Its loss would be a major blow to biological diversity. This isn't a twig—it is a branch on the tree of life. To lose it would be so depressing. Yet nothing has been done for thirty years."

There was to be no feel-good ending. The voyage that started out as a search ended as a farewell. Over 1,600 kilometers through the middle and lower reaches of the Yangtze, all the way to Shanghai, they failed to spot a single baiji. Soon after the expedition ended, the species was declared functionally extinct.[42] Man had wiped out its first dolphin. The conservation dream team was too late.

I look back on the baiji expedition as the biggest story of my journalistic career. More than tsunami, earthquakes, World Cup tournaments, or G8 summits, the end of a species after twenty million years felt terrifyingly momentous. This was not just a piece of news. It was even more than history. It was an event on a geological timescale with disturbing implications for our own species. What were we doing to our world? How could we assume our species was developing and becoming more civilized when an animal once worshipped had been wiped out by neglect, greed, and human filth?

Yet the story never made the front pages. Tragic as the news was, the baiji was just the latest species on the eco-scrap heap. Nobody felt affected. Nobody felt personally responsible. The West blamed China.

China blamed illegal behavior. Everyone blamed economic development, but who wanted to sacrifice that for a dolphin with squinty eyes?

Growth, it seemed, had a price. Modernization was messy. The development model—pioneered in the UK, then Europe, North America, and Japan—was to get rich first, clean up later. Sometimes, as in the case of the baiji, the fix came too late, but the idea of progress was based on the assumption that humanity would eventually get it right. According to this view, the left-behind flag bearer was just an unfortunate casualty of development.

But I was no longer convinced by such reassurances. Progress no longer sounded quite so admirable. I would travel farther along the trajectory of modernization to look in more detail at where it was taking us, and why. The drivers of development could be found on the fast-evolving coast of the southeast. Perhaps at my next destination, Guangdong Province, I would discover how the export of blame, waste, and responsibility had become one of the dirtiest businesses of globalization. The rules and regulations intended to curb this weren't working, but what did this have to do with the rest of us?

Southeast
Man

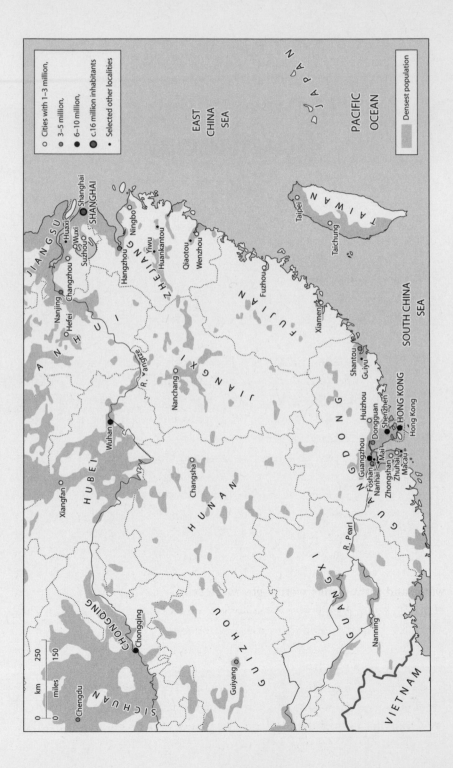

5

Made in China?
Guangdong

Guangdong is where China and your life intersect.
—*Alexandra Harney*[1]

The children at Mai Middle School had probably never heard of Tesco and they could only imagine the luxuries offered by Britain's biggest supermarket chain. But though their village was five thousand miles away from the nearest UK High Street, they could see, feel, and smell the consequences of globalized consumer culture.

On a tree near their classrooms, a snagged blue-and-white Tesco shopping bag fluttered in the warm semitropical breeze like the flag of a distant empire. The gates of a neighboring factory were decorated with huge plastic banners advertising a discount that would be worth a week's wages in Mai: "£20 Off Tesco Mobile Phones If You Spend More Than £40 in the Store." The stream beside their school was choked with carrier bags and plastic wrappers from the other side of the world. Staring up from the fetid water and filthy banks were logos for Tesco, Wal-Mart, Argos, and even Help the Aged. A bold mission statement on the charity shop's green-and-white bag vowed to fight "Poverty, Isolation and Neglect."

It was a decent sentiment, I thought, as I stood in the midst of the illegally dumped garbage. I could imagine my mother feeling good filling a shopping bag like that with secondhand clothes. She would think her shopping was making the world a better place; that it was a form of recycling that helped the aged and the planet at the same time. It would upset her to think people on the other side of the world were paying an environmental price for her charity.

Nobody in Mai was asking for handouts, though the average income was considerably less than Britain's state pension. Locals wanted something far more basic: clean air and water.

"The river is foul—we can smell it from our classrooms," Wang Yanxia, a pupil at the middle school, told me during a noisy breaktime. "When it rains, the water floods onto the path and the stench is everywhere."

Her friend Cui Yun said it had been like this since she had entered the school three years earlier. "My mother worries about my health. Lots of people get sick."

The school was on a street full of small recycling firms that served as the intestine of the global economy, breaking down the world's discarded plastic bags, bottles, and wrappers into tiny reusable parts. Most of the firms were little bigger than sheds, outside which stood blackboards detailing the type, color, and quality of the plastic they dealt in. Migrant workers from Anhui, Sichuan, and Guangxi sifted by hand through hundreds of thousands of tiny plastic pellets, picking out discolored flecks and bits of fluff. The recycled plastic was suitable only for weaving into low-grade sheeting, such as the ubiquitous red-white-and-blue coverings on building sites and the cheap carryalls used by migrants when they travel. One of the traders told me she bought semiprocessed bags for 9,000 yuan a ton (around $1,286) and, after painstakingly cleaning up the contents, sold the plastic for 10,500 yuan.

The cost was ditches full of garbage and a population full of health concerns. The village doctor said the area had an unusually high incidence of respiratory diseases that might be attributable to pollution. But he said locals were willing to pay the price. "This is a sensitive topic. Of course we want a gardenlike environment, but people here have to make a living." A migrant laborer who was walking past the filthy stream agreed. "I don't care about the environment. If your stomach isn't full, how can you worry about your health?"

I was in Guangdong to examine the environmental price China had paid since opening up to global capital and markets. In 1979, this southeastern province was the first to trade with the outside world, and it had since become one of the richest regions in China. Much of its wealth was generated by regurgitating the muck of the global economy either in the form of garbage for recycling or outsourced dirty manufacturing. Fittingly for our globalized age, it was part economic miracle, part environmental tragedy. This was where most of the planet's toys and shoes were made, where Apple outsourced much of the production of its iPods, where Wal-Mart filled its shelves, where Britain's shoes and America's toys and everyone's Christmas decorations were made. Since the start of China's economic reforms in 1978, Guangdong's economy had grown more than a hundredfold to the point where it was bigger than that of Turkey, South America, and Finland.[2] If it were a country, it could join the G20 of the world's richest nations. It was also home to many of the dirtiest and most polluted places on the mainland. The expression "filthy rich" could have been made for Guangdong.

My intention was to sift through the province's rubbish dumps to see where the filth came from. It was a muckraking exercise in both senses, a very deliberate search for the dark and dirty side of development, both in China and overseas. Digging for dirt is as much a part of a reporter's role as reflecting background trends and describing the details of everyday life. Getting a balance between these elements is one of the biggest challenges of the job. To have any chance of achieving that, it is necessary to get out of the office and into the field. Stories rarely turn out as expected.

There was no shortage of places to investigate in Guangdong. Among the palm trees and factories of this semitropical manufacturing region were clusters of contemporary *Sanford & Son* businesses that dealt with *yang laji,* or foreign rubbish. Shopping bags and bottles were shipped to Shunde and Heshan from London, Rotterdam, and Hong Kong for chopping, melting, and remolding into pellets. In the electronic waste communities of Guiyu and Qingyuan, old computers, televisions, and home appliances from the United States, Japan, and South Korea were stripped down and broken up. On a bigger scale in Dongguang, Zhang Yin's wastepaper empire has made her the richest self-made woman in the world, overtaking Oprah Winfrey and J. K. Rowling.[3]

There seemed to be little stigma attached to waste. As I left Mai, my driver told me he was grateful for the foreign garbage. "In Guangdong, when we call someone a rubbish man, it's a compliment," he told me. "It means they have money."

On a long, flat gray road, we passed the gates and buildings of countless factories and industrial parks, most of them joint ventures with foreign investors. Major international brands had home appliances, textiles, shoes, furniture, plastic bags, toys, and knickknacks manufactured and packaged far more cheaply here than in their home countries. When the goods were sold overseas, most of the profit went to the foreign brand owner and the retailer. A tiny share of the revenue remained in Guangdong, though the original product and its wrapping often made its way back here after it was used and discarded in the West.

After an hour's drive, we reached the outskirts of Shunde, where the compressed bales of Dutch Kinder Eggs, Italian diapers, French Lego, and other European trash were stacked on the roadside. Reflecting the close proximity of Hong Kong and its British legacy, much of it was from the UK—Tesco milk cartons, Marks & Spencer's cranberry juice, Kellogg's cornflakes boxes, Walkers crisp packets, Snickers wrappers, and Persil powder containers. It was not just a compression of paper and plastic but of marketing slogans: "They're G-r-r-reat!" "Aah! Bisto," "Whiter Than White."

In trade terms, it made perfect sense for the waste to be shipped across the world for recycling. Historically, British and other foreign merchants had always found it easy to fill their ships with goods on the route from China, but they often sailed in the opposite direction with empty cargo holds. When the economist and demographer Thomas Malthus foresaw the rise of Chinese manufacturing in his 1798 *Essay on the Principle of Population,* he correctly predicted that this would lead to a trade imbalance because Britain would have little to offer in return. The gap, he said, would have to be made up with "luxuries collected from around the world."

What that meant in practice was that my country became the world's biggest drug dealer. British and Dutch merchants had already begun selling Indian-grown opium in Guangdong, then known as Canton, which was at the time the only open trading port in China. In the twenty years up to 1839, imports of this "luxury" narcotic surged fivefold, prompting the Qing emperor to impose a ban. The British prime minister, Lord Palmerston, responded as any self-respecting underworld boss would do by using force to protect and expand his business.[4] Using coal-powered gunboats for the first time, the Royal Navy seized Hong Kong, blockaded the Pearl River, sank dozens of Chinese ships, and forced the Qing emperor to open up Shanghai and several other ports to foreign trade. For China, the crushing defeat in the First Opium War was a rude introduction to carbon-capital power. The ancient civilization never entirely recovered from the shock.

At the time of my visit, there was once again a huge trade imbalance. But this time, the shortfall was being made up not by drugs but by garbage.[5] The economics were logical. It was cheaper to send a container of waste from London to Guangdong on an otherwise empty ship than it was to truck it to Manchester.[6]

Adam Smith, the father of capitalism, would probably have considered this business as usual. In the eighteenth century, he described how China's poor were so wretched they ate rubbish: "They are eager to fish up the nastiest garbage thrown overboard from any European ship. Any carrion, the carcase of a dead dog or cat, for example, is as welcome to them as the most wholesome food to the people of other countries."[7]

But sending waste to the other side of the world was fraught with environmental, health, and ethical hazards. Although recycling could save more carbon emissions than simply dumping the waste in a landfill, the rubbish shipments put an irresponsible distance between consumption and its consequences.[8] People in other countries were being exposed to risks and pollution that wealthy foreign consumers were not willing to accept themselves.

The garbage had been building up for decades. In the mid-sixties, the philosopher Alan Watts was among the first to anticipate a global waste crisis as he contemplated the incipient consumer culture of the United States and western Europe: "Can any melting or burning imaginable get rid of these ever-rising mountains of ruin—especially when the things we make and build are beginning to look more and more like rubbish even before they are thrown away?"[9]

Since then, landfill sites in Europe, North America, and Japan have been filling up almost as fast as they were dug. The alternatives were not much better. Incinerators might reduce rubbish to ash, but, unless operated at very high temperatures, they foul the air with dioxins and other toxins. Meanwhile, we—the global consumer class—were buying ever more goods in ever more layers of wrapping.

Rather than cut down on consumption, which would hurt economic growth, governments encouraged citizens to recycle, which appeared to be a clean, efficient alternative to burning and landfilling. But all too often this meant sending the waste overseas, particularly to China.[10] The rubbish was not supposed to be dumped. That was prohibited by EU and U.S. law, but shipments of nonhazardous waste were permitted for recycling.[11]

This loophole allowed rich nations to deceive themselves that they were cleaning up, even though little or no effort was made to ensure the shipped waste was dealt with properly at the other end. In effect, much of it was swept under a Guangdong carpet.

Not surprisingly, the dubious ethics involved prompted comparisons with the opium trade.[12] But the Guangdong authorities were as indifferent to illegal waste as their Cantonese forebears were to illicit drugs. Perhaps the province's geography has shaped its destiny. Lying close to foreign borders and far from the center of state power in Beijing, the control-dodging character of the region is encapsulated in the expression *shangao huangdiyuan,* "the mountains are high and the emperor far away." This far south, the authority of the state is stretched to its limits. A locally based UK diplomat once told me she proposed a collaboration with the Guangdong officials based on new energy efficiency laws that had just been passed by the state. The response: "We don't think those laws apply to us."

Weak governance and dire pollution go hand in hand. China's political system is neither dictatorship nor democracy. For the environment, it contains the worst elements of both. At the top, the state lacks the authority to impose pollution regulations and wildlife conservation laws, while at the bottom citizens lack the democratic tools of a free press, independent courts, and elections to defend their land, air, and water. The gap in between is filled by local governments, township enterprises, migrant workers, and foreign corporations, many of which are focused on economic growth at the expense of all else. The result is neither red nor green; it is black or gray. Money is concentrated in this bulging middle belt, which is also the main source of corruption and pollution. With such weak regulation and political accountability, rubbish can be sent to Guangdong in the name of nonhazardous recycling, but the end result is often toxic rubbish dumps that damage the health of local people.

Guiyu is the world's computer graveyard.[13] To get there, I drove through giant manufacturing towns I had never heard of, including Chendian, which billboard after billboard of giant seminaked women declared to be the global center of bra production. Farther along the road, the skies darkened and rain began tapping on the taxi roof. I passed a funeral procession. The mourners wore transparent plastic macs over their traditional white funeral garb as they walked through the drizzle. Soon after, I reached the town where motherboards went to die, where hard drives were softened up, and memory cards were erased beyond the reach of any Control Z. The streets were stacked with green circuit boards, computer casings, and reams of cables, leads, and wires. Locals sat among mounds of brightly colored plastic, hand-sorting the waste by shade and type.

Stopping and talking to locals was risky. The dirty conditions and low wages made e-waste a sensitive topic. Several journalists had previously been detained here. At least one team had been attacked.[14] I asked the driver to park on a side road, where my Western face and the taxi's out-of-town number plate would attract less attention. I wandered over to a makeshift outdoor workshop where a bare-chested old man was sorting through huge earthenware pots of tiny plastic pellets under a net awning. The colors were separated in tubs of chemical compounds: green pellets sank, purple floated to the surface. It was a smelly, time-consuming process for which the man earned about 40 yuan per day. He said he had been processing waste from around the world for twenty years, but his garrulity ended as a crowd gathered. The old man asked me to leave: "No journalists. I already get into trouble from time to time with the tax authorities."

It was a similar story in dozens of small warehouses nearby. In one, a child was helping to strip circuit boards. In another, a woman removed whatever white plastic she could find from a pile of computers and printers for 20 yuan (about $3.00) per day. Next door, two Sichuanese women earned 36 yuan for a thirteen-hour shift, picking apart motherboards. "We know it might be toxic, but what can we do? It's a job," one of them told us. "We're not scared."

They should have been. Studies have revealed that the amount of lead in the blood of children in Guiyu is 50 percent higher than limits set by the U.S. Centers for Disease Control and Prevention, which could result in retarded mental development. Workers are also exposed to cadmium, chromium, polyvinyl chlorides, brominated flame retardants, and mercury—a toxic cocktail that can cause brain damage, cancer, or kidney failure.[15]

Many of these chemicals leak from the hundreds of millions of computers, mobile phones, and other devices discarded overseas.[16] Efforts to make manufacturers share responsibility with retailers, consumers, and governments for the lifespan of their products have had only partial success.[17] American companies often falsely claim to be recycling domestically while actually shipping e-waste to China and elsewhere, using shell companies in Hong Kong and Singapore. Interpol has identified waste smuggling as a thriving business for crime organizations worldwide. Eddy Zheng, who studied the e-garbage problem at the Guangzhou Institute of Geochemistry, believes the rapid increase of e-waste coming into China might be out of control: "The government does not have resources to stop this. Many foreign companies take advantage of this to illegally import e-waste into China."[18] He is scathingly sarcastic about foreign efforts to restrict the trade. "The U.S. is too generous in its contribution to China's environmental contamination," he said.[19]

On the road out of Guiyu I saw a banner proclaiming, "Protecting the Environment Is Enriching Life." As was often the case in China, the ideal of the propaganda was the opposite of reality on the streets. It was aspirational. The country's political system was well described as "government by slogan."[20]

Recycling could be less of a hazard with better governance, but Guangdong's economic success has been achieved with speed and energy, not caution and regulation. That is part of its attraction to foreign capital. Since 1979, when the port of Shenzhen was chosen as one of the pioneer economic development zones, Guangdong has been at the forefront of China's spectacular transformation. It was here that former paramount leader Deng Xiaoping launched his famous southern tour in 1992, when he urged the nation to follow Guangdong's example. Reform, he said, should not "proceed slowly like women with bound feet, but blaze a trail and press forward boldly."

The province has thrived on the shifting ideological border between old-style mainland communism and the capitalism of neighboring Hong Kong, its main conduit for trade and investment. Ethics have been contorted by the province's itinerant, border culture. As well as building one of the most spectacular and dynamic economies in the modern world, Guangdong has pioneered a model of corrupt, land-grabbing, labor-abusing, environment-degrading development. For a journalist, it is a gold mine.

How manufacturing costs were kept low is one of the province's dirtiest secrets. Manufacturers are often contractually obliged not to reveal which companies they make products for because the value of brands could be destroyed if consumers are informed about factory conditions. Weak governance helps companies cover up, but the people of Guangdong knew better than anyone the real worth of luxury-brand bags and footwear because they make many of the components.

Due to weak governance, the province has become a counterfeiting center as well as a manufacturing hub, sometimes turning out the knock-offs very close to the original. The city of Shantou on the northeast coast is notorious for copying products made in foreign-invested factories.[21] The cultural fakery also applies to art. At Dafen, 3,000 counterfeit painters produce Rembrandts, Picassos, and Dalís at the rate of fifty masterpieces per day. You can haggle down a copy of Vincent Van Gogh's *Sunflowers* to a mere 50 yuan.

Income disparities are more glaring here than most places in China. On one side is Hong Kong, which has the tenth-richest population on the planet. On the other is Guangxi, one of the poorest provinces in China with an average income twenty times lower.[22] Lodged between these extremes, Guangdong is a hotbed of tension and crime. Corruption is rampant.[23] "Black society" gangs, such as the Triads, are traditionally strong in this region, partly because of Canton's tribal culture but also because of the proximity of the gambling dens of Macau and the opportunities of underworld business in Hong Kong. Many local governments and businesses employ thugs. One night in Shenzhen, a row over an inflated bar bill ended up with two friends and me being chased by a gang of more than a dozen heavies. They surrounded our taxi, smashed my glasses, and badly beat up one of my friends with sticks and belts. It could easily have been much worse.

Far more violent tensions were found at the shifting boundary between urban and rural Guangdong. Pressure often exploded to the surface, particularly when farmland was requisitioned for expanding cities and industrial estates. Like many correspondents, I had spent much of my time in China interviewing dispossessed farmers in Guangdong, which was on the front line of the land disputes. Governance, the law, and farmers' interests were sacrificed in the name of economic expediency so land could be secured for more factories, showrooms, and dump sites. The illegality of the authorities' actions was evident in their attempts to cover up what they were doing. In Xiangyang, I was detained by police, who admitted they had intercepted my phone calls to local protesters. In Taishi, two rural activists were put under house arrest to prevent them from speaking to me.[24] To avoid getting another in trouble, I had to dash through an emergency exit and hide in a restaurant toilet for thirty minutes to avoid detection.

In Sanshan, residents were so desperate to appeal to the outside world about the confiscation of their land that they took the risk of sneaking out of their villages at midnight, being interviewed through the early hours, and then returning just before dawn. Some passed on messages and pictures through intermediaries. Others agreed to meet in parks where they could check whether any of us were being followed. Other interviews could only be conducted by phone—frequently switching prepaid SIM cards because the police might be listening in. This, in what was supposedly the most modern and open province in China.

Guangdong had other dirty secrets. It was a hub for the illegal trade in endangered species. Stallholders, restaurants, and chemists competed to offer the most unusual wildlife dishes and medicines from the traditional pharmacopoeia described in the previous chapter. Markets teemed with more exotic creatures than many zoos. The stalls sold snakes, scorpions, salamanders, and dozens of species of birds and turtles, some of which were endangered. Rare animals were once partially protected by their price. In the past, only the rich could afford such delicacies. But with the rise in wealth, many were being mass-consumed into extinction.[25]

I had a soft spot for the pangolin, a cute scaly anteater that was much in demand for its tasty meat and because its scales were thought to regulate menstruation and to help mothers lactate. The creature had once been common in Guangdong, Yunnan, and Guangxi but was now extremely rare in China. To meet the growing demand, hunters moved to neighboring Cambodia, Vietnam, and Laos; then, when the pangolin populations of these nations were decimated, they pushed ever farther south down through Thailand and the Malay peninsula to Indonesia. The last healthy populations in the remote jungles of Java were also coming under threat.[26]

The smuggling of these beasts was highlighted in May 2006, when a rickety wooden vessel lost engine power off Qingzhou Island off the coast of Guangdong. After the coast guard boarded the abandoned boat, they discovered 5,000 of the world's rarest animals, many so dehydrated from the tropical sun that they were close to death. Crushed inside 200 cages on this 25-meter craft were 31 pangolins, 44 leatherback turtles, 2,720 monitor lizards, and 1,130 Brazilian turtles. They also found twenty-one bear paws wrapped in newspaper.[27] The cargo would probably never have been discovered if it were not for the engine failure, and many more are undoubtedly smuggled in undetected.

Weak governance was at the core of the problem. Police investigations into illegal wildlife consumption were stepped up, but they made limited progress.[28] In 2006, a waitress at one Guangdong restaurant did not think twice before confirming to my assistant, who was posing as a customer, that pangolin was indeed on the menu. Three years later, after countless other supposed crackdowns, we found another restaurant offering pangolin at 1,000 yuan (about $143) per kilogram. "You need to pay in advance and then we will find one for you," said an employee. "We can cook it in a hot pot or braise it in soy sauce."

As illegal restaurants and markets were closed down, others opened up elsewhere or were pushed underground. At 4 a.m., in a dark suburb of Taiping, about an hour's drive from downtown Guangzhou, I found exotic-animal traders covertly doing business out of sight of the authorities and conservationists. The three long rows of sheds they occupied resembled a cramped and dirty zoo filled with wire cages: long and tall for the herons, flat and low for the civet cats. Ostriches had room to move their necks but not their bodies. Local conservationists told me there were similar markets throughout southern China.

Such is the passion for the exotic in Guangdong that local markets had accidentally become biochemical laboratories. Viruses were mixed and remixed as cages filled with civet cats, wild boar, snakes, frogs, and rare birds were stacked close together in enclosed, humid areas. SARS—and quite possibly bird flu—were thought to have originated here.

Guangdong is also where new modes of behavior are tried out. As in California, what happens here today often spreads to the rest of the country tomorrow. This is the home of sexual pioneer Li Li, a philosophy graduate and bedroom activist, who—using her better-known pseudonym Muzimei—became China's most celebrated sex blogger and the first to podcast her lovemaking. It is also a hub of the world's adult toy business, of which China controls 70 percent. In Shenzhen, I visited a sex-toy factory, where bored production-line workers were sticking fake pubic hair on rubber vaginas, testing the circuits on unfeasibly large vibrators, sticking studs on sado-masochist outfits, and waiting for the end of a shift spent monotonously making cheap thrills.

Prostitution is a less legal but far bigger part of the sex business. In Shenzhen, it reaches an industrial scale in streets filled with pink-lit windows displaying the charms of young "masseuses" and "hairdressers," each marked with a number like an item on a restaurant menu. In Guangzhou, I interviewed a karaoke hostess who rented out her womb to a childless Hong Kong couple while making money on the side through prostitution and blackmail. In Shenzhen, I got in touch with Azhen, a twenty-four-year-old *ernai* or second wife, who lived in a flat paid for by a sugar daddy. Hers was a common story. Housing estates near the border were heavily populated with mistresses of rich men in Hong Kong. "No woman wants to demean herself, but there is no social safety net," Azhen told us.[29]

The same might be said of China's place in the global economy. Foreign money and weak domestic regulation have turned Guangdong into a place where overseas companies can illicitly ejaculate emissions and pollution and indulge in energy-intensive behavior while pretending to be clean at home. This is where the developed world dodges its own rules. Rubbish is not the only environmental problem outsourced to China. Carbon is also being dumped as international manufacturers shift production of dirty, energy-intensive goods to Guangdong and beyond.[30] Far away and out of sight of independent courts and a free media, governments and international corporations use China to sidestep the Kyoto Protocol and other international treaties on environmental and labor standards.

Pan Yue, the deputy minister for environmental protection, noted the hypocrisy of wealthier nations: "Developed countries account for 15 percent of the world's population, yet use over 85 percent of its resources. They raise their own environmental standards and transfer resource-intensive and polluting industries to developing nations; they establish a series of green barriers and bear as little environmental responsibility as is possible."[31]

Guangdong is where many of these dubious environmental accounts are hidden. Just as in the Qing dynasty, when corrupt local officials put British opium dealers above their own people, the province is now selling itself as a haven for carbon cheats and waste-regulation dodgers. This is a major reason why China has overtaken the U.S. as the world's biggest emitter of greenhouse gases: between 15 and 40 percent of the country's carbon dioxide output is attributable to the production of exports.[32]

Local people do not receive a fair share of the benefit. Half of the factories are partly or wholly owned by foreign investors, and Chinese partners, when present, are on a far from equal footing.[33] Yet, they are the ones paying the environmental price. Guangdong has one of the worst acid-rain problems in China.[34] The Pearl River, which flows through Guangzhou, was classified as too contaminated for human contact for most of its length for ten years until 2008.[35] In that year, there were more smoggy days here than at any time since the start of the People's Republic in 1949.[36] The haze often spread to Hong Kong and other neighboring regions.

But Guangdong is trying to escape its reputation as the global economy's toilet bowl. The provincial government has moved dirty factories farther inland and nurtured domestic high-tech industries in Guangzhou and Shenzhen. Among the most impressive is Build Your Dreams, a battery-and-electric vehicle manufacturer that became the first company in the world to mass-produce a plug-in hybrid car in 2009. Guangzhou's attempts to turn green are also evident on the skyline, where the seventy-one-story solar-and-wind-powered Pearl River Tower stands proud as the world's most energy-efficient superskyscraper. Its low-emission, environmentally friendly credentials are, however, compromised by the identity of its owner: China National Tobacco.

The city has committed billions of yuan to cleaning up the water and air. To demonstrate the improvement, the Guangzhou mayor, Zhang Guangning, led thousands of people in a swim across the Pearl River in 2006, the first such event in thirty years. But the crossing was only possible thanks to a series of temporary fixes, including the shutdown of factories and the flushing of dams in the days leading up to the swim. Even with these emergency measures, participants complained the water was bitter, oily, and smelly.

The problem is that Guangdong—like China, like developing nations through history—prefers to deal with the environmental symptoms rather than the economic causes. Instead of closing down or cleaning up dirty factories, it just relocates them farther inland. Instead of cutting waste-water emissions, it builds more treatment plants.

Efforts to improve the environment also face a new challenge from the rapid increase in domestic waste as China's populace grows richer and millions more consumers join the resource-hungry, throwaway lifestyle of the developed world. The average person in China discards a third less rubbish than their counterparts in Europe and almost one half less than those in the United States.[37] But they are catching up fast. The amount of domestic refuse more than doubled in the decade after 1998.[38] Yet there are few specialized facilities for dealing with hazardous waste, which means toxins continue to contaminate groundwater and soil resources.

The old problem of foreign dumping persists because Guangdong's governance is weak, and developed nations remain as hypocritical as ever. After a series of embarrassing British media reports in the mid-2000s about the trade in recycled waste, the Chinese government was shamed into shutting down districts like Nanhai, which had been a major plastic and metal recycling center. It also prohibited imports of foreign waste. But, as usual in this province where gaping holes could be found in even the most draconian legislation, the businesses found a way around the regulations. They simply moved on and ignored them.

The concrete was still wet when I arrived at Shijing Village, a refugee camp for rubbish recyclers who had been forced to relocate after the government clampdown. The scrap-dealing community had recently set up their new base in the middle of the countryside in an attempt to avoid prying eyes. Many of the sheds were only half-completed, but the task of buying, selling, and sorting rubbish was already in full swing. The operation was remarkably specialized. One area was dedicated to green and red hotel welcome mats and elevator carpets marked, as was popular in China, with the different days of the week. Another stack of rubbish consisted entirely of the bases of revolving chairs. In other areas, sorters made separate piles of broken black buckets, discarded lids of shampoo bottles, and shoes of every shape and size.

I was thrilled. The junk was a journalistic treasure. I could recycle it for a story proving that the ban on waste imports had been evaded yet again, and that the cleanup of the recycling industry was merely a cosmetic exercise that pushed the problem from the suburbs into the countryside. It had taken a long time and a lot of luck to find. Earlier in the day, we visited Nanhai, but the former recycling hub was eerily deserted. The streets were swept clean and the small sheds shuttered up. The only sign of what the area had been was a foul stream and a handful of dispirited locals for whom the UK media's reports and the government's sudden concern about the environment were a financial disaster.

"It's a terrible blow because we only started this business last year. We get no compensation. All we can do is wait and hope the government allows us to restart business," said one old man, Ding Chunming, who used to process plastic bottles and bags. Others were less patient and optimistic. There were rumors that less law-abiding recyclers had moved to a new location. My assistant, my photographer, and I got nowhere in asking the authorities where that might be. We wasted so many hours searching that I considered giving up and going home.

But by then our taxi driver had entered so completely into the spirit of the hunt that he took the initiative. In the next town he stopped at the first car-scrap dealer on the roadside and, without any prompting, made up a completely fictitious story about us being foreign businessmen looking for a place to sell overseas rubbish. Within minutes, he had directions for Shijing. I sat in the car, a passive conspirator in the deception but its main beneficiary.

For most of the two-hour drive to Shijing we argued over the journalistic ethics of this pretense. "You'll never get any real news in Guangdong if you come clean that you are a journalist," the cameraman—a veteran in the region—told me. I initially claimed the moral high ground, asserting that journalists should speak as well as write the truth. But I realized my words were hypocritical. I was benefiting from the falsehood, so I should either abandon the project or take part in the deception. I chose the latter, justifying this to myself as a small wrong to expose a bigger one.

Minutes later I was lying myself, posing on the phone as a British plastic-waste dealer and hearing from a potential business partner in Guangdong that we could evade the ban on foreign rubbish by bringing it in through Hong Kong. He offered me $100 a ton.[39] By the time we reached Shijing, I had jettisoned my qualms and entered fully into my new fake role.

Most of the rubbish recyclers were unconvinced by my act and treated me with understandable suspicion. There was no hostility but considerable concern about the presence of a foreigner in a place that no overseas businessman was likely to visit. The people we met were at the bottom of the social ladder. They had been moved on once because media coverage about "dirty China" embarrassed their government. Seeing us, they feared the same thing would happen again. A local businesswoman, who gave her name only as Ms. Liang, guessed immediately that I was a journalist and begged me not to write a critical story. "We have only just got here from Nanhai," she told me. "I have never dealt with foreign waste. I can't do it now and I won't do it in the future."

But another, more credulous, man told me he was willing to strike a deal if the price was right. He did not realize he might be incriminating himself to a journalist. My ability to deceive had improved.

I left with a miniscoop and a major feeling of guilt.[40] The Guangdong recyclers were clearing up the world's mess, yet they were treated as if they created it. Pushed ever farther out of sight along with the rubbish, they helped to maintain the illusion of environmental improvement in developed Western nations and rich cities like Beijing, Guangzhou, and Shanghai. In reality, there was no cleanup, just a widening of the distance between consumption and its consequences. This was the opposite of responsible self-governance, but Guangdong—despite its lawless history—was not primarily to blame. Sniffing around the province's waste dumps, I had found a stinking pile of hypocrisy. The stench followed me all the way home.

6

Gross Domestic Pollution
Jiangsu and Zhejiang

Local governments have more revenues, the per capita income is a
lot higher and many farmers have turned themselves into workers
or even entrepreneurs, but what was once paradise on Earth has
been degraded into dumping grounds of industrial waste.
—Yang Jike, Chinese People's Political Consultative Conference Standing
Committee[1]

The road to riches is paved with empire-building ambitions in early
twenty-first-century China. Dirt tracks widen to eight-lane superhigh-
ways. Isolated villages swell into globalized cities. And Gross Domestic
Product—that triumph of human quantity over natural quality—expands
outward in a widening ripple of concrete, steel, and smoke. The heretics
of the age warn that expansion is hitting an environmental limit. The idols
find new ways to break industrial ground. In Jiangsu, the wealthiest province in China,[2] I traced the environmental tracks of some of those economic pioneers.

My journey began, unexpectedly, in a stretch limousine that had been
sent from Huaxi Village to pick me up. It was an incongruous sight among
the taxis lined up outside the airport, and I wondered briefly if I was being
secretly filmed for a send-up video as the driver opened the door into the
spacious leather-upholstered interior.

I could not help grinning. My host, an official with the Huaxi propaganda department, frowned. Not wanting to offend, I tried to explain.

"I'm sorry, I've never been in a car like this before and I didn't expect one here. In my mind, stretch limos are for Hollywood idols and business tycoons. Yet here we are on the way to a model communist village. This is lavish hospitality. Thank you!"

Deputy Secretary Sun Haiyan smiled politely. He then addressed my misconceptions: It should not come as a surprise, he said, to find a limousine in Jiangsu Province. China was no longer poor and we were not going to just any model community; we were on the way to Huaxi, the "Number One Village" in the wealthiest province of the fastest-growing nation of the early twenty-first century.

We drove for forty minutes in embarrassing comfort through the floodplains. Then suddenly, in the distance, nine massive gold-roofed pagodas rose up out of the rural landscape. Fields gave way to an industrial estate. We passed through streets of shops and then row after row of symmetrical, large but rather tatty pale-blue houses.

We stopped in front of the largest of the pagodas, a hotel. I was checked into the presidential suite, easily the biggest room in which I have ever slept. We were then treated to a lavish lunch of globefish, tapertail anchovies, and more than a dozen other delicacies. In case I had missed the significance of the limousine, this was my chance to be impressed.

Huaxi was proud of its achievements. A pioneer of rural development, it had been at the front line of the semilegal town-and-village enterprise movement in the 1980s that went on to become a driving force of the national economy. By turns surreal, impressive, and alarming, it was an early home to communists with stock options, farmers pushing back the boundaries of industry, and farmers cruising around in luxury sedans.

The eccentric glory of Huaxi encapsulated every quirk and contradiction in modern China, then magnified and distorted them like the image in a fairground mirror. It was a communist Utopia ten years past its sell-by date reinvented as a pioneering capitalist community. It was a Potemkin model village boasting its very own White House and Forbidden City. It was also a model of unsustainability, dependent on relentless expansion to treat its residents to European cars, lakeside mansions, and trips to Hawaii.

Thirty years earlier, most residents were farmers living in small, one-story houses. Few could afford a bicycle. By the time I arrived, they were shareholders with an average living space of more than 450 square meters and at least one family car provided by the village, which had a fleet of

500 vehicles, including twenty Mercedes-Benz sedans and, of course, a stretch limo.

Although everyone on the Huaxi family register was classified as a farmer, many had become wealthy industrialists able to live off their capital and the work done by migrant labor. Residents received a yearly salary of more than 10,000 yuan, a bonus of 70,000 yuan and dividends of more than 150,000 yuan. On paper, their income was more than twenty times the national average.

Unlike in Guangdong, governance was not an issue at this local level. Far from it. Under the benevolent dictatorship of the old village chief Wu Renbao and his sons, the streets were clean and the local workforce was tightly disciplined.

The Wu family's grip on village life was little short of feudal. They were Big Brother, Big Daddy, and Big Grandpa rolled into one, controlling everything from village-hall politics and corporate strategy to nursery schools and the propaganda theater. Under their strict leadership, holidays were rare even on weekends, entertainment was considered an unwelcome distraction, and no one was allowed to take their paper assets out of the community. Locals were free to leave, but only if they left their assets behind. They accepted Wu's rule because he kept raising their living standards. In this way, he led their entire town up the economic value chain. As I learned from the old patriarch, it had been a tough, dirty journey.

I joined Wu at a performance in the Ethnic Minority Palace, the theater at the center of the village's cultural and propaganda activities. On stage, the play was about—what else?—the glories of Huaxi. The dancers lip-synched a song about the benefits of more cars and DVDs in front of a backdrop of the town with giant neon characters that spelled out the slogan "Number One Village in China."

During the show Wu was constantly interrupting to shout orders to the performers and deliver a running commentary to a group of visitors. I was told he also wrote the script, a sign that, although nominally retired, the old cadre could not completely give up a lifelong urge to choreograph the community.[3] Why should he? Wu's force of personality had defined the character of the village for more than forty years.

Afterward, the great man granted me an audience. Legs splayed and leaning back on a folding chair, he gruffly explained how he created the Number One Village in China. It was hard to make out. Wu's dialect was so thick that my translator occasionally needed a translator, but the story was well known. Wu's biography was a classic tale of modern China. From swineherd to industrialist, and from political persecution to entrepreneurial opportunism, Wu led his community along the long, dirty pollution chain from pesticide to aluminum to steel. It was not a forced march. Wu kept his followers going by offering ever-greater incentives.

"In the past," he said, "when we lacked food, our biggest hope was just to get enough to fill our stomachs. Then, when we had enough to be full, we wanted better-quality food. After that, we wanted everyone to be able to eat all they wanted. Now villagers aim for five things: cash, a car, a son, face, and a house. We can provide all of this, so our mission must be something greater." Today, Huaxi's priority is not food but ideology. "We are the Number One Village in China. Our aim is to make all of China rich."

Expansion underpins what Wu calls the "Huaxi model." A speck on the map, it initially accumulated capital through the heavily polluting pesticide and aluminum industries. It then became one of the first Chinese villages to list on a stock exchange and the first to franchise its brand, renting the Huaxi name to tobacco grown in Yunnan (another cause of the loss of old-growth forest noted in chapter 1) and a hotel chain in Beijing. More recently it had started to upgrade its steel-milling machinery and begun exporting across the globe.

Wu's life mission could be boiled down to two words: wealth generation. For him, it was the only ideology that mattered. The seventy-nine-year-old was from a generation that had lived through enough upheavals for several lifetimes. Occupation, revolution, liberation, starvation, persecution, and exploitation—he experienced them all. For him, imperialism, communism, Maoism, and capitalism were not abstract terms in a textbook but ideas that had shaped and reshaped his existence. Perhaps because he knew them so intimately, he had little truck with labels: "It doesn't matter whether it is a new kind of ism or an old kind of ism, our aim is to make everyone rich."

Old Wu was becoming a legend in China. According to officially sanctioned biographies, such as the modestly titled *Brilliant Wu Renbao,*[4] he started work at the age of eleven, swilling out pigsties by day and nursing his boss's paralyzed son by night for an income of 40 kilograms of rice per year. This earthy beginning was to prove an asset after the communists took power in 1949. With impeccable class credentials, Wu rose quickly through the party ranks to become village chief and established Huaxi's first commune in 1961.

The party loyalist proved himself a pragmatist, a risk taker, and a rule breaker.[5] While the rest of the country was turning its back on capitalism during the Cultural Revolution, Wu secretly established a hardware factory. To conceal its existence from visiting officials, it was built in a swamp and surrounded by trees. This subterfuge was to cost Wu dearly. On New Year's Eve 1967, Red Guards hauled him into the village square and accused him of being a Capitalist Roader. "It was the toughest time of my life," he recalled. "In a single night, I was stripped of my official titles, publicly condemned, and saw my sons savagely beaten. One is still paralyzed. I'm a very firm believer in the Communist Party and socialism. But that period was a test for me."

Wu's real skill was in knowing when to buck prevailing trends and push at the boundaries of risk. In the early reform period of the 1980s, nearly every commune in China was returning land to farmers, but Wu did the opposite. He requisitioned dozens of plots and established a pesticide factory. It was dirty and polluting, but it turned over 2 million yuan a year. Textile mills and other plants followed as Huaxi blazed a trail for the thousands of town and village enterprises that sprang up across the country during this period.[6] The environment was not given a second thought. By 2000, town and village enterprises accounted for more than half of China's pollution.

In Jiangsu, local government-run businesses expanded faster than anywhere, at one point employing almost a third of the population. Huaxi kept ahead of the pack thanks to Wu's knack of reading the political tea leaves. In 1992, he watched a TV broadcast of Deng Xiaoping's famous pro-entrepreneurial speech during a tour of southern China. Immediately, according to his biographers, he foresaw a surge of economic activity and ordered village officials to borrow every yuan they could lay their hands on to buy up aluminum and other raw materials. Within three months, goes the story, the price of aluminum tripled. But his admirers fail to mention the environmental cost. Aluminum smelting is one of the three heaviest-polluting and energy-intensive industries in China. The worst was steel. This was the business that Huaxi moved into next.

The village bought milling equipment and blast furnaces. This was the trend at the turn of the century as China's economy became increasingly driven by resource- and energy-intensive industries that were no longer economical in the West because of tightening environmental regulations and increasing labor costs.[7] Much of the equipment was made locally, but entrepreneurs from Jiangsu and Hebei also snapped up old blast furnaces from the Ruhr, dismantled them, and shipped them piece by piece to towns and villages on the other side of the Eurasian landmass.[8] Though reported in Europe at the time as an alarming shift of industrial power and jobs, it was also a relocation of pollution and carbon emissions. China quickly overtook Germany, Japan, and the United States to become the world's biggest steel producer with more than a third of the global market. That fulfilled another of Mao Zedong's dreams, but the great news for China's economy was awful for its environment.[9] Steel soon came to account for a tenth of the country's energy demand and a similarly large proportion of its acid rain and carbon emissions.[10]

In Huaxi, the steel mills held pride of place. We crossed Textile Bridge—named after the garment-making industry that was another of the village's main sources of revenue—passed smokestacks and giant mounds of coal, then rolled up at the gates of a factory. As we donned our yellow safety helmets, the manager—inevitably, one of Wu's grandsons—proudly told us Huaxi Steel was the biggest company in the village.[11] He took us to the flat-bar production line, where the heat shimmered above the long belt on which steel strips 100 meters long were fed along rollers to a cutting machine. Five years earlier, the young Wu told me, China had to import flat bars, but now Huaxi sold them for 3,000 yuan ($429) apiece. "Those are not piles of steel," he said. "They are piles of money."

The mix of communist politics and capitalist economics was well named as GDPism. Everything was sacrificed for growth. Though Huaxi took this to extremes, it was far from unique. The coastal belt from Jiangsu down to Guangdong had become the workshop of the world. From the Number One Village I traveled south to Zhejiang, another rich coastal province that was famous for its entrepreneurial, rule-breaking spirit. I got an immediate introduction to the ethos when I took a bus across the border. My assistant asked the woman at the ticket booth how long the journey would take.

"It should be five hours but it can vary quite a bit," she said.

"What do you mean? By how long?" I asked.

The saleswoman was vague. "It can be a number of hours."

"Why? Because of traffic?"

"It depends on circumstances. But you had better hurry. The next one is about to leave."

We rushed to the bus. It was a little shabby and, to my surprise, we had bunk beds instead of seats. Why? If the journey took five hours, we ought to be there before dark. But as we quickly learned, the schedule, like any other rule, it seemed, went out the window if there was a chance to make money. Five minutes outside the bus station we made our first unscheduled stop. The driver popped out and came back with an armful of boxes. Mysterious, I thought. Ten minutes later we halted again so the driver could pick up a few bags. From then on we constantly stopped and started, but strangely it was usually only the driver who got on and off. The route was peculiar too: no highway, but several side streets and even an industrial estate. What was going on? I was beginning to get frustrated. At this rate, we would never reach our destination on time.

The passenger in the neighboring bunk noticed my unease. "Relax. The driver's just making a little money on the side."

"Eh?"

"Doing deliveries. Picking up extra fares."

"Is that allowed? Is it normal? What about us, the passengers? Don't we get a say?"

He shrugged as if my question was absurd. "Don't worry. He'll get us there eventually."

Nobody else seemed in the least bit bothered, though we seemed to have the Warren Buffett of the bus-driving world as our driver. He had business every few kilometers along the road. After a couple of hours, my patience ran out.

"Come on," I said to my interpreter. "This is ridiculous. We won't arrive until morning at this speed. Let's get a taxi."

We bailed out at the next town, flagged down a cab, and set off on a highway flanked by farm fields and factories. I breathed a sigh of relief. Finally, we were making progress. No moneymaking detours would slow us now. Foolish me. The entrepreneurial spirit blew in with the sea breeze in this part of China. Drivers of taxis, no less than buses, were masters of squeezing a few extra kuai from their fares. We crossed the broad expanse of the Yangtze and then a couple of hours later our driver pulled up along-side another taxi, wound down the window, and started talking.

"Why have we stopped? What's going on?" I asked my assistant.

"They are haggling," she replied.

"Over what?"

"Over us," she grinned.

"What?!"

"Our driver wants to sell us. This other driver is from Yiwu and wants to go back home with a paying passenger so he is buying part of our fare. Don't worry, you won't have to pay any extra."

I was outraged, then amused. As we hauled our luggage out of one trunk into another, I laughed at the indignity. We had been haggled over like cabbages in a market. This was human trafficking! But I marveled too at the business mentality of Zhejiang.

"Obviously, they haven't heard the saying 'The customer is god'?" I grumbled. "I just hope we fetched a good price."

The entrepreneurial spirit reached its apex at our destination, Yiwu. If China is the workshop of the world, this was its showroom. Selling every-thing from hair clips and costume jewelry to engine parts and cranes, the town's local market had grown from a few dozen street stalls fifteen years earlier to become the world's biggest commodity trading center. Yiwu was often described as the modern equivalent of the bazaars on the old Silk Road that provided exotic goods to the world. That might have been true in terms of scale, but not quality.

Yiwu was more like the planet's dollar store. The six hangar-sized malls contained 34,000 stallholders, selling a stunningly colorful smorgasbord of goods.[12] Almost all of the merchandise was cheap junk. The variation was staggering: corridors full of bead shops, rows of glitter sellers, alleys full of plastic crocodiles and inflatable guitars, forests of fake plants and plastic flowers, football pitches full of every size and color of ball imagin-able. There was no discrimination, no religious boundaries. In the alleys of portrait peddlers, every god and cultural icon was framed and for sale, often displayed side by side: Jesus Christ and Harry Potter, Buddha and Bob Marley, Krishna and Luke Skywalker, Koranic scripts and Shrek, Mao Zedong, and Madonna. I saw two shaven-headed Buddhist nuns from Wutaishan in Shanxi who were bulk shopping for prayer beads, Bud-dha icons, and amulets at 7 yuan ($1) apiece. Soon after, we came across

Muslims from Gansu looking to make large orders for scrolls and framed Koranic scripts. Business, it seemed, was a great spiritual leveler. Yiwu enshrined the modern global values of mass production, mass consumption, and low quality.

Its goods were in great demand. Wholesale purchasers came here from the Middle East, Russia, and eastern Europe.[13] These modern, mini–Marco Polos snapped up containers of accessories for resale in gift and souvenir shops in Europe, the Middle East, and Japan. Local business leaders hoped this was just the start. Over copious cups of green tea, Hu Yanhu, the chairman of the China Trade Centre's operating company, told me Yiwu wanted to become the world's biggest supermarket.[14]

"We offer more variety, have a good reputation, the transport is convenient, and the price is low. Buyers can make a big profit here. You can get stuff here for one yuan and sell it in the UK for a pound."

"How do you make the price so cheap?"

"Because Chinese labor costs are low, because we are a window for small- and medium-sized enterprises, because we are big and benefit from economies of scale."

Such advantages had speckled the countryside of Zhejiang, Jiangsu, Fujian, and Guangdong with manufacturing communities that dominated global markets. Billions of the world's teeth were being brushed with bristles from Huangzi, the toothbrush town. Its cigarettes were being lit by the sparks of Zhangqi, the cheap-lighter capital. Countless necks were decorated by the tie-makers of Shengzhou, feet supported by the shoe factories of Wenling, and breasts uplifted by the bra-strappers whose arresting billboards I had encountered in Chendian. These manufacturing hubs helped China's exports double at twice the speed of Britain at the height of its industrialization but at a cost of increasing dependence on overseas markets, and an influx of polluting, energy-intensive industries.[15]

The lexicon had yet to catch up with China's transformation. Driving through Zhejiang, we passed village after village. At least, that is what they were called and how they were designated on the map. But, like the Number One Village in China, these communities were far removed from the small, rural settlements usually conjured up by the word. For a start, many of them were bigger than the average European town, and they were heavily industrialized. And, as in Huaxi, the residents were still classified as "farmers" (another semantic anachronism), but most seemed to work in factories rather than on farms and were more used to handling pig iron than pigs. They were no longer cultivating the land, they were gobbling it up, expanding output, building market share, getting ahead.

We drove next through hills and forests to the town that fastened the crotches of the world: Qiaotou. Few people outside the local county had heard its name, but in twenty-five years this humble community had destroyed most of its international rivals to become the undisputed global capital of buttons and zips. Crops had been cleared for factories, farmers had become industrialists, and the river—the Ou—which used to be a clean source for irrigation, had deteriorated into an outlet for industrial waste emissions, some of which occasionally dyed the water purple and blue.

The first small workshop in the country was established in 1980 by three brothers who picked their first buttons off the street. Twenty-five years later, the town's 700 family-run factories were churning out annually 15 billion buttons and enough zips to circle the world 5,000 times. Starting out with little capital, few resources, and the disadvantage of a remote location, the farmers decided to compete on the basis of cheap labor and a willingness to tolerate the smell and pollution associated with plastic and metal manufacturing.

"Qiaotou chose the zip-and-button industry because it is labor-intensive and flexible. You can start a zip business with just a few hundred thousand yuan capital. That suited us. We are a very small town surrounded by mountains. We didn't have an industrial structure," said our host Ye Kelian, the quietly impressive president of the biggest firm in the town and head of Qiaotou's chamber of commerce. He was one of the more unassuming business heroes of a rags-to-riches generation. When he started Great Wall Zipper Group in 1983, it was only the second factory in the town. It had eight workers and one machine. But it could not have timed its rise better. Qiaotou began popping buttons just as China started dressing up. Out went the Mao suits and in came wardrobes of Western clothes. Overseas buyers rushed in. Three out of every five buttons in the world were now made in the town and a good share of the zips. Great Wall Zipper employed 1,000 people, ran three factories, and claimed assets of 80 million yuan (around $11.5 million).

Ye took me on a tour of the factory. It was a mirror of the town— functional, scruffy, and industrious. The lower level was thick with an acrid smell. Emissions of heavy-metal pollutants and dyes had eased thanks to an investment in new technology, but the problem had not gone away either here or in the button-making plants. Qiaotou was still dependent on the dirty manufacturing processes of leather-washing, paint-spraying, resin-dyeing, and metallurgy. Locals reported that, on the worst days, flakes of white plastic filled the air. A refinery had been built to deal with scrap resin, but it too became a source of pollution. The local government repeatedly promised a cleanup, but there was a limit to how much firms in this industry could do without losing competitiveness.

Ye explained how the movement of the zip business had tracked countries in the early stage of industrialization. "Zips were invented in Germany. For years, Germany, Italy, and the U.S. were the main producers. But then Asia quickly took over. First Japan, then South Korea, then Taiwan, and now the mainland. Today, China has 80 percent of the world zipper market. Developed countries don't manufacture zips anymore." The reasons were obvious: the business was dirty and labor-intensive and the profit margins were low—exactly the sort of job that countries outsourced as they moved up the value chain. Foreign companies wanted to produce and source in China because environmental and health-and-safety standards were as low as the price.[16]

The true costs were never accounted for on corporate balance sheets. But they were written on the landscape and stained into river systems. Rapid industrialization degraded the quality of the water, air, and soil. The Grand Canal, which flows through Jiangsu on its route from Shanghai to Beijing, was so thick with foul-smelling green gunk that, as we saw earlier, it was too polluted to use for the South-North Water Diversion Project. Taihu Lake, a famous beauty spot, was choked each summer with blue-green algae blooms, a sign that the water was contaminated by nitrogen.[17] Rivers and lakes sometimes became so contaminated that drinking supplies were temporarily cut. The coastal provinces became notorious for "cancer villages" and other clusters of disease, usually near chemical factories (see chapter 9). Birth defects in Jiangsu soared, a trend that doctors attributed to pollution.[18] As the economy expanded, the media reported a litany of contamination cases that continued month after month, year after year.

Protests were also erupting in many parts of China as industrial ground was broken.[19] The main complaint was the seizure of farmland for development, but fear of industrial toxins was another factor. In 2005, environmental concerns sparked 5,000 mass incidents involving at least 100 people, 128,000 smaller disputes, and more than half a million letters and complaints.[20] The environment protection minister Zhou Shengxian blamed public anger on pollution and called on local environmental bureau officials to stand up to violating companies.[21]

But there was little incentive for them to do so as their salaries were paid not by the state but by local governments that wanted to protect industry. Even if they cracked down and imposed penalties, the sums were often so small that it was often cheaper for a factory to pay fines than install expensive wastewater and emissions-treatment equipment.[22] With corruption endemic and little other means of political expression, illegal protest and violence were commonplace and often more effective than using the law. With no democracy, China's government was being held accountable by riot.

I witnessed this in Zhejiang in the aftermath of a pitched battle between roughly 2,000 riot police and 20,000 villagers, who were protesting against an industrial plant. The *South China Morning Post* had been the first to report the battles in Huankantou, sparked by a chemical factory that locals blamed for ruining their crops and their health.[23]

Three journalists had been detained by police in the area a day earlier.[24] To minimize the risk of that happening, I set out late at night, leaving my interpreter behind in case there was trouble. If I needed interpretation, we would have to do it by mobile phone. The precaution proved unnecessary. The police were in no position to seize anyone in Huankantou. They had completely lost control. I arrived after an hour-long taxi ride through dark streets and countryside, covering my head and pretending to be asleep at tollbooths and anywhere else I saw police. As we approached the town, there were more and more people milling about on the road. In the center were huge crowds but not one policeman.

Most of the people were riot tourists. Although the domestic media had been ordered not to report the demonstration, word had spread that the authorities had suffered a rare and bloody defeat. Residents had put the deputy mayor and more than thirty police in hospital (five critically injured) and defended their community from what they saw as a toxic invader. The mood was euphoric, almost festive. Order had broken down. Children had not been to school for days. Roadblocks barred the route to the chemical factory at the heart of the dispute.

Locals were so proud of their victory they offered guided tours of the battleground, marshaling visitors through a school car park full of smashed police buses and burned-out cars, streets full of broken bricks and discarded sticks. Some carried loudspeakers and bellowed chaotic instructions to try to keep the crowds moving along. In a supposedly authoritarian nation, the anarchy and defiance were astonishing.

"Aren't these villagers brave? They are so tough it's unbelievable," my taxi driver said. "Everybody wants to come and see this place. We really admire them." A fashionably dressed young woman who had come with friends from a nearby city agreed: "We came to take a look because many people have heard of the riot. This is really big news."

The origins of the riot were hazy.[25] Frustration had been simmering for some time. Locals accused corrupt officials of seizing land for the industrial park—built in 2002—without their consent. They blamed toxins from the chemical plant for ruined crops, malformed babies, and contamination of the local Huashui River. They petitioned the government and hung banners outside the chemical plants.

One read: "Give me back my earth, I want to live; give me back my earth, I want to be healthy; give me back my earth, I want my children and grandchildren; give me back my earth, I want to eat; give me back my earth, I want my environment."

Another: "Poison gas gets released, the people are crying, the corrupt officials get rich, the people suffer all their lives." It was signed, "The People of China."[26]

The village chief reportedly refused to hold a public meeting to hear these grievances. Attempts to petition the central government also proved fruitless. They had lost faith in the authorities. "The communists are even worse than the Japanese," one man told me.

Amid the mood of triumph were concerns about a backlash. One old woman ushered me inside her home to see a collection of trophies from the battle. "I am scared," she said, as she revealed two dented riot police helmets, several empty gas canisters, a policeman's jacket, and several truncheons and machetes. "This is getting bigger and bigger."

In the center of a crowd of locals beside a wrecked bus, one middle-aged woman won a cheer of approval by calling for the government to make the first move toward reconciliation. "It's up to them to start talking," she said. "I don't know what we would do if the police came back again, but our demand is to make the factory move out of the village. We will not compromise on that." The bravado was to be short-lived. After the authorities regained control, nine alleged ringleaders were given prison sentences of between one and five years, according to their lawyer Li Heping. Few details of the incident and the arrests were ever published in the Chinese media.

The industrial expansion went on. But the pollution, inefficiency, and instability indicated that something had to change or China would accelerate into an ecological wall. At a state level, the response was Hu Jintao's "Scientific Outlook on Development," which officials told me could be translated more simply as "sustainable development." Among the regions, Zhejiang and Jiangsu went further than most to put this ideal into practice. Like Western nations before them, the provinces had become rich through dirty industries and now they wanted to clean up. Zhejiang's capital, Hangzhou, reinvented itself as a service-industry, information technology, and tourist hub—a transformation that was symbolized by beautifying the lakeside scenery and improving water quality. Jiangsu became a leader in the field of solar energy, centered around Suntech, the world's biggest manufacturer of photovoltaic panels.

Local TV stations, newspapers, and web portals increasingly turned their attention to environmental problems. Some offending companies were named and shamed. A few even apologized.[27] Zhejiang announced tighter controls on pharmaceutical, chemical, cement, and other toxic industries. Jiangsu introduced China's first emissions trading system and promised to close more than 2,000 small chemical plants that failed to meet environmental standards. What was most striking—though unremarked upon by the government or local media—was that the authorities had clearly known for years that these firms had been violating the rules and destroying the environment. There was also no mention of similar punishments for midsized and big polluters, which generated more income and exercised greater political clout.

Often, these "cleanup" measures turned out to be a different means of expansion. As with the recycling businesses of Guangdong, many dirty industries simply moved into the hinterlands. Others found new tricks to dump their waste through concealed pipes or by discharging at night. A year and a half after the supposed crackdown on polluters in Jiangsu, the city of Yancheng had to shut off water for a million people after carbolic acid—including the carcinogens hydroxybenzene and phenol—was found in the city's water supply.[28] Even in Zhejiang, which has gone further than most to improve the situation, officials caution that there would be no qualitative change in the environment until 2020.[29]

The situation was similar at a national level. The government's noble aspiration to move the economy onto a sustainable track was belied by industry's ever-increasing consumption of land and resources. Beijing's mandarins experimented with strategies to ease energy intensity and reduce pollution.[30] They tweaked caps on power and water prices to more accurately reflect the costs of maintaining supplies and quality. They also attempted to make energy-intensive industries, such as steel and cement, pay extra for power, but these efforts were often compromised or ignored. Local authorities did not want to hurt the competitiveness of businesses paying taxes and, more often than not, bribes.

Efforts to make polluters pay or to account for environmental costs faltered because of weak governance. This was evident in the central government's failed attempt to introduce a "green GDP." As the name suggested, this policy aimed to factor long-term environmental costs into calculations of economic growth. It was a hugely ambitious plan that could have set a precedent worldwide. Trials were conducted in several provinces. But three years later, when local officials realized this would almost negate growth in their accounts, they torpedoed the scheme.[31]

The central government could have overruled them if it had been united on the policy. But it was complex to implement, and politburo members had their own reasons for wanting to scrap the plan. With no electoral mandate, the Communist Party depends on economic growth for legitimacy. If "green" accounting sliced several points off GDP growth, the party's authority would suddenly look very shaky. Going green too rapidly was a political risk. Instead the leadership incorporated some of the "green GDP" goals into other areas, such as promotion assessment for cadres, but economic calculations were left untouched. China would remain addicted to growth. In the words of the environmentalist Ma Jun: "The plight of the 'green GDP' project reflects the current conflict between the environment and the economy."[32]

To an extent, these were growing pains. Optimists argued that China was following a well-trodden path of development that would eventually take it out of the industrial mire. A former editor of *The Economist,* Bill

Emmott, predicted that China's environmental problem would prove no more insurmountable than those overcome by Japan and South Korea. Like them, he wrote, China would be able to afford a cleanup once it grew richer.[33] At that point, a time-proven market solution would kick in: first, a newly created middle class would refuse to tolerate the old dirty industries; second, newly generated wealth would fund a cleanup; third, companies would move up the manufacturing value chain by developing cleaner high-tech and service-sector businesses; and finally, higher-polluting industries would be sent out of the cities, or—even better—out of the province.

It was a comforting prospect, but this model relied on those at the cleanup stage being able to sweep the accumulated dirt of development under a new and bigger rug. When this process reached China, it had already been expanding for two centuries. By the time places like Zhejiang and Jiangsu were trying to clean up, the waste was getting too big and the rug too small.

Like Europe and the U.S. before them, Japan and South Korea improved air and water quality by investing heavily in clean and efficient technologies, by moving their dirtiest industries overseas (mostly to China), and by expanding their markets to provide alternative jobs. China cannot easily do the same. It is less wealthy relative to its size and less efficient in generating wealth. Attempts to expand its domestic market are limited by the increasing scarcity of raw materials, which has raised both commodity prices and trade tension. And, as a latecomer to industrialization, it cannot easily dump its waste elsewhere, because the planet's dumps are already full to overflowing.

Reckless GDP expansion has made the economy bulkier but less healthy. In 2007 the World Bank estimated the annual cost of pollution in China at 5.8 percent of its GDP.[34] Take that away from the official figures and the "miracle" of Chinese growth shrinks to a level similar to that of Europe or the United States.

The 2007 estimate was conservative, taking into account only health costs, lost man-hours, 700,000 premature deaths a year, and damage to infrastructure and crops. Adding the costs of erosion, desertification, soil decline, and environmental degradation raises the figure to 8–12 percent of GDP, which would push China's economy into reverse gear.[35] Factor in climate change and the country's expanding consumption of nonrenewable resources around the planet and it becomes conceivable that China's environmental crunch contributed to the global financial crash of 2008.

It appears obvious that growth cannot continue endlessly on a planet with finite resources, but back in Huaxi, the Number One Village in China, there was little prospect of any relaxation of the pace. Indeed, a new generation had new ideas about expansion. On my final day I met Wu Xie'en, unanimously "elected" village chief, local Communist Party general secretary and, of course, the son of Wu Renbao, the founding father.

Adopting the official language of "Scientific Development," he told me that a clean environment was a form of wealth and spoke of his determination to shift the village's economy onto a more sustainable path. But his priority remained social stability and fast growth. Even the national economy was laggardly in comparison with Huaxi's. In the two years before my visit the turnover of the village's companies jumped from 10 billion yuan (about $1.4 billion) to 26 billion. Wu predicted it would double again within three years.

"Anything that creates wealth is OK," he told me. "The most important thing is to be open to new ideas, to do what works. It doesn't matter if it is socialism or capitalism, both have advantages. China is changing. The countryside is changing. So is our way of thinking. Everything is improving."

To celebrate the village's sixtieth anniversary in 2021, he was planning to build a 118-floor skyscraper that would be taller than the Empire State Building. The cost, at 250 million yuan, was, he said, "no big deal for us."

Huaxi represented more of a trajectory than a model. More than any single strategy or ideology, it was underpinned by a belief that living standards would keep jumping forward. Nobody minded mixing communism, capitalism, Maoism, or even Wuism so long as the end result maintained that most essential of modern Chinese "isms": optimism. Confidence in change, in the belief that anything is possible underpinned the country's growth and ensured a degree of public tolerance for pollution and other negative side effects. To maintain belief in this materialist dream, Wu Renbao and his family—like the politburo in Beijing—had to guarantee constant expansion. This could not go on forever.

In the previous thirty years, the original village of 1,500 households had swallowed twenty-six surrounding villages to secure more land for development. Including migrants, the population had swollen to more than

60,000. Residents were financially locked in to growth. Every year the villagers received a bonus, and every year 80 percent of it had to be reinvested in the commune.[36] On paper, they were all rich, but their wealth took the form of shareholdings that they could never cash in. Anyone who left was forced to forfeit 90 percent of their paper assets.

But why would anyone want to leave a community that aimed to create a Utopia within its ever-widening borders? On my last day I was given a final tour of the village. At the center were the nine giant pagodas. Around them were rows and rows of houses, lined up in blocks like battalions of troops on a parade ground. Each block represented a different phase of development, a different level of affluence. The oldest homes were white villas, built in 1989. They were small but still significantly larger than most Jiangsu farmhouses. Next to them were streets and streets of uniform pale-blue two-story homes, which were considered the height of luxury when they went up in 2000. In the latest development, however, the wealthiest residents were moving into three-story European-style mansions with manicured lawns by the edge of an artificial lake. It was as though a century of economic expansion, architectural progress, and rising consumption had been compressed into twenty years.

The world's greatest monuments had been given similar treatment. Huaxi World Park, located on the highest hill in the area, was a tourist resort with no tourists. Everybody appeared to be too busy working to see its wonders, which included a 10-kilometer-long reproduction of the Great Wall that curled between the fir trees on the hillside. The placement of other monuments was suggestive of Huaxi values. At the top of the slope was a symbol of Chinese power and autocracy, a scale model of the Forbidden City in Beijing that covered an area the size of a tennis court. At the bottom were foreign symbols of freedom and democracy: replicas of the U.S. Capitol, the White House, and the Arc de Triomphe.

Less than ten years old, these wonders of the world were already showing signs of wear and tear. The paint was flaking. The concrete was stained. They reminded me of the tatty theme parks and tourist resorts that had been hastily thrown up in Japan during the peak of its economic bubble. For locals, though, Huaxi World Park was proof of the glory of the Number One Village in China. That empire continued to grow. At the top of the hill my guide, Deputy Secretary Sun, pointed to slopes owned by a neighboring village. "We will expand there next," he said. "We plan to use that land to cultivate flowers." After pesticides, aluminum, and steel, the "farmers" of the Number One Village were finally reverting to horticulture.

Perhaps one day, I thought, Huaxi will be a blaze of color. But for now, the Number One Village was mostly a monochrome gray of concrete, steel, and haze. Industry had put money in pockets, food on tables, and Buicks in garages, but I was quite happy to leave the stretch limo and the presidential suite behind.

Before I left, there was one last site I had to visit. "Huaxi Road" was a red-carpeted arcade that celebrated the wealth of the village's original residents. The paint was flaking and the carpet soiled, but the displays were impressive. Suspended from the ceiling every few yards along a concrete path was a large portrait of a smiling family next to a detailed list of their household assets: the value of their property, average level of education, number of members of the Communist Party, and how many TV sets, fridges, computers, cars, motorbikes, and mobile phones they owned. It was astonishingly detailed, a public boast of rising living standards, of new money. It was a monument to materialism.

I looked for the portrait of my guide, Deputy Secretary Sun. Before liberation, the poster said, he had lived in a house of 40 square meters. Now his home was more than ten times bigger and he owned shareholdings and bank deposits worth 710,000 yuan ($101,428). The poster also listed one car, one computer, two mobile phones, two air conditioners, a camera, two TV sets, a stereo, a fridge, two phones, two motorbikes, a washing machine, and a set of redwood furniture. Knowing that he had come from a poor background, I told him how impressed I was. He shrugged, and not just from modesty.

"It is a little out of date," he said. He now owned a lot more.

7

From Horizontal Green
to Vertical Gray
Chongqing

Every five days for the next forty-two years, we will build a city of
over a million people. Where we put them will be crucial.
—*Joel Cohen, demographer*[1]

While industrial villages like Huaxi expand outward to become towns
and cities, hundreds of millions of people from the countryside are
drawn in to work on the construction sites and assembly lines they create.
The result is momentous.

For the first time since the dawn of civilization, *Homo sapiens* has
become a predominantly urban creature. Until 2008, the planet's population was split almost right down the middle: 3.2 billion in the cities, 3.2
billion in the countryside.[2] Since then China has shifted the balance deci-
sively away from the fields and toward the skyscrapers. Our species has
taken a step further than Darwin anticipated. We have not evolved to fit
our environment, we have changed our habitat to suit ourselves.[3]

Nowhere is the staggering urbanization of the world more evident than
in Chongqing, the Coketown of the early twenty-first century. Centered
on a large finger of land between the dark waters of the Jialing River and
the chocolate-colored Yangtze, this former trading center has become the
world's biggest municipality with 31 million residents, more than Iraq,
Peru, or Malaysia.[4]

Many outsiders have never heard of it, yet it is on its way to becoming one of the planet's megacities, with an urban population of 10 million that is on course to double again before 2020.

I wanted to get a snapshot of how this affected people and their environment, so I spent a day there—just the sort of day, in fact, when humanity passed the balancing point on its millennia-long journey out of the countryside.

I woke at 5 a.m. and set out in the rain to the poor district of Qiansimen. In the hour before dawn, it had a distinctly Dickensian feel. Puddles filled the dark narrow alleys, flanked on either side by tall ramshackle tenements. An old man's wrinkled faced glowed orange as he warmed himself over a brazier.

Nestling between the port and the commercial center, this area was the home of Chongqing's most distinctive and traditional population—the *bangbang* army, a 100,000-strong crew of porters who bore the city's weights on their shoulders. Arriving from the countryside with no skills and minimal education, they picked up the cheapest of tools—a bamboo pole (or *bangbang*) and some rope—and hung around the docks, the markets, and the bus stations waiting for goods to carry up the steep slopes of this mountain port.

I had arranged to meet one of them, Yu Lebo. He had just woken up in the cramped three-room apartment he and his wife shared with three other couples, all of whom were porters, cleaners, or odd-job men. There were two double mattresses on the floor in one room, separated by a thin curtain, a third in a tiny room next door and another in the kitchen. Yu scrubbed his face, grabbed a bamboo pole hanging from a hook on the wall, and headed out into the rain and the dark. "We want to move out and get a place of our own, but we don't have the money yet," he said once we were outside. He explained why he had come to Chongqing four years earlier: "I used to be a farmer, but I could not afford to raise my two children. So we left them behind with relatives. I see them two or three times a year."

On an average day, Yu earned about 20 yuan ($3) for twelve hours' work. Most of this, and the money his wife added as a cleaner, went on rent and food, but as long as they remained healthy they could send enough money home to buy clothes and books for their children. The remittances were vital. Education and health care—free in the days of Mao Zedong—had become the biggest burden on the rural community.

Yu's first job of the day was in the Chaotianmen market, where he had to carry several huge bundles of goods. Each was probably heavier than the short, slim porter, who weighed just over 50 kilograms. The stallholder paid him 2 yuan. "Not bad," Yu said. "Sometimes they are heavier. Sometimes we get paid less." Average incomes in the city were more than three times higher than in the countryside,[5] but inequality was widening everywhere. I asked Yu if he regretted coming. He shook his head. "No, my life is a little better than it was when I first got here. Then, I only earned 10 yuan a day. This city is changing so fast. It is getting richer. But our lives are not keeping up. Cities are good for the rich. If you have money you can do anything. If you don't want to carry something, you just hire a *bangbang* man."

Even after dawn, the sun remained hidden behind a thick haze. The giant movement of humanity that was Chongqing was about to get into full swing, working, building, consuming, discarding, developing. If today was typical, builders would lay 137,000 square meters of new floor space for apartment buildings, shopping centers, and factories. The economy would grow by 99 million yuan ($14.1 million). There would be 568 deaths, 813 births, and the arrival of 1,370 people from the countryside. Each year, the city limits were being pushed farther outward as the urban population grew by half a million, the equivalent of all the people in Luxembourg being added to the municipal register.

This represented a massive change from the Mao era, when the government tried to halt, and at certain periods even reverse, the shift to the cities.[6] In the thirty years from 1949 to 1979, the urban population actually declined relative to the birthrate as Mao moved people into remote regions to grow crops. By 1980, only 100 million people lived in cities, and the household residency system tightly restricted movement from one area to another. This policy changed completely during the next ten years, when Deng Xiaoping unleashed the biggest and fastest migration in history and more than 400 million farmers moved into towns and cities.

The story of modern China is the story of that movement. Low-paid, routinely abused, and often working in appallingly dirty and unsafe conditions, migrants provided the human fuel for China's spectacular economic growth. Most returned to their hometowns only once a year, during the spring festival, when they could expect a hero's welcome as they arrived with striped nylon bags full of gifts for their families and envelopes containing their savings. This annual migration is bigger than the hajj, its financial impact enough to make or break a midsized country. In Anhui, the remittances were worth more than the provincial budget.

By moving, people were also reshaping their nation's identity and its relationship to the environment. For 3,000 years China had been a country of farmers. Suddenly, it was a land of city dwellers. Britain has five urban centers of more than a million people; China has more than 120. A few—Beijing, Shanghai, Hong Kong, and Nanjing—are well known around the world. The names of many others—Suqian, Suining, Xiantao, and Xinghua—are unfamiliar even to many Chinese. Building them required cement, steel, and timber. Once complete, homes required electricity for fridges, microwave ovens, TVs, and air conditioners. This was the government's formula for raising living standards.

My next stop was at the municipal office, where Zou Xiaoping, deputy director of the economic relations commission, explained how her city was at the heart of China's vast government plan to address the inequalities between the rich eastern coastline and the poor western interior. The "Go West" strategy, as this policy was called, brought more than 1.4 trillion yuan ($200 billion) of government investment into industrial development, urbanization, and power projects such as the Three Gorges Dam.[7]

"Now is the peak time of the development of western China. Chongqing is in the middle of it. That is why we are growing so fast," said Zou. "We must maintain momentum. This is a crucially important time for our city."

I left Zou's office flabbergasted. Even at the height of Western urbanization in the nineteenth century, there was nothing to compare with the scale and speed of change taking place here.[8] How could space and jobs be found for so many new arrivals? Now accompanied by a government guide, I drove to the city limits and the newly built Lifan Sedan factory in the Chongqing Economic Zone, where newly employed workers were putting together newly designed cars.

"This was farmland a couple of years ago," boasted the proud boss Yin Mingshan. "It is my fourteenth factory, fourteen years after I started business."

I took an immediate liking to Yin. Dapper, twinkly-eyed, and engaging, the sixty-eight-year-old was one of the nation's great industrial pioneers, a twenty-first-century Chinese equivalent to Josiah Wedgwood, Henry Ford, or the Cadbury brothers. Imprisoned for much of the Mao era for his views on free speech and capitalism, he started out in business in 1992 running a motorcycle repair company with a staff of nine. At the time of our meeting, his Lifan company had expanded to employ 9,000 workers.

"China has become a wonderland for entrepreneurs," Yin said as he showed me a scale model of his empire. "There are many people who are doing what I have done."

It was not as easy to build a business in Chongqing as in coastal Shanghai or Shenzhen, where companies could benefit from access to overseas markets, ports, and close supply chains. But, prompted by the government and rising costs, such rich eastern cities had started investing inland. Chongqing was famous for motorbikes; Yin was trying to make it equally respected for cars. He bought a BMW-Chrysler factory in Brazil, had it broken down, shipped it up the Yangtze, and then rebuilt it in Chongqing. He also set up plants in Vietnam, Thailand, and Bulgaria and planned to open a research center in Britain, where his daughter was studying at Oxford.

His creed was one of benevolent self-interest. He wanted his country to become a nation of consumers. "China is too poor. We need high-speed growth. The rich need to increase the income of the poor," he said. "If we improve the living standards of farmers, then they can buy our motorcycles and cars." Within five years, he aimed to more than double his workforce to 20,000. Next to the factory, bulldozers were already churning up fields for another plant.

It was the same story across China as land was gobbled up by factories, roads, and expanding cities. Between 1986 and 2000, about 1.2 million hectares of arable land were converted into built-up areas, mostly small towns of 5,000 to 10,000 people.[9] The loss of farm fields was a common phenomenon in fast-developing countries, but while other smaller nations were able to offset this trend by importing food, this was not as easy for a huge country like China, which had to partly make up for the deficit by reclaiming more land from coastal waters, forests, wetlands, grasslands, and desert.[10]

Driving back from the factory, I counted more than thirty cranes in less than five minutes on the border between the countryside and the city. Just outside the Jiangbei tollbooth, farmers toiled under heavy loads in vegetable fields and women washed their clothes in a stream. Behind them, thirty-story towers were silhouetted against the gray haze. Where the two worlds met was a corridor of rubble as land was cleared for further expansion.

We made an impromptu visit at a building site, where Chen Li, a brash window fitter, kindly delayed his lunch to tell me about his work. He had arrived in the city nine years earlier at the age of sixteen. Since then he reckoned he had worked on between seventy and eighty high-rises. "The buildings are getting taller and better," he said. The improvement in his life was not as evident. Chen lived in a hut on the site, his breakfast was a glass of soy milk and a steamed bun, and on an average day he worked eleven hours for about 50 yuan ($7). "I'm a city resident now. But life is still difficult."

He was helping to build a city that seemed determined to overtake New York. The municipality was erecting a hundred skyscrapers, including the tallest in western China, the Chongqing Super Tower. Once finished, it will dwarf the replica of the Empire State Building that already rises up in the city center.

It was a similar story throughout the country. During the first quarter of this century, half of all the world's new buildings will be erected in China. Fifty thousand of them will be skyscrapers, equivalent to ten New Yorks.[11]

I headed upward to the roof of a tower block, where I met Li Zhiguan, one of the millions now making a living nearer the sky. Formerly a farmer, then a factory worker, Li had recently become one of the many high-wire artists cleaning skyscraper windows, earning him the nickname Spider-Man. We met him at the top of a twenty-four-story telecom office just before he rappelled down the glass on a rope attached to him by a single clip. "It is 100 percent safe. You can go too if you wish," said his boss, He Qing, with a strong German accent picked up studying for an MBA in Mannheim.

With so many towers going up, Li was never going to be short of work. And he had a bird's-eye view of the transforming cityscape. "In six months, there have been huge changes. You can notice it from one week to the next."

The skyscrapers Li saw rising up around him were better for the environment than urban sprawl. Tall, densely populated cities consume less land and allow for greater efficiency of transport, energy, and waste management.[12] China was belatedly trying to reorganize its urban centers after decades of barely regulated expansion, particularly of small towns that threatened to reduce the nation's farmland below the minimum that the government considers necessary for food security: 120 million hectares.[13] To avoid this, the state aimed to concentrate more of the population in megacities and to halt urbanization in the less spoiled and most ecologically fragile regions of Tibet, Guizhou, Ningxia, and Qinghai.[14]

Done right, cities can ease humanity's stress on the environment, according to the demographer Joel Cohen.[15] They already provided homes for half the world's population on just 3 percent of the planet's land.[16] An even bigger proportion could be accommodated if urban expansion was upward rather than outward, if there was good investment in public transport, and if energy efficiency was promoted through urban planning and architectural design. With an extra two billion people likely to join the planet's population by 2050, the best way to make space for everyone is to house them in the sky.

But while compact, clean, vertical cities are the modern ideal in Europe, Japan, and Canada, urbanization in China has long tended toward the 1950s U.S. model of big suburban villas and commuting by car. Thomas Campanella, the author of a book on the country's urban revolution, wrote that the differences could hardly be greater: "When it comes to the environment, China and the West are moving in opposite directions, and at blinding speed."[17] The result, he concluded, was sprawling inefficiency and worsening emissions.

In the future, the government wants to concentrate the population in belts of supercities, including one thick urban string that will thread its way up the Yangtze from Shanghai to Chongqing through Nanjing, Hefei, and Wuhan.[18] To tie these conglomerations together, a high-speed railway is due for completion by 2012. That is just the start. Urban development looks likely to become more intense nationwide. The consulting firm McKinsey advocates the creation of dense urban belts between Beijing and Tianjin, Shanghai and Suzhou, and Guangzhou and Shenzhen. The Dutch architect Neville Mars envisages a day when city clusters will fuse together to create a superintense megaconglomeration stretching from Beijing to Shanghai and along the Yangtze.[19]

Chongqing was trying to set an example of how a city could grow big and stay clean. Its mayor, Bo Xilai, had earned plaudits for greening Dalian with lawns earlier in his career. Now he was trying to go one step further by creating a "forest city." Such was the rush to plant urban trees that other regions complained Chongqing had left no saplings for them. The government also set aside an "ecological shield" region in the northwest of the municipality, from which people were encouraged to migrate to the inner city and alleviate population pressure on the Yangtze.

But the cleanup remained a low priority compared with economic growth. As people move off the land and into the sky, they produce less and consume more. In theory, they become socialized and civilized. In practice, they spend more time shopping and eating junk food.

A nearby shopping center could belong to any city on earth: pedestrianized streets, boutiques, Kentucky Fried Chicken, McDonald's, and a giant screen blaring out pop-jingle ads. As people buy, eat, and drink in ever greater quantities, they produce more waste. Dealing with that rubbish is becoming an ever more pressing problem.

I took a taxi into the hills to see the biggest of the megacity's megarubbish pits: the Changshengqiao landfill. It was an awesome sight; a reservoir of garbage more than 30 meters deep and stretching over an area of 350,000 square meters, the size of about seventy football playing fields.

The waste engineer Wang Yukun told me the city produced 3,500 tons of junk every day. None of it was recycled. Some was burned. Here, it was layered like lasagna: six meters of rubbish, half a meter of soil, a chemical treatment, and then a huge black sheet of high-density polyethylene lining. Three years after opening, the site contained more than a million tons of rubbish.

Once it was full, the city planned to build a golf course on top. The day when people would be driving and putting on top of a mountain of garbage looked set to come sooner than expected. "The site was designed to serve the city for twenty years, but it has filled faster than we expected. I guess it will be completely full in fifteen," Wang predicted.

The same was true for sewage and industrial wastewater, which was contaminating the giant reservoir behind the Three Gorges Dam, a few hundred kilometers downstream, sooner than expected. As fast as the authorities were building wastewater plants, the pollution in the Yangtze was outstripping their capacity. The impact on agriculture and public health was estimated to cost Chongqing about 4.3 percent of its annual GDP.[20]

The story was common throughout China. Move farmers into the city

and their consumption of resources increased threefold and their emissions surged along with their junk.[21] By 2020, when the government aims
to create a *xiaokang shei* (moderately prosperous society), the volume of
urban garbage in China is expected to reach 400 million tons, equivalent
to the figure for the entire world in 1997.[22] With cities already struggling
to cope, that problem looked set to be a new source of social tension and
environmental degradation.

Cleaning the streets of crime was another urban challenge. In many
Chinese cities, the public security bureau was more likely to detain journalists than to take them for a drive. But in Chongqing, the city went so far
as to dispatch an English-speaking officer, Lai Hansong, as a guide. I was
suspicious that he was just another propaganda official, but Lai insisted
he was a regular beat cop who had been patrolling the Yuzhang district
for six years. "It is a low-crime area," he said. "We mostly deal with thefts
or fights." In an average week, he claimed, he dealt with fewer than five
incidents.

It was not what I expected, having heard lurid stories of drugs, prostitution, and organized crime. The city had recently been the focus of violent
industrial protest, and conflicts over land appropriation were common as
the city expanded.[23]

The picture Lai painted was very different: "There are no criminal
gangs in China. Our country has few riots." But someone was clearly worried about something. The police force, Lai said, was increasing every year
and officers had to travel three to a car. Not long after, Chongqing was
rocked by one of the biggest crackdowns on "black society" mobsters in
modern Chinese history. Six gangsters were sentenced to death for murder, machete attacks, and price fixing. Investigators detained more than
1,500 suspects, including the deputy chief of police.[24]

For dinner, I went to meet some of the city's alternative thinkers at a
riverside restaurant. This was a city that dazzled when night fell. The swirling surface of the Yangtze reflected a neon rainbow, brightly illuminated
housing blocks, art deco skyscrapers, and motorway crash barriers that, for
no apparent reason, glowed pink, green, and purple.

My dinner companions included a film director, a publisher, a poet/
cartoonist, and an environmentalist. They laughed at the notion that there
were no gangsters, and some shook their heads at claims that the haze was
just bad weather. Overall, they felt living standards were improving. Cul-

tural development might be slower than material development, "but this is a city of the future," said Li Gong, the poet/cartoonist.

"Compared with ten years ago, the air quality is better. But compare it with other cities in China or other countries and we are still far behind," said Wu Dengming, an environmental activist who founded the Green Volunteer League and helped expose the illegal chemical emissions by local factories and pollution buildup behind the Three Gorges Dam.

Zeng Lei, a documentary filmmaker who spent seven years recording the lives of Chongqing's poorest residents, related unhappy anecdotes of urban life: the *bangbang* man who burst into tears when he returned to his home village for the first time in three years; the housewife who felt so neglected by her family that she hired a team of *bangbang* men to carry banners through the city celebrating her birthday.

Song Wei, a publisher, noted that the evident problems—pollution, loss of heritage, inequality, and crime—were not confined to Chongqing: "We could be talking about almost any city in China."

The similarity of China's cities was a legacy of Stalinist state planning and a sign that aesthetics and heritage preservation were low priorities. During the Mao era, much of the nation's building stock was hastily thrown up according to a tiny handful of designs.[25] The economic reform period was barely any better. Although there was more variety, the rushed spirit of that age meant the quality of design and construction were often awful. At the county level, this created a tatty and tedious urban landscape of almost identical rectangular structures decorated with the same white tiles and tinted windows. As China became wealthier, cities looked to international architects for inspiration, but that often meant urban landscapes came to resemble those overseas rather than having their own distinct identity. Qiu Baoxing, the vice minister of construction, said the damage done to the nation's architectural heritage was similar to that inflicted during the Cultural Revolution. "Many cities have a similar construction style. It is like a thousand cities having the same appearance,"[26] he complained.

Chongqing was not just urbanizing, it was globalizing. Little more than a generation earlier, this had been a city where Red Guards in Mao tunics chanted anti-imperialist slogans. Today, young people with money dressed much like their counterparts in Birmingham, Chicago, or Nagoya. If anything, their values were even more materialistic and consumption-oriented.

After dinner, Spider-Man's boss, He Qing, took me to Falling, which he described as the hottest nightspot in Chongqing. It was Wednesday night, but the dance floor was packed with beautiful people moving to techno music and playing dice. Our table had an 800 yuan ($114) minimum charge, which covered a bottle of vodka, a few imported beers, and a plate of elegantly carved fruit.

He Qing introduced me to some of Chongqing's new rich, including the founder of a candy factory, a restaurant owner, and a bank employee. Without exception they were in their twenties, foreign-educated, and well connected—either through family or political ties—with the city's movers and shakers. "No businessman can thrive unless they have contacts in the Communist Party and the underworld," I was told.

I felt uneasy spending more on a night's entertainment than *bangbang* man Yu earned from a month's grueling work. I was not the only one conscious of the gap. He Qing told me his plan for the future: "Inequality and environmental destruction are the two biggest problems facing China." He wanted to establish a new wind-energy company that would employ migrants to build a cleaner city, using German technology.

I felt sure he would make a killing. Chongqing was growing richer, more densely populated, and more environmentally stressed.[27] The city government said it would pioneer green urbanization. The city ought to look cleaner and brighter as its population prospers. If the urban middle class followed the trend of the West, they might start to eat more eco-friendly vegetarian food and drive smaller cars. Perhaps. More usually, though, cities tend to distance people from the environment and nurture an unsustainable lifestyle. Metropolises are giant blocks of consumption. Their buildings are fitted with air conditioners and modern conveniences that create an artificial climate. Vertical living represents a shift in consciousness from the horizontal, seasonal life of the farmer to a linear drive for progress. Urban residents laugh at farmers, whose lives go around in circles, never getting anywhere, simply following the seasons. City dwellers, on the other hand, pursue career tracks, expect their lives to be endlessly onward and upward. They tend to measure success by how much they can consume. In the future, as resources grow scarcer, more are likely to be left unfulfilled.

There are signs too that people might be turning their backs on the cities. In Guangdong, which was the first to attract an influx of rural laborers

to its factories, companies have begun to complain about worker shortages. Some economists believe China is approaching the Lewis turning
point, at which demand for labor outstrips supply.[28] The lure of the city
had its limits.

Outside at midnight, the bright lights could not mask a seedier side
of city life. Many migrant women worked as prostitutes in karaoke bars
or massage parlors. Their children were left with relatives or sent to the
streets to beg, sell flowers, or sing for money until the early hours. At
a night market, a queue of hawkers offered to clean my shoes, sell me
cigarettes, or pour me soup from a flask. A seven-year-old girl plucked at
my arm and coyly entreated me to buy a rose from her. "Where is your
mother?" I asked. "Oh, she's at work," she replied.

A desperate-looking girl came over, carrying a menu of songs and a bat-
tered, badly tuned guitar. She said she was sixteen but looked more like
twelve. She told me she had been in Chongqing only a few months and
had already decided she did not like it. I paid 3 yuan (44 cents) and picked
the song "Pengyou" (Friend). The young busker stared at some faraway
point as she strummed the one chord she knew and sang out of tune. It
was miserably sad.

Farther along the street, a *bangbang* man wandered into the distance
carrying his bamboo pole. I wondered if he was about to finish work or
start it.

8

Shop Till You Drop
Shanghai

Shanghai was a vast engine of illusions of various kinds. Venture
capitalism going full blast twenty-four hours a day.
—J. G. Ballard[1]

The resident of Number 550 Huaihai Road in Shanghai was a rather
unusual migrant. Born in Wisconsin on March 9, 1959, Barbara Millicent Roberts was the world's most famous supermodel. She drove a Corvette convertible, owned a dream home with a pool, partied with jocks, and
adored shopping. In the U.S., she had been a prom queen and a role model.
In China, she was emerging as an ambassador for consumer culture.

Better known as Barbie, this 30-centimeter-tall icon had spawned a
billion plastic clones and encouraged generations of women across the
world to pursue the 1950s American dream. Fashion was her passion. Her
looks were her life. The world's best plastic surgeons had sculpted her features, given her a gravity-defying bust, and ensured that she would never
grow old. Giorgio Armani, Versace, and Christian Lacroix had personally
designed her wardrobe, but her consumer addiction was impossible to satisfy. Even as she accumulated accessories, furniture, and cars, the world's
most famous shopaholic repeated the same question in the same tinny
tones year after year: "Will we *ever* have enough clothes?"

Barbie was first sold in China in the early 1990s. But it was not until
2009 that she was given her own home in the retail heartland of Shanghai. In a blaze of pink and blond, Mattel, the world's biggest toy company,

marked its leading cash cow's fiftieth birthday by opening the planet's largest Barbie emporium. Covered in pink plastic, the six-story doll's house on Huaihai Road, in the heart of the city's shopping district, became an instant landmark. At the launch party, kung fu star Jet Li and the actress Christy Chung were among the celebrities quaffing champagne and cocktails on a spiral staircase bedecked with plastic blondes.

This was more than a party; it was the launch of a marketing campaign aimed at prolonging and expanding the plastic lifestyle championed by the toy firm. For the Barbie market to continue growing for another fifty years, the doll would have to make it big in China.

I lunched at Barbie's place at the start of what became a social climb up Shanghai's consumer hierarchy. The top floor of the doll's house was a fantastically kitschy themed restaurant with a menu designed by the chef David Laris. It offered Barbie™ Burgers for 60 yuan with Barbie™ pink sauce, Ken's burgers, Pinktastic Pasta, Doll-icious Desserts, and Barbie™ Tini cocktails. The restaurant did not seem to be hugely popular, which might explain the generous promotion offer. Diners who opted for the special meal received a boxed set of Barbie plates and cutlery that they could take home.

I wasn't one of them. But after polishing off a Barbie™ Burger, I chatted to a customer who was delighted at her takeaway tea set. Liu Yunting was an advertising company employee who had come with a friend to mooch around the doll's shop and in-house spa. They could not afford Barbie dolls as kids, but now they could eat, drink, and soak up the Barbie atmosphere. I asked Liu what she planned to do with her new tableware.

"I will use it myself."

"Isn't it a little childish?"

"Not at all. It is cute. This is much better than the stuff for children. We know better how to appreciate it."

Liu was a member of the fastest-growing consumer class: single women—or *xiaobailing* (white-collar princesses).[2] Just like the "office ladies" of Japan, they had high levels of disposable income and a craving for designer labels. Marketing moguls were obsessed by this group. They were the future face of consumer power. State planners forecast that half the population would be middle class by 2020.[3] As this upwardly mobile group was growing, consuming more, and traveling farther, they were getting ever closer to the unsustainable, energy-intensive Barbie lifestyle.

For over half a century Barbie has been the ecological equivalent of a weapon of mass destruction. The doll's plasticity became the subject of much postmodern self-parody in the Barbie emporium. Accessories were decked with English slogans such as "A plastic tan never fades," and the skincare products boasted "plastic smooth" results. Unrivaled in her ability to influence young minds, she was the perfect saleswoman for a fantasy lifestyle that, scaled-up and replicated, was proving calamitous.

The size of Barbie's eco-footprint was belied by her petite slingbacks. With a garage full of cars, a huge home, and a penchant for foreign travel and shopping, her carbon consumption would be off the scale in the real world. If little girls in China grew up wanting to shop, eat, and travel like Barbie, the planet's prognosis would shift from touch-and-go to terminal.

Until very recently, China has been living within the planet's means. If everyone in the world consumed what the average Mr. or Mrs. Wang did in 2007, we would just about stay within the sustainable resources of our planet.[4] Humanity would have a balanced ecological budget.

But, understandably, Mr. and Mrs. Wang wanted to keep up with Mr. and Mrs. Jones on the other side of the Pacific. That was human nature. It was also very bad news for the environment, because if we all ate, shopped, and traveled like those average Americans, we would need 4.5 earths. If we all lived like Barbara Millicent Roberts, the situation would be even worse.[5]

In the United States, appalling damage had been done for decades. The situation was only slightly less serious in western Europe. In China, that Barbie-dream apocalypse was closest to coming true in Shanghai. The city that Deng Xiaoping called "the head of the dragon" was the biggest, richest, most globalized mass of modernity in the country. This was the home of the most luxury shopping malls, the tallest buildings, the nation's first F1 track, the biggest auto companies, the only commercially operating Maglev train, the second-busiest port in the world, and a gathering horde of international salesmen trying to sell the American consumer lifestyle.[6]

The planet's biggest corporations were depending on the Wangs catching up with the Joneses (and the Robertses). The United States had shopped until its economy dropped. Sinking in debt, plagued by obesity, and increasingly dependent on military might to protect its lifestyle, the world's super-consumer was groaning with indigestion. Europe was too decrepit and conservative to take up the slack, so global manufacturers, retailers, and restaurant chains were desperate to stimulate the Chinese appetite.

Shanghai was their beachhead. While information firms and political lobbyists headed to Beijing and manufacturers flocked to Guangzhou, retail giants almost invariably chose Shanghai as the base for their China headquarters and their first showrooms. From Kentucky Fried Chicken, McDonald's, and Starbucks to Louis Vuitton, Gucci, and Chanel, international brands made the city a giant shopping mall. Shanghai's skies were filled with spectacular towers that hosted the offices of global corporations, while its suburbs sprawled outward with the luxury villas of the marketing managers, PR consultants, and advertising executives.

Judging by appearances, Shanghai was a source of environmental optimism. The city has used its wealth to clean up the streets, air, and rivers, to upgrade transport infrastructure, and to relocate polluters.[7] Such was the improvement that the city was often cited as a model in China.

Stroll down the Huaihai Road and the transformation was evident. Most of the colonial-era buildings in this part of the French Concession had been torn down and replaced by boutiques and department stores. Out had gone old family-run stores and local brands, such as Three Gun Underwear. In had come Adidas, Mothercare, H&M, Zara, Costa Coffee, and stalls selling Heineken and Coca-Cola. In quieter side streets, the former residences of the European traders had become upmarket salons for Dunhill and Vacheron Constantin.

Consumers had never had more options. America's Wal-Mart, France's Carrefour, Britain's Tesco, and Japan's Ito-Yokado were expanding in China faster than in any other country. Each year they opened hundreds of new stores in the expectation that Chinese consumption would surge as more rural migrants moved into cities and worked their way into the middle class.

Young urbanites were becoming as enthusiastic about french fries, burgers, and fried chicken as their counterparts in New York or London. When the first Kentucky Fried Chicken opened near Tiananmen Square in 1987, it was seen as a novel Western dining experience. Twenty years later, the company had 2,000 outlets in 400 cities, employing 200,000 people, making it easily the biggest restaurant chain in China.[8] In roughly the same period, McDonald's had grown from one restaurant to 800. Dozens of other fast-food outlets tried to mimic their success. Along with the changing diet came a surge in obesity, diabetes, and heart disease.

As in other countries, the arrival of the Barbie ideal came at a time when real body shapes were moving in the opposite direction. Obese children used to be rare in China. Due to the country's history of famine, plumpness had long been seen as a sign of health and prosperity. Even adults take a certain pride in a bulging belly. Men in the north used to roll up their shirts in the summer to show their *jiangjun du* or General's Belly.[9] But now General's Bellies are everywhere. In Shanghai, they even have a new name: XO Bellies—after the cognac favored by business executives and senior officials. As in the rest of the world, China has rapidly grown obese, with nearly 15 percent of the population overweight.[10] Shanghai is often cited as the worst-affected city.

Diet and weight also affect the health of the planet. The demographer Joel Cohen has estimated that the earth could sustain ten billion people if everyone became a vegan.[11] But the opposite is happening in China. Barbie™ Burgers and the like are part of an increasingly carnivorous diet. As the country becomes wealthier, it moves ever closer to the fattening staples of the United States.[12] Each year, the average American chomps through 124 kilograms of meat, most of it beef.[13] Fattening a cow by a kilogram requires four times as much grain and far more water than fattening a chicken by the same amount. To feed its growing livestock, China now imports huge quantities of soy, much of it from Brazil, which has resulted in accelerated clearance of Amazonian forest and Cerrado savanna for cultivation and a shifting of the irrigation pressure to Brazil and other suppliers of grain. In policymaking circles, this is known as importing "virtual water." In practice it often means exporting environmental stress.

Shanghai's bright cosmetic exterior has been achieved at the expense of the places that provide its resources and deal with its waste. Like many other wealthy cities around the world, the high-protein, high-octane, jet-setting lifestyle is being paid for elsewhere. As the "head of the dragon" grows hungrier and heavier, its ecological footprint is sinking deeper and wider.

At two o'clock on a Tuesday afternoon I stood in front of the imposing colonial facade of Number 18 on the Bund, where I planned to climb a step higher up the consumer ladder. During the colonial era, this had been the center of foreign power. British, French, and Japanese financial institutions built their regional headquarters here in grand styles befitting their claim to empire. By turns art deco, Gothic, baroque, and Romanesque, this promenade on the Huangpu River was home to the magnificent Cathay Hotel, the Hong Kong and Shanghai Bank, several shipping firms, the British consulate, the Jardine Matheson trading house, a number of telegraph companies, a customs house with a replica of Big Ben, and the Shanghai Club, where financiers, military officers, and administrators determined the fate of the natives over gin and tonics at the 30-meter "Long Bar," at the time the biggest in the world.

After the 1949 revolution, the imperialists were kicked out and the communists requisitioned the art deco buildings for party organs and government offices. The pendulum swung again in the 1990s, when the Shanghai Club became a showcase for the nation's reform and opening-up policy. Now the Bund was once again a bridgehead for empires, this time in the form of domestic brokerages and shipping firms and foreign retailers and restaurant franchises.

Number 18 was the former China headquarters of Standard Chartered Bank. It had recently been transformed with Taiwanese money into one of Shanghai's premier adult playhouses. Wandering in through the giant faux Greek columns, I was instantly submerged in marketing and wealth. At one end of the mezzanine level, a dazzling gold panel provided the backdrop for three grinning statues in the *Standard Times* series by the contemporary artist Gao Xiaowu, at the other a guitarist and cello player strummed live Muzak behind a balustrade. I felt out of place with a scruffy beard and no socks. But nobody seemed concerned about dress code. There were even fewer customers than at the Barbie emporium. I was as much of an audience as the Muzakians were likely to get at this time on a weekday.

On the ground floor, the former bank offices had become boutiques for Cartier, Zegna, Boucheron, Patek Philippe, and A. Lange & Söhne. Up above, the sixth-floor roof terrace had been lavishly fitted out as the nightclub Bar Rouge. In between were a French-run restaurant, a contemporary art gallery, and the China headquarters of international designer brands. This, I felt, was where a real-life Barbie would come shopping and clubbing.

My guide was Emily Zhang Huijia, who had been recommended by a mutual friend as a connoisseur of consumption. She was a friendly, intelligent young woman from a middle-class family. Her mother was a hospital accountant. Her father was a lighting engineer for the Shanghai Opera. Emily was the public relations manager for Number 18 on the Bund.

Over a 48-yuan Tsingtao beer (normal retail price 3 yuan), she told me she had been a fashionista since her teens, brought up on *Vogue, Glamour,* and *OK!* magazines. Since entering the luxury-brand industry, she had worked for Gucci, Yves Saint Laurent, and Chanel.

When Emily was a child, her dad bought her a *yang wawa,* a plastic Western doll with curly hair and big round eyes. She called it Fang Fang, dressed it in clothes knitted by her mum, fed it, bathed it, and played doctors and nurses with it.

Barbies were rare in China back then. Only one of her friends, the daughter of a rich real estate agent, could afford them. Each doll cost 99 yuan. That was a lot. "I didn't see 100-yuan notes very often back then," Zhang recalled.

From that age, she raced toward a Western standard of living along with the rest of Shanghai. In 1985, when she was three, her family got its first color television. In 1992, around the same time as the first Barbies went on sale in China, Emily's family bought their first air conditioner. So did everyone in the neighborhood. Then the country.[14]

The Zhangs had their first fixed phone line installed when Emily was six. By the time she was sixteen, they were connected to the Internet. Not for the first time, I was staggered by the speed of change and China's ability to leapfrog ahead with new technology. My family in the UK had a telephone three generations before Emily's, but her parents went online four years earlier than mine.

By 2006, the average person in Shanghai owned two mobile phones, 1.7 air conditioners, 1.7 color television sets, and more than one fridge and spent 14,761 yuan, about 70 percent higher than the rest of the country.[15] Demand surged for everything from cement to wood products. Shanghai residents used almost twice as much toilet paper as the average in developed nations and had a bigger carbon footprint than people in the UK.[16] The city was now consuming beyond the planet's means, and its appetite was still growing by the day.

Rather than being seen as unsustainable, this was more usually described as "good for business." The rest of China was trying to follow suit. It was a matter of economic logic and street fashion. Emily's generation could afford more than the essentials; they could buy style.

"I'm from Shanghai. I'm a Shanghai girl. We don't earn so much money, but we see luxury brands every day. After we see all that good stuff, we don't want to buy anything else."

Emily immersed herself in the luxury industry so she could buy at a hefty discount at stock-clearance and sample sales. Most of her friends were in the industry and they shared information about sales. The first time she went, she blew a third of her salary on Fendi sunglasses.

"It is like a fever. The price is so low that you cannot refuse. I used to go every month and buy a lot. It was like a disease."

Like many a proud shopper, Emily listed how much she saved rather than how much she spent. She was wearing a half-price Dior watch reduced by 2,900 yuan and Chanel shoes knocked down from 7,000 yuan to 950. In her 40-square-meter flat near Fuxing Park, she also had dozens of other bags, accessories, and clothes, including an Armani coat for 999 yuan, discounted from 9,900. Compared with friends, she said she was restrained.

"I've developed the ability to control myself. The problem is, there is always a staff sale; and if you go, you buy."

Her taste for big-name brands sometimes took her to Hong Kong, Bali, Thailand, the Philippines, and Europe, where she could avoid the high tariffs that were slapped on designer goods in China. Besides, shopping and traveling were fun and she could afford both.

In the previous three years, Emily's monthly salary had increased from 3,000 yuan to just under 20,000, putting her firmly in the middle-class bracket. During moments of extreme stress, she would still gorge on a bucket of fried chicken from KFC, but usually she enjoyed haute cuisine and the high life. She ate at restaurants on weekends, had a French boyfriend, played poker every Thursday. Business and pleasure were mixed. Her favorite after-hours hangout, she said, was the building where she worked.

"Bund 18 has the coolest nightclub in Shanghai, so it is probably also the coolest in China."

We agreed to meet there again at midnight, when she promised to introduce me to the city's nightlife.

After dark, the illuminations on the Bund reminded me of London. There was the same weight of history in the spotlit neoclassical pillars and low-rise architecture. My British past offered no such comforting comparisons for the spectacular view on the other side of the Huangpu River, where the futuristic Pudong skyline rose higher into the sky than almost anywhere else on earth. The view managed to be both tacky and awe-inspiring at the same time. Highest among the cluster of spiking, sloping, curving towers was one of the world's tallest buildings, the 492-meter-high bottle-opener-shaped Shanghai World Financial Center, and the red minaretlike dome of the Oriental Pearl Tower flanked by two tinny-looking replica globes. Twenty years earlier most of Pudong had been farmland. Today, it pulsated with light and color. There was no more stunning vista of modern China.

As soon as I stepped out of the taxi, I was approached by a migrant beggar and a drug dealer offering marijuana. Cars were pulling up and disgorging beautifully dressed couples, mostly expat Western men and their Chinese girlfriends. We shared an elevator near a stairwell decorated with discarded bicycles, a work by the artist Ai Weiwei. On the fourth floor, I met Emily in Lounge 18, decorated in "Haute Bohemian" style with walls of candles and faux opium dens. In the cigar lounge, she introduced me to the French food and beverage manager, Julian Desmettre. Over a mojito, he told me how the nouveaux riches from Taiwan, Hong Kong, and Singapore had made the city their playground: "Shanghai is like Paris during la Belle Epoque. This is the city of wealth and style, where people must show their money, where they are judged by how they dress, where they look down on those with less than themselves."

Julian had arrived in Shanghai as a student eight years earlier with just 5,000 yuan in his pocket. Now, he had an Omega watch worth six times that amount on his wrist and wore Zegna shoes and a Hugo Boss suit that he could never have afforded in the past. "My life here is better than in France. I have a big apartment, a cleaner, a compound with a pool and a gym. It is so comfortable, it is almost too much. I am very happy."

He saw a similar change in the city. There were more Ferraris and Porsches than in the past. There was a wider choice of restaurants than in Paris. The supermarkets contained the finest food and drink from around the world, albeit at more than twice the price it would be in Europe. The change was accelerating. "What they did before in ten years, they now do in two. All of the world's big brands are opening stores in Shanghai. There are so many customers here."

Most of the revelers in his lounge were Europeans. The disparity between expats and locals was even more pronounced on the Bar Rouge terrace on the sixth floor, where mostly foreign partygoers drank and danced to techno music, bathed in blue neon light under a fluttering red Chinese flag. They were marketing agents, corporate managers, language teachers, and others in the vanguard of global consumer culture. There were some stylish locals too, but most of the Chinese appeared to be girls paid to dance on the tables, keep the mood suitably scandalous, and encourage the expat customers to buy rounds of shots served in test tubes.

"Where can I meet Chinese partygoers?" I asked Emily.

She was reluctant to recommend anywhere: "There are clubs, but they are the type of place you would find in a second-tier city. The music and décor are not as good, but Chinese men prefer them because they don't want to be near foreigners. Chinese women are different. They are more open. They go where the quality is."

I left alone. Outside the building, a weary-looking hooker touted for business and a dealer offered cocaine for 1,000 yuan per gram. Wandering bars and restaurants, I met a man who claimed to be one of the city's earliest nightclub owners. He claimed to be halfway toward his ambition of licking the nipples of 10,000 women. From others, I learned how bar owners had to pay off the police by taking out a subscription to the monthly public security magazine costing more than 20,000 yuan ($2,857) a copy. They organized prostitutes for their customers and trips to karaoke parlors where hostesses stripped off to sing, and to the saunas on Wuzonglu where masseuses used their soaped naked bodies to wash clients. Shanghai was emulating the consumer sex industry of Tokyo.

There were other reminders of Japan at the height of its "bubble economy." During the peak of its excess in the late eighties, the most notorious binge spending and clubbing took place at a club called Juliana's, where microskirted *wan-ren-bodi-kon-gyaru* (one-length hair, body-conscious girls) would dance on bars as the clientele splashed out thousands of dollars on champagne and whiskey. Now, the same vibe pulsated through China's commercial heartland. While 1980s Tokyo had Juliana's, twenty-first-century Shanghai had Club 88. When I got there at 3 a.m., the club was heaving with scantily clad bodies. A beautiful Asian woman wandered through the throng in fishnet stockings, a garter belt, miniskirt, and skimpy top, casting her blue-contact-lensed eyes toward the ceiling as a drunken girl toppled off the platform where she had been dancing. The tables were packed. On a stage by the bar, a would-be pop idol lip-synched to Michael Jackson surrounded by busty hookers, svelte socialites, shabbily dressed

Europeans, and a couple playing Jenga. The barmen juggled spirit bottles between serving cocktails. Waiters whisked by carrying bottles of champagne in buckets of ice decorated with fizzling fireworks. Faux French chandeliers pulsated in time with the music. Clouds of dry ice billowed up from below the stage. Amid the smoke and the music and the money, Shanghai was having a ball.

The next day, Emily helped me climb farther up the social ladder with an introduction to the head of a thriving marketing agency.

Cindy Tai was a former head of EMI Music in China who had helped to organize the first Rolling Stones concert in Shanghai. Perhaps for this reason, she spoke the language of pop altruism. In near flawless English she told me how her values were changing.

"We must focus on inner beauty, not the luxury outside. If we can all save on what we consume, then we can feed the starving people."

When she was a child, Cindy had a *yang wawa* made of cloth. She had had to nag her mother endlessly to buy it. Even in Shanghai, luxuries like dolls were frowned upon in the postrevolution era. Although it was cheap and ugly, Cindy used scraps of material, spare yarn, glass beads, and colored paper to make it look beautiful, which, even then, meant Western. "My doll had big blue eyes. I painted them myself. And I gave her fake blond hair. We tried to make our dolls look Western because the West was rich, while China was poor."

The doll was confiscated by Red Guards, along with her mum's high heels, soon after the Cultural Revolution began. The only playthings allowed were revolutionary dolls in Mao suits. Cindy and her academic parents were sent to a farm on the nearby island of Chongming, where she turned her musical talent to playing revolutionary songs. "We had enough to eat but nothing to spare. We were very happy if we got a little meat on the table once a week. My parents suffered at that time. I vowed that one day I would buy them whatever they wanted."

That was easy for her now, but, after I told her I was writing a book about the environment, she insisted she had grown out of materialist ambitions.

"My dream now is to create an organic farm. I would like to grow fruit, vegetables, and rice, to raise pigs and chickens. And to have a helicopter to drive me around because the traffic is so bad."

Like many affluent consumers around the world, her idea of environmentalism seemed to be choosing what was healthy for her rather than for the planet. She had blueberries delivered from the local organic farm, baguettes from a French bakery in Xintiandi, and olive oil from Italy. She dined out at least once a day.

Cindy was conflicted by the competing pressures to be green and to be seen. She had recently been thinking of buying a Porsche. After sales agents took her out for a spin on Shanghai's F1 racetrack, she initially put in an order for a 1-million-yuan black Porsche. "It's a novelty thing. Everyone had one, so I felt I had to get one to keep up with the Joneses."

But she said she was having second thoughts. "We keep to a minimum because we want to be green and environmentally friendly. We are very conscious of the environment. We are trying to save the earth so we should not produce a lot of waste. I am very concerned. Everyone is talking about global warming."

At one point she and her French husband had four cars: a BMW, an MG, and a couple of Mercedes-Benzes. Now they had only two, a sign, she said, of their increased concern for the planet. Later in the conversation she revealed her interest had switched to yachts. One was moored near their second home in Cannes. Another was being built.

She may yet get another luxury car. Cindy was already a member of the Shanghai Porsche Club, mainly to keep up with her friends. She checked her mobile phone for a text message about the next event, a cocktail party and awards ceremony hosted by Jaguar and the style magazine *Modern Weekly*.

"They insist I go. I guess they want all the posh people there," she said. Sensing a social-climbing opportunity, I shamelessly asked if I could attend. Her manners were far too good to refuse.

The venue for the Jaguar Gorgeous Award Party was a renovated mansion off Huaihai Road, just a few minutes' walk away from the Barbie store. In cocktail dresses and designer suits, the guests sipped wine in the courtyard, waiting for VIPs to show up, sign the visitor board, have their photographs taken, and be whisked off for a sales pitch for the new 5-liter XKR.

"It is a wow car!" gushed an exquisitely attired PR lady who introduced herself by her Westernized name, Seraph.

I was skeptical. "But you can barely move in Shanghai's traffic. Why would anyone want such a huge engine?"

"Rich people never take the subway. Even if the traffic is bad, they need a car," said Seraph, smiling, clearly deep into her role. "Jaguar is nothing but gorgeous and beautiful."

The description would fit and delight Cindy, who arrived soon after and introduced me to the affable head of the Porsche Club, Li Mingtan. They briefly inducted me into the world of luxury car owners, explaining how the group went driving every weekend to their second homes in the countryside. At times, they also operated as what might be called a rent-a-snob organization, by parking their luxury cars outside branding events. At times this was political. For the tenth anniversary of the Hong Kong handover, Li told me he led a 100-Porsche convoy down to the former British territory to demonstrate the mainland's rising consumer power.

It was a fair statement to make. In the five years before 2009, sales of luxury cars rose fivefold, deluxe villas soared sevenfold, and sales of luxury goods tripled.[17] This was just the start of a spending splurge. The number of wealthy households was forecast to double again between 2010 and 2015.[18]

Li did not seem entirely happy that luxury cars had lost their exclusive cachet. He was one of the first people in Shanghai to buy a Porsche in 2005. Now he said there were more than a thousand on the city's streets. It was a similar story for Bentleys and Ferraris.[19] Keeping ahead of the pack was getting harder. He told me he had recently upgraded from a 3-liter to a 4.5-liter engine.

The Jaguar promotion was not going well. It was too hot. The air-conditioning did not appear to be working and several VIPs grumbled there was nothing to eat but canapés. The live classical music ought to have soothed the audience, but there was a problem with the sound system. Guests held their ears as the shrieking, squealing feedback continued through a speech by the company's chief representative. The tut-tutting was not as loud but probably hurt the ears of the organizers more.

"It's all so superficial," complained a guest from a European embassy. A friend nodded in agreement. I wondered what more they expected.

Consumption was increasingly equated in China with power and prestige. It was not always so. During the Mao era, frugality was a necessity as well as a virtue. Recently, however, conspicuous splurging had become an essential part of the zeitgeist of Shanghai. Taken to excess, it was comical. As the rich used their wealth to keep up with the Joneses, everyone ended up buying the same brands in the same places.

The retail market was becoming less diverse the bigger it grew. Paul French, a marketing consultant at the Shanghai-based Access Asia firm, told me the problem was Potemkin shopping communities designed to create the image of a good life that did not reflect the reality of most people: "They are building more and more malls filled with luxury brands. Like the power stations in Soviet-era Russia, they are being built not because of demand but because of prestige. Every official in China wants one to show their city is on the international map."

These shopping emporiums aimed to generate desire rather than meet needs. Many were scathingly dismissed by locals as *gui gouwu zhongxin* (ghost malls) because they attracted so few customers. Yet these consumer citadels were everywhere. I saw one in Nanjing Road, the former center of the Shanghai retail experience. Like Carnaby Street in London, it had become a pedestrianized parade for tourists and migrants. Locals would not be seen dead there, though the shops contained many of the same brands as supposedly more upmarket spots. I saw them too at Xujiahui intersection, which was ringed by six department stores. Among them was the Orient Shopping Mall, a glass-and-marble monument to spiritual emptiness. Its brands were as predictable as a McDonald's menu: Tag Heuer watches, Folli Follie jewelry, Estée Lauder cosmetics, Rolex watches, Dunhill belts, Kanebo lipstick, Mont Blanc sunglasses, Cartier pens, Dior lipstick, and other high-priced sameness. Passing through the revolving door on a weekday midmorning, I could not see a single other customer. Not even a window shopper.

Outside the polished exterior, under a limpid gray sky, crowds wandered past a Kentucky Fried Chicken outlet, a Coca-Cola promotion tent, a silver pillar dressed up as an Asahi beer can, and the slogan of the Shanghai Expo, "Better City, Better Life."

I wandered under the overpasses and walkways, past the multistory car parks and shopping malls, glimpsing Premiership football on plasma TV screens, inhaling the traffic, and sucking in the capitalized mantras on the advertising billboards: "Beauty Redefined," "Discover the Flavors of the World," "It's the Small Surprises That Touch the Most," "Romance Comes from Little Moments," "Please Follow Us," "Good News to Beef Lovers."

I could have been anywhere. The feelings of familiarity and alienation were borderless. China had joined the party. We were all having a great time, but we were in denial.

There were more of us than ever before and we had never lived longer. We were traveling farther—millions of us covered more ground every year than Marco Polo could have dreamed of in his lifetime. We were burning more carbon and calories—the average human used the energy equivalent of twenty human slaves.[20] And we were eating more—middle-class city dwellers could dine each day on more exotic banquets than any king of old.

Bulging waistlines, expanding landfill sites, and the buildup of toxins in the air and water were not the only reasons this could not last. The Earthwatch Institute estimates that if China's 1.3 billion people were to consume at the same rate as Americans, global production of steel, paper, and cars would have to double, oil output would need to rise by 20 million barrels per day, and miners would have to dig an extra 5 billion tons of coal. If they followed the U.S. appetite, China would chew its way through 80 percent of current meat production and two-thirds of the global grain harvest.[21]

"China is telescoping history. It forces us to focus on what happens when huge numbers of low-income people rise rapidly in affluence," Lester Brown, the president of Earthwatch, told me. "Chinese consumption shows the need to reconstruct the world economy." But the opposite was happening. Global corporations and the communist government were together trying to make China the greatest shopper of them all.[22]

The final stage of my social climb was to the peak of consumer society, where I met the woman who spearheaded that marketing campaign in its earliest stages.

Kan Yue-Sai literally changed the face of China, or at least the female half of it. Born in China, brought up in the U.S., she uniquely rose to fame on both sides of the Pacific as a TV star, an advertising pioneer, and China's first cosmetics queen. She put the first artificial blush on the cheeks of tens of millions of women. Her cosmetics painted their lips, penciled their eyes, established the foundation for generations of Chinese women to look more Western. The finishing touch was a trademark hairstyle—a bob—that is even today known in hairdressing salons across the country as the "Yue-Sai cut."

Sometimes described as a Chinese Oprah Winfrey, she had become the highest-profile socialite in Shanghai. The week before we met, she hosted Quincy Jones, Ewan McGregor, and Halle Berry at a film festival. As well as dropping celebrity names, she put a lot of effort into building up her own. Entering her expansive apartment, I saw a showroom for the House of Yue-Sai brand. While I waited for the great woman, I leaned back on Yue-Sai cushions and the maid brought tea in Yue-Sai cups on Yue-Sai trays.

Given the display of self-love all around me, I unwisely started by describing the previous night's Jaguar party without realizing that Yue-Sai had been not only present but the main attraction. I hadn't been paying attention. So much for my social-climbing skills. She was not amused.

"I was there. I was the first awardee." Her voice rose. She looked genuinely hurt.

We had not got off to a good start. I would have been better off shouting insults at Yue-Sai than failing to pay attention. It was not the last time in our interview that my faux pas was mentioned. I came to think of it in mental capitals as THE SHOCK.

Her reaction was understandable. Yue-Sai was in the vanity business. She had made a living out of being the center of attention. This was more than superficial. Yue-Sai claimed to have created consumer culture in China.

"I was the first one to tell them, 'Go ahead and buy something to make yourself feel good.' It was the early nineties. Nobody wanted to flaunt wealth back then. Nobody had wealth back then. I would sell lipstick for five dollars and sisters would pool their money to buy one. It was the start of consumerism."

Engagingly, charmingly, Yue-Sai told me how she was driven by idealism, how she "colorized" the gray China of the 1980s.

During the Cultural Revolution, cosmetics were condemned as a sign of counterrevolutionary bourgeois habits. The hangover lasted a decade until Yue-Sai began selling lipstick, mascara, and eyeliner. But this was no street-fashion revolution. The order for China to make up its face came from the top. It was a deliberate ploy to distract attention from politics in the aftermath of the bloody crackdown that followed the Tiananmen protests of 1989. Foreign firms pulled out of China en masse. The politburo wanted to show that the country could continue on the path to modernity. They called on Yue-Sai to help.

"At a private dinner with the vice premier, he asked if I would be willing to start a company while everyone else was withdrawing. He told me it would be wonderful and it would look good," she recalled.

"Did you have any doubts?" I asked.

"None. I never doubted that China would open up. The fact that they had invited me to do a TV series and lead them into the world showed that."

"Even after the crackdown in 1989?"

"No doubts. Some even say that my program started the Tiananmen demonstrations because I showed the Chinese people the world."[23]

The political turmoil worked out well for Yue-Sai, who was able to start her business on a field abandoned by many foreign retailers. Like countless firms since, she opened her first stores in Shanghai, before tackling the politically riskier ground of Beijing. In advance of setting up shops in the capital she sought the support of the powerful Women's Federation. The wife of Li Peng, the prime minister who ordered the troops to fire on the protesters, organized a lunch of all the vice premiers' wives to back her.

It was to prove an initiation into a rich elite that she has since helped to expand. Yue-Sai's products were a massive hit. Cosmetics proved a gold mine, particularly in Shanghai, where women spend fifty times the national average on makeup.[24] By the time she sold the company to L'Oréal in 2004, its annual revenue was $80 million. The multinational then made even more money by adding strong skin-whitening agents to their products.[25]

Along with a surge in popularity of cosmetic surgery to enlarge breasts, lengthen legs, and make eyes look more Western, the growth of the skin-whitening industry suggested China was moving closer to the Barbie ideal.[26] Even Yue-Sai, the ambassador of consumer culture, was starting to lament that the world "was becoming all the same." More than ten years after introducing Western cosmetics, she launched a line of dark-haired, brown-eyed Chinese-style dolls.

"I like Barbie, but I thought it was necessary to have a different doll. The idea behind it is to tell Chinese kids that you are beautiful too. The standard of beauty is not just blue eyes and blond hair. It was a revolutionary idea."[27]

Unfortunately, it was also a failure. In toy shops, the doll—inevitably named Yue-Sai Wawa—proved the poor cousin of Barbie, suffering second-class display status if it made it to the shelves at all.

The same proved true of House of Yue-Sai products, which were sold only online. Faced with more market competition and less Communist Party backing, the former cosmetics maven was struggling. She partly blames declining moral standards: "The whole environment has changed because so much wealth has been made by so many people. In all nouveau riche societies, people flaunt their money. Here too. They don't buy a bottle of wine, they buy a case. But all they really know is brand names. It takes a long time to acquire genuine style."

That train of thought took her back to her own credentials and then THE SHOCK that someone, i.e., me, might have overlooked them. "I can't believe you missed me last night."

In an attempt to switch attention, I asked if she would buy a Jaguar after headlining the company's promotion event.

The Yue-Sai cut shook from side to side. "They only offered a ten percent discount. I don't buy for ten percent."

It was not just this doyenne of consumer culture who was occasionally hesitant about splurging. If there was a glimmer of environmental hope in Shanghai, it was that, even here, shoppers had not yet fully embraced Western levels of consumption. Many still preferred flasks of hot tea to cans of Coke. In the big supermarkets, the average basket of goods was smaller than in the West and profit margins were lower. This thrift was not inspired by environmental concerns but by a traditional desire to live within one's means. But that prudence was changing.

I asked Yue-Sai if she regretted her role in promoting an American consumer lifestyle in China, given what has since been learned about the fragility of the environment and the limits of the world's resources.

The question prompted the first silence of our two-hour interview, and then just a hint of self-doubt about her influence on Chinese consumers: "I don't want them to live like in the U.S., but I want them to have a more beautiful life. Of course, I am worried about the environment. Everyone is worried about that, but . . ." Another long silence.

"I can't answer your question well. If you ask me what I am concerned about it is not resources, it is how substandard things are. With the new consumerism, everyone is trying so hard to be corrupt, to make more money. Everyone is squeezing down."

I tried the question again, more directly.

"Do you ever wish you hadn't helped to launch consumer culture in China?"

"No, the government wanted it. China had to open up to the world. If the government didn't want to do it, it would never have happened. When I started working in China in the early 1980s, the leadership was great. They were visionary—"

"But they weren't aware then of the environmental consequences as we are now," I interjected.

"No, they weren't . . . I just read an article about the Antarctic crumbling."

"Do you think it would help to move away from a consumer lifestyle?"

"Consumerism has a good side and a bad side. The key really is to balance it." Then she paused. "Are you blaming me?"

"No, our problems today are not the fault of any one person. There was almost no consumer culture when you started. But now, hasn't it gone too far in the other direction?"

Another pause. "I think you are right. But it is only a small section of society," she said. "And no matter how horrible you think China is today, you should have seen the China I saw twenty years ago. It was truly like a moonscape, totally different. In some ways, it is better now." She pauses again. "But it is true that in other ways China is not better: the ungreening of it, the toxins, the plastic things."

The self-doubt quickly passed. We moved on from climate change and consumer guilt and talked instead about her charity work, about celebrities, about untrustworthy business partners. Her tone was warm. I began to think she might have forgotten THE SHOCK. But then, just as I was preparing to leave, she returned midsentence to that unintended, incomprehensible, unforgettable slight.

"I am so unhappy that you didn't see me last night."

My social climb had hit the ceiling. The worlds of Barbie and the China Doll had converged. In Shanghai, people were under more pressure to look good, to eat expensively, to shop for self-fulfillment. Other cities would follow. The American dream had not yet been realized, but it was drawing closer. Consumption was rising conspicuously, regardless of the fashion for eco-food and green living. On the coast and in Chongqing, I had now seen how trade, industry, urbanization, and other forces of development were all geared toward endless expansion just as in the West. But the planet is a finite space. Something had to give. Where were the stresses being felt? I worked my way next toward the northwest to look at the impact on the land, the water, the air, and the people.

Northwest
Imbalance

★

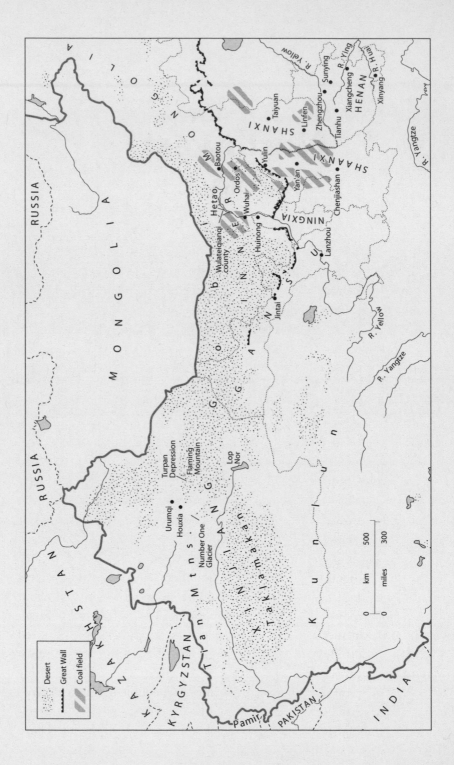

9

Why Do So Many People Hate Henan?

Henan

The country is rather over-peopled in proportion to what its stock can employ, and labour is, therefore, so abundant, that no pains are taken to abridge it. The consequence of this is, probably, the greatest production of food that the soil can possibly afford.
—Thomas Malthus on China, 1798 [1]

China's most populous [2] and, arguably, least popular province lay only an hour by air from the glitz of Shanghai's consumer culture. Traveling from one to the other could be a jolt in more ways than one. Turbulence is usual on the crowded flight paths over the northern China floodplain, but the flight to Henan was bumpier than usual. The shaking of the fuselage forced the Air China cabin crew, who normally wander up and down regardless of the weather, to strap themselves into their seats. All the passengers were gripping their armrests. For the first time in years I felt anxious about flying. Looking out of the window, we appeared to be descending through dense cloud, but suddenly there was a jolt. For a terrifying second I feared a midair collision. But, no, we were in one piece. What was it? Surely we weren't down yet. I could see no sign of the ground. But I strained my eyes and, yes, thankfully, there was the runway. A couple of hundred yards away, I could just about make out Zhengzhou Airport terminal. The steel-and-glass building seemed on the verge of disappearing into the filthy haze

I had mistaken for a dark nimbus cloud. I relaxed. A degree of grimness was to be expected. After all, this was Henan.

"A vision of the Apocalypse," "Hell on earth," "The foulest place in China." When I mentioned I was to visit Henan, expressions soured, distaste rose, and people I would consider liberal, open-minded, and compassionate spewed forth a stream of derogatory comments. Prejudice had become the norm with regard to this crush of humanity. Well-educated Chinese friends casually dismissed people from Henan as greedy and deceitful. Foreign visitors were barely more forgiving. Those who had never been there knew it as a place of AIDS villages and cancer clusters. Even many migrants from the province said they left because their homes were poor, crowded, and polluted. The antipathy so many Chinese feel toward Henan seems to mirror the prejudice that many foreigners express toward China: that it is dirty, overcrowded, and untrustworthy.

I was there to test a theory that discrimination has its roots in population stress; that excess human pressure on the land hurts the health and well-being of those who live on it.

This idea was at least two hundred years old. In the eighteenth century the notorious doomsayer Thomas Malthus argued that too many people on too little land inevitably resulted in a culling of human numbers. He believed people either regulated themselves or disaster would do the job for them.[3] Although he never traveled this far east, the British reverend identified China as the prime example of a population incapable of the self-restraining "preventative checks" that "civilised nations" like Britain were able to apply through religion and education. Instead, he said it was regulated by the "positive checks" of drought, famine, and war. Later Western visitors went so far as to see famine as a necessary evil.[4] China's emperors knew the dangers of imbalance between human demand and environmental supply. The Mandarin word for "population" is made up of two characters, *ren* (human) and *kou* (mouth). But Mao, a believer in strength in numbers, preferred to see each person as two extra hands. It is only in the last few decades that Chinese environmentalists have come to see population as a major cause of their nation's problems.[5] Henan illustrates how the attitude to people power has shifted from admiration to concern.

Historically, this province was credited as the cradle of Han civilization. Tai chi, kung fu, and Chan Buddhism (better known outside China as Zen) are said to have originated here.[6] It was the birthplace of Lao-tzu and other influential philosophers and was a center of political power in ancient times, boasting three former national capitals: Luoyang, Anyang, and Kaifeng. The province once had dense forests and, according to Mark Elvin, more elephants than Thailand,[7] but those beasts have long since been driven away along with the clearance of land for farms, cities, and people. By the Northern Song dynasty (960–1127), Kaifeng was thought to be the most populous city in the world with 2 million people. Frequent famines suggested the capacity of the land and the numbers of dwellers it supported were often out of balance, but as recently as the 1950s Henan was celebrated for clear waters, abundant harvests, and a rich culture.

Since then, the land has come under more human pressure than almost anywhere else in China. The registered population has surged from 42 million in 1949 to over 100 million. Henan's population is bigger than that of any country in Europe and all but twelve of the world's nations.[8] Yet they are crammed into an area of 167,000 square kilometers—the size of Massachusetts or two Scotlands. This has left the province with the highest rural population density in the country, an environment in tatters, and one of the lowest average incomes.[9] Poverty and desperation have made Henan the origin of many of the darkest stories from China: cancer clusters, AIDS villages, slave labor, skewed sex ratios due to selective abortions, birth defects, murder, counterfeiting, and pollution.

As we drove away from the airport, the cause of the dark smog soon became apparent. Smoke curled up from bonfires in field after field. I asked the driver to stop and set off across a field of black stubble to talk to a local farmer, who was burning off stalks after the autumn corn harvest. After sorting the stubble into piles, he ignited the bonfire with a cigarette lighter. It burned quickly, forcing crickets and other insects to flee. The billowing smoke was a negative, inverted image of a snowstorm: a blizzard of rising black flakes. He told me that every farmer burns his field on the same day, and explained why.

This seasonal burn has been illegal for over a decade, not because it fouls the air and adds to China's carbon emissions, but because it is a hazard to air traffic.[10] But the governance problem already noted in earlier chapters is evident here too. The farmers pay no attention. Burning the stubble is the easiest and cheapest way to clear the land and put potassium into the soil. It is an environmentally expensive shortcut. If the stalks were composted and plowed back into the land, their carbon would return to the earth rather than burn into the sky. But that would be too time-consuming for modern itinerant farmers, most of whom labor in the cities and return home for just a few days to bring in the harvest. Because they all violate the regulations at once, the authorities are powerless: it would be impossible to arrest them en masse.

A short distance farther along the road I asked a policeman why he took no action. "This is rural China. This is how things are done," he said, shrugging. "There will be a big fog tomorrow."

Such "backward practices" are supposed to be a thing of the past. The authorities have tried to modernize Henan, but the rush to develop often caused more problems than it solved. With too many people and too few resources, the government often resorted to making money quickly by sacrificing morals, human lives, and the environment.

The last two had long been vulnerable in Henan. When the Yellow and the Huai rivers flood, this province is usually hit worst, often resulting in hundreds of thousands of deaths. During the Sino-Japanese War the Nationalist general Chiang Kai-shek considered Henan so expendable that he ordered his forces to blow up Yellow River dikes to delay Japanese troops, even though it resulted in the deaths of hundreds of thousands of people downstream and left millions homeless. Japan's air force bombed Zhengzhou to rubble. Rebuilt, it remains one of China's least attractive provincial capitals.

Mao Zedong warned that Henan was where rebellions started and dynasties were overthrown, but it was also where he pushed hardest to realize his belief that more people meant more power. Short of economic and military strength in the 1950s, Mao shaped his nationalist goals around the huge population.[11] The founder of the republic's credo was *Renduo, Liliang Da* (With Many People, Strength Is Great). In one of his more idiosyncratic metaphors, Mao compared mothers to aircraft carriers, each capable of launching up to ten fighter-plane babies.[12] To Nehru in 1954, he dismissed the threat of U.S. nuclear weapons because even the world's most powerful bomb would never be able to wipe out the massive Chinese population. From engineering to agriculture, the attitude was the same: throw enough people at a problem and it would be fixed. Little heed was paid to biological limits or natural balance. The consequences were murderous.

To demonstrate people power, Mao was drawn to Henan. During the Great Leap Forward, this was the home of the first people's commune and the boldest agricultural experiments.[13] In 1958—the year that saw the height of Maoist excess—no province went further in applying Soviet-inspired techniques of close planting and deep plowing, or in falsely claiming success.[14] Doctored propaganda images of the era show wheatfields so dense that children could stand on the crop. The slogan of the age was "Learn from Henan. Catch up with Henan!" The reality two years later was a famine that killed up to 8 million people in this province alone.[15] In the worst affected area of Xinyang, corpses littered the fields.[16] Some desperate people resorted to cannibalism.[17] In 1961, an internal party document reportedly described what happened as a "holocaust." Officially the nationwide death toll was 14 million. Historians now estimate between 20 and 40 million people starved to death.

That was not the only way people died. The reckless pace of hydrological engineering of the time, mentioned in chapter 2, was particularly calamitous here. In 1958, a nationwide frenzy of dam building reached its peak in Henan, where a population of farmers was mobilized to build 110 dams in a single year.[18] A decade later, more than half had collapsed, killing countless people. Others lasted longer, though with direr consequences: in 1975, the worst dam disaster in China's history killed around 240,000 people in Henan's Zhumadian prefecture.[19]

Many of these calamities had common causes: a belief that more people meant more power, unrealistically high expectations of the land's fertility, and regional party lackeys who took their leader's wildest plans to absurd extremes, lied about results, then silenced any critic who dared to reveal the truth.[20] After 1978, much the same could be said of the embrace of dirty industry and reckless get-rich-quick schemes that were touted as the best way to lift Henan's huge population out of poverty.

We drove east, through the haze, across the floodplains to one of the worst-affected areas. The Huai River basin is home to 150 million people who live among its tangle of tributaries and irrigation canals. Near Henan's border with Anhui Province, the villages here were crushed together, along with the people. Junctions were strewn with rubbish, and wider social problems were evident from a giant billboard depicting an emaciated man and a screaming entreaty: "Don't use drugs!" More people migrated from these two provinces than almost anywhere else in China.[21] It was the human pool that filled cities like Shanghai with cheap labor. There was little reason to stay. This area was often deluged by floods. In the postreform era, it had also become synonymous with pollution and sickness.[22]

During the eighties and nineties, poor but venal local governments in the Huai valley were in such a rush to industrialize that they accepted and protected heavily polluting companies, such as paper mills, tanneries, and chemical plants. It was a huge risk to the health of the population, though perhaps not fully understood at the time.

Local governments did not want to miss out on the economic development that was making other parts of China rich. Environment protection officials joined "investment soliciting delegations" to promise industries that they would not face the tight controls seen in richer areas.[23] Outside companies were willing to invest, to provide jobs, and—almost certainly—bribes. Many were joint ventures with multinationals that could not get approval to site their production in countries with more stringent environmental standards. Among the worst culprits was Lianhua (Lotus) Gourmet Powder Company—a joint venture between the local government and Japan's Ajinomoto—which was China's biggest producer of monosodium glutamate food flavoring. Every day the plant discharged 120,000 tons of wastewater. Pollution slicks of up to 70 kilometers in length were common. The Ying, a Huai tributary lauded by the Tang dynasty poet Li Bai for "crystal clear" headwaters, became a cesspool.

Almost 100 "cancer villages" have been identified in China, most of them near polluted waterways. From the mid-1990s, pioneering Chinese journalists began investigating a belt of them along the Huai River basin. Reliable information was hard to come by, locals were often intimidated, and many NGO officials and reporters were reluctant to talk on the record. Before my trip, a Chinese journalist advised me not to visit because it might put people in jeopardy. "After I published my story, my sources were constantly harassed by local public security officers. I wish I had never written the piece," he told me.

Another journalist, Deng Fei, has mapped those affected villages.[24] The scientific basis for the cancer village tag is mixed. There have been few epidemiological studies and much of the evidence is anecdotal. But at the very least, these villages can be considered clusters of fear. Such concerns are well founded. Nationally, cancer rates rose rapidly after the launch of economic reforms, and in 1997, this disease became the main cause of death in China for the first time. It causes one in five deaths, up 80 percent over the past thirty years. Lung cancer, caused by smoking and air pollution, is the biggest killer. Diseases of the digestive system— associated with water pollution and food contamination—have also risen sharply.[25] Worst affected are the 700 million people living in the country- side, who are poorer and less likely to have access to piped, treated water than urban dwellers. Compared with the global average, Chinese farmers are almost four times more likely to die of liver cancer and twice as likely to die of stomach cancer. Environmental standards are dire in many areas, but nowhere else has a worse reputation than the Huai River basin. Anec- dotal or not, the locals have solid reasons to be fearful.

In the poor district of Xiangcheng City, the residents living between a coal-fired power plant and the Lianhua factory were not sure whether to worry more about the polluted air or the contaminated water they had been breathing and drinking for a large part of their lives. For much of the previous twenty years another Huai tributary, the Yun, that ran near to their homes had been choked with chemicals, while the air above, they said, had been tinted green on the smoggiest days. At the local industrial primary school, everything from windowsills to the leaves on the trees was coated in fine black dust. A cleanup was finally under way, but for many it was too late.

"The rich folk have already moved out. Just a couple of hundred fami- lies remain. It has become a slum," said one local woman. "Among those left behind, almost everyone over the age of forty has some kind of dis- ease . . . We have complained about the pollution but no one cares. Our county is too remote and too poor."

Many residents in this sprawl of wide gray streets believed the pol- lution was deadly. A short distance downstream at Shi Zhuang Village, a factory worker named Shi Yingzhong was mourning the death of his father from cancer the previous year. The illness had brought financial disaster to an already poor family, which was now saddled with crippling medical bills. Shi's share of the outstanding debt ran to about 25,000 yuan—a huge sum for a man who earned just 1,000 yuan per month. His wife received even less for her work on the family's fields.

Shi was resigned rather than angry, but he had no doubt about the cause of his father's death. "It was the polluted water," he said. "We used to drink from a well just four meters deep. Then the water became dirty so we had to go deeper and deeper. Now it is more than forty meters, but the water is still not clean."

Yet many locals remembered a time not so long ago when the Huai was considered a blessed river. Perhaps the most famous of them is Huo Daishan, who has led the battle again pollution in Henan.

Huo smiled as he recalled nearly drowning in the Huai as a three-year-old. "There were lots of kids diving in the river and swimming around. It looked really exciting so I decided to join in. In I went, then down, down under the water thinking 'Isn't this fun!' Especially after a little while when I could see a blaze of lights in my head. Only later did I realize this meant I had fallen into a coma."

He came to love the river that nearly killed him. During his childhood in the 1950s it was a source of drinking water, irrigation for the fields, fish for the table, and, once he had properly learned to swim, fun. There was romance too. His grandmother took him to a nighttime wedding ceremony on the water. As musicians played and fireworks were set off from brightly illuminated boats, the bride was rowed in from one side and the groom—stripped down to his shorts with just a red ribbon in his hair—had to dance his way slowly across the water from the other direction, his swaying movements the only source of power for the boat. "It was extraordinarily beautiful," recalled Huo. "Even in films, I have never seen anything like it."

That cultural tradition disappeared. The population grew, the economy changed, and so did the river. By the mid-1980s, the banks of the Huai were punctuated with factories. In 1987, when Huo was assigned to photograph the river near his childhood home, the waters were black. It stank. Dead fish floated on the surface. The silk trader's son lacked the vocabulary to describe what had happened. "Back then, we didn't even know the word 'pollution.'"

Locals expressed the change in aphorisms and songs. The people of this area are proud of their cultural heritage. When they are happy, they write ditties and wistful ballads. When sad, they do not just grumble, they sing lamentations. In the late 1950s, this literary talent was channeled into propaganda slogans for their homeland.

"Though you may walk thousands of miles, you will never find beauty to compare to the Huai River" went one. "When we have a good harvest by the Huai River, no one in the entire country will go hungry" ran another.

Forty years later, with the river filthy and the land contaminated, the wordsmiths turned out more cynical lines:

> In the fifties, we washed our food in the clear river,
> In the sixties, we irrigated our fields with its waters,
> In the seventies, we saw our river turn black and oily,
> In the eighties, we watched dead fish float to the surface,
> In the nineties, we too started to fall sick.

The government knew a catastrophe was taking place and tried to act. In 1995, the country's first river environment protection law was enacted to clean up the Huai. The ranking State Council member for the environment, Song Jian, proclaimed boldly, "We must be ready to sever our limbs when bitten by a poisonous snake," to show his willingness to sacrifice polluting industries. But the local government had other ideas. They were not going to abandon companies like Lianhua, which employed 8,000 people and had the host city as a majority stakeholder. The cleanup campaign proved only that laws in China are easy to ignore and rhetoric is often the opposite of reality. Lianhua continued to dump ammonium nitrate. Tanneries and chemical firms discharged other pollutants. The black slicks grew longer and fouler. At the peak, the stench grew so noxious that children at nearby schools had to wear masks in the classroom. A sharp rise in tumor cases prompted Huo—then working for the *China Environment Daily*—to coin the phrase *aizheng cun* (cancer village). Soon similar clusters of disease were being identified up and down the river. Downstream in Anhui Province, the deadly impact on health was exposed by independent journalist Chen Guidi in his article "Warning of Huai River."

Others followed. Soon the names of the Henan cancer villages—Mengzhi, Sunying, Chenkou, Dachu, Duying, Huangmengying, Xiditou—were notorious across the country.[26] Along stretches of the river, the cancer rate was more than twice the national average, but locals had no choice but to drink the stinking water. They would boil it, then skim the scum off the top, but the metallic taste never left. Huo says the calamity hit home hardest when his friend, a local village chief, was struck with cancer after downing a liter of contaminated well water in a bid to prove to locals that he was willing to take the same risks as them.

As late as 2004, the state environmental protection agency was insisting the Huai had been cleaned up. Living by a river that was still evidently foul, locals responded with a new slogan: "We have filthy officials and filthy water. For clean water, we need clean officials."

Huo switched from journalist to activist, exposing factories that were secretly discharging wastewater in the night, and mocking officials who spoke of a cleanup. It was a dangerous move. His family started to get death threats. One day, on his way home from taking pictures of the Lianhua factory, he was beaten up by thugs.

But the media attention was starting to pay off. In 2004, the leaders of the four worst-affected provinces along the Huai agreed to new controls for wastewater. Dozens of factories were closed. The Henan government spent 325 million yuan on drilling 700 new wells into superdeep aquifers. Even the Lianhua MSG factory had cleaned up. It was such a model that other factories were told to copy its example. When I visited the Huai several years later it was no longer black. It did not stink. Some brave souls had even resumed fishing. The subject of cancer, however, remains sensitive. In 2007, the World Bank issued a preliminary report suggesting 750,000 people die each year from pollution in China. This figure was removed from the published document at the urging of the government. It did not even include cancer deaths.[27]

At Mengjian Village I ducked into a courtyard house to talk to a local farming family, who described how the disease had ravaged their community. "Everyone knew someone who had cancer. But now there is a big change. It is like two different worlds. The environment is much better," said Mr. Wang, the head of the family. He credited the government for drilling a well into a safe deep aquifer 500 meters below the surface. The old well, 30 meters deep, is still contaminated. "A frog would die if it jumped in there for even a second," he said.

Others told a similar story. The old problem of water contamination had been replaced by a new one of water scarcity. Pressure from a growing population and expanding industry had resulted in overuse and contamination of rivers and shallow wells across northern China. The deep aquifers could only be a temporary solution. They are a nonrenewable resource, like oil. Pumped at huge cost, they led to subsidence and—if close to the sea—intrusion by brackish water.[28] This meant more stress on the land. Already under intense pressure from above, it was now being sucked dry down below.

Environmental stress was to blame for the prejudice directed toward people in Henan, according to Yan Lianke, Henan's most famous modern wordsmith. The controversial author was the master of dark, absurdist fiction inspired by the deterioration of his homeland. Yan began his writing career as a military author employed by the People's Liberation Army to pen morale-boosting stories for the troops. Instead, his first novel, *Xia Riluo* (1994), related the tale of two military heroes who steadily debased themselves. Yan was thrown out of the army in 2004 after publishing *Shouhuo* (*Enjoyment*), which satirized the bizarre wealth-creation schemes of many local governments. In that award-winning novel, desperate county officials in Henan were so short of resources that the only way they could think of developing their economy was to set up a freak show and buy Lenin's corpse from Russia as an attraction for the growing "Red tourism" market. More scandalous still was Yan's next work, *Serve the People*, which was banned altogether in China. This was not surprising given the plot, which revolved around a Cultural Revolution–era affair between an army officer's wife and her lover, who smashed up images of Mao Zedong and urinated on his little red book to reach new heights of sexual ecstasy.

I met the iconoclast in a bookshop teahouse. He was soft-spoken to the point of shyness, but his eyes blazed with a compassionate fury as he described his latest project: a book about his family in Henan. To understand the turmoil of the past fifty years, he said, it was necessary to look not just at politics and economics but also at the relationship between the environment and people.

He described the changes in his family home in Tianhu, which had swollen since his childhood from a village of 2,000 to a town of 7,000. "The creek that once flowed in front of our home has dried up. The old peach grove has been chopped down. Villagers used to drink from a well three meters deep. Now they go down fifteen and don't always find water. When the wind blows hard, the sky is filled with so much dust from the nearby cement factory that we have to cover all our belongings with sheets."

On an individual material level, Yan said this was good. "We live in concrete homes now instead of mud hovels, the roads are tarmac instead of dirt, but when you consider the environment as a whole, there has been severe damage." And it has affected human health. Every year he heard of more cases of cancer.

Since his childhood, more than 80 percent of the trees in his village had been felled, and even the Yellow River had at times been reduced to a trickle. A still greater loss, he said, was of the tenderness the villagers formerly felt for the earth. "In the past the land was owned by farmers. They could trace it back to their ancestors, so they loved it and cared for it. But now all they have is usage rights. And even those are often taken away when the local government wants to build factories. So farmers take a different view. Now they think, 'Why not exploit the land so I can improve my life?'"

Yan's words were reminiscent of what is arguably the greatest novel in English about rural life in China, *The Good Earth* (1931) by Pearl Buck. Based on the Nobel Prize–winning author's experience in Anhui (which neighbors Henan) from 1917 to 1920, the book tells the story of a poor hardworking farmer and his wife, who endure famine and urban migration before securing land and making a better life for themselves. Their children, however, do not appreciate the value of the soil and, at the end of the book, scheme to sell it off. This prompts a furious tirade from the father, who loves the soil as if it were his own flesh and blood:

> *"Now evil, idle son—sell the land! It is the end of a family—when they begin to sell the land. Out of the land we came and into it we must go—if you will hold your land you can live—no one can rob you of land—if you sell the land, it is the end."*

This story of development resonates through the ages.

Yan believed China had cut its ties to the land in the eighties and nineties, when everyone "went crazy" for money. "The army, farmers, government officials, everyone was trying to get rich." Yan even questioned his own brother, who suddenly became so wealthy at that time that he was able to build a big new home. Where the money came from remained a mystery. "He used to go out who knows where and return with a lorry full of logs," he recalled.

The rush for cash was responsible for Henan's—and arguably China's—worst health scandal: a blood-farming disaster that left hundreds of thousands of people infected with HIV. It started in the late 1980s, when local health authorities, along with every other branch of government, were suddenly told to generate profits. Short of other resources, Henan's officials tapped the population. They started milking veins.

Vans were converted into miniclinics and driven out into the country-side. Ambitious farmers established themselves as "bloodheads" (brokers) to meet the demand among both buyers and sellers. For an 800-milliliter donation, villagers were paid 45 yuan (worth about £3 or $6 at the time), enough to feed a family for a week. Realizing they could earn more by giving blood than from tending the land, they lined up several times a week to make donations. By the peak around 1995, Henan had become one of the nation's blood farms. The methods were either monstrously irresponsible or criminally negligent. In some cases, soy sauce bottles and plastic bags were used to store the blood. Some farmers sold so often, Yan said, they became dizzy and had to be turned upside down to get the blood into the tubes. Plasma was extracted and the remaining blood pumped back into people's veins so they would be able to donate more frequently. In the rush, basic hygiene procedures were sacrificed and the blood they got back wasn't always entirely their own. As a result, innumerable donors became infected with HIV. Disaster once again threatened to cull the population.

I had seen the consequences firsthand at one of the villages in 2003. It was my first visit to Henan and appeared to confirm every malicious word said about the province. It was the most depressing place I have ever been to, not least because the authorities were putting more effort into a cover-up than a cure.[29]

I traveled with an experienced fixer and AIDS activist who helped me sneak in without being detected.[30] We drove through a seemingly end-less expanse of flat stubble-brown fields to Xiongqiao Village, where resi-dents infected with HIV had fought with riot police the previous week to demand compensation and treatment. A local contact insisted we wait at his home in a nearby town until nightfall. Then, under cover of darkness, we drove deep into the countryside, bumping along a rutted mud road until we saw the torches of our guides flashing in the middle of a field.

We stopped. The guides—Chang Sun and his wife—whispered instructions to keep quiet in case someone overheard and informed the authorities, then led us into the village. Apart from squelching feet, the only sound was a chorus of frogs and the crackle of firewood. The blaze was part of a funeral ceremony. Chang told us it was the tenth in the tiny community that year, all of AIDS victims.

Many others seemed certain to follow. Chang told me his wife was infected; so were his mother, his aunt, his cousin, his cousin's wife, their neighbor, and possibly many of the children. Chang's father had died of AIDS the previous year, his three-year-old daughter the year before that. His first wife threw herself down the village well in 2000 after a doctor told her she was no longer worth treating because she had the virus. The flat brown vegetable fields were steadily filling with mossy green burial mounds.

"It is our custom for strong male adults to carry the coffin, but so many people are sick or dead that there aren't enough of us left," the thirty-five-year-old farmer told me. "So now it is the old people who are doing the burying."

Chang took me to see his cousin, Ming, who had started to show symptoms of the disease a few months earlier. Since being diagnosed, he spent most of his time lying on a bed held together by string, watching snowy black-and-white images on an old television set. The only other light was a naked bulb barely bright enough to read the fading newsprint that served as wallpaper.

"Almost everybody did it," Ming said between coughs. "We would sell extra if there was a marriage ceremony coming up or if we wanted to build a house. The most I ever did was four donations in a single day."

Death and darkness filled Chang's small house, which was literally built with blood money. The mood was set by the black-framed picture of his late father and in the funeral poems for his first wife and child that were pasted on the walls: "The wide land weeps for those we have loved and lost."

The disease was spreading across generations. The teacher of a nursery school for orphans in nearby Houyang told me all the school's thirty-eight children had at least one parent who was HIV positive, and many were likely to have contracted the infection in the womb. Only three of the five- and six-year-olds had been tested. All three were positive.

I could think of no grimmer illustration of how China's short-term rush to riches had drained natural resources and contaminated human lives. In such an overcrowded and overutilized land, I could see why the local government was desperate to relieve poverty. After you have cleared your trees for cropland, then ruined your cropland for factories, when your rivers ran either dry or black, what was left but blood?[31]

Deeper problems of poverty, overcrowding, and environmental stress continued to emerge in other forms. A government-sponsored tree-planting program had pushed forest cover from 9 percent to 15 percent in Henan. But Yan said some areas near the AIDS villages had recently suffered a wave of illegal logging. Unable to find work, some people with HIV were cutting down the roadside trees planted as a windbreak. The planks were sold to coal mines for shaft props. Drive through the countryside near Kaifeng, said Yan, and the rows of stumps on stretches of the roadside showed all too clearly how environmental fatigue and human stress fed on one another.

He believed the pressure was reaching the breaking point. "The land gets tired too. But there is no attempt to relieve its burden. Every time I go back home, another patch of ground has been cultivated. Even the little plots outside our homes that used to be untended are now filled. And the croplands are expected to yield two harvests a year. The land must be exhausted."

The stress on the land has been growing for millennia. As the author James Kynge put it: "Chinese history is very much less the story of multiplication than of long division. The experience of having to share scarce resources among so many people has at times been inconvenient and at times traumatic."[32]

After serving an advanced agricultural civilization for so long, the land might well be weary.[33] The weight of humanity had grown. Until around 1650, China's population fluctuated between 50 million and 200 million, rising in times of peace and prosperity and slipping during periods of natural disaster and war.[34] Confucianism, which has its roots in Shandong, encouraged propagation. Mencius believed having no children was one of the "three most impious acts."[35] But there is also evidence that family-planning policies were used in ancient times in the form of birth-spacing decrees.

The population began to rise soon after the Manchus seized power in 1644 and changed the tax system to encourage births.[36] Along with the introduction of new high-yield crops and relative peace, this created the conditions during the Qing dynasty for the population to almost triple

between 1700 and 1850, when it passed 400 million.[37] Malthus was wrong
to assume that the China of his age ignored the preventative checks of
demographic self-restraint. The severity of the country's measures would
have stretched the imagination of even the sternest British Protestant. In
the mid-nineteenth century, the mandarin Wang Shiduo recommended
the death penalty for men who married under age twenty-five and women
under twenty, and suggested tax incentives for infanticide of second
daughters.[38]

Thanks partly to the demographic restraints of infanticide, gender
imbalance, and homosexuality,[39] growth flattened briefly, particularly during the wars of the mid-twentieth century, but jagged upward after Mao
took power. Communist rule ushered in a period of peace, prosperity, vac-
cination campaigns, and a basic medical system provided by a new army of
"barefoot doctors." When the first census for decades was taken in 1953,
the government was astonished to learn the population had surged to 583
million—more than 100 million beyond expectations.[40]

How to deal with the consequences became the subject of fierce political debate. The demographer Ma Yinchu warned in 1957 that overpopulation was jeopardizing the country's development.[41] A family-planning
policy was tentatively introduced, the marriage age raised, and a condom
factory built.

Mao, however, jumped to a contrary conclusion. The founder of the
People's Republic could never accept that more people might mean more
problems. Ma was condemned as a rightist and a Malthusian because he
advocated controls. Mao advocated big families as the foundation of a
strong nation, even giving medals to women who bore large numbers of
children. So far as he was concerned, capitalism rather than overpopulation was to blame for the miserable condition of the masses.

Despite the starvation of tens of millions of people after the Great Leap
Forward, the 1964 census showed the mainland population had swollen
by 100 million. Mao blocked publication of the results. Families grew at a
faster than exponential rate. At the peak during the Cultural Revolution,
there were 4 births for every 100 people in a single year, one of the highest
birthrates ever recorded worldwide.[42] Forty years later, the results are still
evident in families across China. People born in the sixties usually have
at least three siblings, and often four or five, while those in their twenties
have none. By 1970, 20 million people were being added to the population

every year. By then even Mao had to grudgingly accept that people power had its limits.[43]

Mao's U-turn coincided with a remarkable moment in human history. Sometime around 1965–70 the fecundity of our species peaked. In that small window of time, just after the summer of love in the West and the Cultural Revolution in the East, the growth rate of mankind hit a high of 2.1 percent per year. After that it plunged by half. Our species was rapidly slowing down and aging.

The causes were both physical and social. China's family-planning policies were a factor in Asia, along with the widespread introduction of the contraceptive pill in the West. But less obvious forces were also at work. After that peak, women became less fertile and men had lower sperm counts. The more wealthy and educated we became, the fewer children we were likely to have and the later in our lives they would be born. Half of us moved into cities. Instead of focusing on growth, more people were worrying about conservation and sustainability. Our species was showing all the signs of middle age. We were becoming less virile and less virulent. For those who believe James Lovelock's Gaia Theory of the earth as a living organism, it was as though our numbers were being regulated. But whether it was by divine accident or human design, the trend was clearly downward.

In China, birth control was state policy, ruthlessly enforced. The reduction in population was dramatic. Though Mao flip-flopped repeatedly on family-planning policy, his successors introduced some of the most draconian targets in the modern world. In 1971, Premier Zhou Enlai launched a "birth planning" program as part of the socialist planned economy. Production of children, like grain or steel, became the subject of targets and quotas in the government's five-year plan. Couples were told to marry later, limited to two or three children, and required to wait three to four years between births.[44]

It worked. In the following decade the birthrate declined more precipitously than at any time before or since.[45] But the government, advised by a group of rocket-scientists-turned-demographers, decided even this was not enough to slow the momentum of the population. In 1979, the State Council introduced an even tighter family-planning program, commonly but somewhat misleadingly known as the "one-child policy."[46] This required a mass mobilization that dwarfed later campaigns against SARS,

HIV, or avian influenza, suggesting it was far tougher to contain people than any disease. Between 1971 and 2001, doctors carried out 151 million sterilizations and 264 million abortions, sometimes as late as the eighth month of pregnancy.[47] The government is proud of the results. Without the family-planning policy, it estimates China would have an extra 300 million people, per capita GDP would be about a quarter lower, and the country would drain even more of the world's resources.[48]

Population restraint is good for the environment,[49] but even in Henan, where the demographic pressures were shockingly apparent, I found it difficult to accept the violent means and distorted ends of China's family-planning policy: forced abortions, property seizures, abductions of relatives, and the binding and handcuffing of pregnant women.[50] In many parts of the world and other parts of China birthrates had fallen without such brutality.[51] The family-planning policy also exacerbated traditional gender imbalances. Henan had one of the most skewed populations in China. The ratio of boys to girls was about 1.35 to 1. In some villages, it was above 1.5 to 1. This was largely because more girl fetuses were aborted here than anywhere else in the country. Demographers estimated there should be almost half a million more girls in the 0–4 age group in Henan.[52]

The population crisis was not looming in Henan. It had already hit. Once fertile, the soil was losing nutrients through overfarming and floods that rubbed salt into the province's wounds by salination.[53] Farmers responded by pumping more chemical fertilizer into the soil than anywhere else in China.[54] The lack of iodine and excess lead in the earth were blamed for lower-than-average IQ levels in the province.[55] More farmland was irrigated by wastewater here than anywhere else in China, lowering yields, tainting produce, and posing serious health risks. As in Zhejiang, environmental problems in Henan were blamed for an increase in birth deformities.[56] Aquifers were depleted as farmers and engineers dug ever deeper wells to find uncontaminated water. The population was fleeing in droves.

Malthus's grim theory remains as relevant as ever. China's population is on course to grow bigger and older over the next forty years. Worldwide, the demographic pattern is similar. As human numbers continue to swell, the globe will seem ever smaller, more crowded, and—as Yan described the land—more weary. Henan, then, is far from unique. In fact, it may prove to be a focus not of prejudice but of self-loathing. The despised, disaster-prone province encapsulates not just what China is doing to its land but what overpopulation is doing to the planet.

The reckoning is still to come. In the years ahead, China's family-planning policies will amplify existing demographic distortions still further. The country faces a future in which tens of millions of adult men will be unable to find a bride, in which one grandchild will have to look after two parents and four grandparents, and in which by the predicted population peak of 1.5 billion in 2030 the majority of people will be living in cities.

How will farmers cope with the growing hunger for food, the extra elderly relatives they will have to look after, and still find time to care for the soil? The one-child generation will need more machinery and more fuel. That will require greater exploitation of underground resources, because most of the heat and power in China comes from a single source. Coal.

10

The Carbon Trap
Shanxi and Shaanxi

When the age of decadence arrived, people cut rocks from the mountains, hacking out metals and jades. They extracted the pearls from oysters, smelted copper and iron ores . . . They hunted by setting the forests ablaze and fished by draining dry the pools.
—*The Book of the Prince of Huainan*[1]

Cold, dark, silent. Close to death. Buried in the depths of a collapsed, illegal coal mine, Meng Xianchen and Meng Xianyou knew they had been given up for dead.[2]

The rescue effort had been abandoned. The two brothers could no longer hear the sound of mechanical diggers, drills, and spades above their heads. Dismayed and exhausted, they had stopped yelling frantically for help.

How long had it been? Hours, days, weeks? There was no way of knowing. When their mobile-phone batteries died, they lost all track of time.

And place. With the silence and the darkness came disorientation. They were unsure which way led to the surface and which led deeper into the mountain. They had little evidence that they were even still alive. It was like being dead, but lost inside your own tomb.

Aboveground, their families were already preparing a funeral. In accordance with tradition, relatives had started burning "ghost money" for the two brothers to spend in the other world. Negotiations had begun with the

local authorities about compensation. Yet down below, the Mengs stub-
bornly refused to die. Driven by a powerful instinct to survive, they fought
against the earth and the darkness, against death itself.

The brothers started digging. They hacked and shoveled, using a single
pick and their bare hands. They were only a few dozen meters from the
surface, but despite twenty years of mining experience, they were so panicked and confused by the darkness that they started to worry they were
tunneling deeper into the mountain. They changed direction once, twice,
three times, before deciding to head straight up.

With every hour that passed they grew wearier and more depressed.
It grew harder to dig, exhausting even to crawl. They filled water bottles
with urine. The taste was so foul, they could only drink in small sips and
felt like crying after they swallowed. Desperately hungry, Xianchen took
to nibbling finger-sized pieces of coal, not knowing it had zero nutritional
value.

Yet they kept digging. Their companionship was a source of comfort
and strength. They slept in each other's arms to stave off the cold and told
jokes about their wives to maintain morale.

"My wife will be happy after I die. She can find a rich husband in
Shenyang to replace me," mused Xianchen out loud, then laughingly con-
tradicted himself. "But then again, she is an ugly woman with two children
so it will be hard for her to remarry."

Humor does not get much blacker than laughter in a collapsed coal mine.
But it kept them going for six days, until finally, miraculously, they scratched
their way to the surface. Weak and close to starvation, they emerged blinking
into the light, then staggered to the village where they were met with a hero's
welcome and incredulous joy that the dead could rise from their tombs.
They were carried off to the hospital, where the doctors treated their damaged kidneys and journalists bombarded them with questions. The mine
owner, meanwhile, was on the run. Aware that the standard bribes would
not protect him from a deadly accident investigation, he had fled as soon as
he heard of the collapse.

The survival of the magnificent Meng brothers made front-page head-
lines in Beijing. Their experience captured the Chinese zeitgeist of the
past thirty years—gritty, poor, dirty, illegal, dangerous, willing to go to
almost any lengths to get ahead, ill as a result, but surviving long after
being written off. They had been trapped in a carbon hell in which they

dug, ate, inhaled, and were almost suffocated by coal, yet they had lived to tell the tale.

China finds itself in a similar predicament in the first decade of this century. Demand for energy continues to grow and most of it comes from underground. The economy is utterly dependent on coal. It provided 69.5 percent of the country's energy, a greater degree of reliance than that of any other major nation.[3] Cheap coal generates electricity for Beijing, Shanghai, and Chongqing, fires the steel mills of Huaxi, powers the production lines of Guangdong, and allows consumers in the West to buy Chinese goods at a knockdown price. No other fuel has such an impact on the environment. And nowhere is this more evident than in Shanxi Province, where I went to see how the black subterranean dust fouled the skies above what had been the most polluted city on earth.

Linfen had held that unenviable title for most of the previous decade. Shrouded in a spectral haze, the city lay at the heart of a 20-kilometer industrial belt, fed by the 50 million tons of coal mined each year in the nearby hills. When the pollution was at its worst in the late nineties, the average daily level of particulate matter in the air was over 600 parts per million, far off the hazard scale.[4] The New York–based Blacksmith Institute ranked the city alongside Chernobyl on a list of the planet's ten most contaminated places.

Approaching this blackest of black lands, the smog was so thick it seemed to consume its source. On the outskirts of the city, smokestacks belched carbon and sulfur into the putrid mist that enveloped them. Iron foundries, smelting plants, and cement factories loomed in and out of the haze as we drove along the roads leading into Linfen. The skies were as grim as those of Zhengzhou during the postharvest burn-off, but here it was not a seasonal phenomenon. When we stopped in the outlying village of Liucunzhen, locals told us they lived most of their lives in smog.

"We only see the sun for a few days each year," said Zhou Huocun, a community doctor, as we looked out over a washing line of dirty clothes hung across the walls of his brick-built courtyard home. "The color of our village is black. It is so dirty that nobody airs their quilts outside anymore so we are getting more parasites." He had seen a steady increase in respiratory diseases among his patients as the air quality had deteriorated over the years. The unborn were at even greater risk. Shanxi's birth defect rate is six times higher than the national average (which is itself three to five times the global norm). One industry was to blame.[5]

During the past half century, Shanxi has accounted for about a third of China's coal production. The province alone digs up more than twice as much as Britain did at the peak of the Industrial Revolution.[6] Along with neighboring Shaanxi and Inner Mongolia, it is part of the so-called Black Belt in which the majority of the country's 5.2 million miners labored.

The impact was evident everywhere. Convoys of coal trucks jammed the roads, spilling black dust into the air and onto the ground. The landscape was dotted by more than 2,000 slag heaps. The digging of a warren of shafts and empty pits had hollowed out over 5,000 square kilometers of land and left a fragile crust to support homes, schools, and roads. Subsidence affected 950,000 people whose homes and workplaces were built on land sinking into old pits.[7] The industry was no respecter of Shanxi's rich history. Ancient Buddha carvings at the Yungang Grottoes in Datong were coated in acidic soot. A section of the Great Wall had been demolished by a colliery owner so his trucks could bypass a tollbooth on a nearby trunk road. The damage done by coal to human health and the environment in the province in a single year was estimated at 29.6 billion yuan (over $4.2 billion) in 2005.[8]

Yet the coal industry was growing so fast I could taste it in the air. Between 2003 and 2008, the power sector expanded at a rate of more than two new coal-fired 600-megawatt plants per week, adding more to the grid each year than Britain's entire installed capacity after two centuries of development.[9] If China's development was indeed a "miracle," as it was often described, then this fuel was an essential ingredient. The whole world was having to inhale it.

The more I looked into the industry, the blacker it seemed. Over the years, I had talked to black-faced miners at the mouths of illegal pits, descended deep down the shafts of huge state-run collieries, consulted labor activists, and interviewed mine owners and policymakers.

The picture that emerged was of a deadly, filthy industry that was trying to clean up but repeatedly mired by market pressures, weak oversight, and the demands of an economy that was desperate for more fuel. To boost profits, mine owners had been cutting corners on safety and environmental measures. Collieries destroyed arable land and grazing pastures, eroded topsoil, worsened air and water pollution, increased levels of river sediment (raising the risk of floods), and accelerated deforestation (especially if the coal was used to make charcoal). The country's most pressing environmental problems—acid rain, smog, lung disease, water contamination, loss of aquifers, and the filthy layer of black dust that settled on many villages—could all be traced back in varying degrees to this single cause.

Then there were the losses caused by global warming. China recently overtook the U.S. as the world's biggest emitter of greenhouse gases because it is so dependent on this fossil fuel.[10] For each unit of energy, coal produces 80 percent more carbon dioxide than natural gas and 20 percent more than oil. This does not even include methane released from mines, for which China accounts for almost half the global total, or spontaneous combustion of coal seams, which burn 100 megatons of coal each year.[11]

Coal is compressed history, buried death. Geologists estimate the seams of anthracite and bituminate in northern China were formed from the Jurassic period onward. Within them are the remains of ferns, trees, mosses, and other life-forms from millions of years ago. Though long extinguished on the surface world, they still—like ghosts or the Meng brothers—possess form and energy. Consider coal with a superstitious eye and foul air might seem a curse suffered for disinterring preancient life. Described with a little poetic license, global warming is a planetary fever caused by burning too much of our past. But whether we prefer these archaic formulations or modern science, the conclusion is the same: the more we dig and burn, the worse we breathe.

Given the low priority the Chinese coal industry places on ecological and health concerns, it is little surprise that safety standards are also appalling. The country's collieries are the most dangerous in the world. Since the start of economic reforms, the equivalent of an entire city of people has died underground. More than 170,000 miners have been killed in tunnel collapses, explosions, and floods, a death rate per ton at least thirty times higher than that in the United States.[12] Countless more will perish prematurely of pneumoconiosis, also known as black lung disease, because there is little or no protection from the dust in the enclosed tunnels. Mine deaths are so frequent that if the Meng brothers had been less stubborn about surviving, the collapse at their pit could easily have gone unreported. All that is unique in their story is that they emerged to tell the tale. In many other cases, the bereaved have been silenced by mine bosses, censors, and local officials terrified that these underground horrors would come to light.

I saw that at Chenjiashan in Miaowan, a mining community in Shaanxi (distinguished from its neighboring province only by its extra "a") and the scene of one of the worst mining accidents in recent memory, when 166 men were killed in a pit explosion. I was there to interview a group of the bereaved at the small brick home of one of the widows. Less than an hour after I arrived, a neighbor burst into the room with a warning: "Someone has snitched. The security men are coming. Shut the door, close the curtains, and stay quiet." Moments later we heard footsteps outside, then a rap on the door. A mother squeezed her child tightly to her breast to muffle his cries. An older woman held back sobs, her eyes red with tears. Two others sat on a bed, exchanging anxious glances.

I was worried. By talking to a foreign journalist, these people could get in trouble. But I was angry too. The women were not subversives; they were widows and bereaved daughters. At small, unregistered mines, deaths went unreported because the owners, often in collusion with local officials, bought off or threatened the victims' families. But this was a legal colliery. Why where the victims being treated in this way?

"It's said there is blood on every piece of coal in China," one of the widows had told me earlier. "My husband used to talk about the danger all the time. But we are very poor. We have children. What else could we do?"

The 800-meter-deep pit at Chenjiashan had a particularly bad reputation. Four years earlier, thirty-eight men had died there in a gas explosion. Five days before the latest accident a fire had broken out underground. "We came up, but the bosses told us to go back. We didn't want to, but we had to," said Li, a miner who had lost his brother in the explosion. "We all needed the money and there is a penalty of 100 yuan for refusing to go down."

The managers, who had reportedly been promised a hefty bonus to increase production, ordered the men to keep working even though it had become hard to breathe underground. On the morning of the accident, Li had been preparing to start his shift when workers came running out of the shaft saying they had seen thick clouds of smoke. "Every miner knows that means there's been an explosion," he said.

Many widows said they could not hold a proper funeral. "Our husbands' bodies are still underground," said Mrs. Zhang. "But when we went to ask the mine supervisor for action, the security men beat us. One woman was hurt so badly she is still in hospital."

I feared the same might happen again. As the footsteps crunched around the widow's home, we tried to stay silent and pretend no one was in. But one of the children thought it was a game and yelled out loudly. The footsteps moved off, perhaps to call a superior. I had to leave quickly so these people would not be seen with me; so they could deny that we had met.

On our way back to the car we were quickly spotted and followed, first by one man, then three, then five. The goons kept their distance. None of them was of high enough rank to confront us. If we could get to the car before their superiors arrived, we might have been able to flee the village unimpeded. But the vehicle was locked. The driver had wandered off for a cigarette. We had no choice but to wait as a crowd gathered.

The police arrived. We were led away for interrogation. Whom had we been speaking to? What was our purpose? Why didn't we get permission in advance from the authorities? Didn't we know we had committed an offense? Four hours in detention. One of the junior officers came across as sympathetic. He asked the routine questions, but he did not push to find out which villagers we had spoken to. Perhaps he was a local man who did not want to get his neighbors into trouble. Perhaps he already knew who had been talking.

We were led off to a meet a foreign affairs official. More questions. I asked them why they were treating the victims as criminals, while those responsible for more than a hundred deaths were still free. It was dark by the time we were let out. The officials were getting hungry. They couldn't find anything to charge us with and keeping us longer was not worth a missed dinner.[13]

The high death rate was a simple matter of economics. Life in China was cheap, while coal was increasingly dear. In calculating compensation for the victims of the Chenjiashan blast, the state estimated the value of a miner's life at 51,000 yuan (around $7,300). An extra 20,000 yuan was paid as a widow's allowance and another 20,000 yuan for an unrecovered body. By contrast, mine operators were reportedly promised a 400,000 yuan bonus if they could raise output by 400,000 tons in the last two months of the year. The math was brutal. They could afford at least three deaths and still come out with a profit. There were no reports of punishments for any of the mine operators who forced their men into a burning pit.

Soul-destroying materialism is the theme of *Blind Shaft,* one of the darkest and strongest Chinese films of the past ten years. It tells the tale of two migrant miners who literally make a killing from unsafe illegal collieries. From the descent down the mine in the opening scene to the final shot, the director Li Yang presents an unrelentingly bleak view of how humanity is debased by the dark and narrow physical and moral environment. The central characters, Tang and Song, cheat their way from pit to pit, murdering fellow miners and then claiming to be family members so they can demand hush money from the colliery bosses.

Their cash is blown on school fees for their kids and hookers in a country where education is supposed to be free and prostitution illegal. In one scene they go whoring in a karaoke brothel, where they sing "Long Live Socialism." The prostitute sneers at their backwardness and croons the same song with rewritten lyrics: "Americans are taking over China with their dollars."

The con men befriend a naïve sixteen-year-old boy whom they line up as their next victim. Song has qualms about killing the teenager. To delay the day of reckoning he tells his partner the boy must have his first drink of baijiu, smoke his first cigarette, and lose his virginity before he can be killed. But such glimpses of humanity disappear when they return to the pit.

Coal and money degrade the characters and the land. Li bribed colliery bosses to let him film in real mines in Shanxi and Hebei. On the surface, the dusty, windswept landscape is unfailingly devoid of life and color. It is the setting for a moral apocalypse. If humans are to survive here, they must sacrifice their humanity.

Blind Shaft was banned in China. This was not the glory of modern development the government wanted people to see.

But the country was trying to clean up its mines and its skies. Linfen, the model of so much that was wrong, was in the front line of the charge. On the orders of the central government, it was closing down small, illegal collieries and the worst-polluting factories. I dropped in at the city's environment bureau to ask whether these measures were working. The director, Yang Zhaofen, had progress to report. Of a sort. "Linfen is no longer the most polluted city in China," he announced proudly. "It is the second worst."[14] The city had dropped below Urumqi, but I wasn't sure if this was because Linfen was getting better or Urumqi worse.

The local government was taking countermeasures. As in many other cities, it was switching to gas-powered central heating instead of coal. Yang told me they had already shut down hundreds of small mines and were in the process of closing 160 of 196 iron foundries and 57 of 153 coking plants. Small, dirty, and dangerous plants were to be replaced by large, cleaner, and more carefully regulated facilities. But I had heard that before. Over the years, local governments announced coal-mine closures as often as crackdowns on markets of pirated goods. Neither usually lasted long. As soon as the price rose and attention shifted, the illegal mines and fake DVD shops reopened. Yang insisted it was different this time because the changes were being driven by business (nobody wanted to invest in a polluted place), bureaucratic self-interest (local officials needed to meet "green targets" to be promoted under a national reward scheme), and shifting political priorities. Cleaner skies and safer mines were a focus of the central government's Scientific Outlook on Development.

"We have more power than before," Yang said. "The mayor says we can sacrifice economic growth in order to improve air quality. That used to be unthinkable."

Outside, there were signs of change. Many factories appeared to be closed: not a wisp of smoke emerged from their chimneys. Over the previous year, Linfen's residents had breathed fifteen more days of "blue sky"[15] air than during the preceding twelve months. But it was progress from a low base. Official statistics noted the air was unhealthy for 163 days of the year. Even those data were hard to verify. A political haze obscures the subject of pollution. In another off-the-record meeting, a local government official and a people's representative told me about the city's problems and the difficulties of dealing with them. But neither was willing to speak officially. It was too sensitive a subject, they said. It seemed that the authorities were genuine about pushing for a clear-up and had orders to do so from on high, but old habits would die hard. Precedent suggested many of the closed factories and mines would reopen. As long as the demand for coal persisted, the risks to the environment and health would not go away. Not long after I was there, 254 villagers were killed in a mudslide after a mine's waste pond burst its banks.[16]

The next morning as we were leaving Linfen, I made a bet with my assistant how long we would have to drive before we saw blue skies again. Ever the optimist, I guessed two hours. She opted for three. Neither of us came close. We never did escape the haze in Shanxi. It lightened slightly as we lifted out of the Fen River valley but persisted all four hours to Taiyuan Airport. Even on the plane, we failed to climb above it. The pilot saved fuel by flying at a low altitude, entirely through the smog. When we landed forty minutes later, the familiar murky shroud was there outside the plane to meet us. It was almost comforting.

Satellite images of northern China show this is far from unusual. In the energy-intense seasons of winter and summer, when millions of heaters and air conditioners are switched on, all it takes is a few windless days and a murky haze thickens over Shanxi, Shaanxi, Hebei, Henan, and Beijing. It is usually darkest in Shaanxi, where the smog becomes trapped by the Qinling mountain range. Traffic is only partly to blame. Coal-fired industrial boilers, furnaces, and home heaters are the main source. They belch out 85 percent of the country's sulfur dioxide,[17] which—mixed with another coal by-product, soot—forms the acid rain that now falls on 30 percent of the Chinese landmass, ruining crops and corroding buildings.[18] The World Bank estimates the damage caused by acid rain at 37 billion yuan every year.[19]

Air pollution is appalling in almost every city in China. The toll on human health is enormous.[20] Barely 1 percent of the urban population breathes air considered healthy by the World Health Organization, and it is worst in northern China. The result is premature death, lung cancer, bronchitis, and other respiratory and cardiovascular diseases. Another high-risk group are poor peasants who slowly poison themselves by heating their homes with dirty coal. But the full risks are obscured. The toxic buildup of lead, mercury, and other heavy metals in the soil and water near coal plants and smelting factories is not usually measured. Entire communities are being poisoned without realizing it.[21]

Yet coal mines are as much a part of China's civilization as paddy fields. Mining and industry have been crucial in ensuring the longevity of the Middle Kingdom. Despite its reputation as an agricultural civilization, for most of the last 2,000 years China has been by far the biggest producer of coal and iron in the world, a status lost only temporarily in the early nineteenth century when Britain began industrializing. It is no coincidence that the country's recent return to great power status has come at a time when it is once again number one in these basic industries and when large numbers of peasants are working below rather than on the surface.

People in northern China have been burning coal since the Neolithic era 10,000 years ago, which is said (by the China Coal Information Institute) to be a first for the world. The fuel was a source of power and survival. Coal was used to smelt iron as early as the Warring States period (475–221 BC), when it was considered essential to mass-produce weapons. By the Song dynasty (960–1279), smithies were so expert at steel production they could equip an army of a million men with swords, armor, and steel-tipped arrows.

The black fuel was the basis of the world's earliest military-industrial complexes. In the late sixteenth century the army commander on the northwestern frontier, Tian Le, sent out excavation teams into the mountains to search for the ore and trees needed to smelt iron for weapons. He requisitioned foundry workers from Shanxi and Shaanxi to help. Their success was lauded in dispatches.

"In Hexi, the region where the wars are conducted, iron smelted in the morning can be put to use the same evening," wrote an admiring deputy. "The barbarians within our frontiers have repeatedly been given a bloody nose in recent times, and have been sticking out their tongues in astonishment, speaking of an 'iron wall'! When they now further hear that we are smelting iron here, won't they be inclined to behave themselves?"[22]

As in films and art today, the misery and dangers of mining were another frequent theme of poems. Few are more evocative than Wang Taiyue's description of environmental destruction and the grim life of a copper miner in the eighteenth century:

They gather at dawn, by the mouth of the shaft
Standing there naked, their garments stripped off,
Lamps strapped to their heads in carrying baskets,
To probe in the darkness the fathomless bottom.

Grazed by the stone's teeth, the sharp-edged projections,
They grope down sheer cliffs, and across mossy patches
The hot months tempt them with harsh epidemics,
When poisonous vapors mix with hot gases

In the chill of the winter, their bodies will tremble,
Hands blister with chilblains. Their feet will be chapped.
Down the mine for this reason, they huddle together,
But hardly revive, their life's force at a standstill . . .

The wood they must have is no longer available,
The forests shaved bald, like a convict's head. Blighted.
Only now they regret—felling day after day,
Has left them no way to provide for their firewood.

Worse still, as the mountainsides' bellies were hollowed,
The subsidence this caused demolished the rocks,
And smashed them to fragments, like scattering pebbles,
As, in one death, a few hundred perished.

Their spirits were heard, in the depths of night, wailing,
As their ghost fires were flickering, chilled in the gale.
How worthless, alas, is a human's existence,
Its price even less than a chicken's or piglet's.[23]

This lament echoes the coal-mining literature of many other nations, where appreciation for the warmth and power the fuel provided was mixed with horror at the conditions of miners and industrial pollution. In English, the earliest record of urban smog dates back to 1661, when the British diarist John Evelyn penned "Fumifugium," an appeal for the government to clean up the air of London. In words that would sound familiar to the residents of early twenty-first-century Linfen, he noted:

By reason of the excessive coldness of the air, hindering the ascent of the smoke, was so filled with the fuliginous steam of the sea-coal, that hardly can one see across the street, and this filling the lungs with its gross particles exceedingly obstructed the breast, so as one would scarcely breathe.

The smog worsened during the Victorian period. In 1852, Charles Dickens vividly described the "London particulars" in the opening of *Bleak House*:

Smoke lowering down from chimney-pots, making a soft black drizzle, with flakes of soot in it as big as full-grown snowflakes—gone into mourning, one might imagine, for the death of the sun.

It was not until 1956, after a "great smog" killed 12,000 people in 1952, that Britain cleaned up its skies with the Clean Air Act and a shift to oil, gas, and cleaner coal-burning technology. China has found it harder to escape the carbon that appears to choke the sky and the sun.

With 20 percent of the world's population and an economy that continues to grow, China needs huge amounts of fuel. Deposits of oil and gas are small relative to the country's size, but coal is abundant.[24] Unfortunately, it is mostly of low quality and inconveniently located in the northwest, the opposite end of the country from where it is most needed: the manufacturing belt of the southeast.

The cleanest solution would be to transform the fuel into electricity or gas near the source and transfer it via power lines or pipes. But this would mean the mining provinces receiving even less economic benefit.[25] So the coal has to be transported by train, barge, and ship at huge extra cost to the economy and the environment. Coal accounts for 40 percent of the freight on China's railways.[26] On the track from Shanxi through Beijing to the southeast, I counted in astonishment as double locomotives pulled a train of more than two hundred cars each loaded high with more than 60 tons of coal and ash. There was another ten minutes later. Then another. A million tons could pass along a single line in a day.

Millions of dollars flow in the other direction. China's spectacular economic rise can be tracked by the volume of coal mined, freighted, and burned. During the Mao era, colliery production was held back by centralized price restraints that turned coal into red ink. But after the market reforms of the late 1970s and early 1980s, digging mines suddenly became the quickest way to get rich. The wealth of Shanxi's colliery bosses was notorious. The problems caused by coal were not entirely their fault—the state's control over extraction rights and frequent crackdowns encouraged mine owners to cash in as quickly as possible and with minimum concern for safety. But mine owners were a reviled group who were accused of having blood on their hands, ruining the land, and being the epitome of bad taste. Young people who drove flashy cars, wore loud clothes, and treated people badly were taunted as being "like the child of a Shanxi mine owner."

Pan Yue, the deputy environment minister, described the bosses as little more than parasites. "Coal-mine owners from Shanxi Province indiscriminately extract coal and dig up the land, creating pollution. As a result they become extremely wealthy. Once they have polluted Shanxi, however, they do not stay there. Instead they move to Beijing, where they buy luxury villas and push up house prices. They have also pushed up property prices in all the coastal regions of North China. If these areas then become polluted, they will no doubt move to the U.S., Canada, or Australia and cause inflation there too. They create pollution, but are removed from its consequences. They take all the benefits of polluting industries, but pay nothing toward the cleanup costs."

The true cost of the mines never shows up on balance sheets. For the mining provinces, it is a curse. They receive far from a fair market price because the mines are owned by the state and the colliery owners get the rights to profit from extraction. The prosperity of cities like Shanghai and Beijing is based on cheap energy from provinces like Shanxi and Shaanxi, which are left with the environmental and health costs. One influential study estimates the environmental and social costs associated with China's use of coal at about 7.1 percent of the nation's GDP in 2007.[27] As an increasing number of people in China are saying, "Something has to change."[28]

Industry forecasters agree. Without a long-term strategic plan, the country's reserves will be exhausted before the end of the century.[29] The government has responded with a drive for more efficiency, the key focus of "Scientific Development." It has closed small private mines and opened automated megacollieries. It has replaced small old thermal plants with supercritical and ultra-supercritical generators equipped with scrubbers and other technology to reduce emissions of nitrogen dioxide and sulfur dioxide (though it has not always been properly used).[30] Policymakers are studying the possibility of a carbon tax. More public funds and utility cash are being invested in "clean coal" technology. Along with the tightening of safety standards, this has begun to drive up the cost of domestic coal, as has Shanxi's introduction of an ecological restoration fund. Indeed, as prices soared in 2008, many factories in the southeast started importing from Australia and elsewhere.

Abandoning coal completely is not, of course, an option, as I learned in a discussion with Xiao Yunhan, an energy visionary at the Chinese Academy of Sciences. "Nobody likes coal, even in China. But do you have a better solution for our energy supply problems?" he said. He expected consumption of coal to double over the following ten years. For at least another two decades, China would be trapped in a coal-dependent economy.

"Even if China utilizes every kind of energy to the maximum level, it is still difficult for us to produce enough energy for economic development. It's not a case of choosing coal or renewables. We need both," the senior scientist said. "We have to use coal, so the best thing we can do is make that use as efficient as possible."

Unlike the Meng brothers, people will not be expected to eat lumps of anthracite, but industrialists are expected to find new ways to consume carbon. In addition to installing newer and more efficient power plants, China is also ahead of other nations in developing and adopting Integrated Gasification Combined Cycle (IGCC) technology that turns coal into gas, removes impurities, maximizes efficiency, and can capture carbon. In the future, Xiao predicted plants will be able to turn coal into gas and diesel, capturing and eventually sequestrating carbon dioxide emissions. Some of the technology is at an advanced stage of development.

"That's my idea. At Shanxi and Shaanxi, coal-to-oil and IGCC will be integrated into one system. In this regard, China is ahead of other nations. The U.S. is only talking about this," he told me matter-of-factly over a cup of green tea.

The technology is expensive, but Xiao estimated that China could build and operate IGCC plants for about a third of the price of the U.S. In the near future, he predicted China would have to choose whether to invest primarily in supercritical plants, which burn coal efficiently, or IGCC facilities that dealt more effectively with carbon. The latter are more expensive, but price is not the only consideration. "The uncertainty of climate change constraints is a factor in deciding which plants we build," he said. "If we don't need to worry about CO_2 emissions, then supercritical plants make more sense. But if we are concerned about carbon dioxide, then IGCC is the best. This is the big decision we must make in the next five to ten years . . . Sequestration will be the final solution for carbon dioxide control. But before that we should try other things."[31]

"Isn't the priority in the long term to reduce demand?" I asked.

He shrugged and smiled. "We cannot deny people a happy life."

"But we also must not deny future generations a happy life," I said.

"True," he replied.

I returned to the Black Belt soon after. Driving through Shaanxi, the farther north I progressed, the duller the colors of the landscape became. After a few hours I hit the stunningly morose moonscape of the loess hills, pocked with cave dwellings, many still in use. That bleak beauty gave way to a scattering of dirty, cinder-block homes that lifted and thickened into the city of Yan'an. Farther north still, the dark yellow contours gave way to a flat scrubland. It was almost desert. I had to close the window because the air was filled with grit. I wondered whether the haze in the sky was pollution or the dregs of a sandstorm. At Yulin, where part of the Great Wall had been knocked down and replaced by a row of shops and apartment buildings, coal was piled up here and there on the roadside. The town looked filthy.

Moving on, I saw sand dunes and dry riverbeds. Coal production was taking scarce water supplies from agriculture. Dust devils danced on the road ahead, curling and coiling in the wind. At Shenmu, just before the provincial boundary with Inner Mongolia, I stopped at a service station, where trucks laden high with coal lined up for gas. It would be at least an hour before my car reached the front of the long queue for the pumps, so I wandered around and got chatting to a coal wholesaler. Zhang Guoluan was dour-faced but content with life. Why? Because his income had risen fivefold over the previous five years thanks to a surge in demand for coal. But he knew it would not last forever.

"I guess our country might stop using coal one day. It is already being phased out in the big cities because of the pollution it causes," he said matter-of-factly.

I asked if he was worried about losing his job.

"No. If that happens, I will just return to my old life as a farmer."

I filled my tank and pressed on. Zhang's job was safe, I reflected. Demand for coal would not fall anytime soon. Power would always trump sustainability. Educated farmers no longer wanted to work underground because it was too dangerous, but both state mines and private collieries were hiring poor, uneducated workers, often from ethnic minorities, to do the dirty work, just as the West had done for centuries. Mine safety might improve but so would productivity. Local pollution might ease, but carbon emissions into the global atmosphere would continue to rise. For decades, hot, suffocating dregs of preancient life would enter the air in ever greater quantities.

China would remain trapped in carbon with appalling consequences for itself and the world. My thoughts returned to the Meng brothers, who seemed unlikely ever to fully recover from being buried alive. What had happened to them? I asked my assistant to call and ask. Meng Xianchen had moved to Xilinhaote in Inner Mongolia. He was a gatekeeper at a relative's coal mine and still complained of fatigue. He escaped the carbon but not its effects. Nor had he lost his instinct for survival. "If you want a full interview," he said, "you have to pay."

I sympathized. But I would see and hear worse. As I was to learn in neighboring Gansu, coal digging was surpassed only by water mining as an environmental threat to China. Both were unsustainable. Together, there was no more destructive combination.

11

Attack the Clouds!
Retreat from the Sands!
Gansu and Ningxia

No matter how hard mankind tries to transform nature, the largest plots of cultivated land are often overtaken by the elements: the wind and the sand which turns them into dunes, neither arable nor edible.
—Ma Jun, author and conservationist[1]

Flying into Gansu was like landing on the moon. The plane descended through a rugged corridor of barren, gray-brown mounds that swelled up on either side and stretched away into the horizon. Bereft of trees and water, the corrugated landscape looked utterly desolate. Inside the hills, there was no sign of human activity. The earth seemed too dry to support life.

Overcultivation had left mountains naked. Mines, factories, and farms had drained streams and fouled rivers. Many wells no longer held water. Sand dunes threatened farm fields.

The same was true of much of the country.[2] The droughts were getting worse. The shortage of water in northern China was the most pressing environmental problem facing the country and it prompted some of the most desperate remedies. Man had been fighting a battle against the desert here for centuries. Now, thanks to a squandering of resources, dire pollution, and climate change, humanity was in retreat on several fronts.

Guo Yuchun and Wei Guohu were the last to abandon their village at the foot of the Great Wall. They did not want to leave. Although the river that irrigated their crops had dried to a trickle and the dust storms were growing fiercer, they preferred their ancestral home to the new house provided under a government resettlement program. Living with scarcely any water was tough, but so were the old couple, who during their long lives had survived many deadly droughts and famines. But, in the end, even they joined the exodus, though not because of the elements.

"It got too lonely," Wei told me with a broad smile that he seemed to save for his saddest comments.

Wei was eighty-four years old. He sported chunky, round dark glasses of a sort popular among old men in northwestern China and stroked a long, wispy beard that made him look like the guru in a kung fu movie. He was not used to visitors. They were few and far between in Jintai, a remote county on the provincial border between Gansu and Ningxia. This area is so dry that many villagers padlock their wells, even though they leave the doors to their homes open.

Wei and his wife had left their village the previous month. The couple's new home had been hard to find. We had driven for three hours through some of the bleakest scenery in China to reach it. The area was almost devoid of human life. Over a 50-kilometer stretch I saw a single mining truck, an old brick kiln, three tethered asses, the dust of a nomad riding his horse up a distant mountain track, and, surreally, two workers in fluorescent orange jackets sweeping an empty road with straw brooms.

Even after reaching Wei's village we struggled to follow the directions to his home. The hard brown land of gravel, loess, and sand lacked obvious features by which to navigate.

After going around in circles for a while, we reached a cluster of newly constructed brick dwellings with solar panels on the roofs. They were smart, but the residents clearly had more time and less money than the farmers I had seen in Henan. The stalks from the harvest were carefully bundled and stacked outside every home rather than burned in the fields.

Everything felt new and transient. Wei's children and grandchildren showed us into a house that smelled of plastic and fresh paint. The furniture was still covered by the factory wrapping and the ceiling light was a fluorescent lamp rather than the naked bulb that was more usual in a farmer's home. Even the wall portrait of Mao Zedong was shiny and plastic-coated. The colors were so garish that the dead chairman appeared to have transmuted into an Indian deity with lipstick and eye shadow.

The family were warm hosts, plying my assistant and me with fruit and tea as we waited to be properly introduced to the old couple. Wei seemed to find my assistant, with her city ways, almost as strange as a foreigner. When he shook her hand, he held on for almost a minute, scrutinizing her smooth fingers and palms so carefully that it was unclear whether he was trying to read her future or envying a past so evidently free of manual labor.

But, later, as he smoked and smiled, his wife, Guo, did most of the talking. During their childhood, she said, they often had no money for clothes and no food at all. Wei's young brother died of starvation during the famine of 1930. Thirty-one years later, after the Great Leap Forward, there was another. Guo recalled starving people from neighboring villages dropping dead in the streets as they went out to forage for food. Ten years earlier, they had suffered again: when their son and his wife, who already had two children, broke family-planning regulations by having twins, half the family's land and furniture was confiscated as a punishment.

Life was still tough today. Guo told me about conditions in a neighboring village deeper in the hills. "There are droughts nine out of ten years," she said, "so they learn to make one harvest last a decade."

"Why don't they move like you did?" I asked.

"The authorities are doing it in stages. It isn't easy to find land for everyone. And not everybody wants to move."

I asked her to take me to their old home. It was a twenty-minute drive across a rutted, blasted landscape of crumbling orange earth, gray grit, and splotches of white alkaline discoloration. Bleakly beautiful though it was, I struggled to imagine how such an environment could support human life, or life of any sort.

We drove alongside a dry riverbed that usually flooded just once a year for just four or five hours and then trickled dry. On the far bank I spied several dozen mud-brick buildings in various stages of collapse. It looked like an ancient ruin.

"That's where we lived," Guo said.

We got out of the car, walked across the riverbed, clambered up a bank dusted with white alkaline deposits, and entered the ghost village. Eight hundred people had lived here a few years earlier, but it was now in the process of being repossessed by the elements. All that was left of the community were crumbling walls, torn paper windows, and fading New Year decorations on the doors.

Guo's was the only one still locked. She opened it up and invited us inside. The house was spacious and well proportioned with a large court-yard. In its day, it would probably have been the best in the village. But the poverty was evident in the rough earthen floor and the newspapers used to insulate and decorate the walls. There was no running water, no electric-ity. "This was our light," said Guo, holding out an old Red Bull can with a kerosene wick sticking out of the opening.

The area was barely fit for human habitation. In the winter the ground froze and snow often blanketed the land. In spring and summer the village was frequently buffeted by sandstorms that choked the lungs and scratched the faces of residents. Guo said these had become more frequent and more frightening in recent years. Crops had become harder to grow. It was drier, warmer than in the past. There was less rainfall. Life was unbearably tough.

I was surprised that I had not yet seen the Great Wall, even though one of the oldest sections was marked on the map as being next to the old village. Considering that the wall was widely (though incorrectly) believed to be the only man-made structure visible from space, it seemed strange that it was not obvious. I asked Guo where it was.

"It is just outside, though it is not easy to make out," she replied.

That proved an understatement. Long before the village, the Great Wall in this area had been claimed by the harsh environment. All that was left was a snaking mound of mud that blended into the landscape. The heaped-earth ramparts had been abandoned more than a century ago and were now covered in gravel and scrub. Guo had to point out where they once stood, the swelling of red earth that I had just crunched under my feet. Visible from space? It was barely visible even as I stood on top of it.

The same thing was happening to mankind's best-known fortification as was happening to the rest of northern China. The threat of drought and desertification was evident the entire length of the Great Wall, from Xin-jiang in the far west to Hebei on the east coast, over 6,000 kilometers away.

China's ancient fortifications are far more complex and environmen-tally significant than is commonly understood. Contrary to its singular name, the Great Wall is a series of ramparts and spurs, as well as the main trunk that snakes across northern China. In part, they are made of little more than mud. Elsewhere, they are impressive brick structures.

Construction of many of the best-known stretches began in the Qin era (221–206 BC) to keep out northern invaders. Over the following centuries, the walls were widened, lengthened, and strengthened. This massive engineering project separated two cultures and ecosystems. The settled Han agriculturalists of the southern plains wanted to protect their fields from the roaming Mongol pastoralists of the northern steppe. The wall marked the boundary between their two differing approaches to nature: fixed control versus nomadic anarchy. The cultures reflected the environments: fields and valleys against sand dunes and grassland. The wall was an attempt to keep both the climate and the enemy at bay.

It was unsuccessful on both counts. The wall was breached by both at various times in history. Mark Elvin, an environmental historian, has linked the territorial power shifts with climate change.[3] In extended eras of low temperatures—such as the Little Ice Age—the Mongolian nomads were driven south to escape the cold and find new grassland and food sources. During warmer periods, the Han were able to expand their fields northward. The Great Wall was once a boundary between China and Mongolia, but the territory of the Han now stretches hundreds of kilometers farther north. The sands, however, are not so easily conquered. For decades, northern deserts have been invading southern arable land. The Great Wall was no defense. More than half of the original structure is either buried, crumbling, or torn down.[4]

Standing on the crenellated outline of the buried ramparts, I could see why William Lindesay, one of the first to walk the length of the wall, described it as "the backbone of a dinosaur."[5] The structure here was the broken relic that seemed to belong more to archaeology than history.

Guo and Wei were part of a mass retreat to the southeast. After centuries of land conquest and reclamation, the government was moving millions of people off fragile land that could no longer bear their weight. Pan Yue, deputy minister of the state environmental protection ministry, estimated that desertification would force the resettlement of 186 million people, about one in seven of the population.

Guo accepted that there was no choice: "We had to move because there was no water. There were times when we couldn't grow things for ourselves so we relied on government support. But in the new place, life is better. We can grow our own food because they have diverted the Yellow River to ensure we have enough water."[6]

We said farewell and wished the eco-refugees luck. Driving back to the main road, I saw the massive plumbing operation that made Guo and

Wei's new lives possible. The fields were flanked by concrete channels, intersected by steel pipes, and overshadowed by a giant elevated water tank. These hydroengineering works represented a fallback line of defense against the sands. But this barrier too was vulnerable because it depended on China's most overused and abused resource: the Yellow River.

Even before the rush of modern development there were few harder-working waterways on the planet. For almost half its 5,465-kilometer length, the world's sixth-largest river passes through desert sands, loess, and arid grasslands, nurturing 140 million people. Without the "Mother River," as it is also called, there would be little cultivation in these dry northern plains and China as we know it would not exist. The Middle Kingdom emerged between the Great Wall and the Yellow River. Both are vital elements in the battle against entropy. Ultimately, the skeleton of Han civilization is made up of walls and dikes.

Since ancient times, emperors have tried to harness the Yellow in the fight against the desert. It has proved a fickle ally. The river bears the burden of thousands of years of environmental degradation. No other waterway in the world carries as much silt.[7] Most of it comes from the Loess Plateau, which is a France-sized monument to erosion. The fragile soil here was formed by layers of windblown dust accumulated over two million years and held in place by trees and other vegetation. But about 5,000 years ago, soon after man began felling trees and clearing land for cultivation, the loess returned to its windblown state. Stripped of its protective layer, billions of tons of orange loess dust are carried off by the river, hence its name. One theory has it that the first mention of Huanghe (Yellow River) came in the Han era around 2,000 years ago, when the water started to discolor.

The soil erosion has turned vast expanses of Gansu, Inner Mongolia, and Shaanxi into dust bowls. Beijingers feel the consequences every spring when the city is buffeted by sandstorms. The riparian communities along the Yellow are more likely to suffer in the summer, when the combination of sediment buildup and floodwater used to make the river writhe destructively up and down the delta.[8] Accumulated downstream, the silt raises the surface of the water far above the land, with often devastating consequences.[9] Millions have died in the roughly 1,500 floods recorded in the Yellow's history, hence its other nickname "China's Sorrow."[10]

Ancient rulers were judged by their ability to tap and placate this river.

Even today, the giant dam at Sanmenxia is inscribed with the words "When the Yellow River is at peace, China is at peace."[11] The saying is attributed to the legendary emperor Yu (c. 2100 BC), who is seen as the first in a long line of hydroengineering leaders that continues to this day.[12] The challenge they face now is not how to tame the river but how to keep it alive. With more hydro plants, thirstier cities, and ever greater demands from agriculture, the Yellow has come close to choking.[13] Just how near became shockingly apparent in 1997, when it failed to reach the sea for 226 days. If that was not bad enough, the artery is also growing more polluted.[14]

An ancient folk saying predicts the Yellow will one day lose its (dis)color. The phrase *Shengren chu, Huanghe qing* (When a great man emerges, the Yellow River will run clear) was once an aspiration. Now, however, this seems so unlikely that the saying has become the Chinese equivalent of "And pigs might fly." Far from becoming clearer, the spurt of industrial growth in recent years has made the river so polluted it has at various times run not just yellow but pink, green, red, black, and brown.[15]

From Wei's village I drove to see the source of the worst contamination, the border between Ningxia and Inner Mongolia. The water along this stretch cooled and cleansed the thickest cluster of heavy industry I had seen in China. In return it received hot, dirty emissions that left the water so polluted that it was designated too toxic to touch.[16] The buildup started near Huinong City, where the banks of the river were punctuated by smokestacks, cooling towers, fertilizer plants, plastic factories, and paper mills. More dramatic still were the scenes on the other side of the city's bridge as we entered the industrial hellhole of Wuhai. Dust, smog, and exhaust fumes commingled so densely between the barren gray mountain slopes that it was at first hard to make out what was happening on the rocky plain between. Closer up, giant signs for the metallurgical plants and chemical refineries could be made out looming among the tangle of electricity pylons. Giant trucks rumbled out of the gates, churning up grit into the foul-smelling air as they joined an eight-lane jam of mobile tonnage. Farther along the road, smoke poured in hundreds of narrow streams from chimneys atop the long, identical rows of Lowrey-esque redbrick homes.

In just ten years, this blasted outpost had swollen from four factories to five hundred.[17] Dozens more were under construction. It was awe-inspiringly grim. Farther on, sand specters whispered across the road, curling patterns on the tarmac. Tumbleweed bounced madly in our path. Cyclists and pedestrians wore face masks but still grimaced in the grit and sand. On the roadside, fields gave way to dunes, and thick clouds of sand blurred visibility at ground level, though I could see blue skies above. "This is nothing," said our driver. "In a real sandstorm the sky grows so dark that you can't see more than twenty meters."

Areas of land were still being farmed, but the soil was so degraded that only sunflowers could be planted. When I saw the first patch of alkaline discoloration, I thought it was a sprinkling of snow. But the pale blotches came from the fertilizer and industrial pollution that had seeped into the soil. The white earth appeared to have been sterilized.

In other areas, the pollution was black. We stopped at Wulateqianqi County, the site of a recent contamination incident. The collapse of dikes at two paper-mill containment ponds released a tidal wave of toxic sludge across farmland, two villages, and a stream that flowed into the Yellow River. Fifty-seven homes were destroyed and crops ruined.[18]

I arrived unannounced at the home of Yang Kuan, one of the affected farmers. He was welcoming. Word went around family and neighbors. Soon a small crowd were sitting on the kang[19] telling me their story.

The gathering was noisy. Feelings were running high as the family recalled the black wave that swept through their lives. Before the incident, the paper mills, Saiwai Xinghuazhang and Meili Beichen, had been ordered to shut down because of their repeated violations of emissions regulations. An earlier spill had killed tens of thousands of fish in the Yellow River.

But, as was often the case in China, the companies ignored the order and continued to operate. On the day in question, it looked as though a rainstorm would flood the mill's containment ponds and contaminate the Yellow River again. Fearing fines and more criticism, the management channeled their pollution onto farmland instead. There was no warning to local people.

Scraping a living in the dry north had never been easy. After the incident, it became almost impossible. Yang took me out to the fields to see the consequences. It was bitterly cold, but he wanted to show me the land he had lost to the stinking black waters.

"It is ruined. We used to grow corn and wheat, but now it is not really even fit for sunflowers. Nobody wants to buy from us anyway because our crops have been tainted," he complained, shaking his head, then repeating himself, "We can't grow anything now."

A short distance away, a coal-fired power plant belched smoke into the sky. Part of its energy would go to the paper mills, which were still in business.

The village well was still too polluted to drink so the family had to use the foul water from the taps. The small government allowance they had received by way of compensation was due to run out in a year.[20] "After that I guess we will have to steal or beg," Yang said. "We have no other income."

Pollution and drought feed off one another. Contaminated streams and wells worsen water shortages. Rivers with low volumes and weak flows are less capable of flushing out toxins. Both threaten the fertility of the land and the health of the people. Both are evident across northeast China, where temperatures are also rising because of climate change.

Of the 600 cities facing water shortages in China, the vast majority lie either along the Yellow River Delta or in the lands that stretch north from there up to and beyond the Great Wall.

As the quality and quantity of surface water declines, people mine deeper and deeper for alternative supplies. The water table in northern China is falling by more than a meter a year, forcing farmers to dig deeper wells and cities to suck ancient aquifers dry. That is unsustainable. These underground resources might take hundreds of years to be replenished. Tang Xiyang, one of the founders of the green movement in China, described the trend to me in apocalyptic terms: "The Yellow River civilization has been destroyed. People cannot survive on that river anymore."

With 140 million people having to do just that, government mandarins also appear to feel a sense of crisis. Many of their hugely expensive and socially convulsive countermeasures smack of desperation. The relocation programs have spread ever wider, and their hydroengineering projects get bigger and bigger. The South-North Water Diversion Project, detailed in chapter 3, is the biggest gamble yet. Although the massive plan would transform the hydrology of China and possibly much of Asia, engineers felt they had no choice but to press ahead. Northern China could no longer pump water vertically from a few hundred meters underground, so it had started channeling it horizontally hundreds of kilometers from the south. The diversion project was a reinforcement operation.

"This is the only way to solve the water shortage problem," Sun Feng, director of the Yellow River Conservancy Commission, once told me. "The western leg is the only one that transfers water directly into the Yellow River so the whole basin will benefit."

The big outstanding problem is one of quantity rather than quality. The Yellow's volume is falling as demand rises. The river accounts for just 2 percent of the runoff in China, yet irrigates 15 percent of the country's crops and supplies water to 12 percent of the population.

At the Yellow River control center in Zhengzhou, the allocation of water among the nine provinces it passes through is marked on another wall-sized screen. The proportion has been fixed since 1987 based on a long-term estimate of 58 billion cubic meters of runoff every year. That has proved a massive overestimate. This year, the runoff is forecast to be less than 50 billion cubic meters. In 2003, it fell below 45 billion. The provinces are supposed to share the impact of the shortfall equally. Yet Ningxia, Inner Mongolia, and Shandong take more than a billion cubic meters of water above their allocation every year without permission.

The loser is the ecosystem. Twenty-one billion cubic meters of water each year are set aside for sediment flushing and maintenance of nonhuman life on the river. This is the area of the water budget that is cut whenever provinces go over their limit. The Yellow River Conservancy Commission has recently conducted research that shows the value of keeping water for wildlife and nature, but they need more power to put this into action.

"Some provinces and reservoirs don't obey our instructions. They ignore us to generate electricity," says Yu Xiubo. "It's a problem. We lack punitive measures."

Dispersal of authority across agencies and provinces has not helped. To tighten administration, the central government is drafting a Yellow River Law that would give more power to the river's administrating body. There are also plans for a Digital Yellow River that would allow bureaucrats based in Zhengzhou to remotely control and monitor sluice gates and irrigation channels along the entire length of the river. Currently this is possible only in the lower reaches.

This demand-side solution faces fierce opposition. No province wants to accept a cut in water supplies at a time when they all want to boost industry and agriculture. The latter is by far the biggest drain on the river, accounting for 90 percent of the diverted water, some of which is taken hundreds of kilometers into the desert. Yu and his colleagues are dispatched to sluice gates during times of drought when the Yellow River Conservancy Commission has to impose a potentially life-determining judgment on water supplies.

"It can be very dangerous," says Yu. "In the past, our engineers have been thrown into the river by angry residents. In the early days after 1999, nobody wanted to accept us. Upstream residents didn't care about low-stream demands. They said that, historically, they could always take what they wanted."

Better regulation of demand is the best option, but upstream provincial governors are reluctant to accept tough controls on a resource that they have always taken for granted. A politically easier solution is to increase supply even if it means huge expense, waste, and environmental stress.

The world's largest military has been mobilized too. In the battle against the elements, the People's Liberation Army is in the front line. Troops are often dispatched after natural disasters. The People's Armed Police are responsible for forest firefighting in the southern provinces. Ahead of the Olympics, thousands of troops were sent to dig an artificial training lake for a rowing team in Shaanxi.[21] The navy was deployed to clear up algae that threatened the Olympic sailing events. The air force has variously been used to break up ice dams and spread tree seeds in aerial afforestation missions. But perhaps most striking are its attacks on the clouds. No country in the world pummels the sky with the verve of China. In 2006, there were 590 weather-modifying sorties nationwide. Gansu, one of the driest, poorest regions, had fewer clouds to aim at than most, but its pilots logged sixty-one hours of flight time chasing cumulus.

The gates were locked when I arrived at the Gansu aircraft rain enhancement base. It was winter. The cloudbusting season was over, but one of the caretakers, Ma Dubin, offered to show me around. He was a local man and something of an authority on the strange science of weather modification.

Cloud-seeding experiments began in the United States in 1946, when General Electric (the company that also gave the world hydrofluorocarbons and leaded gas) launched the first experiments. Western scientists soon became skeptical about the results, but the Soviet Union enthusiastically adopted and improved upon the technology. China has now taken it on with a degree of alacrity seen nowhere else on earth.

Inevitably, the start of operations was in 1958—the Great Leap Forward year when, as we have seen in several chapters, China tried to conquer nature with a burst of dam building, sparrow killing, tree felling, and desert greening. Mao Zedong gave the project his stamp of approval: "Man-made rain is very important. I hope the meteorological experts do their utmost to make it work."[22]

The first cloud-seeding flights were in Gansu and Jilin, where the air force was dispatched to take on the clouds. In the earliest attempts, cannons fired catalytic chemicals into the heavens. Chinese scientists were pleased with the results, estimating the increase in rainfall at 10 to 25 percent. This prompted the government to enact a law encouraging local governments to "enhance leadership over weather modification." Nationwide, there are now more than thirty provincial-level offices dealing with rain creation, employing over 50,000 people with a budget in excess of $100 million per year.[23] No other country in the world comes close in matching the scale of this unapologetically man-made climate change.[24]

In Gansu, the rainmaking season ran from March 1 to the end of October. During that period, a small squadron of ten pilots moved into the dormitory to be on permanent standby to shoot down approaching clouds. There were three main buildings at the center. The first was the command center, where meteorologists analyzed data from local weather stations. Next to this were accommodations for the pilots, who had a weight machine, table tennis, and a billiard table to while away the hours between missions. There was plenty of free time. On average, they were scrambled only four or five times a month during the summer.

The third building was the storeroom for the chemicals and munitions used to bust the clouds. Outside it was a stack of empty pellet crates from a former weapons plant, Factory No. 556 in Wuhai, that had been converted to manufacture weather-modification devices. On the floor nearby were half a dozen rusting 37-millimeter shells that had been customized to deliver chemical catalysts into the sky. Whether fired from antiaircraft guns below or dropped by planes from above, the aim was essentially the same: to load the clouds with silver iodide or liquid nitrogen that would thicken the water droplets to the point where they became heavy enough or cool enough to fall as snow or rain.

Using these munitions was tricky. No two clouds were ever the same. Even a single cumulus changed constantly as it blew over varying landscapes at different altitudes across a range of temperatures. Some water was colder than ice. Some rain evaporated before it hit the ground. The variables were so great that scientists in many countries doubted cloud-seeding could ever work, but in Gansu as elsewhere in China, it was adopted with gusto.

"It is very effective. We have centers like this all over the region. We are very advanced," my guide explained. "Don't you make rain in your country?"

I replied that, in Britain, everyone complains because it is too wet.

"You are lucky. Our land is very dry. We need extra rain. There are rockets or pellet-firing guns across the region. If we see a cloud, we will try to make it rain."

Weather modification was applied on a massive scale to clear the gray skies before important political events, such as the 2008 Olympics and the parade for the sixtieth anniversary of Communist Party rule in 2009. But its main use was as a short-term fix for alleviating drought. In some areas, the competition for clouds caused bad blood between neighboring communities. In central Henan Province, five arid cities raced each other to induce precipitation over their areas. In one case, officials from Zhoukou complained bitterly that Pingdingshan had intercepted a downpour that had been heading their way. By the time it arrived in their region, only the dregs were left.[25]

Ma Dubin enthusiastically lauded the talents of his country's weather-modifying scientists, but he was less upbeat about impact of other forms of development on his own life and environment when he took me for a short walk outside the base to the home where he was born.

It was a cave, one of dozens that pocked the red loess. Carving houses into the hillsides was the norm here for centuries, but all the residents had been moved into brick homes over the previous twenty years. Ma missed the old way of life. In the cave, he said, each family had more space and the community spirit was stronger. The fuel bills were lower too because caves were warm in the winter and cool in the summer.

"I'd go back if I could, but it's not the way things are done these days. Cave dwelling is seen as too poor and backward," Ma sighed, crumbling some of the dry red earth in his hands.

Water was a perennial problem. In this regard, technology and economic development had brought only mixed benefits. When Ma was a child, wells had to be at least fifty meters deep to find an aquifer. Lugging up the heavy buckets was such a tough job that villages used mules to pull water up from underground. Now, however, the government piped water to their homes from the Datong River in neighboring Qinghai Province. The taste was salty. "We can drink the water, but it is not as sweet as before," said Ma.

The immense engineering effort needed to plumb these arid hills was evident everywhere. A long, dry concrete channel curled around the foot of the hills on its way from the distant river to the fields it irrigated in the spring and summer. The slopes were painstakingly terraced with young fir trees, the base of each carefully guarded against the elements with a rampart of earth. Iron pipes ran up and down the dusty yellow hillsides to provide water to these thirsty plants. The authorities had clearly invested a huge amount of money and labor to keep trees alive in this inhospitable environment. Was it worth it? Ma had no doubt. "Yes. It may look a little yellow now. But come back in the summer. Everything is green. The scenery looks very good."

Many disagreed. The rockets and planes, pipes and terracing were part of the nation's battle against the desert. Political careers and big sums of money were being made and lost on expensive projects. But there were divisions within the ranks about how the campaign should be waged.

Driving from Zhongchuan to Lanzhou, I got a better idea of the scale and the expense of the project. For more than half of the 90-kilometer journey the red hillsides had been terraced, irrigated, and planted with trees, none of which looked particularly robust. The natural climate had always been tough for vegetation. Now the environment was being made worse by hundreds of brick kilns that lined the sides of the road, filling stretches of the long corridor with smoke. The kilns had been worked with convict labor since 2005, when most young locals migrated south in search of higher-paid work. The bricks of the new China were being made with loess dust and prisoners' sweat.

The scraggy knee-high pines on the slopes received more government attention than many of Gansu's impoverished children. Keeping the plants alive so that visitors to the province got a good first impression after flying into the airport had cost the city more than 1 billion yuan and used up precious supplies of fuel and water from the Yellow River.

Local scientists were appalled. In Lanzhou, I visited Wang Tao, the director of the Cold and Arid Regions Environmental and Engineering Research Institute and one of the chief strategists in China's battle against the desert. He did not bother to hide his contempt toward the tree-planting project I had just driven through. "I have been opposed from the beginning. The local government asked my institute to prepare this project ten years ago and we refused. So they found an external organization to do the planning. But it is too expensive. You cannot make such dramatic changes to the environment in such a short time."

In the summer, he said, the green trees and shrubs made for a pleasant landscape, but the conditions were so tough that half of them needed to be replaced every year.

"The intention was good. They wanted to improve the environment. But they rushed their decision, misjudged the costs, and failed to act on the results. It was a mistake."

Other Chinese academics complained, but the project was locked into place by political and financial interests. "Once started, it can't be withdrawn, so the project has to be maintained," said Wang, shrugging. "It seems ambitious but it doesn't work. It is against nature. We human beings cannot change the landscape. It works in a few areas if we pay a high price. But to do it over, the whole of the Loess Plateau is another story."

Wang's specialty was aeolian desertification, or wind erosion. This phenomenon was associated with economic loss, political instability, and social upheaval. From the 1950s to the 1990s, Wang said, China experienced a similar problem to that seen in the dust bowls of the U.S.A. in the 1930s, or in the USSR in the 1940s. He had photos of the enemy assault, vast, menacing dust storms of red, white, or gray particles that billowed out like tidal waves or mushroom clouds. He then showed images of the aftermath: homes deluged by sand, roads blocked, and farmland ruined. Most spectacular were the images of the Great Wall being breached by the northern sands.[26]

The problem was not new, but it had become much worse over the last fifty years of the twentieth century. During that time, an area almost twice the size of Britain had turned into wind-racked desert, threatening 170 million people. Climate change was adding to the stress by making the north steadily hotter and drier. But, overwhelmingly, he said, the main cause was human activity.

As the combined number of China's human population and head of livestock tripled, what was left of the topsoil was stripped away, exposing the dust to the gales that blew across the plateau.

"It really is like the title of that film . . . How do you say it in English?" Wang asked.

"*Gone with the Wind*?"

"Yes, that's it. Gone with the wind."

This was an enormous threat to the nation's food security. About a third of the organic carbon in the soil of northern China was lost, which meant more artificial fertilizers were needed to maintain harvests. If the drought intensified, Wang feared harvests could decline by 20 percent and Gansu could start to resemble the most devastated parts of Africa.

To help the earth recover, he and other thinkers at the institute advised the government to adopt an approach that was almost the opposite of the thinking during the Great Leap Forward. Rather than attempting conquest by throwing people, fertilizer, and water at the desert, Wang favored a strategic retreat. In essence, it was Taoist. Doing nothing was an effective action. That meant paying farmers in the most arid areas to abandon their cropland. This allowed shrubs to return and the soil to recover naturally, which eased the demand for irrigation.

"We stop farming the land. We allow it to recover as grazing land. Sometimes we help it artificially. But usually we just leave it. We don't even need water. Normally it can recover by itself after five or ten years. Our former director proposed turning the affected areas into a huge national park, like the ones in the United States.[27] If it was only used for sightseeing, the land could recover in twenty or thirty years."

For a while it seemed to work. The dust storms eased. But demand for arable land was growing. The Taoist policy of paying people to allow farm fields to return to their natural state was shelved. The Foolish Old Men once again took over from the Useless Tree philosophers. Instead of trimming the demands on the land, the government shifted back toward boosting supply. Anti-desertification efforts focused on tree planting, water diversion, and high-tech allocation of the Yellow River's resources.

But more land needs irrigating, more power stations need cooling, and more city dwellers need drinking water. As coal production is ramped up in Inner Mongolia, as urbanization accelerates in Henan, and as irrigation expands in Shandong, the river's resources look likely to be spread ever thinner.

Attacking the clouds might help. But without greater efforts at conservation and tougher measures to curb pollution, the desert could subsume stretches of the Yellow just as it has claimed sections of the Great Wall. The geographic frontiers of human activity are written in water and erased with sand. China is making ever more desperate efforts to control both, but a third factor is making this increasingly difficult: a changing climate.

12

Flaming Mountain, Melting Heaven
Xinjiang

We have to understand just how big the risks will be if we do not manage climate change. They are not risks of discomfort and inconvenience. They are risks of destruction on a massive scale of the relationship between human beings and the planet, which will affect profoundly where human beings can live and thus result in big moves of population and extended conflict.
—*Nicholas Stern, author of the* Stern Review on the Economics of Climate Change[1]

When Zhao Songling set out for heaven in 1959, he could not have realized how important his adventure would seem half a century later in awakening China to the impact of climate change. In fact, the science student barely even knew where he was going.

In his fourth year at Peking University, Zhao was dispatched to Xinjiang by the Chinese Academy of Sciences. The far-western region was the target of a massive campaign to "open up the wastelands." True to the spirit of the Great Leap Forward, when Mao declared war on nature, it was a quasi-military operation. The soldier-settlers in the *bingtuan* (production/construction) PLA corps were on a mission to turn desert into farmland and produce food for a hungry, fast-growing nation.

His new home was an alien environment. Zhao was a Han from the densely populated coastal plains. Xinjiang was a land of Uighurs, Kazakhs, and other ethnic groups spread sparsely across an area seven times the size of Britain. Nowhere on the planet was farther from the sea. Nowhere in China was hotter.

Over centuries, the locals had developed lifestyles suited to their climate. Many Kazakhs were nomadic herders who followed the seasons in their movements up and down mountain pastures. The Uighurs were oasis dwellers used to conserving scarce water supplies. The new settlers, on the other hand, had been brought up in the irrigation culture of the floodplains. Faced with the challenge of cultivating extensive tracts of arid land, they farmed as their ancestors had done: diverting rivers, streams, lakes, and any other source of water they could find.

During the Great Leap Forward, even that was considered inadequate. In the China of 1959, mankind was believed to have unlimited potential, the earth unbounded fertility. All the soil needed was water. There was plenty of that locked in the mountains as snow and ice. The challenge was how to get it down to the plains.

Zhao joined an exploration to the Tian (heaven) Mountains with five other scientists, ten mule drivers, and two PLA soldiers to guard against wild animals. Setting out from Urumqi, the regional capital, and traversing hundreds of kilometers west to Aksu, theirs was the first systematic study of glaciers in Xinjiang. It was to stimulate some of the earliest debates in China on climate change and mankind's impact on the environment.

Zhao's group was simply investigating the ice fields, but scientists elsewhere were already attempting to milk the mountains. Under the instructions of senior government scientist Zhu Gangkun and Soviet advisers, several glaciers in the far west were targeted for accelerated melting.[2] The military tried bombing the ice, but that wasted munitions. In Gansu, scientists attempted a slightly more scientific approach: they blackened the ice with coal dust to make it absorb more heat.

Spreading coal dust across a sea of ice and snow was no easy task. For more than a month during the summer of 1959, thousands of workers at six locations in Gansu trudged up and down the slopes to the snow line bearing sacks of the stuff.[3]

As irresponsible as this seems today amid fears that global warming is melting the world's ice, in the 1950s, this was considered heroic, patriotic work. Propaganda posters of the time showed scientists in planes dropping grenades on ice fields, a fitting image for the prevailing ethos.[4] Greenhouse gases were unheard of. Nature was something to be overcome rather than protected; mountains were remote, daunting objects to be conquered. This way of thinking was evident in other countries around this time too. In the United States in 1962, the Humble Oil Company, which later became Exxon, ran a double-page advert in *Life* magazine that claimed, "Each Day Humble Supplies Enough Energy to Melt 7 Million Tons of Glacier!" For the U.S. firm it was a figurative boast. In China, it was—for a while—state policy.

The result of this bold thinking was disaster: yet another of the Great Leap Forward's ill-conceived experiments. Across the country, similarly reckless policies decimated food production and led to a devastating famine. The glacier melting operation was less deadly, but it proved to be a complete waste of time, money, and effort.

"The Gansu team were heavily criticized and their work was stopped," recalled Zhao. "Their original intention was good. They wanted to solve the problem of drought. Coating snow with coal dust really did provide more water in the short term, but in the long term it made things worse."

That lesson, learned in the distant mountains of Xinjiang, was to become still more relevant fifty years later, when the entire planet was coated with so much carbon that the mountains once again started to melt. Zhao's mission, which marked the birth of glaciology in China, ensured that China understood the consequences.

The first ice field they encountered, unimaginatively named Urumqi Number One, has become a benchmark for climate change in China.[5] Retracing Zhao's steps on a journey to the west, I learned that the measurements taken here since the 1950s have done more than anything to convince a skeptical nation that it needs to act on global warming. In Xinjiang, one of the nation's most strategically important regions, climate change was becoming a national security issue.

My plane touched down in Urumqi Airport close to midnight. I was thrilled to arrive. Central Asia was a region that my Anglocentric education had neglected, but its geography and history were compelling.[6] Until the advent of ocean travel, Xinjiang—then known as East Turkestan or Uighurstan—was the often tumultuous meeting place of East and West.

Physically, the region's angular features are formed by a horseshoe of mountain ranges, the world's third-biggest desert, and two giant basins, each home to a predominant culture: Kazakh nomads in the northern Dzoungar, and Uighur oasis dwellers in the southern Tarim.

Sited at the center of the Silk Road, the great trade route across the continent, Xinjiang has been traversed by Marco Polo and pillaged by all of the great historical rampagers: Attila the Hun, Tamerlane, Alexander the Great, and Genghis Khan. Spies and explorers, including Francis Young-husband, intrigued here during the Great Game era, when Britain and Russia dueled for control of central Asia.[7] The territory was rarely stable for long. As I was to find out, it was also highly vulnerable to migration and climate shifts.

The causes and effects of global warming are rarely so closely juxta-posed as in Urumqi and its glaciers. European, American, and Japanese cities are far from the polar ice caps where the greenhouse gases they emit wrought their greatest damage. But in China's far west, carbon and its consequences sit side by side.

Xinjiang, which means New Dominion, is the nation's fossil-fuel front line, containing a third of the nation's known oil and gas reserves and the biggest untapped coal deposits. Once burned, the impact of this carbon will be felt at the world's physical extremes, many of which are found in Xinjiang. Drier, wetter, hotter, colder, lower, higher, and bigger than almost anywhere else in China, this Uighur Autonomous Region is an ideal loca-tion to assess the changes in the planet's climate. Yet it has become a global blind spot because it is one of China's highest-security areas.

Those who have heard of the region tend to associate Xinjiang with desert, but that is only part of the ecological picture. As well as being home to the deepest depression after the Dead Sea and the biggest body of sand after the Sahara, the region is a moisture trap. Its mountains, several of which rise over 7,000 meters, receive more precipitation each year than the annual flow of the Yangtze River.[8] Much of it freezes. This makes the region an important part of the "Third Pole," the central and southern Asian mountains that contain the third-largest body of ice on earth.[9] China is home to 46,000 glaciers, more than any other country, but they are shrinking fast in both size and number as temperatures rise faster in the mountains than anywhere else in the country. Two-thirds are expected to disappear in the first half of this century.[10] Many are in Xinjiang, where the

Altai and Tian ranges in the north and the Pamirs and Kunlun in the south have seen their snow lines retreat by about 60 meters between 1960 and 2000.[11] During the same period, the sparsely populated wilderness on the fractious western border of China has been transformed by a spectacular burst of fossil-fueled activity and an influx of the Han ethnic majority. There are few places on earth where industrialization and globalization have arrived so suddenly.

Chinese children are taught that the region has been part of their country's territory since 60 BC.[12] But the degree of control has fluctuated enormously, and often been interrupted completely, owing to the mutable and porous nature of Xinjiang's borders, which touch on eight nations.[13] Sovereignty has been more sharply defined in the modern era but remains hotly contested. Today the region is autonomous, but only in the Chinese sense, which is to say the predominantly Uighur local population is free to do anything Beijing likes. The state's demands on the region have increased along with its strategic importance. In the nation-building 1950s, Mao's war on nature prompted the first waves of quasi-military pioneers to grow fruit and grain in the desert. Amid the political turmoil of the 1960s and 1970s, Xinjiang was part of the front-line defense against the Soviet Union. Since the 1990s, the government's focus on economic growth has driven a new wave of migrants to develop the cotton and oil industries under the "Open the Northwest" and "Go West" strategies. Each successive influx has heightened environmental and ethnic pressure.

Even on the drive from the airport to the center of Urumqi, the region's cultural complexity is apparent. On road signs, Han Mandarin characters sit above sloping Uighur script. On the skyline, domed mosques and minarets peep out among office blocks. On the streets, there is an eye-catching ethnic mix of Kazakhs, Russians, and, of course, Uighurs, the easternmost of the Turkic peoples. Green eyes and brown hair are common here. More men have facial hair, though because this is a mark of the Uighurs' unique ethnic and religious identity, even a mustache is forbidden among officials—a mark of Beijing's insecurity regarding the region. Xinjiang is the only region in China where a teacher can be fired for growing a beard.

People even live on different clocks. To enforce a sense of unity, Beijing insists that all of China uses the same time. For Xinjiang, more than 3,000 kilometers west of the capital, this means the summer sun does not officially rise until 9 a.m. and sets as late as midnight. Unofficially, locals keep Xinjiang time, which is two hours behind Beijing. It can be confusing. When we arranged a car for the journey to the glacier, we first had to agree which of the two clocks to set our alarms by.

At 8 a.m., Beijing time, the road outside the hotel was free of traffic. Locals on Xinjiang time had yet to wake. But our driver, Wu Shibao, was up and waiting. He was used to switching between two clocks and cultures. As we set off, he told us his family history. It was a typically modern story of Han settlement and environmental stress. Turning down the car stereo, he told us he was born in Xinjiang, but his parents were Han. In the 1950s, they had left their homes in distant Anhui in response to a call from Mao Zedong to "bolster the border areas."

The change wrought by successive waves of migrants became apparent as we drove. Compared with the low-rise mud-brick homes and alleys of a traditional Uighur community, the broad roads, tinted windows, and rectangular buildings of Urumqi marked it out as a settlers' city. More than 80 percent of the 2 million residents were Han. The provincial capital was one of an increasing number of areas in Xinjiang where Uighurs had become a minority in their own land. We drove for about an hour, passing from gray urbanity through pale plains, and then to the thickening color of irrigated cropland.

The roadsides were a reminder of history. This land was once lightly touched by humanity. In 1950, while the rest of China was overcrowded, Xinjiang was home to only 5 million people. But the wide-open spaces were impossible for Mao to resist. He began diverting part of the country's rising population into Xinjiang. The propaganda version has it that most of the newcomers were *mangliu* (blind migrants), who were driven by idealism to the far west without knowing what to expect. But many clearly went with their eyes wide open. Huge numbers were fleeing poverty and starvation in overcrowded eastern provinces such as Hunan, Henan, and Anhui. Others, such as the poet Ai Qing, were escaping political purges. Many more were sent by the state. In the 1950s and 1960s, thousands of teenage women were recruited as brides for the lonely pioneer soldiers. Their self-sacrifice is celebrated in the state media as the story of the "Eight Thousand Hunan Maidens Who Went Up Heaven Mountains." A less idealized version of their experience suggests they were deceived into going west with false promises of Russian lessons and technical training, only to find out when they arrived that their fate was to be shared out among the older, senior officers.[14]

During the Cultural Revolution, the stream of people became a flood when Mao encouraged students to go "up to the mountains, down to the countryside." In a reverse of the urbanization that China is experiencing today, the slogan of that idolatrous age was "The Farther from Father and Mother, the Nearer to Chairman Mao's Heart."[15] Nationwide, 20 million people went into the countryside. The populations of Xinjiang and Inner Mongolia surged.

The state rallied the pioneers with a call for the idealism and patriotism found in other countries during call-ups for national service during wartime. But those sent to strengthen the border areas ended up using shovels and tractors more than guns and tanks. They converted an area the size of Israel to farmland by irrigating arid plains or requisitioning land from Uighurs.[16] In the Taklamakan desert, grain yields reportedly quadrupled in four years, from 1.5 million kilograms in 1966 to 6.5 million kilograms by 1970. The results were proclaimed as a triumph of revolutionary will, but the environmental cost was enormous.

For countless centuries, runoff from the snow-capped mountains gave Xinjiang one of the highest water-to-people ratios in China. This kept oases lush with Euphrates poplars, tamarisk, and calligonum.

But the settlers diverted the rivers for cash crops, particularly in the 1990s when cotton, along with oil, made up the two halves of Xinjiang's "black-and-white economy."[17] By then Chinese scholars were already warning that Xinjiang's environmental carrying capacity was being pushed to the limit. There was a precedent of what could go wrong in nearby Uzbekistan, where cotton production had devastated the Aral Sea. But for policymakers in Beijing, a bigger priority was to dilute the ethnic population. The new arrivals needed work. Cotton was the short-term answer, but this meant a huge extra demand on the Tarim and other rivers.[18] Countless wadis dried up. The ecological balance was disrupted. Uighur communities were forced to move. Many rare species, such as argali sheep and brown bears, were decimated.[19]

To the environmentalist Ma Jun, the uncontrolled irrigation was more than just a waste of resources: "This is clearly an ecological crime. Its victims are the plants, animals, and birds."[20] Large areas of Xinjiang were desiccated. Lop Nor, once the second-largest saltwater lake in China, was effectively soaked up by trillions of cotton buds. In the late 1950s, two-meter-long fish swam in its waters. By 2006, even the smallest species were struggling to survive in what had become a trickle in the desert close to the military's main nuclear testing ground. With it went the Tarim tiger, the large-headed fish, huge numbers of Bactrian camels, and a greenbelt of poplar forests.[21] With the tree barrier gone, the Taklamakan and Kum Tagh deserts joined up, forcing *bingtuan* units to abandon their barracks and fields. They arrived in the 1960s to "defeat the desert." They left in the nineties, having surrendered more land to the sands than when they arrived.[22]

During our first stop on the road, I chatted to a young woman wearing a headscarf who had just moved to a new village after marrying a local man. I congratulated her and asked how she liked her new home. "It's good. This place used to have a bad reputation for being poor, but incomes are rising thanks to tourism," she said. The problem now was not money but water for the family farm. Every ten days she had to apply for an irrigation permit at the local Communist Party office. If approved, her family received a card entitling them to use water for three hours each day, after which they had to divert the irrigation channel toward another permit holder.

At that point we were interrupted. An official wearing army fatigues strolled over indignantly. "Stop that. No journalists here." Not wishing to make any trouble for the woman in her new home, I left without complaint. I asked driver Wu why the locals were so sensitive. "This is a military zone and you are a foreigner." I hadn't noticed on the way in, when all I had seen were newly constructed tourist lodges, but, sure enough, on the nearby hills were clusters of khaki buildings. A short distance down the road was the Nanshan military airport.

As we drove out of the restricted area, Wu told me he too had been forced to retreat from the land. Before he became a taxi driver, he had inherited the farm his parents created in the wilderness. At first he made a decent income growing leeks and peppers. But around 1998, the land deteriorated and the crops failed year after year. The earth had become useless within two generations.

As we talked, a syrupy pop song popular at the time played repeatedly on the car stereo. Its English lyrics conveyed the zeitgeist of mutability:

> They say nothing lasts forever.
> We're only here today.
> Love is now or never.
> Bring me far away.

I asked Wu the name of the singer, assuming he must be a fan because the track had been playing all the way from Urumqi. "I don't know, I just downloaded it on my computer," he said, shrugging.

A wall of lush green hills rose up ahead of us. The road climbed and dipped through a narrow gorge flanked by steep granite slopes and dense pine forests. After the two-dimensional flat pastels of the plain, there was a pleasing variety of shape and color above, below, and on either side. I had time to enjoy it. Our car was twice held up by flocks of goats being shepherded along the narrow road by Kazakh herders on horseback. Such scenes would soon be a thing of the past. Earthmovers and mechanical diggers were laying the foundations for a new highway that would speed tourists through the valley without interruption.

After thirty minutes the pastoral scene on either side of the ravine gave way to an industrial horror story. The valley widened, the light dimmed, and the air thickened. This was no mountain mist or low cloud. It was a putrid haze. The source was an anti-Shangri-La, a dirty secret hidden in the hills: the Houxia power plant and concrete factory, which appeared to be competing with one another to belch the most sulfurous smoke into the sky. Their chimney stacks were too short to lift the gas above the roof of the valley, so the smog gathered denseness, shrouding the dormitories of the workers and the black heaps of coal waiting to be fed into the furnaces.

This industrial estate was another legacy of Mao's push into the borders. Factories like this were part of preparations for war against the Soviet Union in the 1960s and 1970s, when the chairman declared a "Third Front" in the country's most remote inland regions. His plan was to scatter China's industrial base so that it would be safe from bombing. Soldiers and students set about building roads and factories in rural idylls. It was a major cause of disruption of local ecologies.[23]

We drove onward, upward, and out of the smog. Almost immediately the scenery returned to a bucolic state. The road climbed beside steep gorges, through thick pine forests, and up onto alpine meadows. A familiar muzziness told me the altitude was around 3,000 meters. On the roadside, I spotted the round white yurt of a Kazakh family. We were getting close. The space-seeking nomads dwell in an increasingly narrow band of land just below the snow line and just above the limits of Han settlement. As in Yunnan, the Tibetan Plateau, and elsewhere, an ethnic minority was being pushed farther to the geographic fringes.

The herdsmen roamed the slopes looking for fresh pastures for their sheep and goats. Their movements were seasonal, driven by the weather, which made them more sensitive barometers of climate change than sedentary urban dwellers.

A few miles on, we entered a grassy plain surrounded by glaciers. In the midst was a Kazakh family erecting a yurt for their summer camp. They allowed me to film them as they tied thickly padded walls to a metal frame. The material had to be heavy to keep out freezing mountain winds and was tied in place with wire twists rather than cord knots. Bahebieke, the young head of the family, supervised the work and, between puffs on a cigarette, explained in rudimentary Chinese what was happening. He said the family were moving to this summer camp a week earlier than the previous year and almost a month earlier than five years ago because temperatures were rising. The winters, once bitter and long, were getting shorter and milder.

"It has become warmer, especially these last two years. That glacier used to come all the way down to the road, but now it stops halfway up the slope," he said, pointing to the wall of ice several hundred meters away.

Warmer climes meant less hardship. Life had improved in other ways. The family had recently acquired a solar panel that gave them enough electricity for a lightbulb and a radio. Bahebieke had switched from a horse to a motorbike. The China mobile signal was so good in the mountains that he could keep in touch with family members working in the city by phone. Their livestock was growing. Looking over to some animals grazing by a meltwater stream, Bahebieke said his family now tended 400 sheep.[24] But bigger herds did not necessarily equate to greater wealth.

He was worried about the mountains he roamed. "As the glaciers melt and the temperature rises, there is less snow and rain. That means less grass. The sheep are not able to get fat. This is the problem we face. For a herdsman, that is a great loss."

Other nomads had found a new way of making money. For the final ascent to the glacier, I stopped by a couple of yurts to hire a padded jacket and pay for a motorbike ride up the final few hundred meters to the ice field. Fifty years earlier, Zhao and his expeditionary team would have taken hours climbing this rutted, winding track. We juddered up in ten minutes. At the top, overlooking Urumqi Number One, I felt a guilty exhilaration. I was privileged to be in this breathtakingly beautiful place, yet I had come to look for signs of decline. It seemed disrespectful. And difficult. I suddenly realized my inability to grasp the scale of the changes taking place. I knew the history of the glacier's retreat, that the two lakes of ice had been one giant sea until they split in 1993. I had read that it was thinning at a rate of six meters a year. And I had been told that the water dripping from the glacier could have been locked in place for hundreds, maybe thousands, of years. I knew this ancient natural legacy was being wasted and degraded. But, standing in front of the glacier, it still looked utterly huge and magnificent. As at the Three Gorges, perhaps I could not appreciate what had been lost because I had never seen the former glory.

Locals, though, had watched the diminishment of the ice with growing alarm. Ashengbieke, my Kazakh motorbike taxi driver, was only eighteen, but he said the glacier had split in half and changed color since his childhood. "While I was growing up, it used to be very cold here. It used to snow in summer, but now it rains instead. Because of the air pollution, the glacier turned black. It used to be pure white and the two snowfields were joined as one."

I clambered down a slope to get within touching distance. Up close, the glacier had a cold sensuality. Gnarled, twisted, and crevassed, its deepest, darkest cave concealed a fragile moistening stalactite. The sounds from within rose in intensity from a simple, steady drip, drip, drip near the top to a roaring torrent below. Thirty meters from the main wall, the flood of meltwater cut a tunnel under the dirty gray ice, leaving only a blotchy, wafer-thin crust on the surface. Near my feet, a chunk of ice the size of a piano had fallen from above. Farther down the slope, a lake-sized slab had been isolated from the main glacier. Cut off like a weak animal from a herd, it was being slowly worn down by the heat.

But was this the impact of climate change or just the normal seasonal melt? I belatedly wondered if I was on a fool's errand. What could a layman conclude in a few hours about a phenomenon that had to be put in the context of millennia? In the Arctic, global warming was strikingly evident as ice fields collapsed into the ocean and polar bears were stranded on floes. In the mountains, the changes were, well, glacial.

But the incremental movement of the ice had been meticulously tracked since Zhao's expedition in the 1950s. At a monitoring station a short way down the valley, I met his modern counterpart, Zhang Enzi, a bespectacled glaciologist who had spent the past five years measuring the thickness and length of the five glaciers in the area, as well as the temperature of the air and the ice. Every day, he and his colleagues took readings at 7:45 a.m., 1:45 p.m., and 7:45 p.m. Their results suggested that "glacial" was no longer quite such an appropriate adjective for "slow."

Zhang was a friendly, worried young man and a believer in anthropomorphic climate change. He told me the ice had been retreating by between eight and ten meters each year. Warmer weather had changed patterns of precipitation. For the first time since records began, rain rather than snow had recently fallen on the peak. There were lakes of melted water at the top of the glacier and more frequent avalanches. The ice was discolored from clouds of soot, also known as black carbon, that billowed across the world from wood fires, diesel engines, and smokestacks in developing nations.[25] The effect was just as it had been with the coal dust in the 1950s. Even the Number Five Glacier, which was less vulnerable because it sat in the shadow of the mountain most of the day, had started to shrink for the first time. At the current pace of thinning, the entire glacier field would be gone within 100 years.

That would be a calamity for Urumqi. The glaciers served as solid water reservoirs. Mountains captured snow, rain, and atmospheric moisture during the summer rainy season and slowly released it during dry winter months. This regulating function was particularly important to Xinjiang's provincial capital, which was flanked by vast deserts. Once the mountains started warming and the glaciers melted, rivers downstream were first at risk of flooding and then, years later, of drying up.

"It's very frightening," Zhang said. "This will create huge problems for Urumqi's drinking water supply."

But the danger was not widely understood, he told me. For at least twenty years, the extra meltwater would seem a bonus. People would get used to having more to drink and irrigate with than usual. Many doubted climate change was a problem.[26] Others saw it as a boon.

A similar range of views is evident at a national level. Talking to scientists and policymakers in China over the years, I have found the debate about global warming to be less urgent than in developed nations. Nobody doubts change is occurring, but the degree of human—particularly Chinese—responsibility is often questioned, as are the likely consequences and the need to take action. Many expressed a feeling of injustice because China was often blamed for being the world's biggest emitter of greenhouse gas. This was understandable. As a latecomer to industrialization, China can claim a lower historical responsibility than developed nations.[27] Relative to the size of its population, its carbon footprint is also just a third or a quarter of that of the U.S. and Europe. A major chunk of its emissions is also used in the manufacture of exports, as we saw in Guangdong.

But there is a growing awareness of the need to take action as the impact of climate change becomes clearer. The 1990s was China's hottest decade in 100 years. I heard from Xiao Ziniu, director general of the Beijing climate monitoring center, that storms were growing fiercer and more frequent in the south, droughts were lasting longer in the north, and typhoons were intensifying near the coast. Rising temperatures were affecting crop production, rainfall patterns, and the pace of glacier melt.

Yet Xiao was not convinced that mankind faced calamity: "There is no agreed conclusion about how much change is dangerous. Whether the climate turns warmer or cooler, there are both positive and negative effects. In Chinese history, there have been many periods warmer than today."

I recalled Mark Elvin's theory about the link between changes in global temperatures and power shifts between different cultures. He observed that cooling often coincided with dynastic crises in China, when the Mongolian nomads of the northern steppe tended to intrude southward.[28] By contrast, Han society, which was based on the irrigation of low-lying plains, had historically thrived during warmer eras when the area of cultivatable land pushed north. This might partly explain the hesitation of

Chinese scientists to consider climate change as a threat. But the warming could shift from the comfort zone.

It was not far from heaven to hell in Xinjiang. At the foot of the Tian Mountains was the Turpan Depression, the lowest and hottest place in China. In classical literature, this was a symbol of murderous heat. During the Tang dynasty (618–907), the poet Cen Shen wrote, "No living thing can dwell on this mountain, Even birds dare not fly over." During the summer months, currents of hot air were said to roll up the barren red sandstone slopes of the nearby Flaming Mountain like tongues of fire. Many travelers passed by on the Silk Road, some recording a climate that always seemed to be summer. The most memorable account was by the Buddhist fabulist Wu Cheng'en of the Ming dynasty (1368–1644). In his novel *Journey to the West,* Flaming Mountain was so hot that the Buddhist monk Tripitaka and his guardian, the Monkey King, were unable to progress on their quest for enlightenment to Gandhara in India. They learned that the only way to cool the earth was to win over Princess Iron Fan. Today, this episode reads like a global-warming parable or at least a potential advertisement for the wind-turbine manufacturers whose blades are now spinning across much of Xinjiang and northwest China.

Climate change was difficult to pin down. It was too complicated and contradictory to squeeze easily into a given formula. In a small number of cases, glaciers were expanding. The dry plains of Xinjiang were getting more rain than in the past. Some research suggested deserts were absorbing more carbon than previously believed. Assessing the impact was also fraught with imprecision. Global warming was rarely solely responsible for anything. Instead, it intensified existing natural phenomena, such as the summer storms, and accelerated many of the worst trends of human development, such as desertification. In some areas, it even seemed to be beneficial. On the coastal plains, Han farmers enjoyed increased yields as a result of the extra warmth and moisture.

The negative impacts tended to be apparent on the geographic peaks and in the economic depressions. The most dramatic temperature changes were found inland, on high ground during the winter. Melting glaciers in Tibet, Qinghai, Gansu, and Sichuan, dried-up lakes in Hebei and Inner Mongolia, as well as ferocious storms and floods in Guangxi, Guangdong, and Zhejiang. In the mountain forests of Sichuan and Yunnan, sensitive species of orchid, insect, and reptile were dying out as the temperature warmed.[29] Off the coasts of Liaoning, striped seal populations were declining along with the icebergs. Among humans, the worst affected were almost always the poorest: nomads who lost their herds when grasslands were engulfed by deserts, farmers on poor land whose crops shriveled up in droughts, and riverside dwellers whose shacks were destroyed in floods. Usually, they were people living closest to nature. Many were Han. But disproportionately, the impact was probably felt most by the ethnic minorities.[30] As they lost livelihoods or escaped to cities, tensions rose. Emotions were particularly strong when indigenous people saw their land and natural resources being taken at the same time by an influx of economic migrants.

People were increasingly drawn to Urumqi because it was becoming the center of oil and gas production in central Asia.[31] The old Silk Road had been reinforced with pipelines, railways, and highways.[32] Driving back along the road from the glacier to the regional capital, the dominance of the high-carbon economy was evident in cooling towers, smokestacks, oil drums, and gas pipes.

On the outskirts of the city, massive refineries, vast storage drums, and a tangle of pipes marked the presence of the world's first trillion-dollar company, PetroChina.[33] With overseas partners, this state-run firm populated the Turpan and Tarim basins with *ketouji* (lit., "kowtowing machines"), the "nodding donkeys" that bow back and forth hypnotically as they pump millions of tons of oil from under the sand.

Viewed from Urumqi, the government's "Go West" campaign to redistribute wealth to poorer inland regions looks more like a "Take East" extraction of energy resources. The flow of oil from the desert and meltwater from the mountains has created a boomtown, but most of the new money has been sucked up by Han settlers.

In the 1950s, Urumqi was a gritty sprawl of 100,000 Uighurs living in two- or three-story mud-brick homes arranged in narrow sand-colored curling alleyways. Poverty was so widespread and health care so rudimentary that people would count themselves lucky to live beyond forty years of age. Traveling here in the 1930s, the English missionary Mildred Cable uncharitably described it as a place possessing "no beauty, no style, no dignity."[34]

Similar terms could be used in the modern age, but for a very different cityscape. As the local economy tore along at a 20–30 percent annual growth rate, Urumqi extended farther across the plains and up into the sky, sucking up water supplies along the way. As the Han settlers poured in, Uighur alleyways gave way to six-lane city streets, square high-rises, and concrete squares. Among the big new water-guzzling developments are the Snow Lotus Mountain Golf Club and the Silk Road International Ski Resort.[35]

The thirst of these luxury sports facilities is slaked by the extra runoff from Urumqi Number One and the 154 other glaciers that feed the river basin. The melt doubled in the twenty years after 1985 and is likely to continue rising for several decades. After that, if the glaciologists are right, Urumqi is at risk of evaporating along with its water supply.

The central government has long been aware of the risks, but it is only in recent years that it has identified the planetary causes. In 2007, it issued the country's first national plan on climate change, spelling out policies for afforestation, recyclable energy development, and a raft of other countermeasures nationwide. Xinjiang's planners have also realized that they need to find somewhere other than golf greens and artificial pistes to invest their water bonanza. They built an eco-park to promote a more sustainable lifestyle among residents, announced plans to build fifty-nine reservoirs to catch glacier meltwater, and were considering augmenting this with subterranean storage pools.[36] But a still more radical plan was also under consideration. To explore it fully, Premier Wen Jiabao dispatched a special envoy with a reputation for earthshakingly ambitious ideas.

Qian Zhengying was very short, very old, and extremely controversial. A former minister of water conservancy and power, she had been in the senior ranks of government throughout the Great Leap Forward. Even after retirement she was a driving force in the Three Gorges Dam project. Few politicians generated such a mix of hatred and respect.[37]

We met for an interview shortly after she had finished a fact-finding tour of Turpan. She had been there to see if Xinjiang's rich coal seams could be exploited. But what she found was China's worst water problem. "We studied every glacier. Because of global warming, we found the small glaciers are melting quickly. So until 2020 the water in the rivers may well increase, but what happens after that when the meltwater is gone?" asked the tiny, wizened figure who managed to fill a giant government chamber with her presence.

As a quarter of the region's water was supplied by glaciers, she said it was vital that the bonus meltwater be used wisely. "We have to be responsible for future generations so we should not start developing at a time when the water income is unusually large. Because later, when water declines, we won't have enough to sustain things."

She had advised Premier Wen that the priority was to restore dried-up lakes, depleted aquifers, and other environmental damage wrought in the past. To do this, she said, farmers should be paid to cease irrigation of their fields because so much water was wasted.

"In Xinjiang, close to 96 percent of the water is used for agriculture. This is the highest share in the world," Qian told me. "This has already caused the destruction of the freshwater ecosystem. In some lower reaches of rivers, there is no longer any water. Some wetlands and lakes have degraded and in some areas the water is severely overused."

I was stunned by her admission that the dash to transform desert into farmland over the past forty years had resulted in a massive waste of water resources and environmental damage. This was an incredible volte-face for the Maoist who had been part of a government that urged Han Chinese pioneers to cultivate Xinjiang and ease the country's food shortages.

Now she wanted to shift farmers off the land and into the cities to raise the efficiency of water utilization. Compared with the relocation program needed for her previous megaprojects, Qian predicted the demographic reengineering would be straightforward. "For the Three Gorges project, moving one person cost 40,000 yuan and it was complicated. In Xinjiang, all that is required is to move people very close to cities and provide them with housing. It will be easier."

That was a dangerous assumption. Water, heat, and migration were a volatile mix. Many Uighurs already felt they were being driven out of a homeland degraded by overcultivation and increasingly fraught with ethnic tension.[38] Both were growing worse. In July 2009, the worst day of racial violence in modern Chinese history left 197 dead and 1,721 injured.[39] The vast majority of the victims were Han settlers. In the future, a changing climate is likely to add to the tension as it forces more people to migrate and increases competition for water and food supplies.

Qian's more immediate concern was the economy. The uncertainties of climate change were making it more difficult to allocate water resources in China. Huge reservoirs she had helped to design near Beijing and Tianjin were getting barely more than a third of the expected runoff.[40] In northern China, she said, the accumulated water deficit was 9 billion cubic meters, which had led to massive depletion of aquifers. Xinjiang's melting glaciers and overused rivers were a particular headache. Instead of trying to feed the nation, Qian said, the region should just grow enough for itself. "In the past, the government officials in Xinjiang were very kind. They felt the country had a food-security problem, so they wanted to produce an agricultural surplus. But now, given Xinjiang's water problem, they should only be required to supply sufficient food for their own use."

Her comments did not mark a late-life conversion to Taoism. Qian's conclusions were based in true Marxist style on economic productivity. Despite the expansion of farming and the mass diversion of water over the past fifty years, Xinjiang's agricultural output remained modest relative to its size.[41] The former minister, who had made a career out of diverting rivers from one area to another, felt the water would be more efficiently allocated to industry and to one sector in particular: coal mining.

"The Turpan area has rich coal deposits but they don't have the water to develop them," she said. "Our study concludes that we should divert some of the water that has been used until now for agriculture."

The diversion of Xinjiang's water from oxygen-producing crops to carbon-emitting fuel is a terrifying prospect for a world already worried about food shortages and global warming, But Qian's vision is in line with China's strategic goals. Economic growth must not be allowed to slow down despite growing concern about climate change. This outlook underlies all of its actions. Ahead of international climate talks in Copenhagen in 2009, the government set its first carbon target. It was an important step, but the intensity goal was a promise to slow the growth of emissions rather than to cut them. Until at least 2030, China expects to be the world's biggest emitter of greenhouse gas.

More and more of it will come from Xinjiang, which contains 40 percent of the country's known coal reserves. They have not been exploited until now because of the difficulties of extraction and the cost of transport. But engineers plan to turn that coal into gas or liquid so it can be pumped east through pipelines. The region, which is already feeling many of the most dramatic effects of climate change, is on course to become one of the biggest sources of carbon entering the world's atmosphere.[42]

Miners and power companies are completing the mission the glacier melters abandoned fifty years earlier. Instead of sprinkling coal dust on the ice, they pump carbon into the air. As Urumqi Number One shows, this is alarmingly effective. Long after we stopped trying, mankind has mastered glacier melting. Unfortunately, when it comes to putting ice back on the mountains, we still do not have the first idea.

In Xinjiang the evidence of climate change and environmental degradation is undeniable, but that is at least a spur for action. Policymakers have started to realize that the current path of economic growth leads toward a dead end. Even Madame Qian is talking about ecological restoration. Elsewhere in China too, scientists and entrepreneurs are looking for climate solutions and profits. Architects, engineers, and urban planners are trying to find a technological substitute to the hydrocarbon economy. Civil society activists are promoting a more sustainable lifestyle. The Scientific Outlook on Development espoused by President Water and Premier Earth aims to create an eco-civilization. But how much progress has China made toward an alternative model of development? In search of an answer I headed to Dongbei, the northeast, to assess the country's capacity for reinvention.

Northeast
Alternatives

★

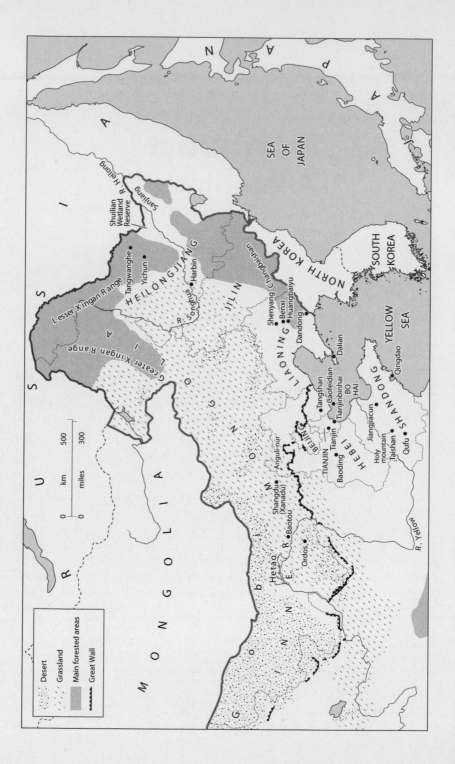

13

Science versus Math
Tianjin, Hebei, and Liaoning

China is a country where once they realize, "Gee, we have to do
something," then they leap forward.
—Suntech founder Shi Zhengrong, the world's first solar billionaire

The egghead leading China's charge toward an efficient, low-carbon
future almost never made it to university. Professor Li Can grew up
during the Cultural Revolution with a politically unfortunate habit: he
loved to study. This went down well with his high school teachers, but, in
those days, it was not much good being a top-level student if you were a
second-rate revolutionary.

By 1975, the nation's universities had been closed for almost a decade.
Business was still frowned upon. For a bright young man, the only career
tracks were through the Communist Party or the government. Lacking the
ideological zeal for either, Li's only choice after graduation was to return
to his home in a remote corner of Gansu and become a barefoot doctor.
His high school education was all the qualification he needed to perform
acupuncture and rudimentary medicine around local villages near the old
Silk Road.

This was a period of massive transition for China, but the changes
almost passed Li by. After Mao died, a new leadership took over. Soon
after, they announced the full reopening of the universities. Li did not hear
about it for weeks because nobody in his village had a telephone or a radio.

Fortunately, the deputy headmaster of his old school remembered the brilliant pupil who had been forced to return to the desert, He cycled 30 kilometers to Li's home to tell him the news and recommended he join the first wave of students to take the Gaokao entrance exam. There was barely any time to prepare and few teaching materials. In those conditions, the future head of China's clean energy research lab did well to come forty-ninth out of 150 students in his region. None of the prestigious universities would accept him. Desperate to secure a place, he applied for a course at a second-rate university in a field he had little interest in.

"I chose chemistry. To be honest, it was not my favorite subject. I had always preferred math and literature, but I thought I would have more chance of securing a place with chemistry. You cannot understand what it was like then."[1]

I had a soft spot for Li's generation. The wave of university students who came of age as the country removed the ideological blinkers of the Cultural Revolution tended to be more open-minded, down-to-earth, and appreciative of education than others. "I can still do acupuncture," the former bare-foot doctor said with a smile as he poured a fresh cup of green tea. He had come a long way from curing desert villagers with traditional medicine.

We were sitting in Li's spacious study in the Dalian National Laboratory for Clean Energy. The research center had just been established to spearhead China's efforts to escape the energy crunch and ease the risks of global warming. Li was the first head. He was engaging company. As he talked about the future of China, the world, and energy, it was clear he had huge ambitions.

"Solar is the most important renewable energy source for China's future. Wind and biomass are good, but their potential is limited. With solar, though, we can do more. There is a lot of land available for solar farms in the deserts of Gansu and Xinjiang. We have calculated that if we covered just a third of those areas with photovoltaic cells then we could meet the current energy needs of the entire country."

That would mean filling the old Silk Road with billions of solar panels. Professor Li's old home in Gansu would become a power hub for the nation. The barren deserts would be transformed into China's greatest asset. If any nation could build such a model it was likely to be China, which had the land, the scale of vision, and the manufacturing resources. It was a thrilling prospect. Li had high-level backing to make it work. The science and technology minister, Wan Gang, told me solar was the best long-term hope.

"The sun has more than enough energy for all our needs, but we currently lack the understanding to utilize that," he said. "Since 2007, we have been using more solar power, and I think we will increase in the future. The priority is to strengthen research and build a strong business model."

But realization was still a long way off. In the short and medium term, the boffins (research scientists) working under Li would work on ways to improve the efficiency of coal. Major experiments were taking place across the country. In some cases the work was more advanced than anything in the U.S. or Europe, suggesting China might one day become a leader in low-carbon technology.[2]

It was heady stuff but exactly what I was looking for in the northeast rust belt, where I planned to put "Scientific Development" under the microscope. Could brainpower and money solve China's environmental problems and make the country a green superpower that could save the world from the accumulated side effects of industrialization and overconsumption? Cities were trying to go green. Industry was moving toward greater efficiency, and the state was planning to ramp up spending on research and development to levels close to those of the U.S., Germany, and Japan.[3] Businesses and local governments were generating a new boom in wind farms, photovoltaic cell manufacturing, electric cars, "eco-cities," and smart-grid technology.

The government had just announced a new front line of the intellectual effort to produce more light and heat with less smoke and waste: the National Laboratory for Clean Energy. If climate change was the biggest challenge facing the planet, and China was the country most responsible for greenhouse gas emissions, then this laboratory was where much of the hope had to be focused in the search for a scientific solution to save the planet.

It was based in the Dalian Institute of Chemical Physics, a reassuringly boffin-friendly environment. Nerdy types wandered through a pleasantly green campus. The only distraction was a giant electronic screen that at first appeared to be made for displaying the latest football scores or stock indices. But look a little closer and the data was good solid science: "Test run of new vanadium redox battery-powered display. Time since last recharge: 30 days, 17 hours." Inside the buildings, the corridor walls were decorated with complex flowcharts and compound diagrams. In the workrooms, students with impressively unkempt hair had their noses deep in lovingly worn research papers and books. The laboratories fitted the 1950s mad-scientist stereotype: semichaotic and crammed full of spectrometers, chemical lasers, and manifold catalyzing experiments, most of which seemed to be housed inside Robbie-the-Robot stainless-steel casings.

The changing role of the institute has tracked trends in resource availability. Founded in 1949, its original goal was to find alternative supplies of energy. Most of the scientists worked on synthetic replacements for oil, which was then in desperately short supply in China. Their role changed completely in 1959 with the discovery of the huge Daqing oil fields in Heilongjiang.[4] After that, the institute quickly reinvented itself as an intellectual resource for the petrochemical industry. By the time of my visit, the wheel had turned again. With more than three-quarters of Daqing's reserves gone, scientists were switching in droves to renewable energy and coal-conversion technology. In their labs, they could see the future and—in the long term, at least—it was green.

China planned to invest about $300 billion to provide 15 percent of its power from renewables by 2020.[5] But far bigger sums would be invested in "new energy," including "clean coal" technology. This would ensure that, for the medium term, the color of development would remain a smoky brown. For the next twenty years, and probably much longer, China would be unable to kick its coal-puffing habit. The government has yet to set a target for when its carbon emissions might peak. Wan, the minister, told me he personally expected the peak between 2030 and 2040. Other officials put it closer to 2050. There was simply no other energy available to fuel the massive economic growth that the government was planning. All the scientists could do was try to ease the damage to the nation's lungs and the world's climate.

But Li insisted a real change was possible. He aimed to use solar energy to convert carbon dioxide into hydrogen, which could then be used as clean fuel. Under his instruction, scientists will focus on catalytic processes to improve the efficiency of coal, through conversion to natural gas, and to deal with polluting emissions, such as sulfur and carbon dioxide, by converting them into other fuels such as methanol.

Many foreign scientists and economists believe it is essential for China to capture and store carbon dioxide so it would not add to the volume of greenhouse gas in the atmosphere.[6] But Li was skeptical. "Burying carbon dioxide is expensive, energy intensive, and potentially dangerous. I think it's better to find a way to convert it into other chemicals that we can use."[7]

This was already being done in the institute's labs, but the processes were decades away from being commercially viable.[8] China's best short-term hope for coal was to improve its efficiency through conversion to natural gas or methanol. Strategic goals were at play too. As Madame Qian had told me earlier, the government wanted to tap Xinjiang's massive coal reserves. This rich vein of fossil fuels had been left underground because of the cost of transporting heavy coal 3,000 kilometers to the factories on the coast. But if the coal could be converted to gas, it could flow cheaply along the west-east pipelines. This would be more efficient, but it could hardly be called clean energy.

I asked Li if he believed global warming was a man-made phenomenon. "The climate has changed. My grandfather told me that his grandfather had told him that our home in northern China used to be a forest. That made a big impact on me. Now our home is a desert," he said. "I haven't personally researched the causes so I don't have firm beliefs, but Nobel scientists say carbon is responsible and I trust them. Even though I am not really a hundred percent convinced, I think mankind needs to err on the side of caution by trying to reduce greenhouse gases."

Again, this was echoed by Minister Wan: "Human activities definitely have an impact on the climate, but the question is how much of an impact. That requires scientific research," he told me. "There are different views about climate change. My role is to create an environment in which scientists can discuss this. Science requires democracy."

As an affected nation and a responsible member of the world community, he said China has to take precautionary action immediately. "The goal is to change lifestyles and modes of production, so we cannot wait for the research findings to come out before we act."

This opened up the business opportunity of a generation. China moved into the clean technology sector at a characteristically rapid speed. From 2005 until 2009, the capacity of wind power generation doubled every year. Car and battery makers promised to outstrip their U.S., Japanese, and European rivals in the race to mass-produce electric and hybrid cars. Plans were unveiled for a more efficient "smart grid" to distribute electricity. Already the world's biggest manufacturer and exporter of photovoltaic panels, China launched a program to install millions of solar heaters and mulled feed-in tariff incentives to further promote solar power. The world's first solar billionaire, Shi Zhengrong, the founder and CEO of Suntech, had previously told me he expected his company to grow into a global energy giant like BP or Shell.

But there was a danger of moving too far, too fast. Low-carbon economic zones sprang up across the country. Municipalities quickly realized they could reinvent themselves and secure investment by talking the language of "eco," "green" and "environmentally friendly."

The northeast needed environmental healing and economic stimulation more than almost anywhere else in China. I was touring Tianjin, Hebei, and Liaoning, the provinces that formed the rusted upper lip of the Bohai Sea. In the era of a command economy, this had been the channel from the industrial blacklands of the northeast to the most polluted sea in China. A decade after the collapse of many old state-owned factories, the sprawling cities and mining villages of this region were trying to reinvent themselves as clean-tech centers and environmental pioneers. The result was part green makeover, part science fiction.

The journey had started in Tianjin, China's third-biggest city and the world's fifth-biggest port. Its name, which means Heavenly Ford, dates back to 1404, when it was still a small trading post. Now a megacity, its reputation was anything but celestial. On the way, my assistant told me a joke. "An enemy bomber is on a mission to blow up Tianjin. He flies across the Bohai Sea but, when he reaches the city, he turns the plane around and returns without dropping a bomb. 'What are you doing?' ask his commanders on the radio. The pilot replies: 'We don't need to waste our explosives. It looks like someone has already destroyed it.'"

Tianjin was still unlikely to be marketing itself as China's premier honeymoon destination, but the city was modernizing impressively. The first surprise was the sleek high-speed train from Beijing that sped along the rails at 335 kilometers per hour, faster than any train I had ever been on in the UK. Advertisements for turbine manufacturers indicated the city's growing role in the wind energy sector, which had doubled in size for five years in a row mostly by putting up turbines along the old Silk Road. Tianjin's ambitions were grander still. It wanted to create a new model eco-city.

I was on my way to a former dump site on the shore of the most polluted sea in China, where the technocratic governments of China and Singapore were pooling expertise and finance to build a new, green urban community of 350,000 people. Due for completion in 2020, it was touted as the most environmentally friendly city in China and an example for developing nations across the planet.

The Tianjin Binhai New Area was more than an hour's drive from the station. We had trouble finding it. The area was not well enough established to merit proper signposts. For most of the previous fifty years, the alkali-polluted flats had been an outlet for industrial discharge pipes. In the middle of that morose expanse we found bulldozers clearing a stretch of land. And in the middle of that was a single, lonely, bright-orange exhibition center, where I went to meet one of the architects behind the project.

Wang Meng was in an office filled with models: balsa-wood shopping malls, Perspex factories, and paper skyscrapers. His job was to scale them up to full size. The young bespectacled planner said it was a childhood dream come true.

"Model making was my hobby. I loved it so much that I used to enter competitions. One year I came fifth out of the whole of Tianjin city with a plane powered by a rubber band. It flew for a minute and a half."

Twenty years on, he was attempting to make a rather more ambitious project fly with alternative energy. The Sino-Singapore Tianjin Eco-City was being billed as a model metropolis, a standard setter that would help the fast-urbanizing nation turn from gray to green. Within ten years it was supposed to get up to 20 percent of its power from renewable sources. Instead of winding up rubber bands, Wang would tap the spinning rotors of wind farms and the geothermal heat contained in the earth.[9] Domestic water use would be kept below 120 liters per person per day, half supplied by rain capture and recycled gray water.

For optimum energy efficiency, every building was be insulated, double glazed, and made entirely of materials that reach the government's green standards. More than 60 percent of all waste was supposed to be recycled. To get car journeys down by 90 percent, a light railway would pass near to every home, and communities would be zoned to ensure everyone could walk to shops, schools, and clinics. It would be greener than almost any other city in China, with protected areas for wild grasses, such as bulrush, hairy uraria, and wild chrysanthemum, and wetland birds, including purple herons, flying snipes, and black-winged stilts. Overall, there would be an average 12 square meters of parkland, grassland, or wetland for each resident. Environmental health would be further enhanced by an on-site water treatment plant to ensure that all tap water was potable, by free sports facilities, and by a commitment to keep particulate matter in the air below 100 parts per cubic meter for more than four out of every five days. That, at least, was the plan.

But Wang, the deputy director of the construction bureau, admitted it would be tough to build a green city the size of Bristol in a single decade. It was not the scale that bothered him. Like many Chinese urban planners, Wang had been playing a real-life version of SimCity, the virtual megalopolis building game, for many years.[10] But the environmental goals were new. And he was not sure if they could be achieved.

Eco-city plans in China were not going well. The most ambitious at Dongtan near Shanghai, which was designed by the British architectural firm Arup, had ground to a halt several years earlier.[11] The Tianjin project had a greater chance of success because it was being run and funded by the central government. China's leaders had invested a great deal of political capital in the project. When Premier Wen Jiabao visited the site, he expressed hope that it would be "practical, replicable, and scalable."

More important, it needed to be genuine. If the eco-label at Tianjin proved to be nothing more than a marketing gimmick to sell up-market real estate, it would quickly become an environmental cul-de-sac. If, on the other hand, it could reach stringent renewable energy, waste recycling, and carbon goals, there was a chance it could be followed by others among the 400 new similar-sized communities that are due to spring up across China over the next twenty years.[12]

On the way out, we passed a scale replica of the project's first phase, a community for 85,000 people. Wang and the rest of his team had until the end of 2010 to turn the model into reality.

"Scientific Development" is about planning the planned economy better, about moving from quantity to quality, about building a new smart model for growth. The country is staking its environmental future on design and technology. This is where the government is playing to its modern strengths. Along with a stronger army and economy, the Communist Party has been trying to build academic institutions capable of matching the West in the "soft power" battleground of thought.[13]

By allying this brainpower with the nation's growing financial muscle, the engineers in the politburo hope to solve the problems of growth with more growth and the problems of science with better science. In this way of thinking, man is not the problem. He is the solution. Everything else—Nature, God, Fate—can be outsmarted. There is no need to step back or slow down. To cope with the multiples of a growing population, rising wealth, and increasing consumption, China needs to reinvent itself. Essentially the challenge is to solve a math problem with science.

The scale of the task was evident as I drove north following the coast of the Bohai Sea, past stacks of containers, more construction sites, the foundations of the "GreenGen" coal-gasification center, a thermal power plant, and then desolate tidal flats and wetlands as far as the eye could see. Soon after crossing the border with Hebei, the land dried and firmed, the road widened, and we saw the telltale construction of another breathtakingly enormous development zone. Five years ago, Caofeidian was a small, sparsely populated island surrounded by tidal flats. Today, it is China's most vast reclamation project. By the end of 2010, the government plans to make this area a model of "industrial ecology" with 300,000 workers, the country's largest coal port, the biggest steel facilities, and a giant petrochemical processing plant.[14] China already has ten of the world's twenty biggest ports. Caofeidian would be another. It would be a base for heavy-industry giants, such as the Huadian power company, PetroChina, and Capital Steel, which previously had plants near heavily populated cities. By relocating and upgrading the furnaces and smokestacks, the government is cleaning up the air and improving efficiency.[15] The latter is essential. China's energy consumption is surging faster than that of almost any other country, but much of it is wasted. For every dollar of economic activity, the country needs three to eight times more energy than developed nations.[16]

The roads were filled with bulldozers and trucks. Pile drivers, pumps, and *ketouji* cut busy silhouettes against the flat, gray horizon. Tens of thousands of laborers were at work on a new home for Shougang, or Capital Iron and Steel, formerly Beijing's biggest polluter.[17] At the sea's edge were newly completed berths for a giant container and coal port. Most of the planned buildings were still only models in the local exhibition center. The building housed so many scale displays of new cities, factories, ports, residential blocks, office districts, and oil facilities that it resembled a giant toy shop. Even if only half of the plans were realized, this stretch of land was certain to be one of the planet's mightiest powerhouses. If the entire project was completed, the 50 square kilometers of Caofeidian would have an industrial output bigger than many countries in the world. The scale of ambition was enormous. But, for me, this was no longer mind-boggling; huge had become the norm.

On a recent visit to London I had a strange sensation as I walked across Waterloo footbridge. The metropolis I had been raised in suddenly felt like a village. St. Paul's Cathedral, so magnificent in my memory, seemed to have shrunk. In scale and significance, it looked puny in comparison with Beijing's CCTV's "Big Trousers" building, the "Bird's Nest" Olympic Stadium, and the "Egg" Grand National Theater.

Visions through time are telescopic. My British past seemed miniaturized, smaller than everything I saw from my Beijing window. But also the Chinese future was magnifying the present. Perhaps this was because I had seen so many tiny models of planned Chinese developments scaled up into giant industrial complexes, office blocks, or residential high-rises. A few years ago, almost every big city in China had its own Mini-Me: a huge model showing every completed and planned building in it. In Beijing, Shanghai, and Tianjin, I felt like Gulliver in Lilliput as I looked down at these dense clusters of little gray plastic buildings conceived by architects and urban planners. Today I find myself staring up at those same buildings, towering above me in steel and glass like grown-up children: outwardly mature but still somehow vulnerable.

Similarly with China's environment, it is easy to lose perspective. On the one hand, the country is taking bigger strides to develop renewable energy than any other nation. But on the other, the benefits are being outweighed by an energy demand that is growing even faster. Like Gulliver, a handful of huge, high-profile, low-carbon projects are being swamped by millions of tiny, barely registered, high-carbon habits. To overcome this, it will not be enough to throw up buildings; lifestyles will have to be redesigned.

We moved inland on the overnight train to the city of Shenyang, the clunky buckle on the northeast rust belt. The provincial capital of Liaoning was formerly the center of the Manchu empire. When the Japanese created the Manchukuo puppet state in 1932, the colonial administration turned

Shenyang into an industrial base, which it has remained ever since. In the 1970s, it was one of China's three biggest economic powerhouses, along with Shanghai and Tianjin, but the city's prestige declined in the following decades along with the fortunes of many state-owned heavy industries.

When I first visited in 2003, it was Grimsville: dirty, poor, and enveloped in one of the country's filthiest hazes. Locals recalled the sky being so full of soot and sulfur that the birds turned black and clothes would fall apart because of constant scrubbing that never managed to remove the grime. To protect their lungs, many wore surgical masks when they ventured outside.

Today, however, Shenyang boasts one of the most improved environments in China.[18] In 2004, it was designated a model city for environmental protection by the China State Environmental Protection Administration. That such a notoriously dirty industrial center could clean up its act gave hope to a nation that the peak of pollution might have passed.

The improvement in air quality has been achieved largely through a mass dechimneyfication campaign. From 2003, the authorities began tearing down smokestacks at the rate of three per day.[19] After practically wiping out the city's small 2–3 ton boilers, the chimney cullers have raised their aim to the 10-tonners. Locals marveled at the change in the skyline as clusters of small stacks were torn down and replaced by fewer, taller, cleaner, more efficient ones that belched their pollution higher into the atmosphere, where it could be dispersed away from the population centers.

The Hun and Pu rivers no longer run black and their banks are lined with trees thanks to a municipal greening campaign. In the north of the city, the Shenbei district has been developed with leafy streets and high-rises topped with solar panels. Nearby, another eco-city is being designed by Tongji University and U.S. architects. Farther south, the concrete campus at Shenyang Jianzhu University's school of architecture has been brightened up by a grid of lush rice fields designed by the country's leading landscape gardener, Yu Kongjian.

Yu's book *The Art of Survival* sets forth one of the most lucid arguments for an ecological rethink of China's development model. He traces the nation's current problems back thousands of years to the first ornamental garden, an attempt to re-create the mythical Land of Peach Blossom at Yuanmingyuan, the summer palace. This vain attempt to improve upon nature, he told me, marked a move away from Taoist ideals. Instead of ecological productivity, he argued, leaders have foolishly spent two thousand years pursuing artifice and consumption. Cities were a symbol of that demise.

"The urbanization process we follow today is a path to death. Chinese culture kills people. It deprives people of productivity," Yu said. "Yet, we carry on with this high culture. We enjoy Chinese gardens with their deformed trees. This is a sick aesthetic."

The Harvard-trained landscape gardener's mix of ancient tradition and radical modernity is immensely popular and increasingly influential in China.[20] Yu's company, Turenscape, is expanding. Government officials consult him about improving what he calls "ecological security," a benevolently self-interested approach to the problem. Its essence is strikingly simple: Don't fix the environment because it looks nice; fix it because your survival is at stake.

Yu advocates restoring natural watercourses, cultivating wild grasses, and rebuilding the "eco-infrastructure." He has declared war on concrete, which he tears up whenever possible. Essentially, he is ordering a strategic retreat by mankind, giving nature the chance to restore itself. His landscaped areas certainly look more attractive than most urban planning of the past fifty years.[21] They are also more productive. At the architecture school in Shenyang, students now plant seedlings every May in the paddy fields he introduced.

"I was asked to do something that was beautiful and unique. So I said, why not grow rice? It costs nothing and it is beautiful in three months," Yu explained in fluent English. "The long-lost tradition of rice culture becomes part of campus culture." Some of the crop is gift-wrapped for visitors. The rest is left for the birds. "To give something back to nature," as Yu put it.

I watched as clouds of sparrows flew back and forth between the trees and bushes in the campus, lightening the atmosphere with twittering and movement. China's environmental thinking had come a long way since Mao declared a sparrow-extermination campaign during the Great Leap Forward.[22]

But the legacy of grim materialism still dominated the cityscape. For all of the recent improvements, Shenyang was still basically an ugly, gray, inefficient city. More than the environment, most residents were interested in earning a good salary and improving their living standards. That usually meant bigger homes, more appliances, and a growing hunger for energy. Over the previous decade, Shenyang's urban population had crept above the 5 million mark and the size of the average home had almost tripled. Those extra people in those bigger houses liked to be two degrees warmer in the winter and two degrees cooler in the summer than ten years earlier, which meant more electricity had to be generated for heaters and air conditioners, not to mention their bigger televisions, refrigerators, freezers, and microwave ovens. As was the case across much of the nation, the housing stock was in dire condition.[23] Building materials were hugely energy-inefficient compared with the more expensive ones used in the West.[24] Solving these problems would necessitate strong leadership at the top of society, a change of values at the bottom, and incentives for businessmen in the middle to make money by selling green products. I met a consultant trying to realize all three.

Dongbei folk tend to be of the hearty variety with a reputation as straight talkers and heavy drinkers. Wang Zhenxin fitted at least part of the stereotype. The Shenyang People's Congress representative had a bluff charisma that would serve him well if democracy ever came to China and forced him to face a popular vote. Without that distraction, he was devoting his efforts to the building of a green energy company.

Like many start-ups, his firm, Xindi Consulting, was a hodgepodge of projects ranging from photovoltaic-walled apartment blocks in the city center to fruit plantations for biomass production in the desert. With barely half a dozen staff, most of them recent university graduates, the firm was full of dynamism but short of personnel. Wang was sufficiently larger than life to fill in the gaps. He served as president, inventor, consultant, and investment manager. He was also the chief lobbyist, using his political position to put pressure on the government to buy solar.

"In China, bottom-up change is impossible, so nothing gets done unless leaders understand the problems. But they don't listen. You have to tell them again and again," he said with a smile. "The People's Congress demanded meetings on solar power every ten days until the government relented. Soon after that, they ordered an extra 150,000 panels." The water in more than one in every twenty homes in Shenyang was now heated by solar power, and the city had set one of the most ambitious targets in China for expansion of this form of renewable energy.[25]

But Wang's proudest achievement as a legislator was the proposal in 2000 of a bill to allow residents independent control of the heating in their houses. This was a radical step away from a fundamental tenet of communism that everyone should be exactly as warm as everyone else. Throughout northern China, public heating comes on line on November 15 and switches off on March 15, regardless of the temperature.[26] The waste is phenomenal. On warm winter days, many people open their windows because it is the only control they have over the heat inside their homes. Wang wanted to end this with a metering system. But his moment of glory was not to be: his bill was amended at the last moment when it was decreed that householders should have neither knowledge nor control of their energy consumption. The proposal for individual meters was blocked. All that was new was an external on-off switch for each house that would make it easier for the power company to cut off individual supplies for nonpayment of bills.

"The system was changed for the benefit of the management companies rather than the environment," Wang said, shaking his head. "The managers didn't want the heat measured because they thought the tenants might complain if some ended up paying more than others."

He consoled himself with the thought that the failed legislation had at least raised awareness of the link between price and demand. But the failure of Wang's bill encapsulates what has happened to the entire Chinese economy. Out has gone the "everyone-the-same" treatment of communism. In has come the "more-economic-activity-the-better" ethos of top-down capitalism. Individual consumers are not given the opportunity to make efficiency improvements that might weaken business growth or social stability. The environment is barely a consideration.

Wang suggested people were used to having their fate decided by others.

"When I was young we had no choice about our field of study. The Communist Party decided everything. I wanted to be a mathematician, but they enrolled me in university as an engineer. It was fate. I am glad now. Energy efficiency has become more and more important."

He insisted he was a public servant first and an entrepreneur second, but if it was possible to combine the two, why not? Money was one of the best incentives for change known to man. As I was about to leave, Wang opened a huge bag of sunflower seeds and invited me to tuck in. "Before you go, I just want to sketch out for you my design for new solar-heating panels," he said. "We have a good thing going here. But we need more foreign investment. Could you be a matchmaker for me?"

I would have liked to help. International cooperation and business incentives will be essential if the world is to descend safely from the peak of fossil-fuel consumption. In global climate-change talks, China's focus is on technology transfer. It wants rich, advanced countries to share or release patents on cutting-edge equipment, materials, and know-how that will improve energy efficiency and reduce pollution. Europe, however, puts a priority on economic incentives for the reduction of emissions of carbon and other greenhouse gases. The United States has tended to take a more market-oriented approach by letting fuel prices rise.[27] This essentially shows each system playing to what it considers its strengths. Europe's proposed solution is politically managed, China's technical, and the U.S. economic. If they cannot find the right balance between their different outlooks and interests, there is a danger that competition to consume resources will surpass cooperation to conserve them. This will not just manifest itself in a hotter, more hostile global climate. It will probably lead to a darker, more belligerent world.

In the border city of Dandong, southeast of Shenyang, I had no need to imagine a planet without energy—I could see this dark alternative future simply by glancing across the Yalu River. On the other side was North Korea, one of the few nations in the world that had slid backward, that had deindustrialized. The difference with China was staggeringly evident at night, when the opposite bank of the river was cloaked in an inky blackness, while the Chinese side was a blaze of multicolored neon, amber streetlamps, car headlights, and illuminated advertising billboards. The Friendship Bridge spanning the river was decked out with fairy lights that pulsed red, green, and purple. But they stopped halfway across. The Korean half of the bridge was black even though it was just a short distance from Sinuju, the second-biggest city in North Korea. The same was true on a national scale. Satellite images of northeast Asia by night showed China, South Korea, and Japan sparkling with broad clusters of urban lighting, while dark North Korea stared out from the middle like a black pupil in the white of an eye.[28]

This was not always the case. In 1970, Pyongyang was one of the most developed cities in Asia. The nation's economy was bigger than that of South Korea. It stagnated, along with much of the former Eastern Bloc, during the 1980s, then slipped into reverse in 1989, when the Soviet Union broke up and stopped providing cheap oil. With few energy supplies of its own, North Korea's industry collapsed, agricultural production plummeted, and an isolated government plowed what little budget it had into the military.[29] By the mid-1990s, millions were starving. Estimates of how many died in the famine range from tens of thousands to more than a million. The biggest operation in the history of the UN World Food Programme eased the food crisis, but energy remains scarce.

To avoid such a future in China and elsewhere, leaders need to prepare for the day when the fossil-fuel tap runs dry. Unless consumer habits change dramatically or technology makes a quantum leap, there might yet come a point when drastic North Korean–style belt-tightening becomes necessary everywhere.

Eco-cities and green buildings could help to allay this risk. But they will not solve China's problems unless similar measures are taken in the countryside, where the majority of China's population live.[30] The average income of the 740 million rural dwellers is 30 percent of that in the city, but farmers are still far richer than ten years earlier. As they buy more household appliances, bigger television sets, and cars, Chinese country folk are gobbling up more of the world's food, energy, and raw materials. Although farmers have traditionally been more conscious of recycling, their modern consumption habits are potentially more damaging because, in the countryside, it is harder to make efficiency gains through public transport usage, concentrated power generation, and shared waste treatment. The agricultural workforce was traveling more, migrating to the cities in search of work, returning for harvests and spring festival. As we saw in Huaxi, the Number One Village in China (chapter 6), village economies are also moving into new areas such as mining, food processing, and manufacturing.

The government would like to make rural lifestyles more sustainable. In the snow-clad hills of Liaoning, officials have collaborated with a local entrepreneur and foreign architects to try to create a model sustainable village. But, as I quickly found out, the results from this marriage of technology and business are anything but encouraging.

The taxi driver insisted we pay 20 yuan extra to go to Huangbaiyu, or

"Yellow Cyprus Valley," because the roads were so bad she would have to drive more slowly than usual. Initially, I suspected she was exaggerating to talk up the fare. But after an hour winding along icy, bumpy, hilly roads, I realized she had been generous. She was also free with advice. Assuming we were foreign investors, she warned us not to waste our money. "Many people in this area will cheat you, so be careful. They promise good returns on all sorts of schemes, but the economy is so bad that most people lose out."

It was a sobering introduction to Huangbaiyu, where a great deal of time, money, and political capital had been invested in what was touted as China's first sustainable village. With the support of Deng Nan, the daughter of former paramount leader Deng Xiaoping, and financial and technical backing from the United States, a local tycoon had constructed forty modern, environmentally friendly homes at a cost of 8 million yuan.[31] Unlike the average Liaoning farm cottage, they were, in theory at least, built with renewable materials, thickly insulated, and powered by biogas. They even had their own wastewater treatment facilities. As the first fruit of the China-U.S. Center for Sustainable Development, Huangbaiyu was initially touted in 2004 as a shining example of international cooperation on the environment. But nobody was boasting about the project anymore. In fact, local officials and businessmen seemed suspiciously reluctant to talk about it at all. Although I applied for interviews weeks in advance, they all insisted they were too busy to see me.

The reason for the reticence became clear as soon as I arrived. Two years after completion, the eco-village was virtually empty. Locals complained the new homes were overpriced and poorly built. The only two residents told me they had moved in under duress. They had no tap water, their ceilings leaked, and they had to cut down trees for fuel because the biogas supply was not working. The developer was so short of cash that he had been forced to sell his entire holding. Locals said the new owner planned to use the eco-village to house workers at a new bronze and iron mine that would soon be carved into the nearby hills. All in all, the project was a disaster.

"There is nothing good about it," said Li Qinghong, one of the two disgruntled residents. "I only moved in because my old home burned down and the authorities told me I would not get any compensation unless I resettled here. I much preferred my old home. It had more space and was built better. In this place, they skimped on construction. The materials provided by the U.S. never got used."

Villagers put much of the blame on the colorful local businessman who wooed Deng's daughter into backing the project. Dai Xiaolong's gift of gab and willingness to take risks were remarkable even in a nation that had come to venerate its entrepreneurs. A former soldier and newspaper employee in the local industrial city of Benxi, he headed north to Heilongjing to make his fortune. After several years he came back with a small amount of seed capital and a head full of big ideas. He persuaded Huangbaiyu's villagers to give him land and money to start a soy-sauce and pickled-cabbage factory. The business soon collapsed, but Dai was undaunted. He convinced the local school to use its tax-free status to set up a distillery. Tianyuan baijiu was a hit, but the success was not enough for Dai, who was in a hurry to get rich. He opened more than a dozen distilleries, then expanded into slaughterhouses, fish farms, and tourist resorts.

"It was great for a while," recalled Mu Baozhi, a teacher at the school. "Villagers who invested 50,000 yuan in Dai's enterprise were getting returns of 9,000 yuan per year. But it wasn't well managed. In the end, it all went bust. Dai ended up owing over a hundred million to his investors."

Mu kindly invited us into his old-style cottage for a hearty lunch of fish, rice, and mountain vegetables. The only insulation was a sheet of plastic taped over the window and a green quilt that covered the door, but the home was far cozier than the empty eco-residences. The old teacher, a Manchu, had lost money investing in Dai's firms, but he still held the entrepreneur in high regard as a big thinker who genuinely wanted to embrace environmental sustainability, albeit as part of a wider strategy to build a personal empire.

"The sustainable eco-project was part of Dai's plan to take control of the whole village," Mu explained. "He wanted everyone to work for him. To do that, he had to provide housing and jobs for everyone. That's where the eco-homes came in. But he failed to attract factories, so there was no employment incentive for people to leave their farmland."

After lunch, we trudged back through the snow to the eco-village. But our talk with the second resident was interrupted. A member of the management team suddenly turned up and insisted we accompany him to the office. Having previously insisted they were unavailable, local officials now wanted to put in their side of the story.

The project coordinator, Xie Baoxing, met us in a room dominated by a large scale model of the eco-village encased in glass. We sat on opposite sides and, at first, I felt we were on opposite wavelengths as he extolled the energy-saving benefits of the project while I recalled the reality of stacks of firewood, empty homes, and unhappy tenants.

"How can it work if the people who live there don't like it?" I asked.

"They are unhappy because their homes burned down. We gave them an alternative place to live. They don't like it. But we can fix the problems. If you come back next year, it will be completely different."

"But it hasn't gone as planned at all, has it?"

"We can't say we are a model. This is an experiment. We are moving ahead through trial and error."

"Do you regret starting this project?"

"No, our country is committed to sustainable development. All business has a degree of risk. The problems here are not so big. We can overcome them."

I sympathized. Xie was not to blame, and he was right that there were bound to be hiccups in the search for a sustainable future. But I departed Huangbaiyu unconvinced that it would ever succeed. If the community was a model of anything, it was how not to construct an eco-village: Dongtan on a smaller scale.

We drove back to the nearest city, Benxi, to track down Dai, but he was busy reinventing himself once again and was nowhere to be found. Having failed to make a fortune with an eco-village, he was now reportedly moving into mining. Nobody considered this a conflict of ideals. It was simple pragmatic materialism, the spirit of the age. Dai was not alone in dreaming up new schemes to be rich in Benxi. The city was another dot on the map where more than a million people were crowding to get ahead. Failing eco-cities were the least of the region's problems.

At the bus station, I was surprised by the unusually tight security. Police were checking every passenger's ID, something I had previously seen only in Xinjiang after a murderous attack on soldiers.

I asked the reason.

"This is China. All sorts of things happen here," a bus conductor replied with considered vagueness.

"Like what?"

"Terrorism."

"By whom?" I hadn't heard of any separatist or religious extremists in this part of China before.

It took five minutes to get an answer. I was told the checks had started the previous year for fear of reprisals from "terrorist" investors who had lost a fortune in a bizarre 33-million-yuan ant-farming pyramid-selling scheme. Many staked their life savings on boxes of ants that they were promised would guarantee them rich returns from the traditional medicine industry. When the scam inevitably collapsed, 36,000 people lost their investment. Some were plunged into bankruptcy. Many protested. Others attempted to travel to Beijing to petition the central government. One committed suicide.[32] The businessman behind the scheme, Wang Zhendong, was sentenced to death, but this harsh penalty failed to placate the enraged investors. The ant farmers are now considered the biggest security threat in Benxi. Salvador Dalí could not have painted a more surreal picture of China's business landscape.

A brighter, more orderly canvas was on display at the final stop on my journey through the former rust belt. Dalian has arguably taken a bigger technological leap than any other city to clean up its environment. Home to 6 million people, this giant port has won accolades and investment over the past ten years as a result of cleaning up its air and opening up its development zones to green energy labs and high-tech companies. I was told that if any existing Chinese megalopolis could claim to be an eco-city, it was Dalian.

I woke up on my first morning in the city to that rarest of treats in urban China: clear skies. Against a sharp blue background, the red national flags fluttering atop government buildings seemed to blaze with pride. Clean, modern, and open, this was smart China at its best. While Shanghai was plagued by an overemphasis on fashion, Guangzhou by money, and Beijing by power, Dalian was blessed by moderate amounts of all three, along with sea breezes that helped to blow away what little pollution was emitted by the high-tech industries that concentrated here. This city boasted the cleanest urban air in China, with all but a few days of the year meeting the national "blue sky" standard.[33]

The transformation was remarkable. Twenty years earlier, Dalian had been a center for heavy industry with air as foul as the rest of the rust belt.

But the collapse of the old state-owned industries in the nineties proved a blessing. The former mayor, Bo Xilai, put parks and lawns on the sites of many dismantled factories (earning the nickname "Grass Bo" in the process), upgraded the city's power plants, relocated the remaining heavy industry outside the city center, and invested heavily in wastewater treatment and public transport, which is now used for 45 percent of journeys— the highest level in China. In the process, Dalian reinvented itself as a clean, modern base for software and informational technology companies from Japan, South Korea, Taiwan, and Hong Kong. Bo, the son of Communist Party "immortal" Bo Yibo, was rewarded with promotion to the post of Liaoning governor, and the city was chosen to host the summer Davos conference.[34] Average incomes in Dalian are high and living standards are considered to be among the best in China.[35]

"We have come to realize that a good environment gives us a competitive advantage," the current mayor, Xia Deren, told me in the Japanese-built city hall. "This is a recent discovery. Practice has taught us the benefits of clean air and water in attracting talented personnel and high-value-added companies."

Xia claimed to be going even further than his predecessor in greening Dalian. By his own reckoning, he spent more than a quarter of his time on policies to reduce emissions and improve energy efficiency. The city was pioneering the manufacture and adoption of hybrid buses and the hydrogen fuel cells that will be necessary if cars are ever to run solely on clean and efficient electricity.[36] The city had also built up one of China's biggest wind-power production bases and won the right to host China's first national clean-energy laboratory. By 2013, said Xia, Dalian planned to go a step further than any other Chinese city in reducing carbon emissions by replacing all of the city's coal-fired power plants with nuclear generators.

I asked Xia if he thought the nation could turn from red to green.[37] His answer was unequivocal. "Yes, we should build a green China. We need to make our country greener and greener. All the top people in the world recognize this. I am confident that we will do more in the future for ecological conservation and sustainability."

It was an encouraging message, though even Dalian still had a long way to go. Wen Bo, a native of the city and member of the Pacific Environment conservation group, warned against taking an overly rosy view of his home.

"The city looks clean because the sea wind blows the pollutants away, but there are a lot of problems that are not visible," he said. "We discharge a huge volume of solid waste into the ocean, which damages marine life, and our dirty factories have been relocated, not closed down, so the damage has simply moved from the urban to the rural environment."

Clearly, there was no perfect model. Nuclear power had well-known risks. Solar energy led to pollution and waste during the manufacture of photovoltaic panels and the refinement of silicon. Up to a third of wind turbines spun uselessly in isolation because they were not connected to the grid. "Clean coal" technology was expensive and carbon sequestration largely unproven. There was a real danger of a bubble forming in the renewable energy sector as local governments rushed to jump on the bandwagon. Yet overall, the push for renewable energy was one of the most positive stories to come out of China in many years. The government was clearly determined to make a technological leap. It was good for business. It was good for national security. And it was good for prestige. In short, it was a power play. China was bidding to own the low-carbon economy of the future.

But this alone did not mean sustainability. China was still ramping up coal production, expanding power-intensive industries, and boosting consumption. Clean energy was just one more area in which to expand. In many ways, President Hu's Scientific Outlook on Development is a rebranding exercise. Rather than genuine sustainability, it is economy lite. As with low-tar tobacco, low-alcohol beer, or low-fat cheese, it tacitly acknowledges the health concerns related to business as usual, but instead of promoting change it has watered down the product, slapped on a new label, raised the price, and aimed for an even bigger market.

The communist engineers in the politburo were trained to optimize production and enhance technology rather than trim demand and reappraise values. Though it has promised to create an eco-civilization, the government continues to prioritize economic growth, social stability, and enhanced national power. Overreliance on technology looks likely to take China further from a sustainable balance with nature.

It was time to return to Beijing. First, a last seafood dinner at a grill-your-own restaurant, then a dash to Dalian station, just in time to catch the 9:45 p.m. overnight train.

Many passengers were already getting their heads down, including an old man in the bunk below mine. But a gruff, middle-aged man opposite was in a garrulous mood. Seeing me open my laptop, he asked what I was doing.

"I'm trying to write a book."

"What about?"

"China's environmental problems."

He snorted. "The problems are caused by foreigners. They pollute here what they can't in their own countries."

"Yes, that's true. But China is also responsible."

"Probably. The pollution is very bad. I live near the Bohai Sea. Have you seen it there? Terrible. It will take decades to clean up."

He asks where I'm from.

"England."

A louder snort. "That's the country that first brought pollution to China."

"We certainly didn't help."

Either tired or disappointed by the lack of verbal combat, he rolled over to sleep.

The next morning, the gruff man was in a mellower mood. We chatted in the corridor as other passengers, mostly men in their long johns, passed back and forth on their way to the washroom. He told me he was a police investigator. A gang of five thieves from Hunan had killed a woman in Dalian during a failed robbery, then fled to their home province. He was on his way to help hunt them down.

"Were the thieves black society?" I asked, using the Chinese term for organized crime.

"No, they were just poor and desperate," he replied. "The economic downturn has made life tougher for a lot of people."

The old man in the compartment returned from cleaning his teeth and joined in the conversation, which took an unexpected revolutionary turn as we approached the outskirts of Beijing.

"Which environment do you like better, Dalian or Beijing?" he asked, staring through the window as the brown fields of the countryside gave way to the gray buildings of the city.

"Dalian," I replied. "It's much cleaner, but I prefer to live in Beijing. My friends are here. It's interesting. Pollution is a big problem, but I think it will improve in the future."

The policeman interjected. "Right, in the past we took investment from anyone. Now we can afford to be more choosy. But clearing up the environment will take a long time because of corruption. Our officials don't follow their own rules."

The old man agreed. "The problem of a corrupt bureaucracy cannot be solved by bureaucrats. We need a mass movement to clear them out. I think there will be one within five years."

The policeman said nothing. His generation had a different view of mass uprisings. The old man, now in his eighties, was in his prime during the triumph of the anti-imperialist revolution. The policeman, now in his fifties, spent his youth watching the abject failure of the Cultural Revolution. While both generations agreed on the need to clear up corruption and the environment, they differed on how it should be done.

Snow started to fall as we pulled into the terminus. A row of cleaners wearing Eastern Star uniforms were waiting on the platform to tidy up the train. The digital clock above their head read 8:25:07. After an eleven-hour journey, we had reached our destination seven seconds behind schedule. China could do the efficiency thing when it chose to. No doubt about that. But, as I was to learn, efficiency could create as many problems as it solved.

14

Fertility Treatment
Shandong

Dao zai shiniao (Tao is found in the shit and piss)
—*Zhuangzi, Taoist philosopher, third century* BC

Relying on efficiency can be dangerous for two reasons. The first is self-deception: focusing on small proportionate gains is often an excuse to ignore a big negative picture.

I learned this from a Zen Buddhist monk in Japan. Masahiro was one of my favorite students when I was teaching English in Kobe in the 1990s. He had recently inherited his father's temple and made a good living from funeral ceremonies, where his chanting and calligraphy skills were put to good use. But apart from that and his bald head, we had a lot in common. Almost the same age, we would go drinking, smoking, wenching, playing football, and singing karaoke together. He would often drive back to his temple drunk in the early hours of the morning. I wondered how he squared this lifestyle with his role as a spiritual mentor. There was only one way to find out.

"Masahiro, can I talk to you about religion?"

"Sure. Anything," he beamed.

"Well, perhaps this is too British a way of thinking. But in my understanding a priest or a monk should set an example. Do you agree?"

"Yes, that's right."

"Yet you drink more alcohol, you smoke more cigarettes, and you have more girlfriends than most people I know. What kind of example is that?"

He laughed. "That's difficult to explain . . ."

"Please try. My behavior is not much different. But you're a monk. Shouldn't you be better? What is the example you are setting?"

He laughed again and leaned back on his chair. "Well, I have an 80 percent rule."

"What's that?"

"I only do 80 percent of what I could. The other 20 percent I hold back."

"Could you give me an example?"

"Well, I could drink ten beers when I go out, but I only drink eight. And I could smoke a hundred cigarettes in a week, but I only smoke eighty . . ."

"What!" I exclaimed incredulously. "Are you saying that makes you a 20 percent better person?"

"It's hard to explain. Buddhism is not easy to understand."

I did not buy the argument at all. Masahiro was a good friend but a dubious Buddhist. He was winging it with this explanation, which sounded a lot like the shopaholic's excuse for splurging in the sales: "I might have spent a fortune, but look how much I've saved!"

A similar mind-set lies behind China's claims of efficiency gains. As in the West, although technology is making energy use less wasteful, it is also encouraging people to use more power. Overall, the result is increased consumption. Scant consideration appears to be given to the fact that resources are finite.

The second danger of relying too much on efficiency is that it stifles creativity and diversity: once something is found to work, it is repeated and expanded to the detriment of all else. I learned that in Shandong, where I went to observe mankind's efforts to improve the fertility of the land and the sea.

When people talk about environmental problems in China, they usually focus on factories and emissions, but it is often farmland and fertilizer that create the biggest problems. The impact is most striking in Shandong. This huge coastal province generates more agricultural revenue than any other.[1] It is China's leading meat producer and its number two supplier of wheat and cotton.[2]

Shandong's history has been shaped by its geography.[3] This is where the Yellow River flows into the Bohai Sea. Confucius was born here around 500 BC and his philosophy of human-centered order has recently enjoyed a resurgence, particularly in his hometown of Qufu.

My journey, though, began at Taishan, the holy mountain where emperors made pilgrimages to beg heaven and earth for the fertility of their land. They were pleading for the Mandate of Heaven.[4] These imperial pilgrimages were made easier in 219 BC, when the tyrant Qin Shihuang had a path built up the mountain. Today, there is a tarmac road and a cable car.

After being winched above the clouds, we joined the tourist throngs wandering through the network of mountaintop temples. At a lower level was a shrine to the Princess of the Rosy Clouds, a Taoist deity believed to help childless women conceive. From there, steep steps led to the 1,532-meter peak, where even the mightiest of men was expected to show humility to the mythical ruler of heaven, the Jade Emperor. The rulers of old could look down from here with a mix of satisfaction and responsibility, knowing they controlled all that they could see across the vast plains and the Yellow Sea. The Taoist emperor Wu was lost for words and famously ordered his stone monument, the Wuzibei, left blank. Mao Zedong, by contrast, was inspired by a glorious sunrise to declare, "The East Is Red."

On the day I reached the top, it looked more of a murky brown. On either side of the meteorological monitoring station to the east of the peak was a double horizon: the first where the land met the smog; the other where the smog met the sky. The moon appeared mockingly beautiful above them both.

Taishan's role had changed. In the era of "Scientific Development," China's leaders no longer prayed for good harvests at the peak. Instead, they relied on the scientists at the foot of the mountain to find new chemical fertilizers and laboratory-engineered seeds. This was the site of the Shandong Agricultural University, which was pioneering China's biggest study of genetically modified crops.[5] It was on the front line of efforts to improve the efficiency of the country's fields.

Shandong grows more genetically modified cotton than anywhere else in China and possibly the world. The U.S. agrichemical firm Monsanto found a willing partner here for its first insect-resistant hybrids. Scientists in the province are also developing salt-resistant tomatoes, soybeans, and rice, designed to grow on saline soil near the coast. Just as in hydroengineering, manufacturing, railway building, and skyscraper construction, China is poised to become a major biotechnology player. With laxer regulations and huge government investment, it already leads the world in GM rice. Scientists predict that half of the country's agricultural produce will be genetically modified by 2015.[6]

Though most of the initial bioengineering breakthroughs have been made in the West rather than by China's agricultural scientists, it hasn't been for want of trying. During the Great Leap Forward in the late 1950s, the government encouraged farmers to experiment with grafting and interbreeding. This led to some bizarre genetic experiments and fantastic claims of success, such as a rooster than could lay eggs, the breeding of an earless, tailless pig, ewes that could give birth to quintuplets, and a pumpkin as heavy as a man. Rabbits were interbred with cows and pear trees grown to produce apples. To save the need to dye textiles, scientists spliced cotton and tomato plants. The aim was to produce red fabric, but the results were closer to fluffy tomatoes.[7] Today, the world sniggers at the crazy excesses of that era, but researchers across the globe are now conducting much bolder and more bizarre experiments.

Even before the Great Leap Forward in the East, scientists in the West were massively expanding yields with a Green Revolution based on nitrogen- and phosphate-based fertilizers, insecticides, mechanization, irrigation, and hybridization. As a species, we soon came to depend on these fertility stimulants. More than half the world's population is now being fed by the extra production from technology and nitrate inputs rather than land expansion.[8]

China was the new frontier for biotechnology. With a fifth of the world's population to feed on a tenth of the planet's arable land, the temptations of biotechnology had always been enormous. Urbanization and industrialization add to the pressures by taking land for factories, roads, and housing blocks.[9] With the population expanding and appetites growing, China faced an uphill struggle to feed itself. As the economist Vaclav Smil noted: "All of the world's grain exports together would fill less than two-thirds of the country's projected demand for food."[10]

Desperate measures were needed to boost agricultural output, but there had been no big productivity breakthroughs for fifty years on the scale of the Green Revolution. Efficiency was made an overriding priority. The result was fields and fields of monotonous monoculture.

On the new motorway from the holy mountain Taishan to the experimental agriculture center at Linyi, I had a feeling of déjà vu. The landscape looked remarkably familiar, though I had never been this way before. Staring at flat brown fields, hazy gray skies, and row after shallow row of uniformly spindly poplar trees was like watching a minute-long clip on a daylong loop. It reminded me of the countryside in Henan, Hebei, and Beijing. On the North China plain, which stretches about 1,000 kilometers from the capital down to the Yangtze, you could travel for hours without feeling any sense of progress because every road looked the same. I used to think this was just because it was flat but then I met Mother Poplar.

That was the media nickname for Zhang Qiwen, the genetics professor who was arguably responsible for changing a bigger chunk of the Chinese landscape than the emperors and engineers behind the Great Wall, the Three Gorges Dam, or the Sky Train railway to Tibet.

In 1980, soon after China opened up to the outside world, Zhang established the nation's first poplar gene pool by importing hybrid seeds and saplings from Canada, the United States, and Italy. She embraced biotechnology with the gusto of a new convert and applied it with the single-minded utilitarianism of an old Maoist. The result was the spread of a now ubiquitous, lanky hybrid of the American *Populus deltoides* and European *Populus nigra,* aka Poplar Hybrid 107.

Developed in Italy more than ten years earlier, this hybrid and its near twin PH108 had failed to take root in most global forestry markets,[11] but in northern China, thanks to Zhang, they came to dominate the landscape more than any subspecies of plant at any time in recorded history.

More than 1.5 billion were planted in just five years, covering a fifth of China's entire forest area. Yet almost all of them were squeezed along roadsides in the crowded North China plains.[12] As a result, from Liaoning in the north down to the Yangtze in the south, this single hybrid is everywhere. There are few more fitting symbols of modern monocultural civilization.

These endless lines of leaves on sticks are the twenty-first century's superefficient substitute for the ancient forests.[13] Imported, artificial, with a sparse canopy and a slender trunk, PH107 was designed for rapid growth without a thought for the wider environment. When Zhang came across PH107, it was love at first sight. The poplar is the cow of the tree world: quick to bulk up and easy to cut down. In China, it is bred for humans, mainly for industrial use or as a protective barrier for crop fields. In ideal conditions—supplied with lots of fertilizer and pesticide—it grows

3 meters a year in height and up to 4 centimeters in diameter, providing 60 percent more wood than a wild poplar.

"It's about production, not ecology," explained Zhang, a robust and kindly woman in a red poppy-patterned cardigan. Though retired, she retained something of the war-against-nature spirit of the Great Leap Forward. When I asked how the narrow canopies affected bird-nesting patterns, she laughed. "I have never thought about it."

A query about cloning and testing techniques provoked a graphic analogy.

"Compare it to a baby. Imagine you [she pointed to me] have ten children with you [she pointed to my horrified assistant]. We choose the best one, chop off its arms and legs, then cut the torso into ten pieces, and plant them in the ground. They should grow up as identical clones, which we then measure as they grow in different conditions."

I'm pretty sure she was referring to branches and trunks when she talked about limbs and torsos, but the language was indicative of a recklessness toward ecosystems and gender balance.

Tree and crop modification has a long history. In China, the ability to bend plants to man's will was seen by the ancients as a mark of civilization.[14] In the modern age, the United States and Europe blazed the trail of hybridization. Professor Zhang simply picked what she considered to be the best of the best. Her selection made her a national hero. On her wall was a group photograph with President Hu Jintao and Premier Wen Jiabao. Mother Poplar was also often lauded in the state media.

PH107 has many good qualities. Poplars absorb more carbon than slower-growing trees, so they can help to tackle global warming. Their cultivation has eased China's reliance on wood from illegally felled forests in Papua New Guinea, Indonesia, and Russia.[15] In smaller numbers, the trees might even be considered attractive.

But their numbers are far from small. The domination of these twin female trees is not just an affront to Taoist ideals of balance and feng-shui aesthetics, it is of dubious long-term economic benefit. Although the hybrids grow fast, they are sickly plants, vulnerable to disease and unable to reproduce. Most are cut down after six years, almost as soon as they start to flower and show other signs of reaching sexual maturity. Zhang described pollen as a form of pollution.

The techniques of modern forestry are no less degrading than the animal husbandry techniques used on giant pandas. This is not wholly

China's fault, but once again it has taken a global trend to a new extreme. Zhang was simply trying to help her country. She told me she was proud of putting poplars across northern China. But I was horrified at the consequences of her work. PH107 cultivation denied sex, destroyed beauty, and replaced local diversity with a superefficient standard.[16] In that final narrow sense alone, PH107 might be considered a good thing. But you could have too much of a good thing.

Zhang was old-school. Trained at the height of the Great Leap Forward, she had wedded Maoist recklessness to Western science to conceive an ugly, superabundant hybrid. But, like the megadams of Sichuan, the wisdom of this approach has subsequently been questioned. A new generation of agricultural scientists is warning that the overcultivation of one efficient crop could result in the choking of everything else.

Professor Jiang Gaoming is one of them. He is a man of the Shandong soil who has grown into an eco-farming evangelist. We met at a banquet, where a relay of genetic engineering professors took it in turns to down glasses of baijiu rice liquor with me, the solitary foreign journalist. Moon-faced and jocular, Jiang joined in with the drinking and the card games that followed, but though he might make small talk with them, his views are utterly at odds with most of the agriculture scientists at his institute.

The next morning, as he drove me to a pilot project along roads lined with PH107, he spoke with passion of his love for his home province and his fury at modern agricultural practices that he believes are destroying the soil and ruining the landscape.

"Everyone in China needs money. They don't care about biodiversity and the environment. A few of us in the science community care because it is our subject, but the government pays little heed. For them, a tree is just a tree."

He railed against chemical fertilizers, pesticides, genetically modified crops, and the plastic sheeting that is spread across the land to trap moisture and heat for the cultivation of garlic. These modern techniques were a form of pollution, he said, that was sucking nutrient-rich, dark carbon out of the soil and turning the land pale. He sympathized with farmers who would do anything to increase yields, but he could not forgive agribusiness and its advocates in global corporations and local government.

"Shandong is number one in China for agricultural production, but this is also where you see the most problems," he said. "Farmers used to be honest. If food was bad, they would withhold it from the market. But now they don't care. They just want to make money. They see the income gap between the city and the countryside and they will do anything to catch up. But though they make poor-quality food for sale, they never eat it themselves."

He said Chinese farmers use twice as much fertilizer and insecticide per hectare as their American counterparts.[17] Despite the health risks, they add arsenic to artificially boost crop yields and melamine to disguise the low level of protein in milk.[18] In the seed market, there were fewer and fewer subtypes because everyone bought the same few high-yield varieties. The same was true of poultry. The tasty native Shouguang chicken had been crossbred with a chunkier U.S. species to increase meat volume, but Jiang said the hybrid was only for supermarkets. None of the farmers want to eat this tasteless lab meat themselves. In a world of mass production, too much of a good thing quickly became bad. The obvious antidote was to make something bad good. For Jiang, that meant making better use of what we normally waste: stalks, husks, and manure.

The fresh rich stink of cow dung assaulted the nostrils at Professor Jiang's eco-farming pilot project in Jiangjiazhuang Village. Cornstalks—usually burned or discarded—were bagged up alongside the road for winter fodder. Inside the building, straw matting was spread across bunk beds. Outside, thousands of insects hopped back and forth across a grasshopper breeding pen. "Very nutritious. We'll try some later," said the professor.

Jiang described his goal as a new Green Revolution, but it was essentially a return to fundamentals. The son of local farmers, he was raised in this village and had watched with horror what modern farming techniques had done to agriculture. He was trying to find an alternative to fertilizer and, encouragingly, the government was willing to fund him. Cue manure, the ultimate wasted resource. China produces more than three times more excrement than solid waste.[19] Most of it flows into rivers and seas, creating a nutrient feast for plankton and algae. Plans are afoot to change this. The government aimed to have fifty million homes using biogas by 2010, some of which would be fueled by animal droppings.[20]

For Jiang, better use of agricultural waste was the best way to ease the problems of global warming and food shortages. He was a manure messiah, a stalk savior who wanted to plow postharvest stubble back into the land rather than burning it and releasing more carbon into the air, as I had seen farmers do in Henan.

"More than half of a plant's photosynthetic carbohydrates are in stalks and leaves. If we use them better, we can ease global warming and make the soil richer," Jiang said with infectious enthusiasm.

He bounced around his walled farm, expressing a childlike joy in the rich, black, plastic-free soil. "Look how big and red these radishes grow with organic fertilizer," he beamed, stooping to pull one up. "And these chili peppers. We get a higher yield with our natural methods than the farmers outside do with agrichemicals." Most vegetables, he admitted, did not grow as fast or as abundantly as they would with the application of nonorganic fertilizer and pesticide, but the difference was small, the quality was higher and, properly licensed, they fetched a higher price in the market because they were safer.[21]

Greenies around the world have been saying much the same thing for years. Jiang reminded me of the jolly, idealistic character played by Richard Briers in the 1970s British TV grow-your-own sitcom *The Good Life*, but instead of an organic garden in a suburban semi, he wanted to introduce eco-farming on a China-wide scale. The aim of the project, he said, was to restore the land to how he remembered it as a child. Essentially, he was trying to re-create a lost paradise with science, government funding, the political backing of the Communist Party, and copious quantities of manure.

There are precedents. The importance of excrement has been extolled in both ancient lore and communist propaganda. Zhuangzi, the most down-to-earth of the Taoist philosophers, held it in high regard. Asked where to find Tao (The Way), he replied, "Dao zai shiniao" (Tao is found in the shit and piss). For Confucians in the thirteenth century, a son's willingness to taste his father's excrement was extolled as a sign of great filial piety. In one famous moral fable, a child discovers his father has a health problem because his turds are sweet.[22] In the twentieth century, at the height of the Great Leap Forward, the model soldier Lei Feng collected the most idealized pile of manure in China's history. As the propaganda legend has it, Lei was so moved by the proceedings of the 8th Plenary of the Chinese Communist Party's Eighth Central Committee that he felt compelled to contribute 500 pounds of manure to the Liaoning People's

Commune. Based on the dung shoveling and numerous other cleaner good deeds by the model soldier, Mao declared in 1963 a "Learn from Lei Feng campaign" for the entire nation.[23] More recently, though, dung has become symbolic of the great rural-urban divide. In the countryside, close to the soil, it is a free boon for growth, but in the concrete environment of the city it is a smelly curse that is expensive to dispose of. If biogas takes off, it won't be in the city.

The changing mores of modern China were apparent as we wandered around the eco-model village. Several homes had been fitted with solar panels on the roofs to heat bathwater, and biogas chambers underground that piped fuel converted from human waste, animal manure, and compost to stoves and lightbulbs. The night soil was collected on an individual rather than a communal basis. Each of the newly fitted homes had its own toilet, a big step up from the shared public facilities of the past. The trend is apparent nationwide: a nation's social change mapped through its toilet habits. When China was poor and genuinely communist, whole communities squatted side by side in public latrines. Today, however, some are reluctant even to share a seat with their own families. I was astonished to see at one luxury housing compound a five-bedroom home with seven toilets—one per person plus spares for guests and housekeepers. Such developments proclaim more viscerally than any political statement the death of communist values.

Jiang did not care where the night soil came from so long as it could be used efficiently. But villagers were not easily persuaded that it could replace conventional modern power and fertilizer. The new system was imperfect. There was a problem with a bio-powered light, and the gas retained an underlying odor that betrayed its origin. A bigger problem was money. Because the government subsidized biofuel, people accepted it. But there were few takers for the stalk-and-manure alternative to fertilizer that Jiang advocated.

The average Linyi farmer, living on an income of 4,000 yuan per year, could not afford to be a purist. They had seen insecticides, chemical fertilizers, hybridized plants, and growth hormones make the difference between starvation and food security within two generations.

Everyone we met in the village shared the professor's family name.

Jiang Su, a farmer and mother, proudly showed off the strong flame from her biogas cooker and the four grunting pigs that provided most of the fuel for it. Jiang Jun, the dour local Communist Party secretary, sat under a poster of Mao and explained that the village, which got its first telephone only in the late 1980s, soon planned to be one of the first in the country to install biogas streetlamps. Jiang Huixuan, an elderly peanut farmer, used to beg in the streets of Qingdao as a child, but now praised chemical fertilizer and plastic field-sheeting for improving living standards.

Most memorable, though, was Jiang Zhoushi, a baijiu-drinking, chain-smoking 104-year-old who puffed her way through almost an entire packet of cigarettes in our half-hour interview. If there is a set of survival genes, Jiang Zoushi must have had the lot.[24] She had lived through several famines, Western colonialism, Japanese occupation, civil war, murderous political campaigns, and eviction by a daughter-in-law during an antirightist movement. In the fight against Japan, her husband had been responsible for shooting local collaborators. During the famine of 1928, she had fought with neighbors to eat the last pieces of bark left on a tree. At that time, she said, she became an unwitting cannibal: "Someone sold us pork soup, but I found a little human finger in it. I knew very well it was from a baby."[25]

No matter which Jiang we met, the refrain was the same: "Life is much better now," or a variation on the theme. Though the professor was trying to wean locals off chemical fertilizers, people were reluctant to give them up. As far as they were concerned, the agrichemicals had kept hunger at bay for more than three decades.

The night before we left, the professor arranged an organic feast. It was an act of hospitality for me and two of his French students, but it was also a propaganda activity aimed at the local Communist Party leadership. He had invited the township chief and other senior cadres to give them a first taste of naturally grown food. The vegetables, all picked from the farm, took longer to cook than expected. The important guests milled around impatiently as chairs were fetched. After thirty minutes the food arrived. It was indeed a feast of more than a dozen dishes, including eggplants, carrots, leeks, radishes, and chicken soup. But the officials picked at it. By their criteria, I guess this was poor fare. At official banquets in China, guests were usually treated to huge quantities of meat and exotic dishes, both signs of how wealthy the host was and how far the country has come from an era in which families considered themselves fortunate to have pork once a year at spring festival.

Baijiu, the fallback spirit reviver, failed to lift the mood, and the conversation remained at the level of formal speeches and polite noises about the food. We toasted each other, drank, toasted again, and drank some more. Between the gulps of throat-burning baijiu, the conversation sputtered along until Professor Jiang produced a bowl of crispy fried grasshoppers. "Just picked from outside," the ebullient host smiled. "Won't you try one?" For a brief moment, insect crunching became a spectator sport with all eyes on the foreigners. It was a consumption dare, like the endless rounds of baijiu. When it was my turn, I paused, took a look at my snack, wondered briefly if I had seen it jumping around earlier in the day, then crunched it between my teeth. It went very well with the organic rice. "Delicious. Can I have some more?"

Despite the taciturnity of the party secretary, Jiang was determined that we should all leave on a high. "Bring your chairs outside. The moon is very beautiful and you can see the stars. There's no pollution here," he said, beaming. "Let's sing some songs." The cadres seemed eager to leave, but there was no escaping Jiang's enthusiasm. We sat. They stood. We sang. They loitered close to their car. Jiang had a fine tenor voice as he crooned "My Hometown Yimeng Mountain," a heartfelt song of praise to the beautiful scenery of Linyi and its abundant crops. When he was done, the French students and I clapped enthusiastically. Even the cadres smiled. It was their excuse to head home.

Why should they be enthusiastic about organic methods? The long-term impact of chemical fertilizers on soil remains fiercely contested throughout the world, hardly surprising given its importance to global food supplies.[26] But there is strong evidence that the soil quality is declining.[27] Depleted of natural fertility and innate virility, the intercourse between humankind and the ecosystem has to be chemically assisted. Humanity relies more and more on artificial stimulants. Effectively we are pumping the land with agricultural Viagra.

Government officials insist they are not worried about food shortages, though Premier Wen Jiabao has privately asked senior former officials to search for new areas to cultivate.[28] There are other good reasons too for exploring alternatives to chemical fertilizers. They pollute waterways, add massively to greenhouse gas emissions, and rely heavily on oil, supplies of which will become increasingly unstable as the earth approaches the peak of supply.[29]

Hydrocarbon inputs have been a crucial element of the Green Revolution that has ramped up agricultural production over the past sixty years. We might not actually eat coal as the Meng brothers did while trapped underground, but we all indirectly consume fossil fuels for food. Oil and coal provide the fuel for fertilizer factories, phosphate extraction equipment, tractors, and distribution networks. The Green Revolution has enabled farmland to produce trillions of extra calories in energy, but the surge in food prices in 2008 suggests the return on technology and chemical inputs may be diminishing. This was the expectation of the author of *Who Will Feed China?*, Earthwatch's Lester Brown: "We are reaching the limits of what plants can do. Plants are not that different from people in this sense," he says. "You can get gains up to a point and then it becomes much more difficult—I don't know of any scientists who are predicting potential advances in grain yields that are comparable with those we saw in the last half century."[30]

Like the poplar, our species is in danger of becoming too successful. By boosting plant yields with nitrates and other fertilizers, human beings have siphoned off almost 40 percent of all land-based photosynthetic capability.[31] Given how much of the planet's energy we are hogging, it is inevitable that other species are declining. The same is true in water systems, where the balance of life is changing due to the runoff of fertility stimulants that mankind pumps into the earth.

My next port of call was the coast. Even the oceans are struggling to meet the demand for food and dilution of waste. The following morning we bade farewell to Jiang and headed off on a four-hour bus ride to Qingdao, a center for oceanic research, fisheries, and beer. This pleasant maritime city of 8 million people sits on the southeastern coast of Shandong. As we arrived, the legacy of the former German treaty port was evident in the Bavarian architecture, the Tsingtao brewery, and the annual beer festival. But the city was moving on with a massive seafront expansion of office blocks and residential towers. Cranes were as thick on the horizon here as anywhere.

Enjoying a crisp coastal breeze, I walked over to the Institute of Oceanology, China's leading marine research organization. The boffins here are
a friendly bunch with a worrying message: pollutants are building up in
the oceans. More contaminants are coming from farms than factories.
As a result, Professor Zhou Mingjiang, the former head of the institute,
believes the main threat to China's coastal waters is not from heavy metal
but from featherlight algae.

Algae are an ancient friend and a new threat. These organisms date
back far longer than humanity, almost to the beginning of life on earth.
They appear naturally, particularly in the summer when the sea is warm,
and could be a source of nutrition for fish and man. But growth patterns
have changed. New forms of algae have evolved. Most worryingly, bright
green and red blooms are breaking out like nasty rashes across a widening
area of lakes and coastlines.

Scientists believe the algae have been stimulated by the sharp rise in
nitrates and phosphates in coastal waters as a result of farm fertilizer runoff, untreated human waste, and the food used to stimulate the growth of
fish and crabs in aquaculture. This has resulted in an alarming increase of
red tides, a manifestation of toxic algae blooms that poison other marine
life, choke oxygen from the water, and block the gills of fish.

This problem was almost unknown at the start of the decade, but of
late the red tides have grown rapidly in both frequency and size.[32] At first,
they were only seen in the summer. But now in the warmer south, the red
tides appear all through the year. In the worst areas, around the Yangtze
and Pearl river estuaries, these harmful algae blooms create "dead zones"
where the water is so starved of oxygen it is unable to sustain other forms
of life.

Farms are the main source of this environmental stress. Fertilizer nitrates
and phosphorus run off into streams and rivers, and eventually lakes and
oceans. It is like pumping marine life with steroids or force-feeding growth
stimulants. The primary benefactors are the organisms first in the food chain,
such as algae and plankton. With the extra nutrition they grow quickly in the
form of green slime on lakes or red tides in the sea, to their own benefit and
their predators' detriment. Some algae have become toxic, but most kill by
suffocation, choking off oxygen and sunlight.

The scientific name for this phenomenon is "eutrophication," a term
that gets to the heart of the risks facing our species and our planet. In

essence, eutrophication means having too much of a good thing. Its origins are positive. The word comes from the Greek εὖ, signifying good or well, and τροφή, meaning nourishment. But like the process it describes, the word has self-degraded. Today, eutrophication is used with reference to stagnant bodies of water to describe an unwholesome combination of aging, overconsumption of nutrients, chemical imbalance, and unwelcome surface growth. The side effects of modern development are nourishing our waters to death.

Inland, the area of lake surface affected by eutrophication has increased sixtyfold since 1970.[33] China's great lakes, Dianchi, Taihu, Chaohu, and Xinlicheng, were now choked each summer with rancid green blooms. To explain why, Professor Zhou, the leading authority on the issue in China, presented three graphs that showed population, GDP, and fertilizer use jerking up in unison after 1980.

Harmful algae blooms are a problem across the globe, associated with modern farming methods, rising populations, and increased use of detergents. The world now has 400 oceanic dead zones. Red tides are frequent in the Baltic and off the southeastern United States. But they can be prevented. Zhou was calling on the government to build sewage treatment plants in every village by 2020, to use fertilizer more wisely, to ban phosphates in washing powders, and to use more organic materials to feed the land.

"This can be solved," he assured me. "In the previous thirty years, we have focused only on development. We had to. Now we have the manpower and the money to think about how to balance development and the environment. That is the basis of 'Scientific Development.'"

China's oceans were certainly in need of a cleanup, but I was not convinced "Scientific Development" held all the answers. Shandong was already spending more on wastewater treatment than any other province, yet it was still surrounded by some of the most polluted seas on the planet.[34] The Bohai Sea is worst affected because it is enclosed on three sides and surrounded by dense populations, heavy industry, and intensive agriculture. Once known as the "Emperor's Fishery," stocks have plummeted as pollution and overfishing have worsened. The prawn catch dropped by 90 percent in fifteen years, clam beds have been decimated, and, in some areas, locals can no longer catch big fish so they are living on small fry and fish eggs. The State Oceanic Administration has warned that the Bohai Sea is so polluted it could "die" in years, by 2016 unless remedial action is taken.[35]

The same is happening with increasing frequency up and down China's 18,000-kilometer coastline.[36] According to the World Wide Fund for Nature, China is the greatest polluter of the Pacific Ocean. Despite government controls, the domestic media frequently carries reports of sewage, fertilizer, and industrial waste being dumped into the sea with often dire consequences for the seabed. In many areas, heavy metals are accumulating in the mud and in the organs of fish.[37]

This highlights a blind spot in "Scientific Development": it focuses on incremental improvements rather than overall limits. Instead of considering accumulated totals or ecological capacity, it sets periodic targets for production efficiency, energy intensity, pollution levels, and carbon emissions. This does not adequately factor in the finiteness of resources and the carrying capacity of the earth. It deals with acute symptoms of development but ignores chronic problems. Despite the government's calls to create a sustainable, cyclical economy, the result has been an ever-greater depletion of resources and an ever-greater buildup of persistent pollutants.[38]

By the time an ecological wall is hit, it is often too late for remedial action. The long-term dangers of this approach can be seen from the pesticide DDT, which although banned in 1983, is even today found in harmful quantities in oysters, mussels, and squid, as are other persistent organic pollutants that were formerly discharged in large volumes in China, as elsewhere.[39]

Fish stocks are also being decimated by the failure to enforce limits on catches. Professor Dou Shuozeng, a young scholar at the institute, watched these trends with a mix of worry and fascination. In fluent American-accented English he told me there were too many fishermen and too many consumers. The yellow croaker, which was once China's most important commercial fish, was now extremely difficult to find in the wild. Farther south, by the Yangtze, he said, the situation was even worse. "Almost the entire coastline is affected," Dou explained. "Resources have decreased rapidly since the 1980s because of overfishing and pollution. These factors have led to the collapse of most commercial fisheries off the coast. Some have almost disappeared."

The government has not been idle, but, as we saw in chapter 4, it has tended to focus on farming rather than conservation. Captive-bred shrimp, flatfish, and jellyfish were released into the oceans under a fish-stock enhancement program. This may have helped some stocks to recover, despite fears that the captive fish—raised on a diet of nitrates and anti- biotics—could weaken the genetic stock of the natural population. The wild ocean, however, was of decreasing concern to China, which was the first country in the world in which fish-farm output exceeded the oceanic catch.[40] Most of the flounder, sea bream, shrimp, and other marine prod- ucts in the markets of Qingdao come from aquaculture, a growing source of the nitrates that algae thrive on.

Dou summarized the trend in terms of size. Large species were in trou- ble. Small ones were thriving. "The ocean ecology is not being destroyed, but it is changing. There are fewer big fish, more small fish. And there are more plankton, photoplankton, and mud dwellers." On an emotional level, it sounded an awful lot like evolution in reverse gear.

Recent studies suggest we ignore plankton, algae, and the micro- organisms present in feces and other waste at our peril. These species played a pivotal role in biogeochemical history. The subject remains con- tentious, but according to one theory, for the first 3 billion years of life on earth, all the organisms were single-celled and incapable of excreting. Then suddenly, about 600 million years ago, the first multicelled excret- ers arrived, laying the chemical foundation for one of the most spectacu- lar bursts of evolution in the history of the planet. The feces-producing creatures ate and processed plankton, starving the bacteria in the depths and releasing a surplus of oxygen that allowed higher life-forms—includ- ing the first vertebrates—to come into being.[41]

While fecal waste may have created the conditions for higher life-forms, algae gunk tends to destroy it. Another theory claims mass extinctions, such as the one during the Cambrian era (about 500 million years ago), were preceded by eutrophication. With an overabundance of nutrients in the ocean, the fastest reproducers (such as plankton and algae) gobbled up everything, starving other species and leading to ecosystem collapse.[42] Once this was completed, carbon started to reaccumulate, paving the way for a new ecosystem with new species to develop. If this is true, the con- notations are worrying for humanity. The algae acted as a biological reset button for the planet. The increase of these fast-breeding organisms in recent years should be taken as a warning of dangerous imbalance.

★

On my last day in Qingdao, I asked a fisherman at the quayside market to take me out in his skiff to fish for lobster. Tan Changhu was glad of the extra income, though his small, single-engine boat was barely up to the task of carrying more than one person. We chugged slowly into deeper waters, pulling farther away from the jagged Qingdao skyline of tower blocks and construction cranes silhouetted in the haze.

Smoking a cigarette and sitting in the bow of his skiff, Tan navigated the still waters, pausing every ten minutes to pour more coolant into the boat's overheating outboard motor. Shouting over the noisy spluttering of his engine, the fisherman told me he was the youngest of five siblings and made the most money. Fishing, crabbing, and shrimping brought in 6,000 yuan a month, more than most white-collar jobs in China. But in recent years catches had declined as more people harvested the seas for a living. He said yapian and snakehead fish were becoming hard to find. The big money was made through aquaculture, the fastest-growing local business.

The vast offshore farms sat a couple of kilometers from the shore, where the surface of the water was pebbled with circular buoys. In 2008, it had been carpeted in blue-green slime. Green tides of algae had been increasing in frequency in these waters for several years due to the extra nitrates flowing in from the shoreline. But this outbreak was exceptional. The first blooms appeared soon after the May Day holiday when the water temperature was unusually warm. Within a month, the blooms grew with astonishing speed to cover an area of 13,000 square kilometers, several times the size of London.[43] The twenty-eight-year-old said he had never seen anything like it.

"I don't know what caused it or where it came from. It was just there all of a sudden, all over the place," he recalled. For him, the slime was only an eyesore. For the local government, then preparing to host the Olympic sailing competition, it was a huge embarrassment. A layer of garish *Enteromorpha/Ulva* slime was not what the authorities had in mind when they coined the term "Green Olympics." [44]

An Ocean Cleaning Command Center was hurriedly established. Tan was recruited with the promise of 280 yuan per day and dispatched to help the clear-up of a beachfront area. He set out at five o'clock in the morning from Qingdao to join a flotilla of more than a thousand boats: skiffs, yachts, trawlers, and speedboats. The vessels came from as far away as Weihai and Jiaodong. He worked twelve hours a day, scooping up the algae with a net until his small skiff was full, then dumping it on the beach for collection. Every day he collected about a ton of the slime. Unlike the red algae, it was relatively harmless, so it could even be sold as feed to pig farmers. Under a summer sun it was hot, hard work, but Tan's efforts were a drop in a bucket. The campaign lasted weeks. Some fishermen fell sick from the effort, but they never completely cleared up the estimated 170,000 tons of algae. Instead, the authorities stretched nets and a barrage across the coastal waters to prevent the gunk from invading the coastline. It did the job. The problem was pushed out of sight. Tan went back to fishing.

Listening to his story, I could imagine a time in the near future when algae would be hybridized, farmed on the ocean, and used as biomass fuel or fertilizer.[45] Replacing the degraded land, the seascape would be divided up into fields of plankton, seaweed, and microphytes. Bigger marine species, now little more than algae-munching vermin or interesting curiosities, would be either wiped out or exiled to aquariums. Algae would be marketed as a health food. Our diets would consist of processed gunk . . .

My fantasy was interrupted by a tinny Chinese pop song. Tan's mobile phone was ringing. Forty minutes from the port, the impressive range of the China Mobile signal was matched by the intrusive reach of officialdom. The call was from the police. "I've been ordered to bring you back to shore," Tan said apologetically. "They say we are not allowed to take foreigners out to sea. You might be trying to leave illegally. I'm sorry." It was absurd. We could never reach the nearest country, South Korea, on a boat that could barely make it to the nearest fishing ground. But we turned around and spluttered slowly back toward the haze-shrouded city. As we chugged along, I considered how desperate someone would need to be to try to escape on such a slow boat from China.

We had lost the chance to fish for lobster, but Tan shrugged, lit another cigarette, and steered his craft back toward port. The fisherman was an optimist. Like the farmers of Linyi, like almost everyone I met in China, he believed life was getting better.

But at what point would "getting better" become too good? Even with fertilizers and intensive farming, food prices were creeping up around the world. Despite aquaculture, fish stocks were in steep decline. Governments in China, Japan, and South Korea were so concerned about shortages they were buying up extra farmland in Africa. The Amazon rain forest and Brazilian savanna were being cleared for soy cultivation.[46] Looming over all forecasts was climate change, which was likely to play havoc with agriculture and cut food production by as much as 40 percent by the second half of the century.[47]

Incremental efficiency gains alone will not prevent the depletion of resources if the number of mouths and the size of appetites continue to grow at current rates. China, and humanity, will soon have to reduce demand to avoid a crisis. "Consume less!" is an extremely difficult message to sell to the public, particularly in Western democracies where electorates are used to being bought off with promises of ever-higher living standards. On the face of it, authoritarian China appears better placed to impose tough political decisions. Might autocratic leadership, mass mobilization, and draconian prohibitions succeed where elected governments seem doomed to failure? I traveled next to the freezing north to consider whether dictatorship could prove to be an environmental asset.

15

An Odd Sort of Dictatorship
Heilongjiang

Let us hold high the great banner of socialism with Chinese
characteristics, rally more closely around the Central Committee,
unite as one, forge ahead in a pioneering spirit, and work hard to
achieve new victories in building a moderately prosperous society
in all respects and write a new chapter of happy life for the people!
—Hu Jintao, speech to the Seventeenth Communist Party Congress[1]

The temperature fell steadily as we rolled north to Harbin on the overnight train from Beijing. I had work to catch up on and was the last in
the cozy compartment to snuggle down. By the time I closed the laptop
and my eyes, I guess we were passing through the dark countryside of
Liaoning. It was a restless night. In the early hours I woke up more than
once because my feet were cold. They were sticking out from under the
small duvet. I pulled them back, curled up as best I could, and went back
to sleep. The conductor woke us at 6:30 a.m. With the light on, I could
see why my toes had been chilly. The window at the end of my bed was
encrusted with icicles. At minus 22 degrees, the temperature outside was
so low that condensation had frozen to the frame inside.

Ice was the main attraction of Harbin, the capital of China's northernmost province of Heilongjiang. Winter was the tourist season. Tens of
thousands of southerners flocked to the city for the exotic sight of slush
on the streets and snow on the roofs. The frozen Songhua River was a
playground of skaters, dogsleds, ice slides, and pony traps. Techno music

blared across the whitescape as cable cars trundled overhead. The highlight came at night, when thickly quilted crowds thronged to the Ice Lantern Festival, where they could wander around garishly illuminated castles and palaces carved out of frozen water. These were no ordinary igloos. Some ice structures were so immense they had their own escalators and elevators. With Disney sponsoring for the first time, the organizers were worried global warming would cut the season short again.

The Cold War seemed a distant memory. But I was in Heilongjiang to measure the ideological temperature. I wanted to see to what extent the world's biggest one-party state could provide a model for other nations to coerce their populations into living greener lives.

A few years ago that would have seemed an absurd, or at least ideologically incorrect, question. Back then, China's opaque, old-fashioned communist dictatorship seemed to be mirrored in the country's dirty and polluted industrial structure. But views had changed dramatically. Following President Hu Jintao's Scientific Outlook on Development, the government claimed to have made environmental sustainability a priority. It was not just a slogan.

The red government appeared to be turning greener by the day. Its Eleventh Five-Year Plan, for the 2006–10 period, was the most environmentally ambitious document in the history of the Communist Party. It promised to reduce pollution by 10 percent, improve energy efficiency by 20 percent, and raise the share of renewables in the energy mix to 15 percent. During that period China announced its first climate-change white paper and Beijing introduced tighter car-emission standards than those of the U.S. Cadres and government officials were told their promotion prospects would depend on meeting environmental targets as well as economic-growth goals. Pilot programs were launched for the introduction of a "green GDP," which would add long-term ecological factors into economic calculations. Beijing introduced draconian traffic control and factory relocation schemes to clear its filthy air in time for the "Green Olympics." National lawmakers passed a bill that obliged local authorities to release pollution information to the public. It looked as though the full powers of the one-party state were being mobilized to create a more transparent and cleaner society. The ideological icing on the cake came when Hu Jintao made the creation of an "eco-civilization" a pillar of party policy.

International opinion was slow to keep up. For years, China's pollution had been derided along with its politics. But suddenly the pendulum of international opinion swung to the other extreme. Prominent foreign commentators began to laud the virtues of authoritarianism. China's ability to get things done for the environment was compared favorably against wishy-washy Western democracies that had to buy off voters with ever greater promises of consumption. In the United States, three-times Pulitzer Prize–winning columnist Thomas Friedman enviously proclaimed, "If only we could be like China for a day."[2] In a *New York Times* op-ed, he opined that America-style democracy was inferior when it came to making tough choices on climate change:

> One-party autocracy certainly has its drawbacks. But when it is led by a reasonably enlightened group of people, as China is today, it can also have great advantages. That one party can just impose the politically difficult but critically important policies needed to move a society forward in the twenty-first century. It is not an accident that China is committed to overtaking us in electric cars, solar power, energy efficiency, batteries, nuclear power and wind power.[3]

It is perhaps a measure of the environmental crisis facing humanity and the gains made by China that such an influential liberal was willing to consider dictatorship as, at least, a partial solution.

Heilongjiang provided, at least on first sight, further evidence for this claim. This is a key location for the biggest "greening" campaign on the planet, which has in recent years planted more trees than the rest of the world combined. It is where the world's biggest army has been mobilized to help protect endangered species such as the Amur tiger. Here too, the one-party state has banned logging and tried to put local and individual interests aside by designating huge expanses of land as nature reserves. And it was in Heilongjiang that a new model of nonconfrontational environmental activism achieved its earliest successes.

Ma Zhong was just fifteen years old when he was dispatched to guard and conquer the Great Northern Wilderness, an expanse of wetlands, dense virgin forest, and freezing winter temperatures that plunged below minus 40°C.[4] The challenge was daunting. Humanity had shunned these lands for millennia. The swamps, impenetrably marshy in summer and ice hard during the long dark winter, were deemed almost uninhabitable.

But a harsh landscape and unfamiliar traditions were by no means the biggest challenges confronting Ma at this moment in history. The year was 1969. For three years, his home city of Beijing had been racked by the Cultural Revolution, which pitted student Red Guards against the army, the party, their parents, and each other. On the northern border, skirmishes between Chinese and Soviet troops threatened to escalate into all-out war. Mao Zedong's solution was to disperse the Red Guards and send millions of students out of the cities and into remote frontier areas to strengthen China's borders and increase food production by converting land to agricultural usage.[5]

Ma was the youngest of a battalion of about 100 "educated youth" from Beijing, Shanghai, Tianjin, and Harbin who were sent to Fuyuan County to convert marshland to farm fields on China's northeastern border with Siberia. The urban teenager suddenly found himself living in one of the world's most desolate landscapes.

The Sanjiang wetlands covered an area the size of Ireland, yet they were home to a tiny indigenous population of just 4,000. Most were Hezhe, the smallest of China's ethnic minorities, a nomadic, shamanistic culture in which the men hunted by sled and the women wore salmon-skin robes threaded together with animal tendons.

"I have never seen such a wild place before or since in the whole world," Ma said forty years later, his eyes lighting up as he recalled the wonder of that time. "It was a unique experience. I was so alone that I could touch nature. I could talk to the forest and the wetland. I learned to hunt and to fish. You didn't need any skill. The fish were so abundant that all I had to do was put the rod in the water to catch something."

When life started to return to something like normal in 1974, Ma went back to Beijing a changed man.[6] He was still determined to master the wilderness, but this time with research rather than labor. When the universities reopened, he committed himself to a study of agriculture. It was not until 1988 that he returned to Fuyuan for a reunion with his fellow pioneers. The intervening fourteen years had seen the death of Mao and the start of the opening-and-reform policy that brought foreign capital and modern technology into an increasingly market-oriented nation. The impact was evident everywhere. When Ma returned to his beloved wetlands, he was shocked. The transformation he had helped begin with old tractors and a band of puny students was superaccelerated with the support of the World Bank, Japanese engineers, and state-of-the-art drainage and channeling machinery.

The consequences appalled him: "Everything had totally changed. The islands of pristine forest in the wetland were clear-cut. There were no fish left in the river. All the other animals were gone," he sighed. "I was very sad. I knew I had started this process. But back then, we were just struggling to survive. We disturbed nature, but only a little. Because there were so few of us, we couldn't do that much damage. We tried to convert the wetland, but we hadn't been able to do it. But when I returned the wetland had been turned into dry land for farming. It gave me a weird feeling."

Ma was forced into a bout of self-questioning. He changed direction. A rising star in academia, he switched his field of postgraduate study from agriculture to the environment. The Sanjiang wetlands became the focus of his research and his political activism. Once again, he was a pioneer, this time as a conservationist.

He quickly moved to the forefront of a new generation of idealists, this time devoted to the environment rather than politics. Ma was influential because he campaigned in a very Chinese way. He knew the one-party system, so did not attempt to confront it, working instead on persuasion and enlightened self-interest. He knew that, post-Mao, the nation was sick of ideology, so instead of appealing to vague ideals he focused on the economic, scientific argument for preservation. He knew the government structure was fragmented and competitive, so he built alliances where he could rather than trying to win over everyone. And he knew that in the New China, money talked, and dollars spoke loudest, so he drummed up financial support from overseas.

On paper, the results were stunningly successful, particularly by the standards of what was then still a nascent environmental movement.[7] In 1992, China won international plaudits for signing up to the Ramsar Convention, an international agreement on wetlands conservation.[8] A year later a national wetland nature reserve was established in Fuyuan under the jurisdiction of the Ministry of Forestry, followed by other state-backed development restrictions.[9] China joined hands with Russia and international NGOs to formulate a management plan for Sanjiang that was expected to establish a model for nature reserves throughout the nation.[10] In 2000, the Asian Development Bank and the Global Environment Fund, which is affiliated with the World Bank, pledged $20 million for biodiversity conservation in the region.

Even the military jumped on the conservation bandwagon. Environmental protection was declared the patriotic duty of the People's Liberation Army as part of its commitment to defend the homeland. Reforestation was declared a militarily strategic goal.[11] Ma's achievements were recognized with a promotion to dean of the Environment Department at the People's University, one of the nation's most prestigious academic institutions. After years in the wilderness, the conservation movement suddenly had a champion, a budget, a pilot project, international financing, and the backing of the state. For once, money, power, and the law were lined up on the side of nature. But even that was not enough.

Anarchy ruled on Harbin's roads. The taxi drivers had taken over. I had never witnessed anything like it anywhere else in China. The drivers asked where you wanted to go and, if the answer was not to their liking or you failed to agree on an off-meter bonus, they drove off contemptuously without a word of explanation. Even if you were fortunate enough to secure a cab, the driver would stop constantly along the way in search of additional fares, cramming as many people inside the car as possible. At first I found the practice immensely irritating, not to mention dangerous and almost certainly illegal, but there was a reason. Metered fares were distance-based, with no allowance made for time spent in the ever-worsening traffic jams that plagued the area. Local people sympathized. Many passengers even wound their windows down and touted on the driver's behalf. Few haggled long over the price. Nobody wants to walk when it's minus 20°C outside.

I was dropped off at the Environmental Protection Department, scene of a similar balancing act between regulatory ideals and people struggling to make a living. Historically, its officials have never been in such a strong position. International concerns about global warming and domestic fears about pollution have enabled the ministry to push through ambitious laws on environmental impact assessment and set meaningful targets for reductions in energy use and toxic discharge. They have named and shamed many polluters, using the media and NGOs to make up for their lack of clout inside the political establishment.[12] As elsewhere, the deputy environment minister Pan Yue proved a genuine force for change.[13] With other like-minded people around him, the environmental protection bureaucracy appeared to be in the ascendant. At a national level, environmental protection work was given ministerial status in 2008. With it came a full vote in the State Council.[14]

But the ministry lacks a strong national network. At a regional level, environment departments continue to answer to local governments. Even more than NGOs, they are obliged to work within the system rather than to expose and oppose its faults.

The EPD's offices were much like those of any other bureau of government throughout China. I was led along uniformly fluorescent-lit corridors past uniformly brown office doors in a uniformly orthogonal building, to the standard interview room, which was square and spacious with calligraphy and landscape paintings on one wall, large low chairs along the sides, and a well-polished table in the middle set with white-lidded cups for the green tea that arrived soon after. Bureaucratic hospitality was pleasingly not so standard, and could sometimes be rather convivial.

Li Ping, the head of Heilongjiang's Environment Protection Department, was in good spirits—a very different mood from his most famous public appearance in November 2005 as the unfortunate official who had to admit to one of the worst pollution cover-ups in the country's history.[15] That had been, he claimed, a turning point for government accountability. An explosion at a China National Petroleum Company plant hundreds of miles upstream in Jilin Province released more than 100 times the safe level of benzene into the Songhua, one of the three rivers that flows into the Sanjiang watershed. Five people died in the blast at the factory, but it was not until more than three days later that people living along the river were told that toxins were coursing in their direction. In Harbin, officials initially announced water supplies would have to be cut off for a few days for "pipe maintenance." The truth emerged just before the 50-kilometer poison slick hit the city, prompting a rush to the airport and railway station by those who could escape and fear and fury among those left behind. The disaster was seen as a watershed for environmentalists. Coinciding with the central government's shift toward a new model of sustainable "Scientific Development," the Songhua spill was cited as an example of everything that was wrong with the old way of doing things.[16]

It had taken similar crises in other countries to strengthen the powers of their environmental agencies. For Japan, it was the deadly mercury poisoning incident at Minamata. In the United States, it was the publication of *Silent Spring* in 1962, when the author, Rachel Carson, revealed previously unknown consequences of pesticide on wildlife. For China in 2005, it looked for a while as if Songhua might become a similar rallying point.

For a short period, journalists enjoyed an open season. Television broadcasts and newspapers were suddenly free to criticize lax environmental regulations and the hardship of ordinary people. The media was filled with images of Harbin residents lining up with buckets and kettles in icy winter streets as they waited for water tankers usually used for road cleaning.[17]

For Li, brought up in a political environment where control and secrecy were the norm, the frenzy of media scrutiny was a shock. "It was a strange experience for me to have to respond to a barrage of questions. I had only seen that on TV before," he recalled. But it was worthwhile. Li told me the media attention brought immediate budgetary rewards. Heilongjiang had been lobbying the central government for ten years for funds to clean up the Songhua. But other rivers, such as the Huai, the Liao, and the Yellow, were considered more urgent. After the benzene leak, however, the Songhua became an instant priority. Within months, Heilongjiang got everything it wanted—13 billion yuan for 116 water treatment plants and other projects to improve the river.[18]

The environment protection minister, Xie Zhenhua, resigned. Nine officials at the CNPC factory were fired and others at the Jilin environmental protection bureau were punished.[19] Li insisted Heilongjiang's government was getting tougher in implementing regulations, but its record was mixed.[20] As one of China's poorest provinces, polluting firms that would be rejected in wealthier areas were more likely to be accepted here.[21] To overcome local government resistance to tighter environmental rules, Li tried to galvanize the media, another change that was supposedly helped by the Songhua spill.[22] "This is a very big change. We want to raise public attention on these issues and to disillusion local governments who think we will protect them."

There was some truth in this heartwarming idea that the one-party state was joining hands with an emboldened media to rein in the excesses of polluters and corrupt local governments. Nationwide, journalists have more power than in the past to expose environmental wrongdoing,[23] and green NGOs are helping to carve out a bigger space for civil society.[24] But there are limits.

As local journalists covering the Songhua spill discovered, the draw-bridge was quickly raised when stories threatened stability. Local government ignored the state's disclosure laws on pollution.[25] Editors were given daily lists of topics that they were prohibited from covering. Journalists were under pressure to self-censor and to put the party before the people. Propaganda departments insisted on positive stories.[26]

China's first national park ought to have been one of them. The bus journey from Harbin to the Tangwang River, a tributary of the Songhua, was six hours due north on darkening, frozen roads lined by snow-covered fields and plantations of young, thin trees in tidy rows. Replanted and patterned in this way, the Great Northern Wilderness looked neither very great nor very wild. The vastness has been conquered. The era of the ideological pioneers lives on in the names of local towns: Red Star, East Wind, and Oppose Revisionism Battalion. But nobody in the bus seemed interested in history. Those eyes that were still open were focused on the bus videos: *Die Hard,* with Bruce Willis, and *Forbidden Kingdom,* with Jackie Chan and Jet Li.

We arrived in the national park late at night. After stepping off the bus, the first vehicle we saw was a logging truck stacked high with felled trunks. "Isn't that illegal?" asked my assistant. It certainly seemed ominous in an area where the forests were supposed to be protected.

The bus driver kindly took us an extra few hundred meters to the entrance of our hotel, so we were not outside long in the cold. Closer to Siberia now, the temperature had fallen to minus 35°C. Icicles formed on my beard. Even inside three pairs of socks, my toes became numb walking the short distance from the bus to the lobby. The receptionist apologized that there would be no hot water until the following day. Never mind. I checked in and crashed out, grateful for the warm bed.

Conservation and tyranny can make happy bedfellows. Although the concept of national parks and other protected areas is usually considered both modern and Western, the northeast of China remained untouched for centuries thanks to autocratic fiat that effectively made this region one of the world's first and biggest nature reserves. In 1668, at the start of the Qing dynasty, Emperor Kang Xi issued a proclamation that anyone who logged, mined, hunted, or fished in the area would be decapitated.[27] The Manchu ruler was motivated by a desire to protect the feng shui of his homeland.[28] Kang Xi ruled during a period of rampant deforestation and land clearance elsewhere in China, but he left Manchuria in pristine condition. It became a sanctuary for tigers, bears, leopards, wolves, wild boar, and cranes. In the eighteenth century, only a million people lived in what now comprises the three northeast provinces of Heilongjiang, Jilin, and Liaoning, a vast expanse of land covering an area the size of France and the UK combined.[29] Harbin, now the biggest metropolis in the northeast, was then a small village. As late as the nineteenth century, when forest still covered 70 percent of the land, the dense woodlands were recognized as the ultimate defense for the nation's northern borders by one military inspector: "The provinces of Jilin and Heilongjiang are full of primeval forests . . . Local tribes are either nomads or hunters and they seldom cut trees. The forests there extend several hundred miles without roads and therefore provide better defense than the Great Wall."[30]

Political change led to the tearing down of this natural barrier and, with it, a steady erosion of the de facto wildlife reserve. When the Qing dynasty weakened in the late nineteenth century, the wilderness was opened up and then carved up by colonial powers. In 1896, during a period when Russian influence was strongest, swathes of trees were destroyed for the construction of the Trans-Siberian railway. After Japan became the dominant regional power, the forest clearance was accelerated to provide fuel and building materials for military campaigns in the 1930s and 1940s.[31] By the time the Chinese Communist Party took over in 1949, the northeast's population had soared to 38 million and Heilongjiang's forest cover had slumped to 45 percent.[32] The worst was yet to come.

The Mao era saw the decimation of what was left of the Great Northern Wilderness. As early as 1956, East German experts were warning China against unsustainable clear-cutting (the complete eradication of all trees in a given area) in Heilongjiang, but they were ignored because Mao was in a hurry to catch up with the economies of the West.[33] As we have seen repeatedly in this book, the greatest damage was done during the Great Leap Forward. In those few years, entire forests of 400- to 500-year-old Korean pines, camphor pines, and Northeast China ash were felled.

The loggers of Heilongjiang became propaganda heroes for supplying half of the nation's timber. Their deeds were lyricized in the "Song of the Lumberjacks":

> I'm an ambitious young man from the Tiger Valley
> Carrying an axe in my hand,

> Chopping down trees on high mountains,
> Giving my precious years to the state.
>
> I'm an educated young man from the Tiger Valley,
> A full-time lumberjack in my hilly town,
> Trained with the best logging techniques,
> This happy life will last 10,000 years.[34]

That "happy life" lasted barely twenty years. In 1984, clear-cutting was banned. By then it was too late.[35] Less than 5 percent of the primary woodland was left.[36]

In 1998, deforestation was blamed for a series of devastating landslides across the nation. Visiting Heilongjiang that year, Premier Zhu Rongji declared, "We must never again cut down so many trees." Logging restrictions were tightened. The state belatedly put its weight behind forest conservation.

In a one-party system, there are no alternative governments and only very weak checks on power. Unable to "kick the bums out," the best and often only hope for reform is that power wielders die or turn over a new leaf. The Heilongjiang provincial forestry department is trying to do the latter. Formerly loggers, they are now trying to reinvent themselves as conservationists by leading the world's most ambitious tree-planting campaign.[37] On paper, this is an impressive example of poacher turning gamekeeper. In 1978, the government in Beijing announced the start of a seventy-three-year plan to rebuild the forests of northern China by planting a "Great Green Wall" that would stretch 4,480 kilometers from western Xinjiang to eastern Heilongjiang, creating the biggest man-made carbon sponge on the planet.[38]

The program was based around a mass mobilization of the sort that only China can muster. The National People's Congress passed a resolution obliging every healthy Chinese citizen older than eleven to plant three to five trees each year without pay.[39] In 1979, March 12 was declared National Tree-Planting Day.[40] Every year since then, forestry officials nationwide have taken up shovels on that date, together with an estimated three million party members, civil servants, model workers, celebrities, and state leaders to plant saplings. The air force has also helped with aerial seeding missions.

This was tree-hugging communism at its most vivid and energetic. Watch the domestic propaganda on such days and you would think China must have the planet's densest forests.[41] That ought to be good news, but the propaganda chief of the forestry department appeared reluctant to share it with the outside world.

Mu Jingjun did not even pretend to welcome an interview. Sneering and occasionally belching as I asked apparently irritating questions about tree planting, conservation, and biodiversity, he said he had none of the answers to hand although we had faxed our request for information long in advance.

Asking for detailed figures produced an impatient sigh. He told me Heilongjiang's forests were the greatest in China and they were growing. The government had banned logging in many areas and pledged to expand coverage to 49 percent of the province within four years. Heilongjiang was in the vanguard of the Great Green Wall project, which, along with afforestation work elsewhere in the nation, added the equivalent of 700,000 football fields' worth of trees nationwide every year.[42]

But it was hard to get a true picture of how effective the measures really are. Many foreign conservationists are skeptical about China's claims.[43] Official figures on forest cover included nurseries and shrublands.[44] Less than half the land designated as "forest" actually had trees growing on it.[45] Chinese academics told me privately that the forestry ministry prevented the publication of scientific papers that challenged their claims of success.

I was not sure if it was a cover-up or merely a difference of values. The forestry department had little time for ecological concerns. Biodiversity was considered an obstacle to reaping maximum economic benefit. Loggers were encouraged to cut below the canopy, remove weeds, and till the soil to prevent rival species from slowing the growth of the trees. But quantity boasts often masked quality shortcomings. Although there were more trees than thirty years earlier, there were fewer species.[46] This made forests weak and vulnerable to disease.[47] Nonetheless, almost every forestry official and academic I spoke to in Heilongjiang and Beijing believed man could improve on nature to ensure maximum economic returns.

The exception was former vice minister of forestry Dong Zhiyong, who told me with unusual candor that the bureaucrats running the ministry had little awareness of the need for biodiversity, even though they were in charge of most of the country's nature reserves. The only reason they have turned to conservation, he said, was because they had no alternative: "We're in a situation where we have no wood to cut. None of the forests are mature enough."

The creation of many nature reserves was heavily influenced by international organizations, such as the International Union for Conservation of Nature and the World Wide Fund for Nature, which were allowed to send delegations to China during the period of opening that followed Mao's death in 1976. Among the first to make contact with them was Wang Song, a zoologist by training who later went on to compile the first Red List of the country's endangered species.[48]

Now retired, Wang recalled the unease among many government officials in those early days. "Some said it was too early to work with the international community, that our conservation systems were too weak. But I said no way. We must hurry. Even then, I knew that China overused wildlife for everything, that people would kill anything for foreign currency."

Since then, progress has been far slower than he would like. "It is a shame. We are much improved, but there is no way to change in one generation. Our country has a long history of overusing wildlife."

Wang bemoaned the loss of forest in Heilongjiang. The plantations of small trees that replaced the old-growth forests were, he said sadly, not the same at all. "A human life is just a fraction of a second in terms of the planet's history, but in my short time I have seen huge changes. I have clearly seen the virgin forest cleared. There are just a few small reserves left. Even now, nobody thinks about restoration of natural ecosystems."

He was encouraged by the increasing willingness of senior officials to discuss the subject. Compared with the past, he said, China had the money for conservation. But the talk and the cash had yet to be translated into action to reverse the devastating changes to China's ecology since the 1950s.

Wang advocates natural regeneration, letting damaged ecosystems recover by themselves. But policymakers prefer engineering projects and big reforestation schemes. With little public understanding of the importance of biodiversity, Wang feared conservation could become an empty fad: "China is very clever. We very quickly pick up foreign terms like eco-tourism and eco-food. But it is mostly nonsense. Look at the Chinese papers. They always write about 'ecological construction.' The word construction means you can do anything you want. We tried to change it to ecological restoration, but nobody would accept this."

When I looked out over Tangwanghe the next morning, it resembled a depressed industrial landscape more than a new national park. Coal smoke poured from hundreds of small household chimneys and a handful of industrial stacks. A shallow haze obscured distant trees. Every minute or so, a three-wheeler taxi or truck stacked with timber blundered through the otherwise quiet, white roads. Logging evidently remained the main source of income for the 40,000 residents of this frontier town, which was carved out of virgin forest in that epic year of 1958.

We crossed the road for a breakfast of gruel and *baozi* at a small restaurant and got talking to the owner, a middle-aged woman, whose parents moved to Tangwanghe when it opened up during the Great Leap Forward. Perhaps a little insensitively, I asked why they came to such a cold and remote place. An old man at a nearby table interrupted: "There was good money to be made here from logging up until about thirty years ago. Then we fell behind the rest of the country." In the early days, the town had been praised by Deng Xiaoping as a model of sustainable forestry because locals planted saplings over the same area that they clear-cut. But the trade-off was unequal. The new trees, mostly white birch and larch, were a poor replacement for the old Korean pines.

The old man told me he continued to cut trees, though there were far fewer than in the past. "It only takes a few minutes with a chainsaw or half an hour by hand."

Tangwanghe is supposed to be an example of smart top-down conservation.[49] Unlike nature reserves, which are often too poorly funded to be effective in protecting flora and fauna, the national park is supposed to generate tourist income to pay for strong management.[50] But the problem is that the area was chosen as a national park not because of its rich ecology but because of its collapsed economy. The nearest municipality of Yichun was classified in 2008 as one of China's twelve "resource-depleted cities," an evocative term that demonstrates how the unsustainable extraction of timber and other resources has left many communities without livelihoods.

The town's young tourist chief, Ma Shengli, drove us to the Stone Forest, explaining on the way that 99.8 percent of the park was forested, albeit with mostly secondary growth. "It is just a trial project. We are pioneers. The idea is to protect the ecosystem on a large scale, develop seven tourist sites, and to help local people get rich," he explained.

We stopped and trudged through the snowy forest, which was predominantly made up of slim young white birch and dragon spruce. There were a small number of old, broad Korean pines, though Ma explained they were usually those with gnarled trunks that were not considered good enough to cut down. It brought to mind my visit to Shangri-La, and Zhuangzi's story of "useless trees" outlasting better-looking specimens. The park had established a sponsorship system for the fortunate if ugly survivors. For 100 yuan, visitors could have their names pinned to a protected tree, some of which were more than 400 years old.

Ma told me there were bears, boar, foxes, and deer deeper in the forest, though I saw no trace of them. The absence of any animal tracks was perhaps unsurprising in the depths of winter, but, apart from a few small birds, the forest was eerily quiet.

Short of wildlife, the park's managers decided their best selling point was unusual granite formations. The building-sized geological formations were unlikely to ever challenge the majesty of the Grand Canyon, but their poetic names were in keeping with a long Chinese tradition of using the imagination to amplify nature. Wandering around the "Kissing Boulders," "Sliver of Sky," "Drunken Tortoise," and "Pine Teasing Golden Toad" made for a pleasant walk, and the views from the hilltops, even of secondary forest, were breathtaking.

But under the forest canopies, the variety of life was diminishing. John MacKinnon, the head of the EU-China Biodiversity Programme, told me China plants more trees than the rest of the world combined. "But the trouble is they tend to be monoculture plantations. They are not places where birds want to live." The World Bank advised China to concentrate more on quality than quantity of its forests.

China's woodlands have been emptied by decades of overhunting, foliage cutting, and excess harvesting of wild plants and fungi.[51] The protection of the military and the powers of the one-party state have not been applied with enough gusto to prevent a decimation of many species.

At the top of the food chain, the world's biggest tiger, the Amur tiger, also known as the Siberian or North China tiger, had been hunted close to extinction because of its value in traditional Chinese medicine.[52] Lower down, the Heilongjiang frog and Northeast China frog were also on the verge of being wiped out because their estrogen is a traditional treatment for fatigue, improving the memory, and strengthening the kidney.[53] The Great Northern Wilderness was becoming the land of dead rivers and hollow forests.

Changbaishan was perhaps the most notorious example. This forest in Jilin, on the border with North Korea, was once one of the most bio-rich places in northern China, home to over fifty species of mammals, including the Amur tiger, sika deer, goral, sable, and black bear, as well as 200 species of birds. This was the subject of one of China's first and most influential studies of the economic value of an ecosystem.[54] International recognition came in 1980, when UNESCO named Changbaishan as a world's biosphere reserve with a declared ecological inventory of 2,277 plants and 1,225 animal species.

The UN body appears to have been the victim of environmental fraud. In 2008, local biologists said they had been ordered to exaggerate wildlife numbers because the real figures were so low they would hurt the image of the nature reserve.[55] Visiting scientists found almost no animal tracks in the park. Feng Yongfeng, one of China's most influential environmental reporters, put it more succinctly: Changbaishan, he told me, is an "empty forest."

The following day, we penetrated deeper into Xiaoxingan to visit a logging camp outside the national park. It was a two-hour drive by bus and then car along a rutted, icy road. The forests were full of felled trees, timber yards lined the roadside, logging trucks added to the traffic, and most of the people we met were cutting, trading, or processing wood. On the bus, a timber merchant offered to show us around. I was grateful for her kindness, but it turned out she had ulterior motives. After calling her husband to explain she would be late home because of a foreign guest, the pretty middle-aged woman hooked up with a young boyfriend. They got friendly in the back of the car as we drove from lumberyard to tree farm.

Finding the lumberjacks was not easy. We stopped every few hundred meters to listen for the buzz of a chain saw, but by the time we caught up with the loggers they had already felled the day's quota of trees and were loading them onto a truck as the snow fell around them. Four men were needed to carry a single trunk of white birch. They lifted in pairs, two at the front, two at the rear, poles across their shoulders tied to steel hooks that bit into the logs as they walked up a pair of parallel planks to the top of the truck.

Their leader, Hou Zhengkuan, gave directions and adjusted loads to ensure the truck was stable. Between logs, he told me incomes had fallen along with production over the previous five years. Now that it was forbidden to fell Korean pines, earnings came almost entirely from the low-quality white birch, which was used for pulp, ice-cream sticks, firewood, matches, plywood, and furniture. He earned 1,800 yuan a month. This was a decline from five years earlier when he was cutting higher-value timber. "The forests are declining in volume. There is less and less wood," he said.

It is the same everywhere in China. Now that the Korean pine has been decimated, most of the trees in the forest are Dahurian larch, which reaches maturity after a hundred years, and fast-growing white birch, which mature in just forty years.[56] But even these species have been logged close to unsustainable levels.

Hou shrugged at the way things had turned out. "After fifty years of cutting, the forests have declined." Loggers, he said, chopped 95 percent less wood than when he started. We next went to see the ultimate diminution of the forests: a small, mist-shrouded factory where huge tree trunks were splintered into 5-centimeter toothpicks. The process was primitively simple. At one end of the workshop, thick logs were peeled. At the other they were diced into thin strips. The transformation was completed along the length of a conveyor belt. The belt was only five meters or so long, but the air was so thick with humidity I could not see one end from the other.

Moisture was the key to the process. The birch had to be thoroughly soaked before it could be stripped and sliced. It was then wrung like a wet rag, filling the air with droplets and turning the factory into a cool sauna.

In the mist, laborers appeared and disappeared like wraiths as they fetched fresh logs, hewed off the bark, then pierced either end of the bare wood with spikes ready for the machine.

Swollen with water, the logs were easily peeled by automated blades, then pressed flat and squeezed dry by a thunderously juddering mangle. Dozens of rings, each representing a year of growth, were unraveled in seconds. A tree was consumed every five minutes.

The clanking machine is like a calculator, doing addition and multiplication for mankind but only subtraction and division for the natural environment. Output—production and profits—are positive. The owner drives a luxury car. Billions of teeth around the world have been picked with the carefully crafted splinters he produces. The input, on the other hand, is entirely negative. Over twenty years, the two workshops in this factory have shredded close to a million trees.

And this is just one tiny old factory that employs a couple of dozen people and cheap, outdated equipment. Multiply that by several thousand and a picture emerges of how much wood is being consumed by China's paper mills, flooring firms, furniture workshops, construction companies, and chopstick makers.[57] Consumption of printing and writing paper have more than doubled since 1995. Hardwood floorings are increasingly popular. China has become the biggest user of pulp and timber in the world. No wonder the factory manager was finding wood harder to come by and more expensive.

The higher prices were inevitable because the government's toughness applied only to suppliers. When it came to consumers, the authoritarian tiger turned into a pussycat. Despite the 1998 logging ban, wood consumption continued to surge along with the growing economy. With China's forests unable to meet demand, buyers had to look to other nations for supplies. From Heilongjiang they did not have to go far.

We drove four hours east to the Heilong Jiang or Black Dragon River,[58] which marks the border with Russia and gives China's northernmost province its name. The water was frozen and gnarled into chunks. On the Chinese bank, several large ships were iced into their berths for the winter. On the Russian side, wisps of smoke curled up from the chimneys of a small settlement. In the middle of the icy expanse a military checkpoint sat on the territorial dividing line. Apart from a single border guard sweeping snow in front of the passport control barrier and a fisherman hacking a hole in the ice, there was not a soul in sight. The Black Dragon was hibernating.

Previous visitors to the border told me the densely populated Chinese side of the river was bare of trees and birds, while the sparsely habited Russian banks were covered in thick forests full of birds' nests. I could not see such a big difference. But local Chinese fishermen shamelessly used this ecological disparity as a selling point. "Buy my fish," said one seller. "They are good. The river is clean. Look over there. That is Russia. No pollution."

But China's environmental problems are spilling over the border.[59] Since the introduction of domestic logging controls in 1998, Chinese demand has destroyed more forest than ever. The only difference is that the trees are being felled—usually illegally—outside its borders, in Siberia.[60] From nothing, the timber trade across this border has suddenly become the most important on the planet.

Since 1998, the volume of wood entering China has risen ninefold, pushing the country up from seventh to second among the world's forestry importers. Already tops for industrial roundwood and tropical logs, China is on course to overtake the United States as the number-one timber importer in all categories.[61]

Following a pattern set in the West, but on a bigger scale with fewer self-constraints, China is snapping up more wood overseas even as it introduces domestic controls. This has accelerated illegal deforestation in South America, Africa, and Southeast Asia. But the biggest supplier by far is Russia, which provides 60 percent of the logs entering China.[62] Much of it is used on construction. As buildings go up in Beijing, Shanghai, Guangzhou, and Chongqing, the vast taiga boreal forests of eastern Russia are being flattened.[63] Siberia is suffering the same fate as China's Great Northern Wilderness. At the harvesting rates of the early twenty-first century, the Russian Far East is on course to be logged out within twenty years.[64]

Day and night, long trains and convoys of trucks bring Siberian logs to China through gateways in Suifenhe, in Heilongjiang, and Manzhouli in Inner Mongolia. Wood is the main freight on the Trans-Mongolian Railway. In China, the imports are used for everything from doorframes to concert halls. When the monks at Wutaishan rebuilt their temple to bolster their bid for UN World Heritage status, they used Russian redwood because no domestic supplies were available.[65]

Wen Bo of Pacific Environment, an NGO which operates on both

sides of the border, told me that China has put huge ecological pressure
on Russia. One side effect of timber smuggling, he said, was an illegal
trade in wildlife. Tiger bone and skin, musk deer, ginseng, and even bears
were sometimes concealed under the logs. He predicted the timber trade
would diminish simply because there was not much top-quality forest left
to cut, even in Siberia. The two countries had repeatedly pledged cooperation to tackle the problems, but governance was even less joined up
across borders and languages. There was very little incentive for China's
bureaucrats and customs officials to act. The country's economic growth
was dependent on deforestation in other countries. There were even tax
incentives for cross-border traders.[66] Given these trends, even the toothpicks might one day be made with Russian wood. Import rules and logging bans in China had completely failed to halt the depletion of the
world's forests.

I left in the morning for the Shuilian wetland reserve to see if the government's efforts to protect nature were more effective in a concentrated area.
The first impression was bleak. The white flatland stretched off to a distant horizon. Reeds pressed through the frozen earth only to quiver in the
icy wind. Hundreds of small birds flocked back and forth from telephone
wires to tree branches. They were the biggest nonhuman population I had
seen in a week. But the landscape felt more suburban than wild. Advertising hoardings, pylons, and farmhouses shared the outer fringe of this
sanctuary.

That was the norm. Throw a stick in Heilongjiang and there was a one-
in-seven chance it would fall in an area designated as a nature reserve,
though much of this land was actually used for farms, yards, or roads.

Judged purely by statistics, the government is doing all the right things.
China has more protected reserves covering a far wider area than any other
country. A fifth were wetlands spread across an area roughly the same size
as England.[67]

In theory, they offer wildlife the full protection of the state.[68] But, in
practice, definitions of reserves are vague and penalties for violations so
low that rules are easily circumvented by developers. Local governments
are often hostile to reserves because they have to pay a share of the running costs while forfeiting the tax revenue that would come from turning

over the land to farms or factories. As a result, most reserves are under-resourced and understaffed, often with people who care little about the environment.

Even the better-maintained wetlands are threatened by pesticides and herbicides and drainage for farmland. A 2005 UNESCO field survey at Lake Xinkai, the biggest lake in northeast China, found that the number of species had declined by 10 percent and wetland by a third. At Zhalong, another of the region's most important reserves, poachers continue to prey on endangered species such as the red-crowned crane. The story was similar across the country. While I was in Heilongjiang, the domestic media reported the slaughter of protected swans in Poyang Lake in Jiangxi Province, one of the world's most important wintering wetlands for migratory birds. The poachers were on a killing spree to satisfy the demand for exotic dishes ahead of the spring festival banquet season.[69] Government protection is no match for seasonal market forces.

I asked one of China's leading conservationists why reserves were so ineffective. Xie Yan, the director of the Wildlife Conservation Society, had been trying to persuade policymakers and the public to boost protection for more than a decade. She said the problem was that the top-down system of establishing reserves floundered on a weak cultural and financial base.

"It is good that China has established so many reserves, but the capacity is very low. The employees' awareness about conservation is very low. They just want a job. They don't love wildlife," she said.

With the exception of Tibet and a few other places where Buddhism was strong, she felt reserve managers had little passion for their work. In many cases they were poorly educated, badly trained, and underpaid. Jobs were often secured through family connections in the party or government, which allowed the staff either to do nothing in terms of patrols or, in the worst cases, to poach themselves to supplement their incomes. Access to exotic dishes and valuable ingredients for traditional medicines became a perk of the position. Xie had visited reserves where the welcoming banquet included dishes made from protected local species.

"If I had power, I would make an order that all government officials should not eat endangered species. They are the biggest consumers. Whenever they have an official banquet, they eat rare animals," she sighed.[70]

Outside of wartime, leaders in all political systems struggle to rein back

demand. Efforts to trim excess often prove temporary, ineffective, or politically suicidal. Supporters of slower growth or more concern for the environment are often marginalized or defeated. As noted in earlier chapters,
this was true two thousand years ago of Liu An, the Taoist naturalist who
is thought to have compiled the Book of the Prince of Huainan. Modern
Chinese history contains similar examples.[71]

The most prominent was Liu Shaoqi, the former president of China
who was purged during the Cultural Revolution. Among his supposed
crimes was *paxingzhuyi* or "reptilianism," a reference to his cautious,
gradualist approach to development. While Mao demanded grand plans
and immediate results, Liu held up a project to dam Dianchi Lake, and
in 1961, expressed alarm at the scale of logging in Heilongjiang, saying,
"How can we face future generations if we clear-cut all these wonderful
Korean pines? We should leave some trees for them."[72] Those words sound
inspired today. But future generations never had a chance to thank Liu. In
1968, he was condemned as "China's number one Capitalist Roader" and
died in prison a year later.

That murderous age is over, but for the environment the situation has
become worse as the power of consumers has grown. After Mao, each successive generation of leaders had less authority than their predecessors.
Hu and Wen do not rule by charisma and fear, but by pulling together
coalitions within the politburo. Local governments have more autonomy
than ever. Industries operate with minimal oversight. The media, the
courts, and the electorate are too weak to hold them to account.

As a result, while there is no Mao at the pinnacle of politics in China
today, there are hundreds or thousands of little Maos in local government
and industry, each with a personal fiefdom, each trying to build an empire,
and each desperate to make their mark with a big project. They appreciate
the central government's attempt to restrain them as much as Mao liked
being lectured by foreign powers. China's political system now exhibits the
worst elements of dictatorship and democracy: power lies neither at the
top nor the bottom, but within a middle class of developers, polluters, and
local officials who are difficult to regulate, monitor, and challenge.

The Ministry of Environmental Protection is too weak to act as a coun-
terbalance. Even after securing full voting status in the cabinet it lacked
the clout and resources of other government bodies.[73] Control over 11,000
lower-level environmental bureaus is patchy at best and in many cases

nonexistent.[74] Only a tenth of China's environmental laws are enforced, according to one legal expert.[75] Only half the funds dedicated to environmental protection are actually spent on legitimate projects.[76] Data that might strengthen the ministry's authority are withheld.[77] Most conservation programs are not under its control. Instead, reserves are usually run by the State Forestry Administration, which favors rare-animal breeding farms, and by local authorities, which often want to use the land for business.

Gradually Pan Yue, the ministry's most visible driving force and one of its main theorists,[78] has been sidelined.[79] In 2006, the "green GDP" programs he established were quietly shelved. A year later, he told friends he had to lie low for a while after being pointedly passed over for promotion during the Seventeenth Communist Party Congress. In 2008, he was stripped of both his powers to enforce environmental assessment impact regulations and his role as a ministry spokesman.[80] The pollution disclosure laws he initiated are now ignored by most local governments.[81]

There are other advocates of change. China's leaders have long been aware of the dangers of waste, inefficiency, and environmental degradation. Government officials constantly talk about policy turning points and new directions. In the 1990s, Premier Zhu Rongji tried to make environmental protection more of a priority.[82] His successor, Wen Jiabao, went considerably further and is widely credited among environmental activists for pushing a green agenda, but he lacks a strong power base compared with other politburo members. His place is likely to be taken by Li Keqiang, who is being handed many of the portfolios relating to the environment and climate change. But authority is diffused. Unable to claim either an imperial mandate from heaven above or a popular mandate from the people below, China's leaders often follow rather than guide development. Laudable laws and praiseworthy policies are not enough. If conservation is to stand any chance of working in China, the government needs to be either a lot more dictatorial or a lot more democratic or, more realistically, needs to secure the support of the market, the media, and a nascent civil society centered around NGOs and the Internet. Without them, the authorities have the power to expand but not the power to conserve. Waste and environmental destruction are inevitable.[83] The emphasis on efficiency of "Scientific Development" reads just like any other propaganda slogan painted on a village wall: it highlights the fact that reality is the complete opposite.

Even Ma Zhong, the pioneer of Heilongjiang's first wetland nature reserve, is fighting a losing battle.[84] Despite international and central government support, his efforts to make the Sanjiang area an example of conservation management failed to win widespread support among locals who preferred to put their land to greater economic use. Demand for food and land is still growing. As farming becomes increasingly profitable, people move in and the government's commitment to the environment is compromised yet further. The population of the three provinces that once encompassed the Great Northern Wilderness is now well above 100 million. The region is a bastion of the state's food security policy. Wetlands and wildlife don't really stand a chance.[85]

"This is the most difficult time to be a conservationist," Ma said sadly. "Few people agree with me. Although it's nice in principle, when people are given the choice of food on the table or the protection of birds, they all choose food. That is understandable."

New cold-resistant hybrids, modern technology, and global warming had turned the Sanjiang area into the rice capital of China. The marshes that Ma helped to convert into dry land for farming during the Cultural Revolution were being reflooded and turned into rice paddies. Nature reserve managers approved the massive expansion of the cultivated land on the dubious grounds that paddy fields are a form of wetland.[86] Far from blocking this expansion into what little was left of the wilderness, the government has encouraged land conversion with tax incentives and price subsidies.[87] Heilongjiang has become the biggest grain producer in China, with a surplus so great that much of it is turned into ethanol.[88]

"In the space of just two or three years, farming on the Sanjiang Plain has become profitable for the first time in more than fifty years," said Ma. "Wetland conservation cannot compete." The math is simple. The value of wetland rises more than thirtyfold once it is converted into farmland.

Yet Heilongjiang's best soil is being degraded. The province once boasted the most carbon-rich earth in China. The black soil was so valuable that it was protected. Under provincial regulations, townships were not supposed to build factories unless they first removed the loam and laid it down elsewhere. But this rule was usually ignored. The topsoil has thinned and paled as a result of overcultivation and excess use of fertilizer.

In some areas in the southwest of the province, the land is suffering the same fate as much of Gansu, Ningxia, and Inner Mongolia and turning into desert. Local journalists told me this was now a bigger problem for the province than water pollution.

More of Sanjiang's wetlands will be converted in the future to compensate for the loss of topsoil and to ensure the nation's farmland stays above the 120-million-hectare baseline that the government set for food supply stability.[89] It is a matter of national security. As the state media has pointed out, the Three Rivers area provides enough food for three cities—Beijing, Shanghai, and Tianjin—as well as the entire People's Liberation Army. Madame Qian Zhengying, the former water minister, told me she believed this had large potential to be expanded further in the future. Against such powerful forces, conservationists like Ma can only hope to limit the damage.[90]

I left Heilongjiang unconvinced that the world could solve its environmental problems by being "China for a Day." Strong government is important. Many of the politburo's declared measures are ambitious and commendable. But they are not enough. Implementation is dire. More nature reserves are being established, more animals are being bred in captivity, and more trees are being planted, but wetlands, forests, topsoil, and wildlife are declining more precipitously than ever.

It is not a question of democracy or dictatorship, but of demographics and culture. As long as there are more people demanding more food and bigger buildings, the pressure to clear more wetlands and forest will grow. Despite its dictatorial reputation, the Chinese government seems even less able to prevent an environmental meltdown than leaders in democratic nations because it is more addicted to growth. When it comes to protecting the environment, the authority of the authoritarian state looks alarmingly shaky.

I had looked at top-down, supply-side, scientific solutions and found them wanting. It was time to consider the grassroots, demand-side, cultural alternatives. And where better to view them than the massive, sparsely populated northern region where more and more of China's problems were being dumped.

16

Grass Roots
To Xanadu

The more I engaged in environmental protection, the more I
understood the importance of democracy and the rule of law.
—Pan Yue, deputy environment minister, "Thoughts on Environmental Issues"

The driver was hurtling us toward Inner Mongolia at a reckless speed.
His handling was good and he was familiar with the roads, but he could
not possibly have known what was coming in the other direction as he
overtook slow trucks on rising, winding bends through the outer dregs of
the Loess Plateau. His only precaution was to keep his hand on the horn
almost as often as his foot was on the accelerator. "I'm coming through.
Get out of the way!" the horn blared. One accident was averted at the last
moment by a sudden spurt of the accelerator and a yank of the wheel,
another by sharp braking and indignant honking.

I was initially fatalistic. But after the first near miss, I became worried
enough to ask him to slow down, which he did for a couple of minutes,
then roared back to video-game speed, talking away the whole time about
his side businesses in a strong local accent. For him, time was obviously
money. Either that or he wanted to make me pay for haggling down the
fare. I took some comfort in the landscape, which was swiftly shifting from
winding loess slopes to flat gravel desert. The scenery was getting uglier,
but at least it was easier to see what was coming on the road ahead.

Inner Mongolia announced itself with a smoke-belching power plant,
piles of coal on the roadside, and a gust of sand-filled wind. I swapped

vehicles at the first opportunity and was soon on a minor road into the Hetao grasslands, relieved to be progressing at a less suicidal speed, with a quiet driver inside the car and empty open plains outside.

I had been looking forward to this trip for some time. A year earlier in Mongolia, the country to the north, I had been awestruck by the beauty of empty space, high, translucent blue skies, and endless green steppe that you could drive or gallop across for hours without seeing a single fence or building. Outside the cities, the only signs of habitation were the white *ger* tents of the nomadic herders who scratched a living on the grasslands.

Few Han care to acknowledge the enormous influence of Mongols on China's history. Much of the country's current territory, wealth, and status are owed to Genghis Khan and his successors. In the thirteenth century, this Mongol led a small army of nomad warriors across Eurasia, bringing almost the entire continent under their thrall and smoothing the way to increased trade between Europe and Asia along the Silk Road. His name has since become a byword for brutality, but he was also a scholar, poet, and philosopher who was sufficiently broad-minded to challenge his own shamanistic upbringing by inviting Christian, Muslim, and other scholars to explain their beliefs.[1]

Genghis Khan was also aware of the need to conserve his home environment. Even while pillaging central Asia, he introduced laws to protect the grasslands of Mongolia. Hunting was permitted only in winter. Burning or excavating the grasslands without permission was punishable by death. Under his rule, the Mongols were said to conserve wildlife better than human life.[2] Such beliefs lasted far longer than the nomad warrior. As in Tibet, Mongolians are Buddhists who revere nature, which is a major reason their economy has been slow to develop and their environment has until recently been among the least spoiled in Asia.

But Inner Mongolia, the Chinese region that spans most of the country's northern border, was very different. Modernity and Han influence were evident in the factories and white-tiled buildings. Large areas of grassland, the traditional home of nomadic Mongol culture, had been converted to agriculture or fallen victim to the desert. Under low gray skies, the landscape looked drained of color.

This was the last leg of my journey across China. What had started with a search for a mythical natural paradise in the southern mountains of Yunnan was finishing with an all-too-real man-made crisis in the flat northern grasslands. This was where the environmental buck stopped. Two hundred years of carbon-driven, capital-financed development had been deferred and outsourced to places like this. The West had pushed its waste and dirty industry on to Japan, Taiwan, and Hong Kong. They, in turn, had dumped the same problems on China's coastal provinces. From there, the ecological stress was transferred to remote inland areas. At each stage, the impact grew bigger. By the time the world's environmental trauma reached Inner Mongolia, it had swollen to staggering proportions.

Polluting factories that cannot satisfy the increasingly stringent environmental regulations of the newly rich coastal regions have found a welcome home in Inner Mongolia, where itinerant local party bosses are anxious to make their mark before moving on to new posts. Clusters of heavy industry have spread up from Shanxi, Ningxia, and Gansu, clogging the U-bend of the Yellow River, which is here so contaminated the water is consistently ranked as unhealthy even to touch.

It is also the new center of fossil-fuel production, taking over from Shanxi's depleted mines even though the quality of coal in Inner Mongolia is poorer and the region has even less water for cleaning and processing the fuel. Engineers have also moved in to exploit the biggest natural gas field in China. Huge wind farms are rising up on the pastures. The land of the nomads is rapidly transforming into a hub of heavy industry. Thanks to these trends and its low population density, Inner Mongolia now has the highest per capita carbon emissions in China.[3]

Most dramatic has been the change in the land itself. Desperate to feed a growing population, the Chinese government tried to cultivate the grasslands. As in Xinjiang, it was a disaster for the environment. Nomads were driven off the plains; settlers moved in and applied the same inappropriate irrigation techniques.[4] The fragile grassland ecosystem collapsed, lakes dried up, and wide areas turned to desert. Inner Mongolia became the main source of the dust and salt-alkaline storms that plague northeast Asia every spring. Mixed with pollution from the growing number of heavy industries in northern China, the particles create photochemical smogs in Korea, Japan, and toxic winds that blow across the Pacific to the west coast of the United States, adding the problem of "global dimming" to that of global warming.[5]

In places the plains had surrendered to sandy dunes. Elsewhere, defensible areas were bolstered with lines of trees and shrubs. Mostly, though, the surface was low grass, gravel, or scrub, hence the generic name *gobi,* which means "stony desert" in Mongolian.[6] Despite fears of sand encroachment on cities and farms, the gravel was more mobile and often more of a threat to habitation.[7] Inappropriate human activity often paved its way. As I had seen in Shandong, Gansu, Xinjiang, and Heilongjiang, overgrazing, overfarming, overpopulation, and misuse of water resources had taken their toll.

If tended well or left completely alone, grass will protect the soil. But beyond a certain point, overused grassland degrades irreparably, and soil becomes as much a nonrenewable resource as oil.[8] Lester Brown of the Earth Policy Institute considers this one of the greatest environmental problems facing the world, far bigger than the dust bowls that devastated the wheat production of the United States in the 1930s. He fears that China faces a calamitous loss of arable land in Inner Mongolia and other northern regions that will lead, at best, to rising global food prices and tensions and, at worst, famine, instability, and war.[9] This is not only a problem for food security. The world's peaty grasslands contain huge amounts of greenhouse gas. If they deteriorate and these gases are released, the effect on the climate could be catastrophic.

In 2002, the State Council warned that 90 percent of China's usable natural grassland had suffered some level of degradation.[10] A huge greening campaign was set in motion in an attempt to repair the damage. Depending on the area, it combined elements of the "Great Green Wall" tree planting I had seen in Heilongjiang, the "grants for green" incentives for farmers to cease cultivation I had admired in Gansu, and the mass resettlement of nomads I had witnessed on the Tibetan Plateau. But government money and mass mobilizations tend to deal with the consequences rather than the usual cause: excessive economic exploitation of areas ill-fitted to agriculture and industry. This was recognized more clearly at the grass roots, where the budding NGO movement started to advocate a different approach.

Among those most familiar with Inner Mongolia was Chen Jiqun, who worked with communities of former nomads who had been resettled into concrete houses on the steppe. Having spent more than thirty years in the area, he told me the problem of land degradation was ultimately one of culture.[11] "China's production system has totally destroyed the northern grasslands and lifestyle. The Han just don't understand the steppe. We should stop sending people into the wilderness. We are not just destroying our own ecology, we are damaging others."

An artist by training, Chen moved to Inner Mongolia during the Cultural Revolution. The situation for students who "went down to the countryside" here was different from those who went to Heilongjiang or Xinjiang. In Inner Mongolia the political violence was bloodier while the war against nature was relatively subdued, at least in terms of land reclamation.[12] Between purges and factional fighting, Chen spent long enough among herders to develop a lasting respect for their understanding of the grasslands.

He believed modern efforts to resettle them were misguided. By taking the nomads off the prairies both here and in Tibet, the government aimed to ease overgrazing. But instead of moving seasonally and relatively lightly across the land, the herders' flocks were now penned in smaller, fixed areas that they quickly chewed into dust. The grass could not recover, so the flocks moved on to destroy other areas.

Alarmed about the impact on milk, beef, mutton, and cashmere, scientists from Beijing were asked to restore the productivity of the grassland. Among their solutions was to douse the prairie with rodenticide in the mistaken belief that the slaughter of pika, rabbits, and rats would leave more nutrients for the cows and sheep. But the rodents were vital to the ecosystem. By burrowing into the earth they made the grassland moister and healthier.[13] When they disappeared, so did many other animals, such as snakes and birds, higher up the food chain. The rodent-control officials belatedly learned that biodiversity was not a luxury but a vital element to sustainable productivity.[14]

Many grassland plant species were in decline.[15] More land was being given over to monocultures of wheat, corn, and grain, but they did not naturally produce more food without massive inputs of fertilizer and diverted water.[16] Nor were cows and sheep fattening up as they once did.[17] Such problems were sometimes blamed on climate change, but it was clearly not the only reason. Just across the border in Mongolia there had long been far better protection of biodiversity of both plants and animals (though in recent years, it too was suffering as a result of the demand from China and other countries for land, minerals, and ingredients for traditional medicine).

Chen focused his efforts on education, but this was not easy in such a sparsely populated expanse. In Wuzhumuqin County, there was just one elementary school for an area twice the size of Switzerland. Using his fine-art training, in 2008, Chen illustrated a book that encouraged the 300,000 former nomads to assert their legal rights over the land. It told the story of Qiqige, a young Mongolian girl who dreamed of a lost idyll of beautiful open scenery, rich wildlife, and horseback rides, then woke up and looked out of her window on a degraded, polluted land divided up into barbed-wire pens for cashmere herds. The book's message was reinforced by a copy of the relevant laws and regulations printed in Chinese and Mongolian that reminded herders of their rights to use the land. Local authorities were so worried by these materials that they ordered police to seize copies and threaten locals who distributed them with arrest.

Chen has always tried to keep the law on his side, turning to the courts when necessary. In 2006, he helped a nomad community to mount a legal challenge against the East Wuzhumuqin Paper Mill, a polluter that had been relocated to Inner Mongolia after an earlier "cleanup" at its original location in Hebei. The nomads won compensation, and the factory was moved on, although the land it had contaminated remained a blight on the area.

Though small in scale, such victories were encouraging. The space for civil society was growing, particularly with regard to environmental issues. Premier Wen Jiabao recognized the need for NGOs and journalists to expose violations of regulations that might otherwise be covered up by local authorities. Pan Yue, the deputy environment minister, championed their cause, noting that the public were the "biggest stakeholders in the environment." The number of NGOs surged.[18] Major international conservation groups established operations in China. Foreign funds provided seed money to domestic groups.

In Inner Mongolia, Chen worked with nomads, Korean charities, and China's oldest legal environmental NGO, Friends of Nature.[19] Its cofounder Liang Congjie, a professor at the Academy of Chinese Culture, was inspired to work on the grassland issues after seeing Chen's Echoing Steppe website of drawings and photographs of a disappearing lifestyle and ecosystem. Liang had built a reputation as the "soul of China's green movement" after establishing Friends of Nature in 1994.[20] Like many of the other groups that followed, it became an outlet for social activists who were unable to press for political changes in the wake of the Tiananmen Square crackdown five years earlier.[21] His message was essentially one of thrift: everyone in China needed to use resources more wisely. People were listening, though not yet in the numbers needed to make a difference.

In difficult circumstances, NGOs had carved out a space for civil society that had not existed before. While traditional folklore was diminishing, new groups were trying to create a modern culture of sustainability. Over the years, I had seen them campaigning on many fronts: in courtrooms, through the media, on websites, sometimes in negotiations alongside the authorities, and sometimes on the streets against them. It was an uphill battle.

The country's most successful environment lawyer, Wang Canfa, told me there were more conservation and anti-pollution laws than ever, but the environment was still deteriorating. "China needs to be ruled by law. At the moment this is not the case. Personal connections often overrule the law. Some environmental laws are useless. We need to educate people, particularly those in power. We need more public oversight. We need to improve information disclosure."[22]

Transparency was the focus of Ma Jun, whose Institute of Public and Environmental Affairs published an online pollution map of China, naming and shaming the worst companies and municipalities. Ma worked with sympathetic government officials and used official data to expose offenders. Yet even after the introduction of a public disclosure law in 2008, the vast majority of local governments failed to respond to his requests for information, despite being legally obliged to do so.[23] In a supportive but depressing note, the environment ministry admitted polluters were able to operate in a "black box" that showed the public interest was not being effectively protected.[24]

Elsewhere in the government, there was evident unease about the growth of civil society. Communist cadres were suspicious of potential rivals, particularly after NGOs played a prominent role in the "Color Revolutions" that swept through the former Soviet Union in 2004 and 2005. Groups were forbidden to set up nationwide networks. Their staff were often interrogated by state security officers. There was an invisible line that bordered their permissible activities. Nobody knew where it was until they stepped over it. Those that became too influential were broken up or their representatives declared persona non grata.[25] Activists who challenged the authorities risked violent retribution and arrest.

I met lawyers who were beaten and threatened with closure, writers who were censored, and journalists who were frustrated that their scoops were spiked by editors either because of self-censorship or on the orders of the propaganda department. I visited three women, the wives of imprisoned activists, who were being harassed and followed by plainclothes police or thugs employed by the authorities.[26] At least seven of my interviewees were later jailed. In many cases, they were at least partly involved in environmental issues but were clearly deemed to have strayed too far toward politics. Hu Jia, the winner of the Sakharov Prize, started out as an environmentalist. He joined student groups doing conservation work in Yunnan and worked with the Kekexili veterans on an eco-tourism program on the Tibetan Plateau. But after he dared to criticize the government's record on human rights in an open letter ahead of the Olympics, he was sentenced to three years in prison.[27]

Others were imprisoned even though they remained focused on green issues. Wu Lihong was declared an "Environmental Warrior" by the National People's Congress in 2005 for his work in trying to clear up the pollution in Lake Tai in Jiangsu Province. He was later accused of blackmail and jailed for three years.

At times, the government seems frightened of its own people. Arrests of activists, Internet restrictions, and the massive domestic security operations around the Beijing Olympics and the sixtieth anniversary of the founding of the People's Republic suggest that the Communist Party is unlikely to ever view civil society as a trusted ally. It will certainly not allow it to grow unchecked. Yet grassroots activism is flourishing.

At one level, this is due to a collapse of ideology. There is a widespread yearning for a new set of values. I have seen it among several young Chinese friends who converted to Christianity, and in older associates who started practicing Buddhism. It is evident in the growing popularity of trips to Tibet, Yunnan, Sichuan, Inner Mongolia, and other minority regions where many Han tourists go in search of a lost spirituality.

People are looking to monks, priests, gurus, idealists, charismatic celebrities, and persuasive bloggers for something more than postmodern, globalized materialism. The environment is not as popular as online nationalism or entrepreneurism, but groups such as Roots & Shoots, Friends of Nature, and Global Village have a growing following.

Many domestic journalists—who are often closest to the problems and the cover-ups—have become environmental activists. Prominent among them is Feng Yongfeng, who runs what he calls a University of Nature that takes people on hikes into the countryside and encourages them to submit research papers for peer review. Many other prominent environmentalists are journalists or former journalists, including Pan Yue and Ma Jun.

Another is Wang Yongchen, a radio broadcaster and founder of one of China's earliest NGOs, the Green Volunteers League. Wang actively proselytizes among media organizations, setting up monthly environmental salons for journalists and field trips to areas affected by pollution, desertification, or dam building. Every year she takes a group to Inner Mongolia to help with tree-planting campaigns. She believes the media fill a gap in the nation's governance structure: "In China, we have law, but sometimes it doesn't work. When that happens, articles, documentaries, and pictures can help to solve the problems."

Despite the hardships facing many activists, she is upbeat. The NGO movement is growing and becoming more ambitious, she feels, as it shifts its approach from public education to influencing business and policymakers.

There are small signs of a pickup in popular culture too. Xiao Wei, the lead singer of the band Catcher in the Rye, wrote the eco-anthem "Green" on his return from a trip sponsored by Greenpeace to see the devastation caused by logging in Papua New Guinea. The single reached number one on the Amazon chart of Chinese music.[28] Another green pop evangelist, Long Kuan, hit the top spot in the Mongolian Cow Sour Yogurt music chart (one of the most influential in China despite its odd name) with a song that attempts to marry wealth and conservation in its syrupy lyrics:

> I am Queen of Lohas, rich in gold and silver
> I love this world, may it never be destroyed
> I am Queen of Lohas, protecting everyone's dreams
> I want my life to be forever sparkling[29]

The song captures the two contradictory elements of a new middle-class Chinese dream: rich and green. Environmental sustainability is marketed as a stylish new form of consumerism. It sells, especially to the urban young. This marketing demographic has its own dedicated magazine, *Lohas* (Lifestyles of Health and Sustainability).

Long Kuan is a passionate vegetarian who is trying to save the planet by encouraging people to eat less meat.[30] For a while, she even arranged regular gatherings of celebrities to try to encourage them into similar habits (until such meetings were prohibited by the authorities).

Yet such small green cultural buds are subsumed by the far bigger and wider trend among consumers to buy larger houses, more furniture, new cars, and electricity-gobbling home appliances. Management guides and fashion magazines far outsell any environment-related publication. Moreover, the pop-culture approach that helped to spread the green gospel in the West is nowhere near so effective in China. Most celebrities are uninterested in conservation.[31] A different approach is needed.

The person who comes closest to providing that is probably Yu Dan, a pop philosopher whose commentary on the Analects of Confucius achieved the rare publishing feat of outselling Harry Potter. Yu, a media studies professor at Beijing Normal University, is one of the country's hottest commentators with a pithy and approachable modern interpretation of the 2,500-year-old classics. She believes her popularity reflects a nationwide questioning of beliefs.

"We in China are trying to reset our entire value system," she told me. "In the 1980s and 1990s, people became lost because they based their lives on money. They became greedy, destroyed the environment, plundered natural resources without restraint, and opened heavily polluting factories."

The environment is a central concern for Yu, who considers herself more Taoist than Confucian. "To develop harmoniously, we need to follow the laws of nature. Of all the traditional Chinese beliefs, Taoism is the most reverent toward nature. Following nature is the ultimate principle."

Yu's eco-evangelism takes second place to her advocacy of stability and respect for order.[32] In this regard, she is a model of modern Chinese political correctness. While the ancients boldly advocated "speaking truth to power," Yu has always stuck to the party line.

The masses, she said, would only be ready for Taoism if they first understood Confucian social values: "After China develops for several more decades and becomes more materially and spiritually aware, then

Taoism can become more popular, but at the moment this philosophy is too advanced."

The idea of Taoism as a philosophy for an upwardly mobile elite is hard to reconcile with the beliefs of Yu's professed inspiration, Zhuangzi, who idealized water because it found a way to the "low places that others disdain." But it is very much in keeping with the plutocratic views of the modern Chinese Communist Party. Replace the word "Taoism" with "democracy" and the lines could have been scripted by President Hu Jintao. Replace it with "environmentally concerned" and the argument becomes a restatement of the canard that China will pollute first and leave the cleanup until after it is rich.

According to Yu, we had to wait patiently until a little more education and a lot more money turned today's socially concerned Confucians into tomorrow's eco-friendly Taoists. But it was not a case of either one or the other. One of the biggest reasons for China's enduring success as a civilization has been the coexistence of different philosophies. It has rarely been either completely Taoist or completely Confucian. The two are emphasized to different degrees during different eras or, indeed, different times of the day. The ancient mandarins were said to be Confucian during working hours and Taoists when they went home. This flexible way of thinking allowed a constant rebalancing of ideas, like having both a governing and opposition party in the national mind.

That balance may well have been jettisoned in the modern effort to overcome national humiliation at the hands of Western industrial powers. China learned the lessons, first of Marxism and now capitalism, the hard way. Its application of both foreign ways of thinking tends to be destructively dogmatic.

This was the view of professor E Yunlong at Peking University's new Ecocivilization Research Center.[33]

"Our primary focus is on establishing a new set of values," he said. "We must globalize our value systems . . . During thirty years of opening up and reform, we learned a great deal from the West. Some things, like technology, have been good, but we also picked up bad habits, such as high consumption and winner-takes-all competition. We must not let these bad habits grow, because if Chinese people want to live luxuriously, then not only China but the whole world will be unable to afford it."

There was a nationalist bent to his argument. "It is a matter of survival," said E. "The main aim of our center is to change the way people think. To educate people, to show them that protection of the environment is a life-or-death issue for humans . . . It is a matter of ethnic protection."

A broader yet more pessimistic view was espoused by Tang Xiyang, a veteran of the green movement. Among the 300 or so people I interviewed for this book, Tang was one of very few Han to describe nature as a participant rather than a resource: "In China when people make policies, we don't ask if nature will allow it or if nature agrees. We should. I have witnessed how China has cut down many forests. At each movement of Chinese history, the forests are the victims."

He believed civilization was fundamentally bad for the environment and had had an increasingly adverse impact in recent centuries, not just in China but across the world: "Humans do not respect nature and history anymore. They think they can do anything they want. That is not the way to respect nature. Nature will take its revenge on mankind."

Tang was an inspiration. I met many other brave, intelligent, and effective environmental campaigners, some of whom worked closely with the authorities such as Ma Jun, Sheri Liao, and Xie Yan, and others such as Dai Qing and Hu Jia who believed the system was the problem. They all made enormous contributions toward raising awareness of environmental issues. But Tang was the most intuitively persuasive, perhaps because he had traveled the world writing about the environment, while most of the others focused only on China. But his beliefs were as traditional as they come. Tang was fond of quoting lines from Zhuangzi:

> *The universe and I came into being together;*
> *I and everything therein are one.*

It is not, he said, that the ancient Taoist sages were smarter than people today, just that they lived closer to nature and understood it better. Since then, he felt, the distance has grown. "The problem is culture. We will never solve anything until we change the way we think."

The search for a new ideal was a central theme of *Wolf Totem,* a bestselling novel about Han pioneers in the Mongolian grassland. The author, Jiang Rong, used his experience of life among the nomads during the Cultural Revolution as a parable for the ecological ignorance and political timidity of modern Han culture. It was one of the most influential Chinese novels of the early twenty-first century, selling more than two million copies, translated into twenty-one languages, and winning more than a dozen awards, including the Man Asian prize, the regional equivalent of the Booker. Yet it is filled with cultural self-loathing.

Far from the image of a confident, modernizing China, Jiang paints a picture of a destructive and insecure race that has neither the liberties of the West nor the natural wisdom of the Mongolian nomads. The semi-autobiographical tale is based on his own experience as a Red Guard sent to East Ujimqin Banner in Xilin Gol, Inner Mongolia, in 1967. From getting lost on the grasslands and finding himself terrified and alone among a pack of wolves to tenderly raising a young wolf cub, the events in the book are based on his life.

The protagonist, Chen Zhen, is a Han Chinese who leaves Beijing in disgust at the Cultural Revolution. He is assigned a job as a shepherd and given a *ger* tent among a family of Mongolian herders. He quickly grows to respect their freedom, natural wisdom, and worship of the wolf totem. By comparison, Chen feels that he is as "gutless" as a sheep:

> He was saddened to have been born into a line of farmers. Farmers had become as timid as sheep after dozens, even hundreds, of generations of being raised on grains and greens, the products of farming communities; they had lost the virility of their nomadic ancestors, going back to the legendary Yellow Emperor.

Jiang draws on the contrast between the two cultures that were traditionally divided by the Great Wall: the agrarian Han in the southern plains and the nomadic Mongols on the northern steppe. In Inner Mongolia, the Han majority's modern triumph is portrayed as a disaster. Development has devastated the habitat of the wolves and turned the grasslands into desert. There are few bleaker visions of the ecological peril created by modern China's development.

It is a provocative work. The book's emphasis on competition, survival, and slaughter went down well with military and business leaders, prompting overseas critics to label Jiang a fascist and a symbol of the rising nationalist sentiment in China. Others dismissed *Wolf Totem* as sentimental and romantic. The idealized portrayal of the nomads has much in common with the "noble savage" motif found in much Romantic literature in the eighteenth and nineteenth centuries, when Europe—like China now—was undergoing rapid industrialization and urbanization.

When I met him, Jiang (whose real name is Lu Jiamin) looked anything but lupine. His thick glasses, thinning hair, and a schoolteacher pullover made it hard to imagine him braving the wild. But the appearance was misleading; when he closed in on one of his passions—politics, nomad culture, or wolves—his delivery grew more animated and a predatory glint came into his eyes. He was a radical liberal who lived his values.[34]

As well as being a former artist, Jiang had been a Red Guard, shepherd, political prisoner, radical news-sheet publisher, Maoist lecturer, and Tiananmen Square protester. He was now defending what was left of the Mongolian grasslands: "China's agricultural traditions are about taking from the environment without giving anything back. This is unsustainable, which is why we are frequently beset by disaster. Our thinking about the ecology is so weak that it has held back the progress of our nation. We need to pay more respect to nature. In my book I wanted to show that nomad culture is very protective of ecosystems."

When he won the Man Asian award, Jiang donated the $10,000 prize money to Chen Jiqun, the grasslands activist noted above. They had been comrades since the Cultural Revolution. They both knew and respected the grasslands and Mongolian culture. The author saw China's current environmental crisis as a turning point. The problems of pollution, sandstorms, water shortages, and disease were so acute they could not be ignored. For the situation to improve, he believed China needed to move away from meek Confucian deference to authority. Officials at the top were still focused on economic growth. Jiang wanted people at the bottom to be more assertive about improving their living conditions. Yet, for all the idealism of Jiang and efforts of NGOs, the reality in Inner Mongolia was that the landscape was being shaped not by grassroots activism but by ever-bigger industrial projects.

On the outskirts of the grasslands, the empty road gave way to a vision of China's future. Ordos rose up out of nowhere in smart rows of tower blocks, new industrial parks, and construction cranes. Built almost from scratch in the desert, the city was so perfectly arranged that, from a distance, it looked like it was constructed from Lego bricks. There was none of the clutter, chaos, and vibrancy of other cities. The streets were deserted. I put this down to the biting minus 20°C winds that cut in from the Gobi. But it soon became apparent that humanity has not yet fully embraced the future that has been built for it by the architects of "Scientific Development."

Ordos is industrializing faster than Huaxi and urbanizing almost as quickly as Chongqing. Its economy is surging at such a speed that the average salary here is higher than in Shanghai.[35] Below its surface lies the biggest gas field in China; on its outskirts is an open-cast coal mine that dwarfs anything in Shanxi. Industrial-scale experiments that will shape the world are under way here. Ordos plans to build a huge wind farm and the world's largest solar plant, which will cover an area bigger than Manhattan and generate enough electricity to power three million homes.[36] This is also the proposed site of an algae plant that would soak up carbon and convert it into biofuel or feed for animals.

But, as elsewhere in China, these green experiments are dwarfed by the investment in fossil fuels. Ordos is the new capital of carbon. Inner Mongolia has overtaken Shanxi as the nation's biggest coal-producing region. Heavy industry has followed the fuel. That trend has given the region the highest per capita greenhouse gas emissions that are more than twice the level in the UK. Yet this region is considered a training ground for future leaders. When President Hu's protégé, Hu Chunhua (no relation), was made governor of Inner Mongolia in 2010, it was taken as a sign that he had been put on a fast track toward leadership of the country in 2022.

The most advanced colliery in the world sits on the outskirts of Ordos. Contrary to the dirty, dangerous, and insufficient image of coal in China, the Shangwan pit churns out more than a million tons per month with just 300 miners and claims a 100 percent safety record. On the outside it was indeed remarkably green. With trees and lawns and barely a speck of coal dust on the ground, the state-owned company's model mine resembled a garden more than a pit.

Before going down, I had to put on a miner's coverall, helmet, and boots. The changing rooms are like those of a five-star sports club. Valets took me to the crisply laundered outfits, white gloves, and a satchel containing an emergency oxygen supply laid out on a cushioned chair. The mine's cheerfully pudgy Communist Party secretary, Wang Tianliang, stripped down to his long johns beside me and extolled the virtues of what was, he said, the most productive single face in the world.

To get to the pit face, we had only to board a comfortable minibus and drive 10 kilometers through a tunnel that was wider and cleaner than the London Underground. There were just a handful of miners at our destination, 355 meters underground. They worked with remote-control devices that changed the direction, position, and speed of a German-made cutting machine that sliced back and forth along a 300-meter coal face. Giant hydraulic supports kept the tunnel stable. "This hydraulic system is one hundred percent made in China," Wang told me with evident pride.

Back on the surface, Wang showed me the control room where a bank of computers ran the operation, all monitored on a wall of CCTV screens. One screen tracked the position of every worker in the mine. Another showed the rail depot, where carriages were filled at the rate of a ton a second before they trundled east to the power plants and factories on the coast.

The mine is run by Shenhua, a state-run firm and the world's biggest coal company. By 2015, it plans to almost double production at this super-colliery. Most of the extra output is earmarked for a nearby experimental facility that could determine the future of China's greenhouse gas emissions and the world's efforts to tackle climate change.

In the glow of a Mongolian sunset, pink and white smoke billowed gently from the gleaming silver pipes of the Shenhua-Ordos coal-to-liquid facility. There was no smell and so little noise from the machinery that the most audible sound was the flap of the red national flags outside the entrance. The facility was as clean and beautiful as industry gets, yet this plant was also an environmentalist's worst nightmare.

Coal liquefaction is a process that is historically associated with desperation. It was developed in Nazi Germany and enhanced by South Africa when antiapartheid sanctions were threatening the country's fuel supplies. Japan, the United States, and several other nations also launched small-scale trials after the oil price shock of the early 1970s. Most were abandoned due to environmental and cost concerns.

But the industrial-scale experiment at Ordos had already produced a million tons of liquid coal in its first year of operation. It used a direct liquefaction technique to "crack" black carbon with hydrogen extracted from water to produce clear diesel. The demands on resources were immense. For each ton of diesel, six and a half tons of water had to be piped from an aquifer more than 70 kilometers away, and more than three tons of carbon dioxide were released into the air.

For many years, the government hesitated about adopting this technology because the production of liquid coal results in almost twice the emissions as producing a comparable amount of oil. But Shenhua planned to expand production fivefold and to build a similar facility in Xinjiang. In nearby Ningxia, the South African firm Sasol was tying up with a local partner to make an indirect liquefaction facility.

As he showed me the plant, Shu Geping, the chief engineer, said cost and insecurity had prompted China to develop liquid coal as an alternative to imported oil. The coal substitute was competitive when oil hit $40 a barrel. In the future, as technology and economies of scale improve, it will be even cheaper. Ultimately, liquefaction technology was a form of insurance against oil price rises, trade conflict, and embargoes.

"This is strategically important for China because we have abundant coal but little oil," Shu explained. "I've read that if the output of coal-to-liquid plants could reach 50 million tons a year, then China's energy problems would be solved."

But it could also completely undermine efforts to put the country on a cleaner growth track. By cheaply filling gas tanks with the world's dirtiest fuel, liquefaction technology could kill efforts to develop electric cars and other forms of clean transport. If adopted on the massive scale envisaged by Shu, it will extend the life of collieries for decades. The world's biggest carbon emitter will have found a new way to fill the atmosphere with greenhouse gas.

Shu, though, insisted his facility could be good for the environment because it is equipped to capture and condense carbon dioxide for possible storage. His plant was about to launch one of China's most ambitious carbon-capture and sequestration projects. In conjunction with a United States partner, it would store 100,000 tons annually in a nearby saline aquifer. That was small beer, less than a thirtieth of the plant's emissions. It was a pilot project that could be scaled up in the future, but I had heard from several scientists and policymakers how reluctant China was to accept the costs of dumping carbon underground when it was far cheaper to pump it into the air.

Unless such attitudes change, it is likely the carbon storage project will end up as another fine-sounding small step toward a cleaner future while the economy as a whole continues to take giant strides toward heavy, coal-fired industry.

The government is still making up its mind on whether to expand liquefaction. Plans for other facilities that would result in Inner Mongolia converting half of its coal—about 4 percent of China's total energy resources—into liquid are on hold. In favor is the oil price. Against are environmental concerns and fears of unsustainability. Ordos's economic growth has been predicated on massively ramped-up consumption of carbon and water. Ordos is surrounded by desert and more prone to drought than Gansu. Up until 2003, water was rationed and residents could use the taps for only three hours a day. Now there are no restrictions because enough water is pumped here from the Yellow River and elsewhere to allow each citizen 130 liters of water per day.[37] While the rest of North China endures devastating droughts, rich Ordos is siphoning off more water than ever.

Elsewhere in the city, I examined another very different eco-project that attempted to address criticism that Ordos was wasting scarce resources. The local government had teamed up with the Swedish government and European scientists to build the world's first dry-latrine multistory housing complex.[38] Six hundred families were using toilets that flushed sawdust instead of water. It was a tricky business. The technology was far from perfect and users needed to have a good aim to make it work.

The technique was explained by Chen Furong, a smart young official from the city's Environmental Protection Bureau who was only occasionally embarrassed by the subject under discussion. In the exhibition center she showed how instead of flushing water the cistern discharged sawdust or wood chips. This covered the waste, which then tipped automatically into a bin in the basement. It was collected once a week and composted for use as fertilizer.

Environmentally, it was brilliant. The apartments in the eco-town used just a third of the water usually required for homes of the same size. Scientists claimed they were the first in the world to mass-compost human waste, which was an efficient use of energy and a good source of potassium, nitrates, and other nutrients for the soil. Professor Jiang in Shandong would have been proud.

But the experiment had a problem: It stank. On some days, the smell was so unbearable that a number of families had moved out. German experts from the World Toilet Organization had been called in for advice. But there was no easy solution.

We visited a group of residents playing cards in a ground-floor apartment. Song Guoying, who lived on the top floor where the smell was worst, felt she was a rat in a toilet laboratory: "When we bought the apartment, the former owners never told us about the special toilets. We just got it because it was cheap. I would never have moved here if I had known about the eco-project. The smell is sometimes so bad I can't sleep."

Most of the residents were content, but officials told me privately they did not expect the eco-project to move to a second phase, once the Swedish planners handed control back to the hosts.

Even if the experiment were to succeed, the unflushed savings would be tiny in comparison with the lakes of water being gulped down by mining and the coal liquefication facility a short distance up the road. The small, resource-conserving international project looked like failing while high-emission, resource-consuming industrial complexes were expanding. Ordos encapsulated the contradictions of "Scientific Development." It was black power, red power, and green power rolled into one. The most successful experiments in Ordos looked great, but they necessitated the consumption of ever more carbon and water. The vision it offered of the future was clean rather than sustainable.

The final full day of my longest journey across China was spent making a 600-kilometer taxi ride through grasslands. The roads were flanked by rolling fields, stretches of barren scrub, and rows of saplings and seedlings. We passed small villages of packed-earth huts daubed with family-planning propaganda and China Mobile adverts. Pulling onto a minor road near Qahar shortly before dusk, we bumped through the most spectacular Mongolian scenery I had seen so far: a broad valley between two knobbled mountain ridges. At the end of a long day, the sun seemed to be in a playful mood, appearing and disappearing behind the peaks like a doting parent playing peekaboo. The twilight lingered for another hour or so, then the stars brightened as we cruised through a sea of grass to our destination—Xanadu.

For three years from 1260, this was the summer capital of the greatest land empire in human history. Kublai Khan held court here in a palatial *ger* on the grasslands to escape the heat of his adopted home in Beijing. A gourmet and lover of the exotic, the great khan required constant stimulation and entertainment. Wealthier than anyone in the world at that time, he sponsored some of the finest theater in Chinese history and invited

Tibetan lamas, Kashmiri magicians, Arabian astrologers, Nestorian Christians, and other great thinkers from his empire to share their philosophies. Poetry of that Yuan dynasty era describes three-day feasts for a thousand guests and dancing girls writhing sensuously in a "heavenly demon dance." Visitors to Xanadu witnessed the most magnificent and cosmopolitan spectacle of the age. Marco Polo, the Venetian trader, was awestruck: "No man since Adam has ruled over so many subjects or such a vast territory. Nor has any possessed such treasure or such power." His imagination may have got the better of him. Many historians suspect the Venetian trader never visited Xanadu.[39] It was hard to equate any kind of grandeur—real or imagined—with Shangdu, as the disheveled town is now called in Chinese. The small town, which I reached late in the evening, was very much a Han community of orthogonal roads, square white-tiled buildings, tinted windows, pink-lit massage parlors, karaoke bars, and a giant billboard from which Dashan, an enviably fluent Mandarin-speaking Canadian, entreated people to buy mobile phones. The biggest development in the area was a new power plant. The second biggest was the Summer Palace Hotel, where we checked in for the night. It was a giant concrete *ger*, a modern pleasure dome.

I felt like celebrating. I had made it all the way from Shangri-La, the longest land journey of my life. It was a moment to celebrate. I asked a taxi driver to take me to the best restaurant in town.

Functional and fluorescent-lit, the Eastern Cloud Attic looked much like any other restaurant in the town, but it offered a slightly wider selection of food. I told the waitress I was in the mood for a feast and ordered frog, snake, pigs' ears, mushroom, mutton, and baijiu. I gorged myself, taking pleasure from consumption rather than the grim surroundings.

The owner, a chubby florid-faced Han, was delighted at the business and the rare foreign visitor. He told me he too was a newcomer to Shangdu: "I have three restaurants in my hometown, but I decided to move here because it has a new power plant. That will bring many opportunities."

He invited me to join his table, where he held court with a dozen friends and hangers-on. There was a cook, a businessman, a driver, and a minor official. We drank baijiu, then toasted each other, then drank more baijiu.

"You are my first English friend. Drink with me in the spirit of international friendship," he said. Then he looked around at his friends and cracked a joke: "You are not Japanese, are you?" he laughed. The hangers-

on grinned. "If you were I would kill you here and now. I hate Japanese."
Guffaws erupted from around the table. I was reminded of the patriot on
the train across the Tibetan Plateau. Was it the harsh environment or did
the pioneers of China's remote regions get their sense of humor from the
same joke book? My celebration was over. I had eaten and drunk too much
and had more than my fill. It was time to return to the hotel.

Kublai Khan was a big man with a huge appetite. The portraits of the Yuan
emperor, as the Sinophile styled himself, show him to be the most corpu-
lent ruler in China's history. He was a brilliant leader but a troubled man.
Under his rule, China's territory was expanded to include Tibet, Yunnan,
and much of Southeast Asia, paper currency was introduced, and water
was diverted to Beijing, which he established as the capital. Yet he was
never embraced by the Han as one of their own, and many Mongolians
hated him because he took on Chinese airs. In later life, the mighty khan
overstretched his empire, overconsumed, and increasingly retreated to the
grasslands where he felt most comfortable.[40] After the death of his son, he
began binge eating, eventually dying in 1294, massively overweight and
suffering from gout. His political legacy was short-lived. The Yuan dynasty
ended less than a century later in famine, corruption, and war. "Toward
the end of his life Kublai became depraved" read the final inscription of a
Chinese exhibition on Mongolian history. "So go all emperors."

Xanadu is a symbol of his confused cultural legacy. Built around 1256,
it was a walled capital the size of Beijing's Forbidden City that encompassed a park, trees for his falcons, and two homes. As well as a permanent marble structure, the khan-emperor also constructed a palace fit for
a nomad: a round, domed structure made of gilded cane that could easily
be taken down and rebuilt elsewhere.[41] Historians have speculated that he
moved between them according to the seasons, but he may also have been
pulled from one to the other depending on whether he was in a Chinese
or Mongolian frame of mind. It cannot have been easy to span a cultural
divide marked so tangibly by the Great Wall. In the West, however, Xanadu
is not associated with confusion or decline. Far from it. The name is synonymous in the English-speaking world with the ultimate escape, a man-

made paradise. This is largely thanks to Samuel Taylor Coleridge's poem "Kubla Khan." In 1798, the poet dreamed of an all-powerful ruler who ordered the creation of "a stately pleasure-dome." Bursting with sexual energy, the verse explored the power of creation and destruction and man's futile efforts to control chaotic nature. It was a dark vision, prophesying floods, war, the eruption of mountains, sunless seas, and lifeless oceans. But it was also ripe with images of fertility, of savageness and magic, of an earth so alive it almost seemed to be breathing:[42]

> *In Xanadu did Kubla Khan*
> *A stately pleasure-dome decree:*
> *Where Alph, the sacred river, ran*
> *Through caverns measureless to man*
> *Down to a sunless sea.*
> *So twice five miles of fertile ground*
> *With walls and towers were girdled round*
> *And there were gardens bright with sinuous rills*
> *Where blossomed many an incense-bearing tree;*
> *And here were forests ancient as the hills*
> *Enfolding sunny spots of greenery.*[43]

It was pure romanticism. Like James Hilton with Shangri-La, Coleridge never set foot in the Oriental paradise he imagined so vividly. He is believed to have written "Kubla Khan" in an opium-induced reverie at a farmhouse near Exmoor in the southwest of England. He never finished. Of the two hundred lines he composed in his dream, he wrote down only a quarter. They were published as a fragment, subtitled "A Vision in a Dream,"[44] which has since inspired—and sold—countless stories, films, and pop songs. Coleridge's incomplete fantasy is now far more powerful than the imperial citadel on which it is based.

The next morning, I visited the ruins that were all that was left of the Great Khan's stately playground. For several decades the site had been completely neglected. During the Cultural Revolution it was part of a closed military region. Such was the panic over imaginary Mongolian independence movements in those days that even the mention of the ancient khans would have been enough to warrant imprisonment or worse. A local farmer told us the land was owned back then by the May 1st Collective.

Most of it was now privately farmed. The owners grew potatoes for Kentucky Fried Chicken. Sand breaks suggested they too were having to fight the encroaching desert.

All that was left of the powerhouse was a square mile of grassy banks and stones on a windswept plain. There was no sacred River Alph, only a trickle on the largely dried-up bed of a stream. If there had ever been "sunny spots of greenery," they had shriveled up or been submerged under the scrub. The only sign of natural life or human activity were a snake asleep among the rubble and some empty beer bottles. There could be few more striking examples of how empires fall as well as rise.

No single factor can explain the fall of dynasties, but environmental historians believe individuals or civilizations often bring about their own annihilation by losing touch with their roots, overconsuming or failing to recognize ecological limits. Initial success often proves the origin of later failure. Perceived strengths turn into fatal weaknesses.

Take the Maya of Central America, whose culture was so prodigious that they expanded to the point of destroying the dense rain forests where they lived and hunted.[45] The fall of Sumerian civilization has been blamed on overrapid urbanization and a bronze industry that polluted their farmland. Alexander the Great might not have been driven to ultimately destructive conquest were it not for the deforestation of his Macedonian homeland.[46]

But perhaps the most disturbing case was that of the Easter Islanders, who outgrew the capacity of their small isolated territory in the South Pacific. Initially successful in food gathering, they had an advanced culture for their age and gave thanks by making giant statues called *ahu*. Logs were felled as rollers to move the giant stones to ceremonial sites. But as the population expanded beyond the carrying capacity of the island, competition for food and materials to build statues intensified. When the islanders' fortunes began to fail, they started to fight and were more desperate than ever to erect statues to regain the favor of their ancestors. The once densely vegetated island was completely stripped of trees. With no wood left for homes, the islanders retreated to the caves. They died out soon after.[47] Such, at least, is the explanation offered by environmental historians. There were other possibilities. But civilizations, it seems, tend to fall much more quickly than they rise. By the time people realize they have hit a tipping point, it is too late to do anything.

Wandering Xanadu, I was almost alone. Modern China was in too much of a hurry to bother with ruins, especially Mongolian ones. I met only two other visitors. One of them, Lu Zhiqing, a sculptor, told me he had come in search of inspiration for a statue of Kublai Khan he had been commissioned to erect in front of Shangdu's Summer Palace Hotel. He was disparaging of the Han attitude toward the past.

"We deliberately neglect chunks of history, especially the contributions made by minorities. Kublai Khan was the greatest of them. In his day this would have been a far more beautiful place. The Mongolians traveled, so they always found beautiful spots with tall grass and plenty of water for the horses."

But Lu was optimistic that modern China was moving in the right direction. He said his income had doubled in the previous five years and the environment had improved: "I am an artist, so I see things in terms of colors. When I was a child, the sky was so polluted that it was often yellow, red, or black. It is better now, but we must do more. What we need in China is more green and more blue."

"But you are a communist. Shouldn't it be red?"

"Ah, that is history. That is from the West, from Marx and Lenin. It was good for the country . . ." He paused. The conversation had turned toward politics, a dangerous subject to discuss with foreigners. Instead, I asked what was the biggest change he had observed in his lifetime. The answer was predictable: "My life has become better. So has the entire country."

We returned to Beijing, driving through another grit storm, skirting the dried-up salt bed that was all that was left of Anguli Lake, and overtaking flatbed trucks carrying turbines to the wind farms rising up across Inner Mongolia. We curled down steep winding roads through the hills, passed the Great Wall, a dam, a coal train, and a half-completed concrete theme park. Every few kilometers, I saw red-armbanded volunteers sitting at the side of the road. I was curious. We stopped to ask what they were doing. "Watching out for forest fires" was the reply. It was a sensible precaution. There had been no rain for several weeks. The hills were dry and brown. The sky was the color of cement. The artist's ideal of more green and more blue did not look as though it would be realized anytime soon.

Peaking Man

1949: Only socialism could save China
1979: Only capitalism could save China
1989: Only China could save socialism
2009: Only China could save capitalism
—Joke doing the rounds in Beijing after the global financial crash

It has been more than thirty years since I prayed for China. During that time, the country's population has surged to over a billion and its economy has jumped far past that of the UK. The globe has not stopped turning, but the comfortable world order I knew as a child has indeed been shaken off its axis.

A new power is emerging in Beijing that represents both the apotheosis of human development and the folly of continuing with global business as usual. As I have shown in these pages, the planet's problems were not made in China, but they are sliding past the point of no return here.

Mankind's capacity to consume has reached a crescendo. There has never been more of us on the planet. Our species has never lived longer. Our footprint has never spread wider.[1] The average human today burns more carbon, travels farther, and eats far more than any of our ancestors. A billion people in the rich nations of Europe, the United States, Japan, and South Korea have taken the world to the brink with their unsustainable consumption. Two billion more in emerging economies like India, Brazil, and Indonesia are pressing up from behind. In between is the Middle

Kingdom, threatening to tip us all over the edge with a population that is now twice as big as that of the entire world in 1750.

It is a tough place to be at an extremely challenging time. Mankind is growing old. The generation born at the historical apex of human fertility in the late 1960s is now hitting middle age. The global population is growing at half the speed it once was. That is an opportunity and a risk. In the long term, the slowdown will be good news for the environment, but during the next twenty or thirty years it adds a demographic challenge to the ecological crisis. Once the current peak-generation era passes, there will be fewer working-age adults to support more elderly in rich nations and more children in poor countries. As a species, we are about to pass our prime.

Our planet too seems to be aging. On the road, I have seen how the earth's lungs—the forests—have been decimated; its skin—the soil—is getting drier and more reliant on chemicals; the pressure on the earth's arteries—the rivers—is higher than ever, owing to blocking dams and clogging pollution. Our energy reserves—coal and oil—are being run down faster than ever. Temperatures are less predictable, and there are more and more unhealthy growths in lakes and oceans. Many nations show some of these symptoms. But they are all apparent in China, where the impacts of development are accumulated, amplified, and accelerated.

Historians may well look back on China and Britain as bookends on the most spectacular and unsustainable passage of development that humanity has experienced. The model of carbon-fueled, capital-driven economic growth probably seemed a brilliant idea when it started in my country in the late eighteenth century. But that was one relatively small nation in a world that was, at the time, home to fewer than a billion people. Since then, the same model has expanded across the globe with barely any consideration for the finiteness of the earth's resources. Like a game of pass-the-parcel, rich countries have "outsourced" the accumulated impact of unsustainable growth to faraway lands and future generations. China currently holds the unpleasant consequences. Not surprisingly, it does not want the music to stop. But it may not have a choice.

An alarming number of the country's problems are spreading across borders to become a global security concern. Nationalism is rising as the environment declines. Dust storms in Japan, deforestation in Russia, and the increased extraction of oil from Canada's tar sands can all be traced back to China. With the population expected to swell by almost 200 million by 2030, resources will come under increasing demographic pressure. Water shortages and pollution are already causing unease in Russia, Kazakhstan, and Southeast Asia. If rivers are diverted away from India, there is a very real risk of a conflict. Unless China kicks its coal habit, scientists say greenhouse emissions will surge, global temperatures will rise, and climate change will create millions more eco-migrants and food supply instability. It is no coincidence that the West suddenly seems more concerned with Beijing's environmental performance than its governance or human rights record.[2]

Fear is not the only reason for this attention. There is also hope that China is modernizing so quickly that it might find a sustainable route up the economic value chain. Compared with the 1970s, China and the developed world have far more in common. Our economies are more mutually dependent. Our tastes are converging. Many of us watch the same DVDs. We drink the same coffee. We eat the same junk food. This brings with it a temptation to assume that as in Europe, Japan, South Korea, and Taiwan, a rise in incomes will eventually bring an improvement in the environment. Under this optimistic scenario, the world's biggest population is now clambering over the hump of the dirtiest, most wasteful phase of economic development. Once China manages to overcome that obstacle, our species can breathe easy. The heavy lifting will have been done. Other developing nations will be able to follow. After the global population peaks, probably around 2040 to 2050, the pressure on the environment should relent.

This is not just wishful thinking. Look and you can find positive signs that, perhaps, just perhaps, China is emerging from the mire. Compared to the past, Beijing is no longer a smoggy construction site. There are fewer cranes and more "blue-sky" days. In Henan and Anhui, the notorious Huai River basin has improved albeit only from an appalling low. Dalian and Hangzhou are becoming as clean and modern as any city in the West. Even Tianjin and Shenyang are smartening up. Nationwide, there are tentative indications that pollution may be approaching a peak, though for the moment perhaps only in some forms and in some areas.

Attitudes are also changing. At China's grass roots, there is a hunger for new ideals to replace the grim materialism of the recent thirty years. The thousands of protests against chemical plants and waste incinerators show the extent of concern about environmental health. If China could blaze a new low-carbon trail of sustainability and energy security, the government could win the lasting affection of young nationalists who are desperate for their country to secure international respect.

That is still a long way off, but a space has opened up with the retirement of the Great Leap Forward generation of scientists and policymakers such as "Mother Poplar" Zhang Qiwen, the Three Gorges Dam builder Madame Qian Zhengying, and General Guo Kai, who calculated how many nuclear bombs would be needed to blast a channel through the Himalayas. Their successors are better educated, more focused on detail, and—thanks to pollution protests and commodity inflation—acutely aware of the consequences of ignoring the environment. Many challenge the megaprojects conceived in the past, though that era is far from over.

A debate is under way in Zhongnanhai, the center of power in Beijing, about the future course of development. It divides along political fault lines: wealthy coastal regions that are moving up the value chain line up against poor western provinces that are the destination for insourced dirty industry; the privileged party elite who run power companies challenge merit-based technocrats who have experienced the consequences of untrammeled growth; and advocates of pollute-now-clean-up-later market solutions tussle with those who call for tighter regulations and increased state intervention. President Hu's Scientific Outlook on Development attempts to bind all these strands together with a promise of sustainable green growth.

China's leaders are proving more adept and ambitious than many of their overseas counterparts in pursuing the opportunities of low-carbon technology, which they see as a new driver of economic expansion and national power. If their most ambitious plans are realized, Gansu's deserts will one day be filled with solar panels, the Silk Road will be lined with wind farms, cities will throng with electric-powered public transport, and bodies of water throughout the country will be divided up into fields of harvestable algae. It is impressive, inspiring stuff. Not for the first time, the country is stirring up extremes of hope and despair. With the government promising enough investment in renewable energy to overtake Europe by 2020, the world's biggest emitter is suddenly being hailed as a budding eco-power. Red China, we are told, is not going to destroy us after all; Green China is going to save us.

The true story is more complicated. Few would begrudge China a savior's status if it could supply the world with affordable clean technologies and set a more sustainable model of development. The government is trying to do just that, but at the same time it is also following many of the worst examples of the old development model, and in some cases making them worse. Like governments across the globe, Beijing's leaders focus on technology and growth rather than ecology and sustainability, which means many problems are just pushed out of sight. The skies above Beijing have become bluer at the expense of the rural areas where factories have been relocated. Environmental problems are insourced to marginal land, reclaimed tidal flats, and poorer western regions. "Clean" hydropower has attracted dirty energy-intensive industries into pristine valleys. Reservoirs of garbage are filling up as the national appetite for resources swells. Despite the surge in renewable energy supplies, China is more dependent on coal than ever. As well as mining record amounts of the fuel, it has also become a net importer.

Rhetorically, "Scientific Development" sounds a little less Mao and a little more Tao but in practice, it is another attempt to manufacture a solution to China's problems. Political engineers rather than natural scientists call the shots. Their approach focuses on the acute environmental symptoms of pollution and energy inefficiency. Meanwhile, they often neglect the chronic problems of resource depletion, heavy-metal accumulation in the soil, and the rising clouds of carbon in the air. The overall trend is that of a dozen small, dirty chimneys being replaced by a single towering smokestack. The result is that local pollution improves but more emissions than ever are pumped into the global atmosphere. China's greenhouse gas output will more than double between 2005 and 2020, despite the government's promise to reduce the carbon intensity of the economy by more than 40 percent.

Instead of constraining demand for natural resources, the government puts more effort into increasing supply. At times its measures appear reckless, even desperate. How else to see the building of dams near seismic fault lines, the development of coal liquefaction facilities, the expansion of genetically modified crops, and the expensive ecological gamble of the South-North Water Diversion Project? There is clearly a strong willingness to experiment, despite frequent failures. Almost none of the eco-cities, eco-villages, eco-cars, and even eco-toilets I have seen are operating successfully on a commercial basis. Several are a disaster. But who would bet against China leading the way in future global experiments in cloud whitening, ocean fertilizing, and genetic modification?

Hopes for a green future are premature. Fears of a red past seem outdated. If any single color predominates in today's China, it is the gray of smoke and ash and concrete, of horizon-blurring smog, of law-obscuring vagueness, and of color-stifling monotony. More species are dying out, more forests are emptying, fish stocks are declining, water shortages are growing more severe, deserts are encroaching on cities, glaciers are shrinking, and the climate is becoming more hostile. Countless millions die each year of environment-related disease. Yet the government is choosing farm animals over wildlife, monoculture over biodiversity, concrete over earth, and weather modification over truly ambitious moves to tackle global warming.

It is difficult to be dispassionate, still harder to claim the truth. Different baselines clearly produce very different expectations. Amid the smog, dust, and algae, I have felt at times that China portends an environmental apocalypse. Yet, more often that not, local people tell me, "Life is getting better." That is probably the refrain I have heard more than any other during the past seven years, often prompting me to wonder which was coloring perceptions more: my western, liberal, middle-aged prejudices or the communist propaganda of the Chinese government.

Whatever the political label, I sympathize with President Hu and Premier Wen. Environmental triage is particularly difficult in China, which can be afflicted by drought, floods, dust storms, and pollution disasters in a single week. That is not the only reason this is no ordinary developing nation. China is a 3,000-year-old civilization in the body of an industrial teenager; a mega-rich, dirt-poor, overpopulated, underresourced, ethnically diverse mass of humanity that is going through several stages of development simultaneously; a coal-addicted powerhouse attempting to pioneer new energy technologies, and a communist-led, capitalist-funded economic giant traveling at unprecedented speed. If that is not enough of a challenge, environmental pressures have forced the leadership to attempt something unprecedented in the world's history: to reengineer an economy before it has finished industrializing.

I doubt they have the authority to achieve this. Despite the politburo's nominally dictatorial powers, it is either reluctant or unwilling to impose any measure that might constrain growth. Indeed, it often punishes those who try to do so. Environmental activists who expose pollution scandals are sometimes beaten up, locked away, or censored. Religions, unions, journalists, lawyers, universities, NGOs, aristocracies, and other independent sectors of society that resisted untrammeled economic expansion in other nations have either been abolished or kept under tight control.

Power resides not at the top or bottom of society, but in the bulging middle band of local party chiefs, factory owners, foreign investors, and outsourcers who have profited most from the lack of environmental regulations. As I saw in Guangdong and Heilongjiang, these Mini-Maos in regional governments do not take kindly to any measure that curtails their expansion. They are the reason the government, despite its authoritarian reputation, is less able to rein in polluters than dissidents.

To counter this, it is often argued that China needs more democracy and a bigger middle class. But people power alone will not solve all of the country's environmental problems. A swelling middle class could make things much worse unless beliefs and lifestyles also change. In this case, the West has set a dire example in dealing with the biggest threat of our age: consumption.

Pollution was yesterday's priority. Climate change is tomorrow's. Both are symptoms of a bigger, more immediate malaise: the unsustainable consumption pioneered by advanced, wealthy democracies, and now increasingly replicated by rich citizens of developing nations like China.

Having visited almost every province in the country, I am far more concerned about Shanghai's friendly shoppers than Henan's snarling polluters. The latter are a recognized problem that can be cleared up with sufficient time, money, and government effort. The former, however, are hailed as potential saviors of the global economy. Nobody wants to stop them. Indeed, businesses spend a fortune encouraging consumers to spend more. Their advertising campaigns have proved devastatingly successful. The energy use of the average person in Shanghai has surpassed that of Tokyo, New York, and London and is now 50 percent higher than the global norm.

The rest of the country has some way to catch up, but that is what the government wants. To provide everyone in China with a Shanghai lifestyle, factories will need to churn out an extra 159 million refrigerators, 213 million televisions, 233 million computers, 166 million microwave ovens, 260 million air conditioners, and 187 million cars. Power plants would have to more than double their output. The demand for raw materials and fuel will add enormously to global environmental stress and security strains.

The story of China is changing. On one hand, it is still partly the heart-warming tale of a poor nation catching up with the West. But it is also increasingly the threat of wealthy individuals and megacities that are gobbling up resources and producing waste at a rate that is as destructive and unsustainable as almost anyone and anywhere overseas. The cultural and economic line between "them" and "us" has blurred. But our shared environmental reflection could hardly be more clear or less flattering.

Faced by the resource depletion and climate change, the world community needs to shift away from nationalist competition to consume, and toward an internationalist cooperation to conserve. If the planet's resources were priced properly for their long-term value to future generations, rather than their immediate accessibility, mankind might just be able to avoid a disastrous fight for what's left. I am not holding my breath. It's a big "might." As the Copenhagen climate conference showed us, no government—of whatever political stripe—wants to raise prices or tell citizens to consume fewer resources.

For China, that is particularly difficult. The leadership has no electoral mandate. It relies on economic growth and nationalism for legitimacy. How can Hu or Wen possibly say to their people, "You cannot eat as much or buy as much as citizens in rich nations"? How can consumers in wealthy countries have the temerity to complain if they do?

Strictly in terms of equality, China should have the same scope to damage the planet in the future as rich nations have done in the past. It should also have the same right to consume. This would be completely fair and utterly calamitous. It would allow China to increase its emissions beyond 2050. By that time, the atmosphere will increasingly resemble an Inner Mongolian stew, presuming nations have not gone to war before that over scarce energy supplies or the right to shop for luxuries.

A better environment needs better values. It is unreasonable to ask China to save the world, but the country forces mankind to recognize we are all going in the wrong direction. Technological progress is essential, but it is not enough. Before we retool our economies, we need to rethink our fundamental beliefs. In this regard, China has much to contribute.

The country's environmental and philosophical history should be more deeply mined. The world's longest-enduring civilization offers lessons in how to sustain, such as the Taoist appreciation of "useless trees" or the growing academic skepticism toward "foolish old men who move mountains."

Ethnic, social, and cultural diversity is likely to be another source of new ideas. Antidotes to materialism can be found in the nature worship of Tibetan and Mongolian Buddhism. There are traces of sustainability in the day of rest practiced by the country's Muslims and Christians. Temples nationwide have some of the best-protected wildlife.

China's ideological mixing pot may also throw up more sustainable practices. As resources dwindle, a new generation of market devotees will look for greater efficiency through pricing mechanisms, while old-school state interventionists will press for tax and feed-in-tariff incentives to manage demand. Communes and work units should join a wider discussion with companies, NGOs, and netizens about how to share wealth, food, and materials.

Individuals—those ones in a billion—can also provide inspiration, whether it be the dogged survival instinct of the Meng Brothers, the innovation of Dalian's scientists, the courage of environmental activists,[3] the preference of Beijing taxi drivers for flasks of tea over cans of Coke, the experience of intellectuals sent down to the countryside, or the self-sacrifice of migrant workers everywhere.

A new outlook is essential. This is not a matter for one country or one generation. Mankind has climbed to a peak in China, but our position is precarious and the view from the summit is appalling. Here, more than anywhere, the world has been unbalanced by superlatives, by billionfold multiplication, by earth-changing jumps. Here, more than anywhere, the current path of human progress looks certain to lead to destruction. Here, more than anywhere, we all need to look forward and step back.

Acknowledgments

Two types of journey are reflected in this book: the physical hauls across China and the mental slog of writing. Neither would have been possible without those who provided guidance, shelter, love, and encouragement along the way.

Setting off on these travels would not have been possible without the *Guardian,* which assigned me to China and later granted six months' book leave for research and writing. The newspaper's independence and commitment to environmental issues have shaped much of the reporting in these pages.

My agent, David Fugate, put me on the path of book writing and made sure I stayed the course with patience and professionalism. I would have dawdled far longer on the early stages of that road were it not for supportive prods by Yang Ailun, Xie Yan, and Lisa Foreman.

The route was determined by a confluence of influences. Tracy McVeigh of the *Observer* commissioned the original journey from Shangri-La to Xanadu in search of China's ideals. Lu Jie, curator of the Long March art project—a neighbor in Beijing's Dashanzi district—inspired the travel-narrative approach. Colin Robertson, formerly of Scribner's, encouraged me to venture further into green territory. Photographers Mathias Braschler and Monika Fischer set the bar for ambitious on-the-road reportage.

During this writing expedition I was grateful for the accommodation and tranquillity provided by Michiko Fukui, Philip Lote, Mary Hennock, and Miwa Okubo. Thanks too to Yoyo Gill for giving up her bed on more than one occasion during my stays at her parents' home in Shanghai.

Along the road, guidance came in many forms. Advice on how to survive a book project was generously shared by Jasper Becker, Jason Burke, Paul French, Rob Gifford, John Gittings, Alexandra Harney, James Kynge, Jo Lusby, Richard

McGregor, Philip Pan, Ilaria Maria Salsa, Catherine Sampson, and Zhang Lijia. During the difficult early months of compilation I was kept on track by Paul Jackson, Dominic Al-Badri, Mary Kay Magistad, Nick Bridge, and Jes Randrup Nielsen, all of whom put in a yeoman's work critiquing the garbled first drafts.

At the editing stage, Henry Volans at Faber was a font of sage suggestions while Trevor Horwood cleaned and polished the manuscript with perspicacity and good humor. Chapters were improved with thoughtful feedback from Sharmilla Beezmohun, Chris Gill, Duan Xiaoli, Tim Johnson, Lauren Johnston, Rupert Wingfield-Hayes, and Yang Ailun, who read some or all of the book despite the busy schedules of people at the top of their game.

Research was greatly helped by several superb blogs and websites. Particular thanks to Isabel Hilton for *China Dialogue,* Xiao Qiang for *China Digital Times,* Roland Soong for ESWN, Jeremy Goldkorn for Danwei, Sam Crane for the Useless Tree, Jeremiah Jenne for Jottings from the Granite Studio, and Rebecca MacKinnon and John Kennedy at Global Voices Online. Covering this much ground would have been difficult without the Internet for reference. Gratitude is also due to those at bricks-and-mortar institutions, such as Kerry Brown at Chatham House, Hugo de Burgh at the University of Westminster's China Media Centre, Kjetil Haanes of the Norwegian Union of Journalists, and Alex Pearson, Peter Goff, and Jenny Niven at the Bookworm.

Specific advice on where to go and whom to talk to about environmental issues was provided by Marcus Haraldsson, Duncan Hewitt, Calum MacLeod, Richard Stone, and Marga Zambrana. As the bibliography and notes show, I have also followed up on stories and tips by many others in the vibrant foreign-correspondent community in China, including Jonathan Ansfeld, Naoko Aoki, Andrew Batson, Lindsey Beck, Chris Bodeen, Henrik Bork, François Bougon, Tania Branigan, Fred Brown, Chris Buckley, Steve Chao, Chi Yin, Dan Chung, Clifford Coonan, Elizabeth Dalziel, Mure Dickie, Bessie Du, Gady Epstein, Tomas Ezler, Maureen Fan, Jaime FlorCruz, Peter Ford, Peter Foster, Emma Graham Harrison, Lindsey Hilsum, Lucy Hornby, Charles Hutzler, Matt Jasper, Kim Rathcke Jensen, Joe Kahn, Sarah Keenlyside, Jutta Lietsch, Benjamin Lim, Louisa Lim, Melinda Liu, Andreas Lorenz, Barbara Luethi, Jane Macartney, Scott Macdonald, Mark and Karen Magnier, Kathleen McLaughlin, James Miles, Tom Miller, Isolda Morillo, Bernardo de Niz, Brad Olson, Evan Osnos, Peter Parkes, Tom Pattinson, Brice Pedroletti, Ted Plafker, John Ray, Peter Sharp, Craig Simons, Richard Spencer, David Stanway, Eugene Tang, Didi Kirsten Tatlow, Mary-Anne Toy, Alan Wheatley, Holly Williams, Jim Yardley, and no doubt some others I have omitted. I will be forever grateful to Stephen McDonell, Robert Hill, Yao Liwei, and Jiang Xin of ABC for finding space in their tent for me during the postearthquake thunderstorm in Yingxiu. Particular thanks to Sami Sillanpää, with whom I shared an office, many great assignments, and an awful lot of bad jokes.

Deeper into the subject and the territory, I was helped by the expertise and openness of professors at Beijing's top universities and the Chinese Academy of Sciences, notably Hu Angang, Li Can, Jiang Gaoming, Song Huailong, Wang Tao, Yao Tandong, Zhou Mingjiang, and Zou Ji. Guidance on specialist issues was also provided by Chimed-Erdene Baatar, Nicholas Bequelin, Arlene Blum, Carter Brandon, William Callahan, Ellen Carberry, Joel Cohen, David Concar, Robin Grayson, Arthur Kroeber, John MacKinnon, Isaac Mao, Charlie McElwee, Todd Meyer, Bob Moseley, Robin Munro, Sidney Rittenberg, Kate Saunders, Andrew Scanlon, Deborah Seligsohn, Vance Wagner, Alex Wang, Wang Fuqiang, Wang Sung, Alex Westlake, Tony Whitten, Matt Whitticase, Julian Wong, Xie Yan, and Nick Young.

On the ground, I have at times been taken on propaganda tours by government officials and on other occasions I have had to use subterfuge to cover sensitive stories with the help of local activists. Many of those who helped have asked to remain anonymous but I can thank the following institutions and groups: Chongqing Green Volunteers League, Friends of Nature, Global Witness, Green Camel Bell, Green Longjiang, Greenpeace, International Rivers, the Nature Conservancy, Traffic, the Wildlife Conservation Society, the World Wide Fund for Nature, the Chongqing and Dalian propaganda departments, The National Development and Reform Commission, and the Institute of Ecological Civilization Research. The International Campaign for Tibet and Free Tibet have also been very helpful.

Among the journalists and conservationists who have provided time or insight are Chen Guidi, Dai Qing, Feng Yongfeng, Jessy Lee, Sarah Liang, Ma Jun, Nie Bei, Tang Xiyang, Wang Yongchen, Wu Chuntao, Wu Dengming, Yang Yongping, Yu Xiaogang, and Zhang Jicheng. I would like to express respect too for the courage of lawyers such as Teng Biao and Gao Zhisheng, and citizen activists such as Chen Guangcheng, Hou Wenzhuo, Hu Jia, Liu Xiaobo, and Zeng Jinyan, who campaign on sensitive issues, including the environment, and have sometimes suffered violent retribution or imprisonment by the authorities.

I would not have made it to the end without the support and understanding of my wife and daughters in Beijing and the words of encouragement from my mother, sister, and stepfather on the other side of the world. Many friends shared warmth, wisdom, or much-needed mickey-taking, but I am particularly grateful to Nick Bonner, Andy Brock, Chen Ying, Jocelyn Ford, Kristen McQuillin, Sumiko Okita, Qin Liwen, Gareth Richards, Wang Chunhui, Wang Xiaoshan, and Yoyo Yoshiko. Special thanks to Murray Sayle, a master of the foreign correspondent's craft, whose essay "Overloading Emoh Ruo" was an inspiration for this book.

Finally, how can I express sufficient gratitude to those who have provided so much fine research and warm companionship over these years? One of the privileges of being a correspondent in China has been working with talented assistants, whose insight, sensitivity, and humor have added enormously to the pleasure and profit of traveling this vast country. Jin Jian, Zhou Xingping, Huang Lisha, Chen Shi, Chen Ou, Chang Yiru, Yu Hongyan, Xuyang Jingjing, and Cui Zheng know best that these pages would not be the same without their interpretation, and that for big chunks of the narrative, the "I" ought really to be "we."

I am in debt to them, to the others named above, and the many other friends and sources I have not mentioned, but whose help has made this book feel, at times, like a collaborative "cloud" project more than an individual work. I take sole responsibility for the interpretation and personal polemic, but ultimately it is cooperation and a shared acceptance of "facts" that moves people. To all those who have contributed, thank you.

Notes

Introduction: Beijing

1. At the time, the population of China had just passed 900 million. Today, it is close to 1.4 billion.
2. There are at least two other equally apocalyptic versions of this story that suggest the consequence of the synchronized jump would be a tsunami or an earthquake that would kill everyone on the planet. All of them may be bastardizations of the apocryphal quote attributed to Napoleon: "Let China sleep, for when she wakes, she will shake the world."
3. Wei Yiming et al., *China Energy Report (2008): CO$_2$ Emissions Research* (Science Press, 2008). The U.S. Energy Information Administration and the Carbon Dioxide Information Analysis Center noted an increase of more than 30 percent between 2003 and 2005.

1. Useless Trees: Shangri-La

1. Found at Ana village, Chuxiong Prefecture (Xu Jianchu and Jesse Ribot, "Decentralisation and Accountability in Forest Management: A Case from Yunnan, Southwest China." *European Journal of Development Research* 16, 1 [spring 2004]).
2. Chen paid the local authorities to clear up the mess, but neither he nor they bothered about the consequences until Chinese journalists revealed that the great director had turned the lake into a dump site. He was fined 90,000 yuan and publicly apologized for his negligence. Local officials were reprimanded, the lake was cleaned up and, two years later, the government banned filmmaking and artistic performances in most nature reserves.

3. Rock's influence may be overstated. Hilton said he studied the essays of the French missionary Abbé Évariste-Régis Huc, whose version of the myth of Shambala located it somewhere north of the Kunlun mountain range between Altai and Tian Shan. This would put it close to the border between current-day Qinghai and Xinjiang, hundreds of miles from Yunnan. But that has not stopped many other areas from attempting to appropriate the lucrative name (Michael McRae, *The Siege of Shangri-La: The Quest for Tibet's Legendary Hidden Paradise* [Broadway Books, 2002], pp. 84–86).

4. Renamed Camp David by President Eisenhower in 1955.

5. Ashild Kolas, *Tourism and Tibetan Culture in Transition: A Place Called Shangrila* (Routledge, 2007).

6. That year, an earthquake struck the area, killing two hundred people and putting the city's unique architectural heritage into the international spotlight. Soon after, Lijiang was granted UNESCO World Heritage status.

7. The trend is provincewide. In 2007, Yunnan province received 4.6 million overseas tourists and 89.9 million domestic tourists (China National Bureau of Statistics).

8. Kolas, *Tourism and Tibetan Culture,* details how the Diqing government's tourist office lobbied for the renaming of Zhongdian in late 1996 by inviting a "search party" commissioned by the Yunnan Economy and Technology Research Center to find evidence backing their claims. The party comprised more than forty academics, including experts in the fields of ethnology, literature, religion, linguistics, geography, and Tibetology. The government persuaded the Diqing Prefecture Tibetan Studies Center to assert that Xianggelila (Shangri-La) was a transliteration of *sems kyi nyima zlawa* (sun and moon of the heart)—a phrase in the local dialect used as a metaphor for perfection in the Bon culture.

9. Logging would probably have been halted anyway because the state banned tree felling in many areas after the floods of 1998 were blamed on deforestation.

10. A year after Xianggelila was renamed, labor teams began construction of a new airport and the tourists surged in. Between 1995 and 2010, the number of visitors increased 400-fold to three million, according to Zhongdian tourist authorities. (Interview with the head of the Zhongdian tourist board.)

11. This view was best expressed by Ye Xiaowen, the head of China Administration of Religious Affairs, who pointed out that central government spending was raising living standards more than the dreamy romanticism of the West.

He concluded: "Life expectancy was 35.5 years, but now it has reached 67 years. This is the real 'Shangri-La'" (Ye Xiaowen, "Shangri-La Has Changed and Tibetans Know It," *China Daily,* December 8, 2008).

12. He was later jailed for his idealism. This is discussed in more detail in ch. 16.

13. Yu's ideas are outlined in more detail in ch. 13.

14. Elizabeth Economy, *The River Runs Black: The Environmental Challenge to China's Future* (Cornell University Press, 2004), pp. 30–31.

15. Sam Crane provided this definition of *ziran*, which includes a translation by David Hinton. A far more recent variation is *daziran*—or "big *ziran*"—which is often used in a similar way to the Western idea of "Mother Nature," according to the China hand Sidney Rittenberg. The concepts of *tian* and *ziran* are fundamental to early philosophical debate in China.

16. Zhuangzi tells the story of a lost paradise as follows:

I have also heard that in ancient times when beasts outnumbered men, people had to build their dwellings in trees in order to avoid them. By day, they would pick acorns and chestnuts; at night they would sleep in the trees. Hence, they were called the "nest people," meaning people living in the nests. In ancient times, people did not know the use of clothes as they collected firewood in summer and burnt it in winter to keep themselves warm. Hence, they were referred to as "people who knew how to survive." During Shennong's reign, people went to bed with a peaceful mind and got up free and easy. They did not know their fathers but only knew their mothers. Living side by side with elk and deer, they farmed and wove for themselves and nursed no ill will against others. This was an age when virtue reached its peak.

Thereafter, the Yellow Emperor ruined virtue by his fights with Chiuyou in Zhuolu, with blood flowing a hundred li. When King Shun and King Yao ascended the throne, numerous official posts were established. King Tang exiled his lord and King Wu destroyed the preceding dynasty. Ever since then, the strong have been bullying the weak; the many have become the prey to the few. Ever since King Tang and King Wu, all monarchs have been usurpers who bring disorder to the people (Zhuangzi, trans. Wang Rongpei, *Library of Chinese Classics,* vol. 2 [Hunan People's Publishing House, 1999], ch. 29, pp. 517–19).

17. The ideal baseline was called the "fundamental norm." Mankind followed the concept of *wuwei* (noninterference by human intelligence) so everything was done in the interests of creation and the constancy of nature.

18. Cited in Roger Ames, *The Art of Rulership: A Study of Ancient Chinese Political Thought* (University of Hawaii Press, 1983), pp. 201–2.

19. Liu is also commonly credited as the originator of tai chi and soy milk.

20. Randall Collins, *The Sociology of Philosophies: A Global Theory of Intellectual Change* (Social Science, 2000), p. 157.

21. Activism was frowned upon, except by the Chimei (lit. "Red Eyebrows"), a contemporary agrarian rebel group sometimes described as the forerunner of secret societies and underworld gangs such as the Triads.

22. Mark Elvin, *Retreat of the Elephants: An Environmental History of China* (Yale University Press, 2004).

23. Ibid., p. 9.

24. Interview with John MacKinnon, head of the EU-China Biodiversity Programme and one of the most experienced foreign zoologists working in China.

25. Yuming Yang, Kun Tian, Jiming Hao, Shengji Pei, and Yongxing Yang, "Biodiversity and Biodiversity Conservation in Yunnan, China," *Biodiversity and Conservation* 13, 4 (2004): 813–26.

26. Forest cover in the province more than halved between 1950 and 1990. The worst logging occurred in Xishuangbanna, where 530,000 hectares were cleared between 1947 and 1980—much of it to cure tobacco (Qu Geping and Li Jinchang, *Population and the Environment in China* [Lynne Rienner, 1994], p. 64).

27. Yang et al., "Biodiversity and Biodiversity Conservation in Yunnan," p. 10.

28. As rubber prices have tripled over the past decade, plantations have boomed in Xishuangbanna. Now covering about 400,000 hectares, they occupy 20 percent of the prefecture's land. Nowhere is safe. China's leading conservation center, Xishuangbanna Tropical Botanical Garden, home to 11,700 plant species, is threatened by the spread of rubber trees (Jane Qiu, "China's Leading Conservation Center Is Facing Down an Onslaught of Rubber Plantations," *Nature*, January 8, 2009).

29. Personal correspondence and Robert Moseley, "Historical Landscape Change in Northwestern Yunnan, China: Using Repeat Photography to Assess the Perceptions and Realities of Biodiversity Loss," *Mountain Research and Development* 26, 3 (August 2006): 214–19.

30. Yang et al., "Biodiversity and Biodiversity Conservation in Yunnan," p. 4.

31. Jianchu Xu, a professor at the Kunming Institute of Botany, and Jesse C. Ribot, a senior associate at the Institutions and Governance Program, World Resources Institute in Washington, agree with Moseley that local autonomy is the best way to protect forest resources and that locals know best how to protect their environments. In ancient times, there were even elections for forest guardians, who risked being replaced if they were not "fair, straight, honest and moral" (Xu Jianchu and Jesse Ribot, "Decentralisation and Accountability in Forest Management: A Case from Yunnan, Southwest China." *European Journal of Development Research* 16, 1 [spring 2004]).

32. Tibetan monks at the Taizi monastery blame themselves for the dramatic retreat of the Mingyong glacier because they feel the sacred mountain's decline reflects a lack of pious devotion on their part (B. B. Baker and R. K. Moseley, "Advancing Treeline and Retreating Glaciers: Implications for Conservation in Yunnan, PR China," *Arctic, Antarctic, and Alpine Research* 39, 2 [2007]: 200–209).

33. Yang et al., "Biodiversity and Biodiversity Conservation in Yunnan," p. 5.

34. Matsutake exports to Japan have made many farmers rich. The business generates more export income for Yunnan than any other agricultural product. In 2005, the province earned $44 million from Matsutake—almost half of which came from Shangri-La (Christoph Kleinn, Yang Yongping, Horst Weyerhäuser, and Marco Stark, *The Sustainable Harvest of Non-Timber Forest Products in China: Strategies to Balance Economic Benefits and Biodiversity Conservation* [Sino-German Center for Research Promotion, 2006]). Studies have shown that production of Matsutake declined from 530 metric tons in 1995 to 272 in 2000. There has been a small improvement since, thanks to the education of villagers and a local initiative to regulate harvesting (ibid.).

35. The price has reached $60,000 per kilogram (Richard Stone, "Last Stand for the Body Snatcher of the Himalayas?" *Science*, November 21, 2008).

36. These brown worm-shaped organisms account for four out of every ten dollars earned by rural Tibetans and provide a bigger boost for the economy than the combined revenue from manufacturing and mining (Daniel Winkler, "Yartsa Gunbu [*Cordyceps sinensis*] and the Fungal Commodification of the Rural Economy in Tibet AR," *Economic Botany* 62, 3 [2008]: 291–305).

37. In July 2007, eight people were shot to death and fifty wounded in one such battle. In desperation, people are foraging for the treasured fruit in ever

more extreme locations. In June 2007, dozens of pickers died after being stranded in a blizzard. Every year, the fungus is being driven higher as the fragile lower grasslands are trampled into desert by the growing hordes of harvesters (Stone, "Last Stand").

38. A cascade of dams on the Lancang (Mekong), including the world's tallest—the 272-meter Xiaowan Dam—were already under construction. Thirteen more were being built or planned on the Nu (Salween) and eight on the Jinsha—the headwater of the Yangtze. Ch. 3 describes some of the consequences.

39. The impact could be felt hundreds of miles away. China's dams were already slashing catches downstream in Cambodia, where people depended on fish for the majority of their protein. For more on hydropower, see ch. 3.

2. Foolish Old Men: The Tibetan Plateau

1. Francis E. Younghusband, *Among the Celestials* (Elibron Classics, 2005 [first published 1898], p. 87).

2. Mao Zedong's closing speech at the Seventh National Congress of the Communist Party of China in 1945.

3. Patrick French, *Younghusband: The Last Great Imperial Adventurer* (Harper-Collins, 1994), p. 223, quotes a letter from Lieutenant Hadow, commander of the Maxim gun detachment, in which he writes to his father: "I hope I shall never have to shoot down men walking away again."

4. Ibid., p. 283.

5. Younghusband, *Among the Celestials,* pp. 15, 246, 254.

6. Tenzin Metok Sither, a spokeswoman for the overseas-based Free Tibet Campaign, told me it would add to the already tense political situation. "This is a highly strategic project that seeks to tighten Beijing's control over Tibet and will serve to further marginalize Tibetans economically and culturally."

7. On December 9, 1973, Mao informed King Birendra of Nepal that China was going to build the railway. In March 1974, construction on the Xining-Golmud section, which had begun in 1960, was resumed. See "The Qinghai-Tibet Railway: 50 Years in the Making," July 7, 2006, www.china.org.cn/english/features/Tibet/174015.htm.

8. Paul Theroux, *Riding the Iron Rooster* (Houghton Mifflin Harcourt, 1988).

9. Caroline Williams, "Where's the Remotest Place on Earth?" *New Scientist,* April 20, 2009. (According to Williams, it is three weeks' journey from Lhasa.)

10. www.dalailama.com/messages/world-peace/a-human-approach-to-peace.

11. Rudyard Kipling, *From Sea to Sea: Letters of Travel* (Cosimo, 2006 [first published 1889]).

12. In an e-mail to the author, Tibetan researcher Tenzin Losel wrote: "Tibet was never a Shangri-La pre-1959, and nor were other places in the world at that time (or today). We Tibetans would never describe it as such. But at the same time we Tibetans firmly deny the 'truth' stated by the Chinese government that old Tibet was the darkest, the most backward and the most barbaric society. Serfs did exist in the history of Tibet, but not the kind of serfs described by the Chinese government who did not enjoy any rights and who were merely treated as animals that can speak. The reality was more a contract-based relationship between serfs and their owners."

13. Since 1965, the central government claims it has financially supported Tibet to the tune of about 97 billion yuan ($14 billion). In the five years up to 2007, the incomes of farmers and herdsmen rose 83 percent. But the government insists that, far from being overrun by Han settlers, nine out of every ten residents are Tibetan. The environmental situation is also supposedly improving thanks to restrictions on logging and a ban on the mining of mercury, arsenic, peat, and alluvial gold. Over the coming decades, Beijing promises 22 billion yuan in investment on 160 "blue-sky" environment projects (Ye Xiaowen, "Shangri-La Has Changed and Tibetans Know It," *China Daily,* December 8, 2008).

14. According to China, this was voluntary. According to the Tibetan government in exile, it was imposed by military force.

15. Interview with John MacKinnon, head of the EU-China Biodiversity Programme.

16. In 2002, the State Council estimated 90 percent of the country's grassland had some level of degradation (Richard B. Harris, *Wildlife Conservation in China: Preserving the Habitat of China's Wild West* [East Gate, 2008], p. 38). Ch. 16 deals with grasslands in more detail.

17. Jane Qiu, "China: The Third Pole: Climate Change Is Coming Fast and Furious to the Tibetan Plateau," *Nature,* July 24, 2008.

18. According to the Free Tibet Campaign, 900,000 have been resettled out of the overall nomadic population on the plateau of 2.25 million. The proportion of resettlements in the Qinghai portion of the plateau is far higher. (E-mail correspondence with Matt Whitticase, spokesman of Free Tibet Campaign.) Reports in Xinhua suggest a higher figure of 80 percent. http://news.xinhuanet.com/english/2008-08/15/content_9343243.htm.

19. The quote refers to herders of Bange County, northern Tibet, who left the grassland to set up a cashmere and yak wool-carding factory in Germu City in neighboring Qinghai Province. Soon, cashmere sweaters named after the largest beautiful lake in Tibet, Namtso, went on sale in the inland market (Xinhua, "Northern Tibet Grassland Takes On New Look," May 19, 2009).

20. "To plunder Tibet of its mineral wealth, the Chinese government first had to clear large numbers of nomads from their land where mines were to be established" (Matt Whitticase, "The End of the Nomadic Way of Life in Tibet?" *Free Tibet,* May 2009).

21. This is on the Chinese side alone (interview with Yao Tandong, China Academy of Sciences).

22. The proximate cause of the changes now being felt on the plateau is a rise in temperature of up to 0.3°C per decade that has been going on for fifty years—approximately three times the global warming rate (Qiu, "China: The Third Pole").

23. Luo Yong, deputy director of China's National Climate Center, estimates that the volume of ice on either side of the Qinghai-Tibet highway has retreated by 12 percent since the 1960s, a trend with worrying implications for the tracks. "By 2050, the safe operation of the Qinghai-Tibet railway will be affected if temperatures keep rising steadily as observed over the past decades," Luo has warned (Chen Zhiyong, "Chilling Prediction," *China Daily,* December 20, 2004). This is also backhandedly acknowledged by a Xinhua report stating the railway will not be affected by climate change for forty years ("Qinghai-Tibet Railway Won't Be Affected by Climate Change Within the Next 40 Years at Least, Says Glaciologist," October 3, 2009).

24. Qiu, "China: The Third Pole."

25. Based on repeat photography study by Greenpeace of images from 1968 and 2007 (Jonathan Watts, "Everest Ice Forest Melting Due to Global Warming, Says Greenpeace," *Guardian,* May 30, 2007).

26. Stephen Chen, "The Tibetan Tundra's Explosive Secret," *South China Morning Post,* October 16, 2009.

27. Harris, *Wildlife Conservation in China,* p. 142.

28. Though small in numbers, Tibetan rangers are more devoted to wildlife than those in other regions, probably because of their Buddhist beliefs. Interview with Xie Yan of the Wildlife Conservation Society.

29. Ibid.

30. Kate Sanders, International Campaign for Tibet, personal correspondence.

31. The "photographer" was Liu Weiqiang, who was under contract to Xinhua. This was the second such scandal. The same year—2007—the forestry bureau in Shaanxi rewarded a farmer for a photograph of a South China tiger, long feared extinct. Soon after it was published online, the hoax was spotted by attentive netizens.

32. "Qinghai-Tibetan Plateau to Embrace 6 More Railway Lines by 2020," Xinhua, December 3, 2008.

33. Kenneth Pomeranz, "The Great Himalayan Watershed: Agrarian Crisis, Mega-Dams and the Environment," *New Left Review* 58 (July/August 2009).

34. Discussed in greater detail in ch. 3. See also Pomeranz, "Great Himalayan Watershed."

35. Since Qinghai was linked to the network in the 1950s, the population increased at least fourfold (Harris, *Wildlife Conservation in China,* p. 28).

36. Xie Yu, "Graduates Offered Cash Incentive to 'Go West,'" *China Daily,* January 8, 2009.

37. French, *Younghusband,* p. 252.

3. Still Waters, Moving Earth: Sichuan

1. It came into operation in 2006, two years before the quake, and had the capacity to generate 3.4 million megawatts of hydroelectric power, enough for a small city.

2. The epicenter was just 10 kilometers away, almost a direct hit in geological terms. An expert from the Nanjing Hydraulic Research Institute told *Caijing* magazine that Zipingpu was designed to withstand earthquakes below level 8 on the Mercalli intensity scale; however, the Sichuan quake (known in China as the Wenchuan earthquake) on May 12, 2008, hit level 11. "It's really a wonder that the dam survived the jolt," he is quoted as saying (Li Hujun, "Zipingpu Dam Upstream of Chengdu Secured," *Caijing,* May 19, 2008).

3. About 1,800 dams were at risk of collapse. According to China's ministry of water resources, 69 were in danger of collapse after the earthquake, 310 were at "high risk," and 1,424 posed a "moderate risk."

4. As of 2008, about 67 percent of Sichuan's energy was generated by hydropower plants (Ma Jun, "Overexploitation of Southwestern Hydropower Unhelpful to China's Energy Conservation and Pollution Control," Reform and Opening-up Study Series: Poverty Reduction and Sustainable Development in Western China [Social Sciences Academic Press (China), December 2008]).

5. Cited in Associated Press, "Sichuan Earthquake Damages Dams," May 12, 2008.

6. Peter Goff and Tania Branigan, "Survivors of Quake Urged to Hang On as Troops Arrive," *Guardian,* May 14, 2008.

7. The water was released at the speed of 800 cubic meters of water per second (Hujun, "Zipingpu Dam Upstream of Chengdu Secured").

8. Shai Oster, "China: New Dam Builder for the World," *Wall Street Journal,* December 28, 2007.

9. "Sichuan," formerly known as Szechuan, means Four Rivers. This is an abbreviation of Four Circuits of the Rivers and Gorges.

10. Interview with Tang Xiyang, coauthor of *A Green World Tour.*

11. Steven Sage argues in *Ancient Sichuan and the Unification of China* (SUNY Press, 1992) that Dujiangyan was the basis for grain surpluses that gave the Qin armies a huge advantage over their rivals.

12. The landmark study on this subject in English was by Karl Wittfogel, who argued in *Oriental Despotism* (Vintage, 1957) that power in Asia is derived from water, creating "hydraulic states." See also Mark Edward Lewis, *The Flood Myths of Early China* (SUNY Press, 2006), p. 47.

13. Li Bing was a real man, but he is often compared to the godlike emperor Da Yu, who defeated the floods by dredging rather than damming, while his son Erlang is portrayed in classical literature, such as *Journey to the West,* as a miraculous sage and nephew to the mythical Jade Emperor (Lewis, *The Flood Myths of Early China,* p. 46).

14. Where, according to an official hagiography, "many female schoolmates found him effortlessly attractive" and he excelled thanks to a "photographic memory" (Andy Zhang, *Hu Jintao: Facing China's Challenges Ahead* [iUniverse, 2002], p. 2).

15. Includes Cambodia's 192-megawatt Kamchay Dam and the 120-megawatt Nam Ting Dam in Laos. Data from International Rivers (www.internationalrivers.org) and Probe International (www.probeinternational.org). Sinohydro has business interests scattered across China, Africa, Southeast Asia, and lately a growing number in central Asia—the state-owned company is currently working on a 150-megawatt hydropower station in Tajikistan, using part of a $200 million loan the Chinese government extended to Tajikistan's main utilities firm, along with projects in Myanmar and Laos (Mark Godfrey, "A Global Hydro Power," *Probe International,* March 6, 2009).

16. Following Mao's comment, a plan was made for an eight-step development project along the upper reaches of the Min, in which the Zipingpu Dam was recommended as one of the first to be built along with Yuzui (later Yangliuhu).

17. Michael Lynch, *Mao* (Routledge, 2006), p. 274.

18. As early as 2001, Li Youcai voiced fears that officials were underplaying the risk of a major earthquake in the region (*China Dialogue,* 2008). Fan Xiao, a chief engineer with the Sichuan Geology and Mineral Bureau, warned about Zipingpu's seismic risks before the dam was completed. Concerns about an earthquake were also raised at a closed-door hearing in 2001 (David Murphy, "Dam the Consequences," *Far Eastern Economic Review,* July 11, 2002).

19. Andrew Mertha, *China's Water Warriors: Citizen Action and Policy Change* (Cornell University Press, 2008), p. 97.

20. Zipingpu was no exception. The project, which was completed with Japanese funding in 2006, displaced 33,000 people.

21. The reservoir was 660 kilometers long, which is a little more than the straight-line distance from Plymouth to Berwick-upon-Tweed.

22. The National People's Congress, usually a rubber-stamp legislature, recorded its biggest-ever "no" vote on this issue with a third of the delegates voting against or abstaining on a motion to approve the dam. But it passed with a majority that would be considered very comfortable in a democracy.

23. Fourteen people were killed in 2004 by a 20-meter wave generated by the collapse of 20 million cubic meters of rock into the Qinggan River, just 3 kilometers from where the tributary enters the Yangtze. In 2006, dozens of landslides occurred along a 32-kilometer stretch of riverbank. Little more than a year later, thirty bus passengers were buried when the earth gave way in Badong County near another tributary into the reservoir. In Fengjie County, where landslides have forced the resettlement of 13,000 people, officials have issued warnings for 800 disaster-prone areas.

24. According to a joint report by the Nanjing Institute for Geography and Limnology of the Chinese Academy of Sciences and Changjiang (Yangtze) Water Resources Commission, landslides and bank collapses have been identified at 4,719 places in the reservoir area. Of these, at least 627 are associated with filling the reservoir. Chen Jiang, "Three Gorges Dam Authority Suspends Reservoir Filling," *Nanfang Zhoumo* (South Weekend), November 27, 2008 (translation by Three Gorges Probe).

25. Jonathan Watts, "Three Gorges Dam Risk to Environment, Says China," *Guardian,* September 27, 2007.

26. Ahead of the Olympics, a time when other dissidents were intimidated into silence or locked up, Dai authored *The River Dragon Has Come!* a collection of essays on the murderous follies of China's dam-building programs. She often cities her father-in-law—a senior water ministry official—warning, "When you build a dam, you destroy a river," though she says the book was more of an exercise in free speech than an example of green activism.

27. Judith Shapiro, *Mao's War Against Nature* (Cambridge University Press, 2001), p. 50.

28. Quality was of secondary importance. There were few checks and balances. It was all about quantity and forward movement, as this quote in Dai's book from Liu Derun, the then deputy director of this office, shows: "Our daily work consisted of making phone calls to the provinces inquiring about the number of projects they were building, how many people were involved, and how much earth they had moved. In hindsight, some of the data and figures we gathered were obvious exaggerations, but no one back then had the energy to check them."

29. In 1952, Mao observed, "Southern water is plentiful, northern water scarce." Nobody could doubt the truth of that statement, nor did there seem any reason to dispute the almost childlike simplicity of his proposed solution: "Borrowing some water would be good."

30. Political opposition came mainly from provinces, such as Sichuan, that would lose water as a result of the plan, according to retired general Guo Kai (interview with the author, November 2008).

31. The city of Tianjin reportedly preferred to build desalination plants, which were more expensive but supplied cleaner water. The cost was 9.5 yuan per cubic meter in 2008, according to Guo Kai.

32. To offset these fears, the government has had to earmark an extra 8 billion yuan to bolster the Han, including diverting water from the Three Gorges reservoir on the Yangtze and along the Xinglong Hinge. These measures—essentially robbing Peter to pay Paul—will require another 650 kilometers of channels to be dug through farmland.

33. The estimated cost of the dams, tunnels, and pumping stations for this complex project is more than 320 billion yuan.

34. Qian Zhengying, former minister of water conservancy and power and the driving force behind the Three Gorges Dam, told me the diversion scheme needed a rethink. "The original plans were made twenty years ago. Since then our society has developed and the natural environment has changed. My view is that we must make a new assessment of the plan for the middle

and eastern legs," she said. Scientists doubted whether the upper reaches of the Yangtze had sufficient volume to "donate" the quantities of water envisaged in the plan.

35. Among the doubters is Zuo Qiting, a professor of hydrology at Zhengzhou University, who told me, "I am not a supporter of megaprojects . . . One way to halt the trend of ever-bigger projects is to evaluate their impact from a wider perspective. We need to look not just locally, but at the national and global level."

36. It is a mark of both Guo's perseverance and the Chinese government's openness to grand schemes that his ideas have received hearings at the highest level. In 1998, the then president Jiang Zemin called for a feasibility study. More than a dozen Mao-era generals from the People's Liberation Army are behind him, including retired air force major general Wang Dinglie, one of the last survivors of the Long March. In 2005, Guo and his collaborator Li Ling published details of the diversion plan in a book titled *How Tibet's Water Will Save China,* based on seventeen years of research. It was put on the politburo reading list, reportedly on the orders of President Hu Jintao.

37. When I met him, the general told me he always knew the scheme was impossible. "The Himalayas are made up of four mountain ranges, two of which are on Indian territory. Even if we blew a hole on our side, they would never approve to doing the same on theirs."

38. Qian Zhengying, the former water resources minister who pushed through the Three Gorges Dam, told me China needs to rethink the way it treats water. "We need to adapt our economic production to follow the natural course of water rather than the other way round" (interview with author).

39. Hydro plants were the main beneficiaries of foreign funds channeled to China under the UN-managed Clean Development Mechanism of the Kyoto Protocol to combat climate change by reducing greenhouse gases (Joe Macdonald, "China Dams Reveal Flaws in Climate-Change Weapon," Associated Press, January 25, 2009).

40. Among the best sources on this is Ma Jun, "Overexploitation of Southwestern Hydropower."

41. Xiao Yunhan, deputy director general of high-tech research and development at the Chinese Academy of Sciences, told me in an interview: "People often forget that when you build a one-kilowatt renewable energy plant you need to build the same size coal plant as a backup. I have read about that in

Sichuan with dams. They need a coal plant as a backup or else they would only have a half life."

42. China now produces more than 80 percent of the world's yellow phosphorus. Since 1985, its output of the compound has risen more than sixteen-fold, while production in Europe has been cut by two-thirds, in the U.S. by half, and in Japan completely eradicated. Yet these rich economies continue to import large amounts of yellow phosphorus, as an ingredient for products ranging from herbicides and fertilizers to steel, semiconductors, and tracer bullets.

43. Even without the coal plants nearby, this is misdirected. Carbon credits are supposed to be given to "additional" generation capacity. But these dams would have been built regardless of the Clean Development Mechanism. There is no additionality.

44. Where the authorities want to build a new dam upstream of the huge hydroelectric plant at Xiaolangdi, which is struggling to cope with the sediment buildup.

45. The "rush" is known in Chinese as *xihequanshui*, literally "to occupy the river." In 2002, State Power Corporation of China was broken into five corporations, each with exclusive development rights over particular watersheds. The biggest of them, Huaneng, won rights on the Lancang (Mekong), Huadian secured rights on the Nu, while Sanxia focused on the upper Yangtze (Mertha, *China's Water Warriors*, p. 46).

46. A former head of Huaneng, for example, was Li Xiaopeng, the son of former premier Li Peng, who drove through the Three Gorges project (ibid.).

47. Kenneth Pomeranz, "The Great Himalayan Watershed: Agrarian Crisis, Mega-Dams and the Environment," *New Left Review* 58 (July/August 2009).

48. "This was the first time in the history of the People's Republic of China that a decision on an engineering project of such magnitude—a decision that had already been reached—was reversed" (Mertha, *China's Water Warriors*, p. 103).

49. I read two days later in a Chinese newspaper that one wealthy resident had paid for a group of the fittest men in the area to rescue a relative in one of the cutoff villages. They reportedly turned back a day later after several were killed in landslides.

50. Though Fan never claimed to prove a link, he said that "Zipingpu has all conditions that provoke reservoir-induced earthquakes . . . We cannot rule out the possibility that building the Zipingpu Dam induced the earthquake

because the epicentre is so close to the dam" (Fan Xiao, chief engineer of the Regional Geology Investigation Team of the Sichuan Geology and Mineral Bureau, quoted in *Southern Metropolitan Daily* and translated by Three Gorges Probe). This possibility was also raised by several other scientists, for example, Richard A. Kerr and Richard Stone, "A Human Trigger for the Great Quake of Sichuan?" *Science,* January 16, 2009.

51. Cited in Kerr and Stone, "A Human Trigger for the Great Quake of Sichuan?"

52. The best-known example was a 6.5-magnitude earthquake triggered by the Koyna Dam in a remote area of India, which killed about 180 people in 1967. Others are Kremasta, Greece (1965), Kariba, Zimbabwe-Zambia (1961), and Xinfengjiang, China (1962) (Antoaneta Bezlova, "Temblor Shakes China's Big Dam Ambitions," Inter Press Service, June 26, 2008).

53. See note 18 of this chapter.

54. "China to Build 20 Hydro Dams on Yangtze River," Associated Press, April 21, 2009.

4. Fishing with Explosives: Hubei and Guangxi

1. Translation by R. Stercks, cited in Richard B. Harris, *Wildlife Conservation in China: Preserving the Habitat of China's Wild West* (East Gate, 2008).

2. Including Bob Pittman from NOAA, Brent Stewart from Hubbs-Seaworld Research Institute, Tomonori Akamatsu from Japanese FRA, Beat Mueller from the Swiss Eawag Aquatic Research, Wang Ding, deputy director of the Institute of Hydrobiology, Wuhan, and Samuel Turvey, Zoological Society of London.

3. The six-nation Yangtze Freshwater Dolphin Expedition was co-organized by the Institute of Hydrobiology, Wuhan, and August Pfluger, the millionaire CEO behind the baiji.org foundation.

4. Clive Ponting, *A New Green History of the World* (Penguin, 2007), p. 15.

5. A baiji-like creature is first mentioned in the ancient dictionary *Erya* in the third century BC. River dolphins are also given semimythical status along the Amazon and Mekong. In Brazil, the boto dolphin is said to take human form.

6. "Bai Qiulian," in the ancient Chinese storybook *Liaozhai Zhiyi* (Strange Stories from a Chinese Studio).

7. The pale, snub-nosed creature first drew attention outside China thanks to a study by Swiss biologist Giorgio Pilleri. Only six have ever been captured

alive. The last of them, Qi Qi, died at the age of twenty-four in the Wuhan Dolphinarium in 2002.

8. In 1986, there were 300 baiji; in 1990, 200; in 1994, fewer than 100; in 1997, an estimated 13. Since then, there have been only two sightings, both unconfirmed.

9. Foreign environmentalists have also blamed the Three Gorges Dam for accelerating the baiji's demise. The scientists aboard the *Kekao 1* said that, compared with overfishing, the direct impact of the barrier was minimal. But it added to the pressure on the animal because less sediment was flowing downstream, which meant fewer of the sandbars formed that were an important part of the baiji's habitat.

10. Yuan/dollar figures should be treated with caution. During the course of my writing, the exchange rate fluctuated considerably. For the sake of simplicity, I have used a uniform conversion rate approximating to $1 = 7 yuan. It is the rounded-up average during the three years before publication.

11. The others were Honghu and Tonglin.

12. Harris, *Wildlife Conservation in China*.

13. China is one of the globe's most important centers of biodiversity. Altogether, there are 613 types of mammals (ranking second in the world), 1,244 types of birds, 3,862 types of freshwater fish, 51,000 insects, 35,070 plants, 9,000 forms of algae, 8,000 fungi, 500 bacteria, 376 reptiles, 284 amphibians (Yuming Yang, Kun Tian, Jiming Hao, Shengji Pei, and Yongxing Yang, "Biodiversity and Biodiversity Conservation in Yunnan, China," *Biodiversity and Conservation* 13, 4 [2004]: 813–26).

14. Interview with Jim Harkness, former head of the WWF in China.

15. Fossil records show the planet has endured five previous mass extinctions, but unlike the previous wipeouts, this one is man-made rather than caused by asteroid impact or climate change. In the last 400 years, 83 mammals, 113 birds, 288 other animals, and 650 plants have become extinct—nearly all of them in the past century. Of the 21 marine species on the list, 16 have died out since 1972 (Ponting, *A New Green History of the World*, p. 170). A quarter of all mammals are now endangered or extinct, as are 15 percent of birds. *Nature* magazine estimates that half of the world's species will be extinct by 2100.

16. "Threats to China's biodiversity come from several sources: uncontrolled deforestation, desertification, overgrazing of rangelands, overexploitation and use of animal and plant resources, atmospheric pollution, poor protec-

tion and overutilisation of water resources in arid and semi-arid regions, invasive plants and animals, overfishing, water pollution, and adverse effects of tourism, mining, wetland reclamation and other human activities. These pressures have led to a greater threat to biodiversity in China than elsewhere. Compared to a global rate of species loss of 10 per cent, the estimate for China is greater, about 15–20 per cent" (John MacKinnon et al., *A Biodiversity Review of China* [WWF International, 1996], p. 12). The UN's Convention on International Trade in Endangered Species of Wild Fauna and Flora (CITES) reports that 189 of the world's 740 endangered species are in China, around a quarter of the total. Between 4,000 and 5,000 of China's plant species are endangered or at risk—about a fifth of the nation's floral diversity. More than half the mammal and amphibian species in China are classified as threatened or near threatened.

The China Species Red List (www.chinabiodiversity.com/index.php) notes that 39.8 percent of mammals are threatened, and 10.8 percent are near threatened. Among amphibians, the percentages are 39.9 and 19.6. Of 1,200 orchid varieties, 99.5 percent are endangered. The "cute factor" is important. One study has shown that funding for protection tends to focus on species with large eyes.

17. *National Statistical Yearbook 2008* (China National Bureau of Statistics, 2008).

18. As of 2005, there was just a single trained wildlife biologist in Qinghai Province, while Gansu had three. The combined area of these two regions is the size of Europe. They had no shortage of geologists and hydroengineers (Harris, *Wildlife Conservation in China*, p. 15). Interview with Wang Sung, former head of the Wildlife Conservation Society.

19. John MacKinnon, head of the EU-China Biodiversity Programme, private conversation, January 2009.

20. According to MacKinnon, "The decimation of wild medicinal plants could threaten the health of millions of people around the world who rely on traditional medicine to treat serious illness, according to scientists."

21. Figures provided by Traffic in 2006 (www.traffic.org).

22. Interview with John MacKinnon.

23. A clause in the law states: "Governments in different levels should set nature reserves in areas and waters where wild animals live and breed." This does not specify that animals should be kept in their natural habitat.

24. Data on captive musk deer tend to be regarded as a state secret, thus even Chinese surveys have difficulty establishing exactly what goes on at musk-

deer farms. All the bears in China produce ursodeoxycholic acid, a bile fluid considered to have medicinal properties, but sun bears are small, so probably produce less bile, and brown bears are more aggressive. So most of the farmed bears are Asiatic black bears (Harris, *Wildlife Conservation in China*, p. 88).

25. Violations of the Wildlife Conservation Law can result in long prison terms, and more than thirty people have been executed for killing or trading elephants and giant pandas (Jeffrey A. Sayer and Changjin Sun, "Impacts of Policy Reforms on Forest Environments and Biodiversity," in William F. Hyde, Brian Belcher, and Jintao Xu [eds.], *China's Forests: Global Lessons from Market Reforms* [Resources for the Future, 2003], p. 181). Despite such harsh penalties, however, the laws remain weak because they are not implemented with sufficient funds, personnel, commitment, or organization.

Responsibility for protecting wildlife is fragmented among at least five ministries. The main responsibility lies with the state forestry administration, which manages most of China's nature reserves, but other parks, zoos, breeding centers, and protected areas fall under the ministry of environmental protection, the ministry of construction, the ministry of agriculture, and the state oceanic administration.

26. The reserve was moved to Bifengxia Panda Breeding Center after Wolong was damaged in the Sichuan earthquake.

27. John MacKinnon, "More than Just Pandas," *Biodiversity Matters Newsletter*, 5 (2008).

28. The success rate is 85 percent.

29. As I later discovered, such practices are commonly used by sheep and cattle farmers across the developed world, though apparently semen-milking with artificial vaginas was preferred because the sperm count and quality tended to be better.

30. The rental fee varies according to the place and circumstances. American and Japanese zoos pay top dollar. In other cases, pandas are loaned for little or no fee as a gesture of friendship.

31. It is not the only controversy. The designation of the area as a nature reserve accelerated deforestation as developers cleared land for hotels and roads. New forest plantations have not provided the preconditions for bamboo growth and so have not been able to serve as a new panda habitat (Harris, *Wildlife Conservation in China*, p. 116).

32. This view was put forward most vividly by Chris Packham, the head of the UK's Bat Conservation Trust and a BBC presenter, who said of the giant panda: "Here is a species that, of its own accord, has gone down an evolutionary cul-de-sac. It's not a strong species . . . Unfortunately, it's big and cute and a symbol of the World Wide Fund for Nature and we pour millions of pounds into panda conservation" (Liz Thomas, "Let the Panda Die Out, Says BBC Presenter Chris Packham," *Daily Mail,* September 22, 2009).

33. Interview with Jim Harkness.

34. Talking to me soon after the release, the scientist sounded like a proud father: "Xiang Xiang is doing very well. His weight has increased by fifteen kilos. We taught him how to choose good bamboo." He told me the panda had been satellite-tracked on journeys of 9 kilometers, a sign of confidence. "We are hoping he will fight with other males during the mating season next year." Unfortunately, that appears to be exactly how the panda was killed a few months later. Markings on Xiang Xiang's body suggest he was pushed out of a tree. It was his second bloody fight of the season. Zhang withheld news of the death for three months (Jonathan Watts, "Captive-bred Chinese Panda Dies in the Wild," *Guardian,* May 31, 2007).

35. Until recently, about half of panda mothers gave birth to twins, one of which usually died through neglect. Zhang says it is very difficult for mothers to look after both twins, because infants are not capable of urinating or excreting until they are six months old. The mother must lick them clean far more often than any human parent changes their baby's nappies. Having struggled with this problem for years, the Wolong team can now almost guarantee the survival of both twins by rotating the babies between their mother and the nursery. Keepers clean the babies by using a cotton swab warmed to the same temperature as the mother's tongue. Thanks also to improvements in artificial feeding techniques, the survival rate is more than 95 percent, up from 50 percent in the 1980s.

36. This was a positive step because many panda communities had fewer than twenty animals, and needed to link up to mate.

37. "A recent paper by Berta Martín-López and colleagues in Conservation Biology reports that the size of an animal's eyes appeared to be people's main measure for determining whether they think an animal is important enough for them to open their pocket books and pay for its conservation" (Tony Whitten, "How Cute Do You Have to Be to Be Safe?" blog on World Bank website, April 8, 2008).

38. "Certainly some species have been driven to extinction since the 1980s, for example, snakes and turtles. In the 1980s, few people ate these animals but since the 1990s, there have been more and more restaurants that serve these exotic dishes. Around that time, China used up many of its domestic animals so it started to eat animals outside China. The situation is getting worse. Snakes and turtles are being taken from the wild. There is a market for them now. The price is going up" (Interview with Xie Yan of the Wildlife Conservation Society of China). Xie cited the case of the yellow-headed box turtle, which is endemic to Anhui. In the 1980s, there were around 2,000 left in the wild. But in the WCS's most recent survey, they found none.

39. This is particularly true in Guangdong and Guangxi, where a common saying has it that people will eat everything with four legs except a chair, everything that flies except an airplane, and everything in the water except a submarine.

40. Jonathan Watts, "Student Activists Try to Save Wildlife on China's Menu," *Guardian,* May 15, 2009.

41. Though this too proved controversial when hunting licenses were auctioned mostly to rich Westerners (Jonathan Watts, "China Puts Price on Head of Rare Animals," *Guardian,* August 9, 2006). This led to a furious online backlash (Xinhua, "Auction of Hunting Quotas Postponed," August 12, 2006).

42. There has been a possible sighting of a lone baiji since, but even if confirmed, it is thought highly unlikely there will be sufficient dolphins to continue the species.

5. Made in China? Guangdong

1. Alexandra Harney, *The China Price: The True Cost of Chinese Competitive Advantage* (Penguin, 2008), p. 17.

2. From 24.5 billion yuan in 1980 to 3.5 trillion yuan in 2008.

3. According to Rupert Hoogewerf, compiler of the *Hurun Report* list of China's richest men and women.

4. Although it was not an illegal trade, since opium use was permitted in Britain. A more eloquent criticism was made in Parliament by the Opposition leader William Gladstone, who described Britain's actions in the subsequent "Opium War" as "unjust and iniquitous . . . to protect an infamous contraband traffic" (House of Commons Debates [Hansard], vol. 53, April 8, 1840, col. 818).

5. Jiang Gaoming, "China Must Say No to Imported Waste," *China Dialogue,* February 8, 2007.

6. The world's largest container ship, the *Emma Maersk,* had recently delivered 170,000 tons of trash to Lianjiao in south China's Guangdong Province.

7. Adam Smith, *An Enquiry into the Nature and Causes of the Wealth of Nations* (1776), bk. I, ch. 8. Like Malthus, Smith judged China without ever seeing it.

8. A report from the Waste Resources Action Programme of the UK suggested that the advantage of recycling over landfilling was so great that it made environmental sense to ship waste halfway around the world for recycling, 1,300–1,600 kilograms of CO_2 being saved for each ton of recycled waste (John Vidal, "Sending Waste to China Saves Carbon Emissions," *Guardian,* August 19, 2008).

9. Alan W. Watts, *The Joyous Cosmology: Adventures in the Chemistry of Consciousness* (Vintage, 1965), p. 63.

10. Between 1999 and 2009, annual exports of waste paper from Britain, mainly to India, China, and Indonesia, have risen from 470,000 to 4.7 million tons and plastic bottles from under 40,000 tons to half a million (Vidal, "Sending Waste to China Saves Carbon Emissions").

11. The Basel Convention on the Control of Transboundary Movements of Hazardous Wastes and Their Disposal came into force in 1992.

12. Jiang, "China Must Say No to Imported Waste."

13. According to Eddy Zheng of the Guangzhou Institute of Geochemistry, approximately 70 percent of e-waste generated worldwide is processed in China. The biggest center for this operation is Guiyu, where, he says, human exposure to toxins is very intensive (talk given to the Foreign Correspondents' Club of China, August 24, 2009).

14. Scott Pelley, "'60 Minutes' Crew Attacked in China While Reporting on E-Waste," *Huffington Post* (Internet newspaper), November 6, 2008. My own party comprised my assistant, Sami Sillanpää of the *Helsingin Sanomat,* and Clifford Coonan of the *Irish Times.*

15. Arlene Blum of the Green Science Policy Institute has conducted extensive research on the health problems related to fire retardants in the U.S. With regulations tightening in other countries, she fears the industry is moving to China (interview with author).

16. In the U.S, 130,000 computers are discarded every day and 100 million cellphones annually, according to Allen Hershkowitz, a senior scientist and authority on waste management at the Natural Resources Defense Council, quoted in "Following the Trail of Toxic E-Waste," CBS *60 Minutes,* Novem-

ber 9, 2008. The U.S. Environmental Protection Agency estimates that Americans produce 2.63 million tons of e-waste each year.

17. In 2008, the U.S. Government Accountability Office condemned the Environmental Protection Agency for failing to identify where 80 percent of U.S. electronic waste is headed.

18. Zheng, talk given to the Foreign Correspondents' Club of China, August 24, 2009.

19. Press conference, August 2009.

20. I first heard this apposite expression from Nick Young while he was head of China Development Brief.

21. So much so that even other factories in Guangdong are worried. When I visited a legitimate production line for the Robosapien toy, I was surprised to find every member of staff being searched on their way out of the gates. "Why?" I asked a manager. "Because otherwise someone will smuggle out a model and then a factory in Shantou will be producing rip-off copies within days."

22. Hong Kong's per capita GDP in 2006 was $42,123; Guangxi's was less than $2,000 (*National Statistical Yearbook* 2007 [China National Bureau of Statistics, 2007]).

23. Nearly 5,000 officials at the county level or above were punished for corruption in one year, state media reported (Mark Magnier, "Corruption Taints Every Facet of Life in China," *Los Angeles Times,* December 28, 2008). Nationwide, corruption accounts for an estimated 3 to 15 percent of a $7 trillion economy, and party membership can be an invitation to solicit bribes or cut illegal land deals.

24. This is also where a former colleague, Benjamin Joffe-Walt, saw a local activist, Lu Banglie, so savagely beaten by thugs that he reported him dead. I went to look for Lu's body and was relieved to find him shaken but very much alive.

25. Xie Yan of the Wildlife Conservation Society told me, "The big demand for wildlife started in the nineties. It existed before but not on a big scale. I think that is related to the economy. People are getting rich and exploring rare dishes. Guangdong is the biggest problem but all of the southern area of Guanxi and Yunnan, it is getting more common."

26. Author's interview with Traffic representative.

27. Jonathan Watts, "'Noah's Ark' of 5,000 Rare Animals Found Floating off the Coast of China," *Guardian,* May 26, 2007.

28. One raid on a restaurant in Guanghzou in 2008 turned up 118 pangolins, 60 kilograms of snakes, and 400 kilograms of toads.

29. Jonathan Watts, "Concubine Culture Brings Trouble for China's Bosses,"
     Guardian, September 8, 2007.

30. Other factors, of course, include cheap labor and a good infrastructure. The
     average hourly salary in Guangdong for manufacturing workers in 2002 was
     57 cents, about 3 percent of the U.S. level, according to Alexandra Harney
     in *The China Price.* She estimates that this is less than handloom operators
     in Britain were paid during the Industrial Revolution (p. 9).

31. Quoted in Zhou Jigang, "The Rich Consume and the Poor Suffer the Pollu-
     tion," *China Dialogue,* October 27, 2006.

32. This single province accounts for a third of China's exports (Harney, *The China
     Price,* p. 15). The National Development and Reform Commission estimates
     that between 15 and 25 percent of all the country's global warming emissions
     result from manufacturing exports. According to Oslo's Center for Interna-
     tional Climate and Environmental Research, a third of all Chinese emissions
     are linked to exports, with 9 percent from manufacture of exports to the U.S.,
     and 6 percent from goods for Europe (Jonathan Watts, "Consuming Nations
     Should Pay for Carbon Dioxide Emissions, Not Manufacturing Countries, Says
     China," *Guardian,* March 17, 2009). If such emissions were factored into con-
     suming nations' carbon accounts, the reductions claimed in Europe in recent
     years would be overturned. The British government's impressive 18 percent cut
     in carbon emissions since 1990 would be revealed as a 20 percent increase.

33. By one estimate, Chinese manufacturers are paid only a quarter of the final
     retail sale (Harney, *The China Price,* p. 15).

34. The power generated for industry here is particularly dirty because coal
     mined in the south contains high levels of sulfur.

35. Data from 2005 (Tang Hao, "Cleaning China's Polluted Pearl," *China Dia-
     logue,* June 28, 2007).

36. Cheung Chi-fai, "Hong Kong Smog Third Worst Since 1968," *South China
     Morning Post,* January 17, 2008.

37. The average American discards 23.4 kilograms of plastic packaging a year. In
     Japan and Europe the figures are 20.1 and 15 kilograms, respectively, while
     in China it is a mere 13 kilograms. Developed countries recognized the
     threats that plastics pose long ago, and responded by using new materials
     and developing recycling (Jiang, "China Must Say No to Imported Waste").

38. Ministry of environmental protection website figures released in 2008.

39. Prices have more than halved since the start of the economic crisis in
     autumn 2008 (*Nanfang Metropolitan Daily,* October 21, 2008).

40. Jonathan Watts and Jess Cartner-Morley, "Waste Land," *Guardian*, March 31, 2007.

6. Gross Domestic Pollution: Jiangsu and Zhejiang

1. Speech to an international conference on sustainable sanitation in Ordos, Inner Mongolia, in 2007 (Shi Jiangtao, "Experts Blame Pollution on Runaway Greed," *South China Morning Post*, August 28, 2007).

2. Depending on how and when wealth is calculated. This accolade has also been claimed at times by Guangdong and Shanghai.

3. Now nominally retired, Wu has passed leadership of the village to his son, but he is still revered as a founding father and exercises influence much like Deng Xiaoping—who dominated Chinese politics long after he resigned all formal titles apart from that of Honorary Chairman of the China Bridge Association.

4. He Jianming, *Jingcai Wu Renbao* (Shandong Wenyi Publishing House, 2007).

5. But the biographies are careful not to position Wu too clearly as a pioneer capitalist. Among his leftist achievements, they cite the setting up of a free village canteen in the early 1970s. Its success was proclaimed when thirty-eight of the fifty-eight women residents put on weight—a sign, if nothing else, of how cosmetic values have changed in China.

6. Town and village enterprises (TVEs) were a driving force in the first two decades after the economic reforms of 1978 as local governments and collectives took advantage of the opening to foreign trade and capital. From 1978 to 1996, TVE employment rose from 28 million to 135 million (Barry Naughton, *The Chinese Economy: Transitions and Growth* [MIT Press, 2007]).

7. James Kynge covers this in detail in *China Shakes the World: A Titan's Rise and Troubled Future—and the Challenge for America* (Houghton Mifflin, 2006). See also Bill Emmott, "What China Can Learn from Japan on Cleaning Up the Environment," *McKinsey Quarterly*, September 2008.

8. Joseph Kahn and Mark Landler, "China Grabs West's Smoke-Spewing Factories," *New York Times*, December 21, 2007.

9. A central aim of the Great Leap Forward in 1958 was to make China one of the world's major steel-producing nations.

10. International Energy Agency figures cited in Kahn and Landler, "China Grabs West's Smoke-Spewing Factories."

11. With 2,400 employees, a turnover of 7 billion yuan (around $1 billion), and an annual output of 1.3 million tons per year.

12. Together, they covered an area more than twelve times greater than the Trafford Centre in the UK.

13. The city estimates that 5,000 foreign merchants have established permanent bases in the city. Each year, another 200,000 visit for short-term sprees.

14. China Commodities City Group.

15. China's exports have doubled in less than five years. The "miracle" Japanese economy of the 1970s managed the feat in seven years; Germany took ten years in the 1960s; it took Britain twelve years after 1838, culminating in the Great Exhibition in London's Hyde Park—the proudest moment in its industrial history—to do the same (Will Hutton, "Welcome to the Great Mall of China," *Observer,* May 13, 2004). However, dependence on overseas markets makes the economy extremely vulnerable to a downturn. At the time of the economic crash of 2008, the economist Michael Pettis estimated that China was five times more dependent on foreign markets to create domestic jobs than the United States was at the time of the Great Crash in 1929.

16. One example is the use of toxic fire-retardant chemicals exposed by UC Berkeley chemist Arlene Blum: "I learned China is putting fire retardant chemicals into all furniture imported into the U.S. and Canada. PentaBDE and other chemical fire retardants considered too toxic to be used in the U.S. are being added at high levels. Scrap foam containing these toxic chemicals is also imported into the U.S. for use in carpet cushion" (Arlene Blum, personal correspondence).

17. Fisherman say whitebait catches have fallen to a fifth of their peak. In 2007, the lake was so fetid that 5 million people in Wuxi and neighboring regions had to use bottled water for drinking and bathing. Local media reported that 6 billion tons of wastewater were discharged into the lake each year and 70 percent of the nearby rivers were heavily polluted.

18. Between 2001 and 2006, the number of babies born with heart defects, cleft lips, and hydrocephalus rose by 50 percent, a fifth of which were attributed to pollution (Stephen Chen, "Birth Defects Caused by Environmental Pollution: First Large-Scale Study Exposes Poisoning Risks," *South China Morning Post,* January 9, 2009).

19. Citizens of conscience who have greater influence than China's chronically overlooked rural residents have no means to escape. He Hongshi, party secretary of Touzen Village of Jiangsu Province, is currently serving two years in prison for leading villagers in their complaints against chemical parks.

An article in the *Nanfang Daily* recounted two cases of such abuse. Villagers from Duigou Village in Jiangsu Province's Guannan County decided to have their river water tested because of noticeable pollution. The results showed that the water was undrinkable for both people and animals. Residents demanded compensation of 40,000 yuan ($5,700) from the chemical plants in the local industrial park. In response, the administrative committee, a government branch, sued them on charges of blackmail.

20. Ma Tianjie, "Environmental Mass Incidents in Rural China," *China Environment* 10 (2008/9), Woodrow Wilson International Center for Scholars. In the most violent reported case, police killed at least three villagers in Dongzhou, Guangdong Province, while quelling a riot over a planned power plant. Two years later, in 2007, thousands took to the streets in Xiamen, Fujian Province, to successfully block plans for a petrochemical plant. In recent years, the government has stopped releasing data on the number of mass incidents.

21. Jonathan Watts, "China Blames Growing Social Unrest on Anger over Pollution," *Guardian,* July 6, 2007.

22. As Elizabeth Economy notes: "The price of water is rising in some cities, such as Beijing, but in many others it remains as low as 20 per cent of the replacement cost. That ensures that factories and municipalities have little reason to invest in wastewater treatment or other water-conservation efforts. Fines for polluting are so low that factory managers often prefer to pay them rather than adopt costlier pollution-control technologies. One manager of a coal-fired power plant explained to a Chinese reporter in 2005 that he was ignoring a recent edict mandating that all new power plants use desulphurisation equipment because the technology cost as much as would 15 years' worth of fines" ("The Great Leap Backward?" *Foreign Affairs* 86, 5 [September/October 2007]).

23. Huaxi Chemical Industrial Park. Though it shares the same name as the "Number One Village in China," they are unconnected.

24. Sami Sillanpää (*Helsingin Sanomat*), Didi Kirsten Tatlow (*South China Morning Post*), and Clifford Coonan (*Irish Times*).

25. Accounts differed. The Dongyang government said about 1,000 police and local officials had been attacked by a mob, resulting in thirty-six injuries and no deaths. Residents claimed 3,000 police stormed the village, leaving several people—including police—killed, dozens wounded, and thirty police buses destroyed.

26. These slogans are included in a detailed report on the incident in the *Phoenix Weekly* magazine, translated by Roland Soong on his ESWN blog. http://www.zonaeuropa.com/20050601_1.htm.

27. In December 2007, the government forced six enterprises to publish an apology in the *Hangzhou Daily*. "We have been found discharging excessive pollution recently. This is because we had not paid enough attention to environmental protection nor fully obeyed the law and regulations, and the pollution treatment facilities were not operating properly." The firms—two paper mills, two electroplating factories, and two printing and dyeing plants—promised to suspend production until they had invested more on waste treatment. "We sincerely apologize to all the people in Hangzhou and are willing to accept criticism and advice."

28. Qian Yanfeng, "Toxic Water Scare Leaves a Sour Taste," *China Daily*, February 25, 2009.

29. The director of the environmental bureau, Dai Beijun, quoted in Xinhua, "Six Enterprises Apologize for Pollution," December 28, 2007.

30. Ch. 15 covers these initiatives in more detail.

31. "The first Chinese province to calculate 'green GDP'—economic production less environmental costs—has concluded it [the economy] barely grew during the country's expansion over the past two decades" (*Financial Times*, August 19, 2004). When asked to explain why the scheme had been aborted, one official observed: "The 'green GDP' really makes the provinces and cities look bad" ("'Green GDP' Mired in Red Tape," *China Digital Times*, March 30, 2007).

32. Ma Jun, "After 'Green GDP,' What Next?" *China Dialogue*, August 8, 2007.

33. As Emmott writes: "Far from being unprecedented, the broad shape and nature of the country's growth from the 1980s onward has been pretty similar to the pattern shown in earlier decades by Japan, South Korea, Taiwan, and other East Asian success stories" (Emmott, "What China Can Learn from Japan on Cleaning Up the Environment"). This assumption follows the Kuznet's curve hypothesis, which suggests that pollution and inequality increase during the early stages of a country's development and then start to decline. Though Emmott did not say so, the same could also be said of the UK or the U.S.A.

34. *Cost of Pollution in China: Economic Estimates of Physical Damages*, report by the World Bank and China's Environmental Protection Agency, Ministry of Health, and Ministry of Water Resources, 2007.

35. Economy, "The Great Leap Backward?" cites water pollution costs of $35.8 billion one year, air pollution costs of $27.5 billion another, and on and on with weather disasters ($26.5 billion), acid rain ($13.3 billion), desertification ($6 billion), or crop damage from soil pollution ($2.5 billion).

36. The annual bonus was usually about 80,000 yuan ($11,400), and 95 percent of their dividends—worth about 200,000 yuan ($29,000).

7. From Horizontal Green to Vertical Gray: Chongqing

1. Speaking at the Nature Conservancy conference ConEx in Vancouver, 2008.

2. United Nations Department of Economic and Social Affairs, "City Dwellers Set to Surpass Rural Inhabitants in 2008," *DESA News* 12, 2 (February 2008).

3. Joseph Stiglitz, the Nobel Prize–winning economist, described this as one of the defining trends of our era. "Revolution of new technology and China's urbanizing process are expected to be the two big events that will affect humankind in the twenty-first century," he noted at a symposium in China in 1999.

4. By administrative fiat. Chongqing had previously been part of Sichuan Province. But it was made into a municipality in 1997 as part of preparations for the Three Gorges Dam, noted in ch. 3.

5. City residents in Chongqing have seen their incomes rise 66 percent in the past five years to just over 10,000 yuan ($1,400) per year, almost three times that of their country cousins.

6. China's urban population increased by only 8.3 percent between 1949 and 1979, 20 percentage points lower than the average for developing nations. This was partly due to the politburo's belief that urbanization was responsible for the famines of 1960 and 1961. However, a bigger factor in that tragedy was the Great Leap Forward, during which farmers were ordered to tear down trees for steel production, slaughter birds that killed pests, and use deep-plowing techniques that ruined soil quality.

7. With 1.6 trillion yuan ($229 billion) spent since 1999, mainly on roads, bridges, dams, and pipelines, this policy is sometimes compared with the Marshall Plan that helped rebuild postwar Europe.

8. As one observer noted, Chongqing's urban population was expanding eight times quicker than that of late-nineteenth-century Chicago, then considered the world's fastest-growing city (James Kynge, *China Shakes the World: A Titan's Rise and Troubled Future—and the Challenge for America* [Houghton Mifflin, 2006]).

9. Deng Xiangzheng, Huang Jikun, Scott Rozelle, and Emi Uchida, "Cultivated Land Conversion and Potential Agricultural Productivity in China," China Academy of Sciences, July 2005.

10. Over this period some cultivated land was added: 24.2 percent of it by reclaiming woodland, 66 percent from grasslands, and 1.9 percent from bodies of water. But this was all obtained at the expense of natural ecosystems. Over the previous forty years, land reclamation has led to the loss of 11,900 square kilometers of coastal shallows, with industry taking more than 10,000 square kilometers of coastal wetlands. Half of China's coastal shallows are now completely destroyed. Despite this, the trend of overall loss of cultivated land has not been reversed (Jiang Gaoming, "The Terrible Cost of China's Growth," *China Dialogue,* January 12, 2007). Chapter 15 considers this phenomenon in more detail.

11. According to a study by the U.S.-based Council on Tall Buildings and Urban Habitat. The planet's most spectacular edifices are now rising up in the East rather than the West. In 2008, six of the world's ten tallest new buildings were completed in China, including the 492-meter Shanghai World Financial Center, which is only slightly shorter than the world's highest man-made structure, Taipei 101 in Taiwan. Both will soon be dwarfed by the 632-meter Shanghai Tower and the 600-meter China 117 Tower in Tianjin.

12. Energy use of New York City is 70 percent of U.S. average because using public transport and heating residential blocks rather than individual homes are more efficient (interview with Joel Cohen).

13. China's urban population has grown in cities of all sizes. However, townships of between 5,000 and 10,000 people are witnessing the fastest growth. Demographic trends in China indicate that (1) the urban population of about 430 million in 2001 will reach 850 million by 2015, and (2) the number of cities with over 100,000 people will increase from 630 in 2001 to over 1,000 by 2015 (World Bank on Urban Environment, web.worldbank.org).

14. "Urbanization Will Be Halted in Tibet, Guizhou, Ningxia, and Qinghai," *South China Morning Post,* January 4, 2008.

15. Interview with Joel Cohen.

16. Only 10 percent of which is arable.

17. Thomas Campanella, *The Concrete Dragon: China's Urban Revolution and What It Means for the World* (Princeton Architectural Press, 2008).

18. Where population pressures are exacting a toll on the environment, according to mainland media. It would also be stopped in nature reserves and

areas that are the origins of major rivers and sources of sandstorms. The favorable areas to live, accounting for about 10 percent of China's landmass, would hold more than 30 percent of the population. Fertile agricultural plains in northeastern, central, and southern China, and flourishing urban clusters centered on megacities such as Shenyang, Beijing, Zhengzhou, Wuhan, Changsha, Qingdao, Nanning, Chengdu, Chongqing, Shanghai, and Guangzhou would start preparing for an enormous increase in residents ("Urbanization Will Be Halted in Tibet, Guizhou, Ningxia, and Qinghai").

19. Interview with Neville Mars.

20. Elizabeth Economy, "The Great Leap Backward?" *Foreign Affairs* 86, 5 (September/October 2007).

21. The average city dweller produces 440 kilograms of waste a year. The effect on emissions is contested. United Nations agencies, former U.S. President Bill Clinton's climate change initiative, and New York Mayor Michael Bloomberg have all stated that between 75 and 80 percent of emissions come from cities. However, this figure is refuted by the International Institute for Environment and Development, which argues that cities account for only 40 percent of emissions, so they are actually more efficient.

22. Reuters, "China Will Sink under the Weight of Its Own Rubbish," January 9, 2007.

23. The previous year, twenty strikers required hospital treatment after police broke up a 10,000-strong protest over layoffs from the Tegang state-owned steel factory. Less than a year earlier, police cars had been torched and overturned in a riot by thousands in the satellite city of Wanzhou. Professor Ye Jianping, head of the department of land management at Renmin University, told me, "The problem is that local officials have too much power, governors are too inclined to measure their importance by the extent of their city limits, and the amounts of money involved are too great a temptation." Other academics say local governments get 60 to 70 percent of the profits from land transfers. Much of it ends up in the hands of cadres and officials—many of whom treat their territory like the fiefdoms of old.

In 2007, Chongqing was the focus of probably the most famous land dispute in China.

24. Initiated by the mayor, Bo Xilai, in 2009 (Jonathan Watts, "A City Fights Back: Chinese Gangsters Get Death Penalty," *Guardian,* October 21, 2009).

25. Jasper Becker goes into detail about this in *City of Heavenly Tranquility: Beijing in the History of China* (Penguin, 2008).

26. Jonathan Watts, "Minister Rails at China, Land of a Thousand Identical Cities," *Guardian*, June 12, 2007.

27. Despite the influx of migrants, even the city's poor district is better than the corrugated iron-roofed slums of India and South America. Such is the mood of confidence that city planners expect the city to reach the state's primary goal of a *xiaokang* (all around, well-off) society five years before the central government's target of 2020. By that time, they say the municipality's economy will have tripled from its 2005 level to reach a per-person average of 77,300 yuan (about $11,000).

28. Named after the economist Arthur Lewis, a Nobel Laureate well known for his studies of labor. According to him, developing countries' industrial wages begin to rise quickly at some critical point when the supply of surplus labor from the rural areas tapers off. This shifts the labor supply from surplus to shortage (Kam Wing Chan, Cai Fang, and Du Yang, *The China Population and Labor Yearbook*, vol. 1: *The Approaching Lewis Turning Point and Its Policy Implications* [Brill, 2009], p. 12).

8. Shop Till You Drop: Shanghai

1. In an interview with Hari Kunzru, October 2007, http://www.harikunzru .com/jg-ballard-interview-2007.

2. Fraser Newham, "China Puts Its Best Face Forward," *Asia Times*, April 6, 2006.

3. Wu Jiao, "50% of People to Be Middle Class by 2020," *China Daily*, December 27, 2007.

4. World Wide Fund for Nature, 2008 Living Planet Report, www.panda.org, 2008.

5. Ibid. A European or Japanese lifestyle is a little less eco-intense than that of the U.S., but it too would be catastrophic on a Chinese scale. The comparison is similar to that of launching 3,000 or 4,000 nuclear warheads. One number is bigger than the other, but it is almost irrelevant as destruction would be total in either case.

6. Shanghai's carmakers account for almost a fifth of the local economy. Its port is expected to overtake Singapore as the world's busiest container port, in terms of cargo handled, before 2012 ("Singapore Remains World's Busiest Container Port," *Port World*, January 11, 2008).

7. Song Ligang and Wing Thye Woo (eds.), *China's Dilemma: Economic Growth, the Environment and Climate Change* (Brookings, 2008), p. 8.

8. As ever, the expansion was superaccelerated in China. In the U.S., it had taken thirty years for the chain to hit the 600-restaurant mark (Warren Liu, *KFC in China: Secret Recipe for Success* [Wiley, 2008]).

9. The term appears to date back thousands of years. When archaeologists excavated the terra-cotta warriors in Xian, one way of distinguishing the ranks of the soldiers was the size of their stomachs. The poor foot soldiers were lean. The officers were distinguished by a more fulsome girth.

10. Though it is nowhere near as bad as in the U.S., where a third of people are obese and nearly two-thirds are overweight (James Randerson, "China's Alarming Increase in Obesity Blamed on More Affluent Lifestyle," *Guardian,* August 18, 2006). In the first fifteen years after the start of economic reforms in 1978, the number of overweight people in China more than doubled to 200 million. A six-year-old boy in China is now 6 kilograms heavier and 6 centimeters taller than his counterpart thirty years ago.

11. Speech at the Nature Conservancy conference ConEx in Vancouver, 2008.

12. The average consumer in China ate 54 kilograms of meat in 2007, up from 20 kilograms in 1980. The country as a whole now chomps through 65 million tons of meat per year, equivalent to 260 million cows, 650 million pigs, or 26 billion chickens (Jonathan Watts, "More Wealth, More Meat: How China's Rise Spells Trouble," *Guardian,* May 30, 2008). A study by the Australian Rural Industries Research and Development Corporation forecasts a sharp rise in demand for meat and dairy in twelve Asian countries—home to more than half the world's population. By 2020, it predicts a rise in beef consumption in the region by 50 percent, pork by 30 percent, chicken meat by 40 percent, and dairy products by 55 percent.

13. Europeans have a leaner diet but still get through 89 kilograms of meat per year.

14. Between 1978 and 2006, the number of air conditioners in China rose 390,000-fold, refrigerators 1,200-fold, and cars 700-fold (*National Statistical Yearbook 2007* [China National Bureau of Statistics, 2007]).

15. Ibid.

16. The 140,000 tons of tissues and toilet paper Shanghai uses every year consumes some 80,000 tons of wood pulp, equal to about 300,000 tons of wood. Wang Yueqin, vice director of the Shanghai Paper Trade Association, noted: "While I am happy to see many young people adopt paper tissue for its convenience, which is a sign to reflect our social development and has helped improve our industry to some part, I am beginning to worry about the large

wood consumption" (Cao Li, "Toilet Paper Demand Upsets Wood Supplies," *China Daily,* February 15, 2005). Figures on carbon usage provided by Nicholas Stern, former chief economist at the World Bank, based on data from the China National Bureau of Statistics, IPCC, and the World Bank.

17. McKinsey and Co., "The Coming of Age: China's New Class of Wealthy Consumers," www.mckinsey.com, 2009.

18. Ibid. Wealthy households are defined as those with incomes of at least 250,000 yuan.

19. "China's Auto Consumption Likely to Surpass That of the U.S. by 2017," Xinhua Economic News Service, April 14, 2008.

20. J. R. McNeill, *Something New Under the Sun: An Environmental History of the Twentieth-Century World* (W. W. Norton, 2001), p. 15.

21. Jonathan Watts, "A Miracle and a Menace," *Guardian,* November 9, 2005.

22. The countryside was also targeted. After the economic downturn of 2008, the Chinese government attempted to spur consumer demand by giving 13 percent rebates to farmers who bought air conditioners and refrigerators.

23. Yue-Sai sounds naïve and self-deluding, but her self-justification has since been echoed by countless multinationals. When criticized for pandering to an authoritarian regime, the response is usually along the same lines as Yue-Sai's: "Our products are opening China to the world. By selling we are doing good."

24. Fraser Newham, "China Puts Its Best Face Forward," *Asia Times,* April 6, 2006.

25. The Japanese firm Shiseido reportedly found that Chinese consumers want even more intense whitening agents than those in Japan (ibid.).

26. Leg lengthening is a painful and dangerous procedure in which surgeons break the legs and bolt either side onto a racklike device, which stretches the bones as they heal over months.

27. Yet, she is self-aware when she explains why Asian features require different makeup. "Being Chinese, we know that we look different from you in the West. I have black hair, dark eyes, a flat nose—I have a hard time buying sunglasses. My skin tone is yellow, my eyes are small and slanted so I try to make up differently."

9. Why Do So Many People Hate Henan? Henan

1. Thomas Malthus, *An Essay on the Principle of Population* (1798), ch. 16.

2. In terms of registered population in 2008. Other provinces claim this title when measured in different ways. Guangdong would be top if migrants are included, Sichuan if Chongqing is included.

3. Ibid.

4. In the nineteenth century the American A. K. Norton wrote, "The numbers of the people must be cut down, and if disease, war and plague are not sufficient, famine may be depended upon to fill up the toll. Herein lies the paramount reality of the China problem" (cited in Jasper Becker, *Hungry Ghosts: Mao's Secret Famine* [Holt, 1998], p. 11).

5. Qu Geping and Li Jinchang, *Population and the Environment in China* (Lynne Rienner, 1994).

6. Though the origins of tai chi are contested.

7. Hence the abbreviated name for the province Yu, a character depicting a person leaning on an elephant (Mark Elvin, *Retreat of the Elephants: An Environmental History of China* [Yale University Press, 2004]).

8. http://news.sina.com.cn/c/2009-01-23/071217101413.shtml.

9. Population density in Henan is 380 people per square kilometer (*National Statistical Yearbook 2008* [China National Bureau of Statistics, 2008]). It is the seventeenth-poorest province in China with an average rural income of 3,850 yuan in 2007.

10. The safety of planes is a high priority in China: many airports put up huge nets around the runway to stop birds from flying into aircraft engines. Conservationists say the nets are deadly, unnecessary, and no longer used in most developed nations (interview with John MacKinnon).

11. Here and in Sichuan, which was the most populous province until Chongqing was made into a separate municipality.

12. Judith Shapiro, *Mao's War Against Nature* (Cambridge University Press, 2001), p. 31. Mao also argued that "an extra belly was also two extra hands."

13. The first people's commune was established in Chayashan, near Xinyang city, in April 1958.

14. Wang Shilong's stunning photographs of the province during that era capture the sense of communalism. In one, thousands of farmers are mobilized as hydroengineers, working in a honeycomb formation to dig vast irrigation channels. In others, workers toss fuel into the roaring fires of backyard steel furnaces and beaming farmers display giant cabbages and armfuls of wheat. Such idealized propaganda—backed by the "Good News Reporting Teams" of Maoist cheerleaders—masked a very different reality.

15. Becker, *Hungry Ghosts*, p. 272.

16. One in eight people in Xinyang died (Yang Jisheng, *Mubei: Zhongguo 60*

Niandai Dajihuang Jishi [Tombstone: A History of the Great Leap Forward], Cosmos Books, 2008).

17. Starvation and cannibalism have a long history in China. The same is true in many Western countries. But memories here are more recent. It is no coincidence that the most common question after saying hello even today is "Ni chi le ma?" (Have you eaten?). See also Becker, *Hungry Ghosts,* pp. 116, 118, for this and the remainder of the paragraph.

18. Henan's apparent success in dam building was the inspiration for Mao to launch the Great Leap Forward, according to Ma Jun, *China's Water Crisis* (Eastbridge, 2004), p. 149.

19. Becker, *Hungry Ghosts,* p. 77.

20. Mao was in a hurry to catch up with developed nations. Henan's leaders were the most enthusiastic in feeding his delusions about the production gains that could be achieved. Other grandiose goals, "Let the River Waters Yield" and "Let the High Mountains Bow Their Heads," started here and spread nationwide in this era.

    The Henan Communist Party secretary Wu Zhifu tried to conceal the leader's failures by restricting travel, locking up opponents, and ensuring the propaganda machine churned out stories of production gains and satisfied farmers. Anyone who dared to reveal that the harvest in 1959 actually declined—instead of more than doubling as the government claimed—was denounced as an enemy of the people. Wu's hold on power was finally broken in 1961 when 30,000 PLA troops moved in, arrested the leadership, and distributed grain. By then, countless thousands had starved to death (Becker, *Hungry Ghosts,* p. 112).

21. Henan exported 21 million migrants in 2008, according to Xu Guangchun, Henan Communist Party secretary (*China Youth Daily,* February 2009).

22. The Huai was the inspiration for the title of Elizabeth Economy's *The River Runs Black: The Environmental Challenge to China's Future* (Cornell University Press, 2004).

23. Ma Tianjie, "Environmental Mass Incidents in Rural China," *China Environment* 10 (2008/9), Woodrow Wilson International Center for Scholars.

24. See http://maps.google.com/maps/ms?hl=en&ie=UTF8&oe=UTF8&msa=0&msid=10434075597844108849 6.000469611a28a0d8a22dd.

25. About 11 percent of cases of cancer of the digestive system are attributable to polluted drinking water (World Bank and Chinese Ministry of Environmental Protection study, *China: The Environmental Cost of Pollution,* p. xiv).

26. Xiditou, with a registered population of 6,000, has a cancer rate of 2,032 per 100,000, almost fifteen times the national average (Mary-Anne Toy, "Waiting for Death in Fetid Cancer Villages," *Sydney Morning Herald*, May 27, 2009).

27. Richard McGregor, "750,000 a Year Killed by Chinese Pollution," *Financial Times*, July 2, 2007.

28. The World Bank estimates the cost of water contamination at 147 billion yuan, or about 1 percent of GDP per year.

29. In the mid-1990s—the period during which most people in China became infected—the central government was still dismissing HIV as a "foreign disease." Even in 2003, when Beijing was starting to acknowledge the problem, Henan's leaders were still in denial. AIDS experts, charity organizations, and foreign diplomats were either refused access to Henan or only allowed to enter under heavy restrictions. Journalists discovered in the area were kicked out immediately.

30. After flying to Zhengzhou, we checked into the hotel late at night because staff are then less likely to report the presence of foreign reporters to the local police (as they are obliged to do). The next morning, we left early and spent an hour finding a taxi with curtains so my Western face would not be spotted on the road.

31. Those who played the biggest part in exposing the disease—whistle-blowing doctor Gao Yaojie, the health ministry bureaucrat Wan Yanhai, and the young activist Hu Jia—were either harassed or thrown in jail. Efforts were also made to silence Yan Lianke. After three years visiting the AIDS villages undercover, he penned *The Dream of Ding Village*. The novel was to be his defining satire, a devastating critique of China's runaway development, the environmental and spiritual horror story of a country that sold its blood along with its soul to foreign consumers.

    The book describes the collapse of the land and the people in painfully beautiful prose: "Days like corpses. Grass upon the plain gone dry. Trees upon the plain gone bare. Crops and fields withered, ever since the blood came. Ever since the blood ran red. The villagers, shrunken into their homes, never to emerge again."

    The novel was blocked. The authorities issued a "three noes" order: no distribution, no sales, and no promotion. But the grassroots campaign to expose the AIDS villages and support the victims had some success. The government now acknowledges the problem and has been providing free retroviral drugs to the people infected.

32. James Kynge, *China Shakes the World: A Titan's Rise and Troubled Future—and the Challenge for America* (Houghton Mifflin, 2006), p. 48.

33. "When I look at today's Chinese landscape, so much of which bears the unmistakable footprint of man, the earth seems not so much bad as simply tired. The lands that make up China have done a yeoman's job in providing sustenance for untold millions, ceaselessly and without rest for a few thousand years. They seem to be asking for a bit of a break" (Richard Harris, *Wildlife Conservation in China: Preserving the Habitat of China's Wild West* [East Gate, 2008], p. 10).

34. Shapiro, *Mao's War Against Nature,* p. 30; Judith Banister, "Population, Public Health and the Environment in China," in R. L. Edmonds (ed.), *Managing the Chinese Environment* (Oxford University Press, 1998), pp. 262–91.

35. Economy, *The River Runs Black,* p. 42.

36. By replacing the poll tax (which penalized families for having children) with a land tax (which encouraged families to breed so they would have more hands in the fields to raise productivity).

37. Becker, *Hungry Ghosts,* p. 10.

38. Frank Dikötter, "The Limits of Benevolence: Wang Shiduo (1802–1889) and Population Control," *Bulletin of the School of Oriental and African Studies* 55, 1 (1992), p. 110.

39. Historically, one in five Chinese males have been lifelong bachelors (James Lee and Wang Feng, *One Quarter of Humanity: Malthusian Mythology and Chinese Realities, 1700–2000* [Harvard University Press, 2001]).

40. Shapiro, *Mao's War Against Nature,* p. 33.

41. Ibid., p. 22.

42. Mortality rates also fell thanks to the introduction of "barefoot doctors" (local farmers who have undergone basic medical training) and a lifestyle free from cigarettes and alcohol, which most people were too poor to buy.

43. After Mao's death, Ma was rehabilitated, and his arguments were accepted. The realization that China has reached an unsustainable size of population came disastrously late. If Ma's suggestions had been adopted in the 1950s, China could have several hundred million fewer people today and many of the country's environmental strains would be considerably reduced. This is reflected in a bitterly worded inscription in Ma's hometown of Shengzhou, which reads: "Criticise one person, give birth to several million additional people" (Shapiro, *Mao's War Against Nature,* p. 45).

44. Philip Pan, *Out of Mao's Shadow: The Struggle for the Soul of a New China* (Picador Asia, 2008), p. 302.

45. China's total fertility rate fell from 5.4 children per woman in 1970 to 2.8 in 1979.

46. The "one-child policy" does not mean every couple is restricted to a single child. The single-child rule is enforced in most cities, but in the countryside most families can have a second child if the first is a girl. Ethnic minorities, particularly in sparsely populated regions such as Xinjiang, are often allowed three children. In 1980, the Marriage Law made procreational restraint a legal obligation for couples. In 1982, this was upgraded to a constitutional requirement. "Both husband and wife have the duty to practice family planning" (Article 49). See Isabelle Attané, "China's Family Planning Policy: An Overview of Its Past and Future," *Studies in Family Planning* 33, 1 (2002): 103–13.

47. Pan, *Out of Mao's Shadow*, p. 305. Near-term abortion is far from the norm, but neither is it unheard of. Chen Guangchang, a blind activist in Shandong, was imprisoned when he tried to draw attention to the sometimes brutal enforcement of family-planning policy.

48. Xinhua, "China's Family Planning Policy Benefits Country, World," October 24, 2008. I have heard rumors that China might try to claim carbon credits for the "one-child" policy: the fix for Mao's demographic mistakes hawked as a gift to the planet.

49. Human numbers are a big factor in environmental impact assessments. In a landmark 1970s study, Paul Ehrlich and others described the relationship formulaically as IPAT (Impact = Population x Affluence x Technology; see www.stirpat.org). Some scholars believe this understates the influence of culture and religion. Others argue that the impact is more direct. Qu Geping, one of the earliest and most influential Chinese environmentalists, describes human numbers and ecological degradation as two sides of the same coin (Qu Geping and Li Jinchang, *Population and the Environment in China* [Lynne Rienner, 1994]).

50. I spoke to a gynecologist in Yunnan who admitted such practices were common in the recent past, although she said they were no longer used.

51. Beijing's mandarins argue that they did not have the educational, financial, or bureaucratic tools to effect demographic change in any other way. But this claim is contentious. Birthrates were falling rapidly even before the one-child policy was implemented. Studies by the United Nations suggested rising incomes and smart economic policies were more effective than coercion in limiting births. Hong Kong, Taiwan, Singapore, South Korea,

and Japan all achieved a lower fertility rate than mainland China without taking such draconian measures.

52. Laurel Bossen, "Missing Girls, Land and Population Controls in Rural China," in Isabelle Attané and Christophe Z. Guilmoto (eds.), *Watering the Neighbour's Garden: The Growing Demographic Female Deficit in Asia,* Committee for International Cooperation in National Research in Demography, 2007, www.cicred.org.

53. Ma, *China's Water Crisis,* p. 14.

54. Henan uses more chemical fertilizer in China than other provinces: over 6 million tons, or 836 kilograms per hectare (Xinhua, "Henan Releases Environmental Data. Good and Bad News for Environmental Protection," June 4, 2009).

55. In Henan and ten other provinces, government studies in 2002 linked the lack of iodine with 10-point-lower-than-average intelligence quotients in the worst affected areas. Measures have subsequently been taken to provide iodine supplements (Xinhua, "More Than 90 Percent of Chinese Residents Using Qualified Iodized Salt," May 16, 2006).

56. It is estimated that in China a baby is born with physical defects every thirty seconds because of the country's degrading environment (Chen Jia, "Birth Defects Soar Due to Pollution," *China Daily,* January 31, 2009).

10. The Carbon Trap: Shanxi and Shaanxi

1. Cited in Mark Elvin, *Retreat of the Elephants: An Environmental History of China* (Yale University Press, 2004), p. 108.

2. The following account is based on interviews with Meng Xianyou, the *Beijing News,* and earlier research for my "On a Diet of Coal, Urine and Grim Jokes, Brothers Tunnel Their Way Back to Life," *Guardian,* August 29, 2007.

3. In 2007, 76.6 percent of all the energy China produced came from coal (*National Statistical Yearbook 2008* [China National Bureau of Statistics, 2008]). The global average is 40 percent (Mao Yushi, Sheng Hong, and Yang Fuqiang, "True Cost of Coal" (Greenpeace, the Energy Foundation, and WWF, October 27, 2008).

4. According to the World Health Organization, the upper limit ought to be 50.

5. "'The fact that the rate of birth defects in Shanxi Province is higher is related to environmental pollution caused by the high level of energy production and burning of coal,' said Pan Xiaochuan, a professor from Peking

University's Occupational and Environmental Health Department" (Phyllis Xu and Lucy Hornby, "Birth Defects Show Human Price of Coal," Reuters, June 23, 2009).

6. Britain produced 292 million tons in 1913, the peak year of production (Ian Jack, "Every Story Looks Different from the End," *Guardian,* September 5, 2009). In 2009, Shanxi's output was forecast at 650 million tons (Bloomberg, "Shanxi's Coal Production to Rise in Second Half, Huadian Says," August 13, 2009).

7. Zhao Jianping and David Creedy, "Economically, Socially and Environmentally Sustainable Coal Mining Sector in China" (World Bank, China Coal Information Institute, Energy Sector Management Assistance Program, December 2008).

8. Institute of Energy Economy, Shanxi Academy of Social Sciences, October 26, 2007. The breakdown is as follows: damage to aquifers and other water resources 7.2 billion yuan, subsidence 2.6 billion, disposal of coal waste 2.9 billion, air pollution 4.1 billion, water pollution 1.8 billion, erosion and other ecological damage 11 billion.

9. This is a conservative estimate. A figure of three plants per week is suggested by Edward Steinfeld, "MIT Report Debunks China Energy Myth," Massachusetts Institute of Technology, October 7, 2008. China has added some 170 gigawatts of coal-fired power capacity in the past two years alone—more than double Britain's entire electricity-generating capacity—and has overtaken the United States as the world's largest emitter of greenhouse gases (Jeff Tollefson, "Stoking the Fire," *Nature,* July 24, 2008).

10. Coal accounts for about 80 percent of China's carbon dioxide emissions (Mao Yushi et al., "True Cost of Coal," October 27, 2008).

11. Vaclav Smil, *Global Catastrophes and Trends: The Next Fifty Years* (MIT Press, 2008), p. 217. In 2007, authorities in Xinjiang put out a blaze that had burned for fifty years and consumed more than 12 megatons of coal.

12. Coal industry statistical yearbooks and figures from former ministry of coal industry (now State Bureau of Coal Industry) and State Administration of Work Safety.

13. This was before January 2007. Since then correspondents have been theoretically free to travel where they wish, but local authorities often ignore the new rules to block coverage of sensitive stories. Tibet remains off-limits apart from rare tours organized by the ministry of foreign affairs.

14. It has subsequently gone to Panzhihua and others.

15. Under the government's definition, a "blue sky" day is when PM10 particulate matter falls below 100 parts per million. This is still double the minimum standard of the World Health Organization.

16. The disaster occurred on September 14, 2008, at the Tashan mine in Linfen.

17. Mao Yushi et al., "True Cost of Coal." Coal is also responsible for 67 percent of China's nitrogen dioxide emissions.

18. Acid rain falls mostly in the south, where the sulfur content of coal can be five times higher than in the north.

19. World Bank and China's Environmental Protection Agency, "The Cost of Pollution in China," 2007.

20. According to the World Bank and China's Environmental Protection Agency, "Cost of Pollution in China," the economic burden of premature mortality and morbidity associated with air pollution in China is between 1.16 and 3.8 percent of the country's GDP. Burning coal releases large quantities of mercury and other hazardous chemicals into the atmosphere. In an enclosed environment, this can have dire health consequences. In Guizhou, cancerous lesions, arsenic poisoning, deformities, and fluorosis—a disfiguring of teeth and bones—have been traced to locally dug coal, which contains a particularly nasty combination of toxins. Nationwide, the sharp rise in lung cancer cases over the past ten years is attributed as much to the use of coal heating in badly ventilated homes as to cigarettes.

21. But when they find out, they are furious, as the spate of riots connected to the lead poisoning of thousands of children in Shaanxi and Hunan showed in 2009 (Jonathan Watts, "Further Anti-Pollution Riots Break Out in China," Guardian, September 2, 2009).

22. Mark Elvin, "The Environmental Legacy of Imperial China," in Richard Louis Edmonds (ed.), Managing the Chinese Environment (Oxford University Press, 1998), p. 112.

23. Ibid., p. 441.

24. China has 14 percent of the world's known coal reserves, the third-largest share by country.

25. Water is also a factor in the dry north as old gasification and electricity-generating technology used water as a coolant (Neville Mars and Adrian Hornsby [eds.], The Chinese Dream: A Society Under Construction [010 Publishers, 2008]). But in recent years, the development of fan-cooled technology has made this less of a bottleneck.

26. Smil, *Global Catastrophes and Trends,* p. 218.

27. The estimated cost was 1.7 trillion yuan in 2007 (Mao Yusi et al., "True Cost of Coal").

28. As Premier Wen noted: "This kind of huge consumption of energy, especially nonrenewable fossil fuel, will not be sustainable" (Bruce Alberts, "Chinese Premier Wen Jiabao Sees Science as a Key to Development," *Science,* November 2008).

29. Zhao and Creedy, "Economically, Socially and Environmentally Sustainable Coal Mining Sector in China." They argue that demand management alone is not enough. Without sustainable mining practices, they believe, the environmental fabric of China will be "irreparably damaged."

30. As at the end of 2007, China had commissioned 226 large supercritical units and nine of the very modern and efficient ultra-supercritical units. These supercritical units operate at higher pressures and temperatures than the normal pulverized fuel coal plants which are in standard use elsewhere in the world, including the U.S. and Europe. Relatively few supercritical units are operating outside China, despite the fact the technology was developed in the advanced countries (Dave Feickert, *China Coal and Energy Update 2009: Cleaner Coal* [Interfax, 2009]).

31. The groundbreaking Chinese firm ENN had a demonstration center outside Beijing in which captured carbon was being fed to algae. The room full of huge pipes of bright green gunk resembled the set of a science-fiction film (Jonathan Watts, "China Recruits Algae to Combat Climate Change," *Guardian,* June 29, 2009).

11. Attack the Clouds! Retreat from the Sands! Gansu and Ningxia

1. Ma Jun, *China's Water Crisis* (Eastbridge, 2004).

2. China has 1.67 million square kilometers of deserts and desertified land. More than a third is desert, a third is gravel gobi, the rest is mostly Aeolian desertified land (interview with Wang Tao, director of the Cold and Arid Regions Environmental and Engineering Research Institute).

3. Elvin notes that the temperature during the golden age of the Tang dynasty was about 1°C higher than today, while the economic and demographic expansion of the Qing dynasty in the eighteenth century came as the planet emerged from the "little Ice Age" (Mark Elvin, "The Environmental Legacy of Imperial China," in Richard Louis Edmonds [ed.], *Managing the Chinese Environment*, Oxford University Press, 1998, p. 9).

4. Chinese scholars estimate that the sections of wall left standing are now around 2,400 kilometers long, down from a high of 6,400 kilometers during the Ming dynasty (1368–1644).

5. William Lindesay, *Alone on the Great Wall* (Fulcrum, 1991), p. 64.

6. Guo and Wei received no financial assistance for relocation, but the authorities gave them 4 mu (2,700 square meters) of former wasteland and piped water from the Yellow River at 2.42 jiao per cubic meter (1 yuan = 10 jiao). They grew wheat and other vegetables and had twenty sheep that they often took up to their old land—10 kilometers away—to feed. Now that life was "better," their nine descendants could earn on average 6,000 yuan per year—about $2.00 per day.

7. Between 1.6 billion and 3.9 billion tons of sediment are discharged into the river every year.

8. With each breach of its banks, the river can also change course. Few waterways have twisted quite so dramatically across continents. Though it now empties into the Bohai Sea, the Yellow previously had its estuary hundreds of miles south and discharged into the Yellow Sea.

9. Dikes had to rise higher and higher to cope with the sediment. In some places, this has created an elevated river, as high as 10 meters above ground level in Henan Province's Kaifeng City. The Yellow's main environmental claim to fame is now that it is the only river in the world that flows high above the heads of tens of millions of people.

10. Several floods have killed more than a million people, most recently in 1931.

11. In 1956, Soviet engineers adapted a Japanese military blueprint for Sanmenxia, the first megadam on the Yellow River and almost exactly halfway along its curling length. Wide tracts of land were flooded, forcing the resettlement of 280,000 farmers. They were told their sacrifice would be worth it to ensure flood controls and hydroelectric power for millions of others. But the dam silted up within ten years, making the turbines redundant.

12. For a more detailed description of the philosophy behind Sanmenxia and other efforts to tame the Yellow, see Rob Gifford, *China Road: A Journey into the Future of a Rising Power* (Random House, 2007).

13. Agriculture is by far the biggest drain on the river, accounting for 90 percent of the diverted water (interview with Yellow River Conservancy officials), some of which is taken hundreds of kilometers into the desert.

14. In 2008, four billion tons of industrial waste and sewage were discharged into the river system, leaving 83 percent of the water too contaminated to drink without treatment. In 2007, the authorities revealed that a third of the 150 fish species that once swam the murky waters are now extinct and fishermen's catches are down by 60 percent.

15. The spectrum of pollution was most vividly seen in October 2006, when a half-mile stretch of river in Gansu ran pink after the Lanzhou Tanjianzi No. 2 Steam Heating Station flushed 2,000 liters of tainted liquid from a broken boiler into the river. To the company's credit, they had added the dye to prevent the water being mistaken for drinking water, but it was not supposed to have found its way into the Yellow. Other firms have no doubt done worse, but not made half the splash because their deeds were colorless.

16. Alarmingly, the definition of this water quality grade (level five) does not say it is too dirty to use for irrigation.

17. Jim Yardley, "Rules Ignored, Toxic Sludge Sinks Chinese Village," *New York Times,* September 4, 2006.

18. Ibid.

19. A raised cement floor heated by burning coal underneath.

20. The government provided a special stipend of 55 yuan for each mu of land affected. Yang's area covered 12 mu.

21. Jonathan Watts, "Silk Road That's Paved with Gold," *Observer,* August 3, 2008.

22. Tom Scocca, "The People's Weather: Officials Are Betting Weather Modification Can Keep the Sun Shining on the Olympics," *Plenty,* April 17, 2008.

23. Ibid.

24. The immensity of China's weather modification forces were evident during the Beijing Olympics, when the sky was assaulted as never before to ensure rain did not put a damper on director Zhang Yimou's elaborately choreographed opening ceremony. As storm clouds approached, the rings of anti-rain defenses around the city were ordered into action. Over eight hours, they fired 1,104 dispersal rockets in what was described by the domestic media as a "successful interception" of the rain belt heading for the stadium. With stratospheric rivals out of the way, Olympic organizers frazzled the sky with a 30,000-rocket pyrotechnic display.

25. The city expected a downpour of more than 100 millimeters but, after interception, had to make do with less than 30 millimeters (Jonathan Watts, "Cities Fall Out Over Cloud," *Guardian,* July 15, 2004).

26. He estimates the losses at 54 billion yuan per year.

27. The former director Zhu Zenda was influential in persuading the government to adopt this policy. Wang considers him a mentor.

12. Flaming Mountain, Melting Heaven: Xinjiang

1. This quote is from a speech that Lord Stern gave at Renmin University on September 11, 2009.

2. Interviews with Yao Tandong, glaciologist at the China Academy of Sciences, and Shi Yafeng, a member of the team. At least six of the locations were in Gansu, according to Shi.

3. Interview with Shi Yafeng.

4. Jasper Becker, *Hungry Ghosts: Mao's Secret Famine* (Holt, 1998), p. 77.

5. The first measurements of Urumqi Number One were taken by explorers in 1953, but it was not until after 1959 that systematic studies of the glacier were undertaken, according to Yao Tandong.

6. I was not alone in my ignorance. One newly arrived colleague from another newspaper admitted that he had never before heard of the Uighurs—the region's ethnic majority—whose name he initially assumed was from a Monty Python sketch.

7. The strategic concerns of empire clearly outweighed the Christian piety of the Victorians. Britain armed and financed a failed Muslim uprising in 1862 led by Yakub Beg, a notorious tyrant. For Younghusband, see ch. 2.

8. 5.8 billion cubic meters (Ma Jun, *China's Water Crisis* [Eastbridge, 2004], p. 205).

9. Together, they cover 60,000 square kilometers and account for 15 percent of the planet's ice.

10. Jonathan Watts, "Highest Ice Fields Will Not Last 100 Years, Study Finds," *Guardian,* September 24, 2004.

11. Ma, *China's Water Crisis.*

12. Rob Gifford, *China Road: A Journey into the Future of a Rising Power* (Random House, 2007), p. 240.

13. Mongolia, the Russian Federation, Kazakhstan, Kyrgyzstan, Tajikistan, Afghanistan, Pakistan, and India.

14. The unidealized version of the story is told by the journalist and blogger Huang Zhangjin, who was born in Xinjiang: "When the first group of female soldiers arrived, it was as if there was a whole pack of wolves fighting over scraps of meat. The middle and lower level officers didn't see so much as

the shadow of a woman, and this made them even more desperate than before. So, there was a large assembly, during which a high-level officer—a new groom himself—made a grand promise: Mao will make good on his word, you can be sure of that. Everyone will certainly be distributed a wife!" Translated by *China Digital Times* as "The Tale of Eight Thousand Hunan Maidens Going Up Tian Mountain."

15. Judith Shapiro, *Mao's War Against Nature* (Cambridge University Press, 2001), p. 160.

16. Ibid., p. 140.

17. Xinjiang came to produce a third of China's cotton.

18. Nicholas Bequelin, "Xinjiang in the Nineties," *China Journal* 44 (2000): 65–90.

19. Richard B. Harris, *Wildlife Conservation in China: Preserving the Habitat of China's Wild West* (East Gate, 2008), p. 136.

20. Ma, *China's Water Crisis,* p. 111.

21. The diversion of the Tarim (Lop Nor's source river) led to the total collapse of the dense poplar forests downstream that had thrived in the area for thousands of years. The roots of these hardy trees go down 10 meters—which allows them to survive in even the worst climatic dry spells. But once the river dried up, the water table fell 14 meters, dooming even these most drought-resistant of trees.

22. Across stretches of Xinjiang there are similar cases of disastrous ecological mismanagement by the settlers. Lake Manas was once a giant body of water covering 550 square kilometers, but it dried up completely after *bingtuan* teams built a reservoir on its main source. Abi Nur, on the border with Kazakhstan, has shrunk by more than half from 1,200 square kilometers since the 1950s as a result of an eightfold expansion of farmland. White salty dust from the exposed bed is carried across the Heaven range all the way to Urumqi, more than 600 kilometers away, eroding the quality of land in between, causing diarrhea in livestock and posing serious risks to human health. With less water to keep the desert in check, sand dunes threaten to take back farmland. In several areas, such as Jinghe, many farmers have abandoned their homes. Sand on the tracks repeatedly forces stoppages on the transcontinental railway that links Beijing with central Asia (Ma, *China's Water Crisis*).

23. They were chosen with three criteria in mind: *shan, san, dong* (in mountains, dispersed, in caves). As often as not, this meant locations where they

would be most inefficient and cause maximum damage to pristine landscapes. With war considered imminent, they were planned hurriedly and rushed into operation. Mao was under no illusions about the bespoiling character of the Third Front campaign. It was, as he said in a memorably earthy 1964 speech, the arse-end of a three-pronged war effort: "Agriculture is one fist, and national defense is another fist. To make the fists strong, the rear end must be seated securely. The rear end is basic industry." Given this analogy, it is no surprise that many of the sites of "Third Front" factories resemble toilets.

24. Which suggests some creative head-counting, given the government-imposed limit of twenty animals per person.

25. The impact of black carbon and brown clouds on the Himalayas is a source of increasing concern (Randeep Ramesh and Suzanne Goldenberg, "Soot Clouds Pose Threat to Himalayan Glaciers," *Observer*, October 4, 2009).

26. In Xinjiang, the pattern of warming and drying is particularly complex. While overall ice cover has declined dramatically, a few glaciers have continued to expand. Much of western China appears to be getting moister. Traditional temperature patterns may be inverting. Winters are warming faster than summers. While the highest, coldest places are melting, the lowest, hottest areas appear to be cooling and growing wetter. Deserts are getting more rain. Some scientists in Xinjiang believe the deserts may be an ally in the battle against climate change. They found that the alkaline ground gulps more carbon dioxide at night than temperate forests. Similar results in the U.S. led some to believe that deserts might soak up half the amount of carbon currently emitted by the burning of fossil fuels. Similar findings have come from studies in Nevada's Mojave Desert, where the sand soaks up about the same amount of CO_2 per square meter as in some temperate forests. If confirmed, this would be good news because almost a third of the earth's land surface is desert (Richard Stone, "Have Desert Researchers Discovered a Hidden Loop in the Carbon Cycle?" *Science*, June 13, 2008, p. 1409).

27. According to the World Resources Institute's history of CO_2 emissions since 1900, China is third behind the U.S. and Russia. http://www.guardian.co.uk/environment/datablog/2009/sep/02/co2-emissions-historical. Earlier starting dates also put China behind the UK and other developed nations.

28. See ch. 11, n. 3 (Elvin, "The Environmental Legacy of Imperial China," in Edmonds [ed.], *Managing the Chinese Environment*).

29. Xie Yan of the Wildlife Conservation Society is extremely concerned about the impact of global warming on orchids and other species because rare species are concentrated in such small bands of land that they cannot easily migrate for survival. "I think there will be big problems caused by global warming. Many species are very sensitive to temperature, such as amphibians. They are narrowly distributed. If the existing nature reserve is not suitable anymore, they could go extinct. Some plants only have 100 or so in some locations. Many are critically endangered. Orchids are extremely threatened" (interview with author).

30. Nomads were blamed by Han settlers for degrading land they and their ancestors had lived on sustainably for centuries. Tibetans, Mongolians, and Uighurs were targets of resettlement programs. Climate change was only part of the reason.

31. Since the completion of a 4,200-kilometer pipeline from the Lunnan field in the Tarim basin to Shanghai in 2004, Xinjiang has been China's biggest supplier of natural gas. Several other vast pipelines have been built or are under construction that will link central Asia's oil and gas fields with the factories and cities on China's eastern seaboard. Engineers have built roads to carry oil through the Taklimakan, a desert where the dunes encroach so rapidly that guards have to be posted every 5 kilometers to maintain the 400-kilometer rose-willow defense line against the sands.

32. More ambitious still, a new Silk Road is under construction. Asia Highway One, as the modern version is prosaically called, will link Urumqi with Istanbul, passing through the resource-rich nations of Iran, Uzbekistan, Tajikistan, and Kyrgyzstan. Political ties are being strengthened through the Shanghai Cooperation Organization, which groups China, Russia, and central Asian states that together control a quarter of the world's oil supplies.

33. The share value passed $1 trillion soon after the firm listed in 2007.

34. Introduction to Urumqi, Frommer's (www.frommers.com).

35. During holiday peaks, their sprinklers and snow machines use enough water every day to fill more than twenty Olympic swimming pools. (Josh Chin and Zachary Slobig, "Xinjiang's Melting Glaciers," *China Dialogue*, March 20, 2008).

36. At U-Cang, in the north of the city, work is under way on an "ecological

park" aimed at nurturing a more sustainable lifestyle among residents. All municipal flowerbeds, lawns, and hedgerows are doused with treated wastewater. The skies are also clearer now that the huge coal-fired power plants have been ordered to wash their coal before burning it. Our driver Wu told us that the smoke from their chimneys has changed from black to white. See also Jonathan Watts, "China Plans 59 Reservoirs to Collect Meltwater from Its Shrinking Glaciers," *Guardian,* March 2, 2009.

37. The state media continues to give prominent coverage to her speeches. Her critics are marginalized. The best known of them is Dai Qing, who accuses Qian of irresponsibility for saying, "The coming generations are bound to have greater intelligence than we do? Let's trust their ability to solve their problems" (Dai Qing, *Yangtze! Yangtze!* [Probe International, 1993]).

38. The overseas Uighur leader Rebiya Kadeer often linked environmental stress to ethnic tension as in this interview comment: "Han Chinese are brought in to water down our population . . . When the Chinese Communist Party first occupied us in 1949, only 2 per cent of the population was Han Chinese. Now, they number 60 per cent. There is also widespread environmental damage. Three lakes have dried up, our natural resources are exploited, and thus, the environment is disturbed too. In the early days Uighurs were able to work in agriculture and earn a living. Now, they no longer have this opportunity because so many Han Chinese have arrived. People resist such suppression" (Florian Godovits, "China's Female 'Public Enemy Number One' on the State of China's Muslim Uighurs," *Epoch Times,* October 29, 2007).

39. On July 5, 2009, decapitations, knifings, and beatings left 197 dead and 1,721 injured, according to government figures. The vast majority of the victims were Han. Uighur exile groups claim the toll is higher and includes more minority victims, but foreign reporters who were given relatively free access to Urumqi were unable to find evidence that large numbers of Uighurs were killed.

40. She cited the specific case of the Miyun Reservoir near Beijing, which had been designed for an annual runoff of 1.4 billion cubic meters of water, but had actually received just 500 million cubic meters.

41. According to government figures, Xinjiang now has 1.4 million hectares of farmland, accounting for 3.3 percent of the national total. Although much of it is used for cotton, the area is also famous for melons and other fruit.

42. Plans for expansion concentrated primarily on San San, Turpan, and Harmi
     ("Expert Says Xinjiang Is the Land of Opportunity for Coal Liquification
     Projects," *Caijing*, September 22, 2009).

13. Science versus Math: Tianjin, Hebei, and Liaoning

1.   Since then, he has had to work harder to prove himself than his peers
     at more prestigious institutions. More than thirty years on, that effort is
     finally paying off. Li is now credited internationally for leading the team
     that discovered ultraviolet Raman spectroscopy technology, a groundbreak-
     ing tool for analyzing energy conversion; and for ultradeep desulfuriza-
     tion techniques that dramatically reduce the amount of sulfur emitted in
     the combustion of diesel. His more recent research on catalysis and solar
     energy has propelled him to a leading position in the clean-energy field in
     China.

2.   China is pushing ahead with key "clean coal" technologies related to the
     Integrated Gasification Combined Cycle and Carbon Capture and Storage
     (IGCC plus CSS), a method which converts coal to nonpolluting synthetic
     gas.

3.   The government's goal is to increase the share of the national budget devoted
     to science and technology to 2.5 percent of gross domestic product by 2020,
     up from 1.4 percent in 2006. If achieved, this share would rank as one of
     the best in the world.

4.   Containing 16 billion barrels of oil.

5.   This figure was cited by Li Xiaoqiang, vice chair of China's National Devel-
     opment and Reform Commission, in a speech on September 7, 2006, at
     Dalian's "summer Davos" meeting. But it may be an underestimate. The
     International Energy Agency in its *World Energy Outlook 2006* noted that
     China will need to invest $3.7 trillion in new energy sources between now
     and 2030 (Li Taige, "Investing in a Better Environment," *China Dialogue*,
     October 3, 2007).

6.   For example, Jeffrey Sachs, founder of the Earth Institute at New York's
     Columbia University, who argued in the 2007 Reith Lectures that the best
     hope for the world was for China to develop or borrow technologies to
     sequestrate, i.e., bury, carbon from coal.

7.   In high concentrations, carbon dioxide can be lethal. In 1986, it bubbled up
     in Lake Nyos, Cameroon, and killed 1,700 people (Nathan Lewis, "Power-
     ing the Planet," California Institute of Technology, 2007).

8. Li uses the energy from solar power to convert carbon dioxide into hydrogen, which might one day be used to power cars. This can be done in the laboratory but is very far from being commercially applicable.

9. All targets in this section are published in the Sino-Singapore Tianjin Eco-City Administrative Committee, Key Performance Indicators Framework 2008–2020 (www.tianjinecocity.gov.sg/).

10. In his previous job in the municipal construction bureau he had helped to redesign the city of Tianjin, which has a population of more than 11 million people. By comparison, the eco-project is modest.

11. The fate of Dongtan looked uncertain as this book went to press. Originally planned to house half a million people by 2040, the first phase was supposed to be ready by the Shanghai Expo in 2010. But construction has yet to start.

12. This is only part of the urbanizing shift, which is expected to bring 400 million people—more than the population of the U.S.—from the country to the city between 2000 and 2030 (Elizabeth Economy, "The Great Leap Backward?" *Foreign Affairs* 86, 5 [September/October 2007]).

13. Wang is part of a vast pyramid of technocratic model-makers. At the top is the hydroengineer Hu. One step below him is a politburo of former engineers and scientists. Under them are a broad network of academic policy-makers in universities, institutes, and research academies. They, in turn, can call upon an army of professors, doctors, postgrads, and other researchers. In the past thirty years, China's universities have churned out 240,000 PhD's, 1.9 million master's graduates, and 14.1 million bachelor's degrees. Since 1995, there has been a fourfold increase in science and engineering degrees, with the latter total in China now greater than that in the U.S. and Japan. The number of students taking science or engineering degrees in China each year climbed from 115,000 in 1995 to more than 672,000 in 2004, putting the country ahead of the United States and Japan; about two-thirds of the Chinese degrees were in engineering. In 2007, Chinese scientists accounted for 32,000, or almost one-quarter, of the 142,000 foreign students receiving PhD's in the United States, more than any other country except India, which accounted for one-third. China's share of the world's published scientific articles soared from 0.2 percent in 1980, to 7.4 percent in 2006, when it overtook Japan for the first time (Declan Butler, "China: The Great Contender," *Nature*, July 24, 2008).

China's ministry of science and technology has reported that 5 percent of the nation's total investment in science is being spent on basic research, according to Bruce Alberts, a professor of biochemistry and biophysics at the University of California, San Francisco. By comparison, the U.S. National Science Foundation (NSF) has reported that 17.5 percent of the U.S. total investment in science was being spent on basic research in 2007 (Bruce Alberts, "Chinese Premier Wen Jiabao Sees Science as a Key to Development," *Science*, October 17, 2008).

14. Project of Comprehensive Development and Construction of Tangshan Caofeidian Eco-City, June 13, 2008, Tangshan government website (www .tangshan.gov.cn/xiangmu.php?id=2278).

15. This upgrade is a major reason for China's success in increasing energy efficiency by about 20 percent, and reducing pollution by 10 percent between 2005 and 2010.

16. "China's Energy Consumption per Unit of GDP Is 3–8 Times Higher Than in OECD Countries" (World Bank Mid-term Evaluation of China's 11th Five-Year Plan, February 12, 2009). Chinese scientists say this is only partly because of inefficiencies. A bigger reason is the structure of China's economy, which is a global base of labor- and energy-intensive industries (interview with Wang Shudong of the Dalian Institute of Chemical Physics).

17. A factory official told visiting journalists in 2008 that the Shougang plant in west Beijing belched out a tenth of the particulate matter in the city's air (Jonathan Watts, "Beijing Goes for Green with Olympic Clean-up," *Guardian*, July 19, 2008).

18. In 2001, the city had 251 "blue sky" days, the water quality of the Liao and Hun rivers was at the worst level (five), and green cover was 29 percent. By 2007, the number of "blue sky" days had risen to 323, the water quality of the Hun improved to level four, and urban greenbelt coverage was over 38 percent. Industrial pollutant discharge had fallen by more than 21 percent since 2002 (data from Shenyang Environmental Protection Bureau).

19. In three years, the city destroyed over 3,000 chimneys and 1,200 boilers.

20. Municipal planners have adopted his designs at Qiaoyuan Park in Tianjin, Tiazhou in Zhejiang, Qinhuangdao in Hebei, and Zongshan in Guangdong.

21. Much of the urban landscape is a legacy of Mao-era reliance on a tiny number of Soviet designs and a thoughtless rush of development in the 1980s and 1990s. The construction vice minister, Qiu Baoxing, has lamented the fact that almost all of China's cities look the same. Orthogonal buildings,

white-tiled walls, and blue-tinted windows (Jonathan Watts, "Minister Rails at China, Land of a Thousand Identical Cities," *Guardian,* June 12, 2007).

22. Because they ate seeds, sparrows were considered one of the four pests during the Great Leap Forward (the other three were flies, mosquitoes, and rats). People were encouraged to wipe them out by making so much noise with pots, pans, and fireworks that the birds were too afraid to land and died of exhaustion.

23. Of the 40 billion square meters of urban buildings, 95 percent are classified as high energy consumers (Pan Jiahua, "Building a Frugal Society," *China Dialogue,* November 5, 2007).

24. "China's buildings are roughly two and a half times less energy efficient than those in Germany. Furthermore, newly urbanised Chinese, who use air conditioners, televisions, refrigerators, consume about three and half times more energy than do their rural counterparts" (Economy, "The Great Leap Backward?"). Regulations are often ignored or geared toward boosting the economy rather than minimizing consumption of scarce resources. There are few mechanisms to check whether people are following the rules. Wang Xue-jun, a professor at Peking University's College of Urban and Environmental Sciences, spelled out the challenges to me in an e-mail exchange: (1) lack of funds for enterprises to improve their energy efficiency; (2) lack of new techniques and experts in energy efficiency improvement; (3) cheap energy makes energy saving less cost efficient; (4) lack of policy incentives such as tax reduction and exemption; (5) improper statistical and reporting systems for energy consumption.

25. Shenyang aims to have 35 percent of households using solar power for water heating by 2015, compared with the national target of 20 percent, according to Wang. It will be tough to achieve. Reaching that goal will require the installation of more than 500,000 square meters of photovoltaic panels. Shenyang currently lags the national average with just 6.3 percent coverage of households.

26. For heating purposes, northern China is defined as everything north of the Yangtze River, much to the annoyance of people in Shanghai who miss out on the benefits of subsidized central heating.

27. Though not consistently. Several administrations have pursued policies to keep gasoline prices low. Even so, energy prices are not capped as they have been in China.

28. On my five visits to Pyongyang since 2002, I have never failed to be struck by the gloom inside buildings and the darkness outside at night. No capital in the world is better for stargazing.

29. The situation was worsened by largely self-imposed isolation, friction with the outside world, and an overemphasis on military spending.

30. Though perhaps not for much longer: Xinhua/NBS, "China's Rural Population Shrinks to 56 Per Cent of Total," October 22, 2007.

31. The Huangbaiyu design is a collaborative work by William McDonough, Tongji University, the Benxi Design Institute, and the China-U.S. Center for Sustainable Development. See also Mary-Anne Toy, "Green Dream Vanishes in Puff of Reality," *Sydney Morning Herald*, August 26, 2006.

32. Richard Spencer, "Man Faces Death for Ant Scam," *Daily Telegraph*, February 16, 2007.

33. In 2008, 360 out of 366 days were under level II on the national pollution index, which means less than 100 parts per million of particulate matter in the air. By Chinese standards this is great. But even Dalian would fail to meet the World Health Organization's benchmark of 50 parts per million for almost half the year.

34. Bo later became China's commerce minister and mayor of Chongqing Municipality.

35. In 2007, the per capita GDP was 51,000 yuan. Dalian regularly tops polls of China's most desirable city in which to live.

36. Shanghai Automotive is working on mass-producing 100 percent electric cars, but they will need a recharging infrastructure that will not be in place until at least 2030. In the interim, China has moved into the hybrid-car field. The Shenzhen-based company BYD—which stands for Build Your Dreams—has built the world's first mass-produced, plug-in hybrid sedan, the F3DM. The car has a gasoline engine that kicks in above 60 kph; up to that point, it runs completely on electricity.

37. Although China plans to build thirty-one nuclear plants by 2020 (Associated Press, "China Begins Building New Nuclear Plant, First in Country's Northeast," August 18, 2007), Chinese energy specialists believe that nuclear power can have only limited use because the country lacks large supplies of uranium and does not want to be too dependent on imports for power. Worldwide, nuclear power cannot solve the earth's energy problems. Nathan Lewis estimates that we would have to build a new nuclear fission reactor every two days for fifty years to meet humanity's demand for power.

But even if that were possible, there wouldn't be enough uranium on the planet to fuel them all (Nathan Lewis, "Powering the Planet," California Institute of Technology, 2007).

14. Fertility Treatment: Shandong

1. In 2007, Shandong's population stood at 96.37 million (China National Bureau of Statistics). The province is home to the country's biggest cement maker, its second-largest oil field, its third-biggest reserve of coal, and its leading brewer of beer.

2. *National Statistical Yearbook, 2006* (China National Bureau of Statistics, 2006).

3. The province was a gateway to the creative and destructive influence of the outside world. At the low point of Chinese power at the end of the nineteenth century, the German navy made Qingdao their base. The failed Boxer Rebellion against foreign influence began in Shandong in 1899. This was the scene of some of the bloodiest fighting against Japanese troops in the 1930s and 1940s.

4. This concept is covered in more detail in ch. 3.

5. The thirteen-year, $3.1 billion program will research dozens of varieties of GM rice, maize, soy, and wheat, according to a spokesperson for the ministry of agriculture. The initiative involves sixty-four projects on GM rice, maize, wheat, and soybean, and the Shandong Academy of Agricultural Science will be involved mainly in the project's downstream work, including genetic transformation and evaluation of the performance of the transgenic plants in biosafety greenhouses and the field, according to Huixia Wu, CIMMYT (International Maize and Wheat Improvement Center) wheat transformation specialist (cited in *Science* magazine, September 5, 2008).

6. The father of China's GM rice program, Professor Zhu Zhen of the Chinese Academy of Sciences, told me this (Jonathan Watts, "Illicit Rice Trade Endangers Biotech Barriers," *Guardian*, June 14, 2005).

7. Judith Shapiro, *Mao's War Against Nature* (Cambridge University Press, 2001), p. 80.

8. Up until the 1960s, for every increase in the human population there was a corresponding expansion in the area of arable land under cultivation. But after that, all the gains in yield came from the green revolution (Joel Cohen, speaking at the Nature Conservancy conference ConEx in Vancouver, BC, 2008).

9. Construction accounted for more than half of the 25,000 square kilometers of cultivated land lost in the 1990s. Remote-sensing surveys show that China's cultivated land area fell from 1,307,400 square kilometers in 1991 to 1,282,400 square kilometers in 2000—from 1.8 mu (0.0012 square kilometer) per head to 1.5 mu (0.0010 square kilometer) per head. Construction accounted for 56.6 percent of the decrease, 21 percent of land was forested, 16 percent was flooded, and 4 percent became grassland.

10. Vaclav Smil, *Global Catastrophes and Trends: The Next Fifty Years* (MIT Press, 2008).

11. Italy was the only other country to adopt it, but not on the same scale (interview with Zhang Qiwen).

12. It is too cold for them north of Shenyang, too hot for them south of the Yangtze (interview with Zhang Qiwen).

13. China now has 7 million hectares of artificial forest—the most in the world—almost a third of which are poplar 107 and 108. China claims greater progress in afforestation than any other country in the world, yet its "success" is based largely on these species and similar "economic forests" of eucalyptus in the south.

14. In the gardens of the Forbidden City in Beijing stand four ancient junipers which were repeatedly split in the middle and the wounds were covered in burlap, then tightly bound in oilcloth so that the base of the trunk split in two parts that met higher up the trunk. The intended shape is the character for "person." Even centuries ago, horticulturalists were shaping nature in man's image.

15. The ministry of forestry has set a target of enough new artificial poplar plantations by 2015 to produce 143 million cubic meters of timber every year—almost equal to the entire amount that China currently imports.

16. This felt horribly familiar. It reminded me of Mao-era architecture in Beijing, all of which was initially constructed according to fifty standard Soviet blueprints. Even this was considered too diverse during the ultraegalitarian Cultural Revolution, when everything was built to one of just four designs. The rural landscape was following the utilitarian path of the postrevolution cityscape (Jasper Becker, *City of Heavenly Tranquility: Beijing in the History of China* [Penguin, 2008], p. 280).

17. Interview with Jiang Gaoming.

18. Interview with Jiang Gaoming. We met in late 2008, soon after the government admitted that melamine, illegally added to milk, had killed at least six infants and left a further 860 babies hospitalized.

19. By one estimate, 2.7 billion tons of livestock manure are produced throughout China every year, 3.4 times the amount of industrial solid waste. But in most places less than a tenth of the manure is returned to the land (Wu Weixiang, Department of Environment Engineering at Zhejiang University, quoted in "A New Livestock Revolution," *China Daily*, December 19, 2006).

20. The World Bank is investing heavily in the project to reduce greenhouse gas emissions, reduce indoor air pollution, and improve sanitary conditions.

21. But there is the problem of trust. In China today, few consumers believe "organic" labels are anything but a marketing gimmick. Their skepticism is understandable. Countless food-safety scandals have been caused by corruption, counterfeiting, and reckless shortcuts aimed at boosting profits. All too often a stamp of approval by the authorities merely shows that the regulatory officials have been paid a big enough bribe. Other checks and balances are missing. Journalists are frequently paid off with "taxi money" bribes. There are no independent courts. Consumer organizations are weak or nonexistent. Nothing is allowed to impinge upon the authority of the party. So if the party approves something, there is no comeback. Many commentators see this resulting "crisis of trust" as one of China's biggest problems.

22. From a book of twenty-four stories about filial piety compiled by Guo Jujing during the Yuan dynasty (1271–1368).

23. Cynics who thought Lei sounded too good to be true were almost certainly correct. Conveniently, however, the selected icon had died a year before the campaign started when a clumsy army colleague backed a truck into an electricity pole that flattened the soon-to-be national treasure. The propaganda authorities had, of course, already recorded his deeds and acquired a "diary" of his politically perfect thoughts. In addition to his dung donation, Lei's altruism reportedly extended to scrubbing public toilets in his spare time, darning the socks of poor farmers, and giving away his meager savings to the needy.

24. She was supported both physically and financially by the villagers, including Professor Jiang. Some locals believed she was a shaman who could cure the sick by touching their heads.

25. Chinese anecdotal history contains numerous tales of people turning to cannibalism during famines throughout the ages, most recently after the Great Leap Forward.

26. In the English-speaking world, Lester Brown and Vaclav Smil are, on one side, warning that falling water tables and overuse of the land are threatening the nation's ability to feed itself. On the other is Peter Lindert, professor of economics and director of the Agricultural History Center at the University of California, Davis, who suggests the depth of topsoil is relatively unchanged in China and the quality may even have improved. See Brown, *The Earth Policy Reader* (Norton, 2002); Smil, *Global Catastrophes and Trends*; Lindert, *Shifting Ground: The Changing Agricultural Soils of China and Indonesia* (MIT Press, 2000).

27. Researchers from the government's Institute of Soil Science in Nanjing have found that soils in fields converted to growing vegetables are becoming dramatically more acid, with average pH falling from 6.3 to 5.4 in ten years. Meanwhile nitrates are at four times previous levels, and phosphate levels are up tenfold (*Environmental Geochemistry and Health* 26, pp. 97, 119). The changes in soil chemistry have been accompanied by an equally dramatic decline in soil bacteria and an epidemic of fungus. The deterioration is worst when the crops are grown under plastic (Fred Pearce, "China's Changing Farms Damaging Soil and Water," *New Scientist,* September 18, 2004).

28. Interview with Qian Zhengying, former minister of water conservancy and power.

29. More use of fertilizers means more nitrous oxide emissions, which are 200 times more effective at trapping heat than carbon dioxide (Smil, *Global Catastrophes and Trends,* p. 225). The rising demand for rice means more methane emissions from paddies.

30. "The Limits of a Green Revolution?" BBC News, March 29, 2007, http://news.bbc.co.uk/2/hi/6496585.stm.

31. Dale Allen Pfeiffer, "Eating Fossil Fuels," October 3, 2003, www.fromthewilderness.com.

32. In 2001, there were six covering a combined area of less than 3,000 square kilometers. Five years later there were more than forty spanning more than 15,000 square kilometers. (Figures based on research by Zhou Mingjiang, former head of the Institute of Oceanology.)

33. Jin Xiangcan, vice director of China Society of Environmental Sciences, said the affected area was about 135 square kilometers in the 1970s, but due to the rapid development of the economy and society, it increased to 8,700 square kilometers by 2009 ("Areas of Lakes Affected by Eutrophica-

tion in China Increases 60 Times in 40 Years," Xinhua, November 6, 2009; http://news.xinhuanet.com/politics/2009-11/05/content_12391302.htm).

34. Wastewater treatment expenditure from *National Statistical Yearbook 2006*. In June 2007, the provincial Maritime Fisheries Bureau confirmed severe pollution off the coast of Shandong at Laizhou Bay, Jiaozhou Bay, the southern Bohai Gulf, and the mouth of the Yellow River. The contaminants were inorganic nitrates, lime phosphates, and oil ("Dark Water: Coastal China on the Brink [I]," *Southern Metropolis Daily,* April 8, 2008).

35. Shi Jiangtao, "Bohai Sea Will Be Dead in 10 Years," *South China Morning Post,* October 19, 2006.

36. At Yanwei in Jiangsu, the stench from polluted water was so bad in 2007 that children had to be sent home from their school. In the far south tourist resort of Silver Beach in Guanxi Province, Xinhua reported the runoff from a shellfish processing plant turned the sea into a stinking red patch of effluent (Liang Siqi, "World's Best Beach Polluted, Stench from Discharge Pipe Unbearable," Xinhua, February 15, 2007 [in Chinese]).

37. In 2006, in the heavily industrialized southeastern provinces of Guangdong and Fujian, almost 8.3 billion tons of sewage were discharged into the ocean without treatment, a 60 percent increase from 2001. More than 80 percent of the East China Sea, one of the world's largest fisheries, was graded at the second highest level of pollution or worse in 2006, up from 53 percent in 2000.

The state news agency reports that the seabed is suffering desertification because of a discharge of sewage and pollutants (Xinhua, "China's Seabed Undergoing Desertification Caused by Pollution," December 15, 2006), although the scale of such phenomena is difficult to gauge. Xinhua, once unreliable because it was merely a mouthpiece for the Communist Party, is now prone to exaggerating environment scares because it is now freer in this area to stir up a circulation-boosting storm. Two scholars told me the damage caused by industrial pollution and overfishing on the seabed is overstated.

All but ten of the fifty-three waterways that flow into the Bohai Sea are rated "heavily contaminated." Together they release 2.8 billion tons of polluted water into the Bohai annually, leading to a buildup of heavy metal in the mud 2,000 times higher than the national safety standard (Yingling Liu, "China's Coastal Pollution Necessitates Rethinking Government Role," Worldwatch Institute, November 8, 2007).

38. The clearest illustration of this was the lead-contamination scandal of 2009. Thousands of children were poisoned by the steady buildup of heavy metals from factories in Shaanxi and Hunan. It arose because the government monitored data only on the daily proportions of emissions; it was not measuring the accumulated total of lead in the soil.

39. "DDT-laced Seafood from China May Pose a Threat to Humans," Underwatertimes.com News Service, May 17, 2007, citing a study published in *Environmental Toxicology and Chemistry.*

40. The 32 million tons of farmed fish produced in China in 2005 was equal to roughly a third of the world's oceanic fish catch.

41. This theory is credited to biogeochemist Graham Logan of the University of New South Wales: Graham A. Logan, J. M. Hayes, Glenn B. Hieshima, and Roger E. Summons, "Terminal Proterozoic Reorganization of Biogeochemical Cycles," *Nature,* July 6, 2002.

42. This theory is put forward by paleontologist Ronald Martin of the University of Delaware: "Secular Increase in Nutrient Levels through the Phanerozoic; Implications for Productivity, Biomass, and Diversity of the Marine Biosphere," *Palaios* 11 (1996): 209–19.

43. Frederik Leliaert, Zhang Xiaowen, et al., "Identity of the Qingdao Algal Bloom," *Phycological Research* 57 (2009): 147–51.

44. Ibid.

45. Algaculture is already under way in several countries, including China. One use is to absorb carbon sequestered from coal-gasification plants. In Japan, a very similar technique is used to harvest nori seaweed.

46. Jonathan Watts, "A Hunger Eating Up the World," *Guardian Weekly,* January 20, 2006.

47. Climate change will have a devastating effect on agricultural production in China. If no measures are taken, the overall productivity of Chinese farming industry may decline 5 to 10 percent by 2030. By the second half of the twenty-first century, the production of major crops in China's wheat, rice, and corn could see a maximum reduction of 37 percent (Lin Erda et al., "Investigating the Impacts of Climate Change on Chinese Agriculture, China-UK Collaborative Project," www.dfid.gov.uk, 2008).

15. An Odd Sort of Dictatorship: Heilongjiang

1. Official translation.

2. Thomas Friedman, *Hot, Flat, and Crowded: Why We Need a Green Revolu-*

tion—and How It Can Renew America (Allen Lane, 2008). Friedman advocates the adoption of China's authoritarian powers as a temporary measure for "one day." In parentheses, he steps back by saying "(not two)."

3. Thomas Friedman, "Our One-Party Democracy," *New York Times,* September 9, 2009.

4. Heilongjiang recorded the lowest temperature in Chinese history of minus 52.3°C on February 13, 1969, at Mohe.

5. Heilongjiang was the front line for 1.25 million of them (Judith Shapiro, *Mao's War Against Nature* [Cambridge University Press, 2001]).

6. The crisis with the Soviet Union abated when Mao met U.S. president Richard Nixon and gained the support of the world's most powerful military.

7. In 1995, Ma won over the newly formed Environmental Protection Committee of the National People's Congress, China's parliament. Senior politicians were impressed by his argument that wetlands are a cost-effective form of flood control, while swamps have a kidneylike function in cleansing polluted waterways and processing toxic waste. The agriculture ministry objected. They opposed any brake on the conversion of land for food production. But Ma was in the ascendant and so, it seemed, was the conservation movement (Joanne R. Bauer [ed.], *Forging Environmentalism: Justice, Livelihood, and Contested Environments* [M. E. Sharpe, 2006], p. 66).

8. This was of international importance as China has the biggest wetlands in Asia. Including marshes, swamps, lagoons, deltas, lakes, rivers, and coastal areas, they cover approximately 25 million hectares, or about 2.5 percent of its territory. See www.ramsar.org.

9. The Sanjiang wetland reserve in Fuyuan was established in 1993, approved as a provincial reserve the next year and a national-level reserve in 2000. In 1999, Heilongjiang was applauded worldwide for taking the lead in wetland protection when it announced the first ban on the development of swamps and watersheds (Cynthia W. Cann, Michael C. Cann, and Gao Shangquan, "China's Road to Sustainable Development: An Overview," in Kristen Day [ed.], *China's Environment and the Challenge of Sustainable Development* [M. E. Sharpe, 2005], pp. 3–35).

10. In 1996, the Overseas Economic Cooperation Fund of Japan conducted the first environmental impact assessment of a natural resource exploitation project in China on the Sanjiang Plain with support from the Wild Bird Society of Japan and the International Crane Foundation (Michael Pickles, "Implementing Ecologically Sustainable Development in China: The Exam-

ple of Heilongjiang Province," *Georgetown International Environmental Law Review,* April 1, 2002, p. 2).

11. Troops lent military boats, telescopes, offices, and observation stations to nature reserve staff. In return, the conservationists taught soldiers to identify the flora and fauna of the region. The July 18, 2000, issue of the *People's Liberation Army Daily* carried the headline "Every Soldier Is a Soldier for Environment Protection" (Bauer, *Forging Environmentalism,* p. 65). Bauer also quotes a military official as saying, "The Russian side is full of forests and their observation stations are hidden in the big trees. Our side has few trees and our observation stations and military moves are exposed."

12. The initial blitzkrieg came in 2005, when the State Environmental Protection Agency, as it was then called, blacklisted thirty projects worth 119.7 billion yuan, then suspended all development approval in four of the worst pollution hotspots: Tangshan in Hebei, Luliang in Shanxi, Liupanshui in Guizhou, and Laiwu in Shandong.

13. See chs. 5, 10, 11, 15, and 16. Pan Yue was advocating the creation of an eco-civilization long before President Hu. Pan was greatly helped by his family's revolutionary credentials. His father, Pan Tian, is an engineer general in the People's Liberation Army and his father-in-law is Liu Huaqing, former commander of the navy. Pan has a journalistic background and worked in the Economic Restructuring Office (Andrew Mertha, *China's Water Warriors: Citizen Action and Policy Change* [Cornell University, 2008], p. 50). He worked inside the government and the Communist Party to ensure that candidates for promotion were judged at least partly on their environmental records, launched an experiment to assess "green GDP," pressed for environmental impact assessments for new projects, and initiated a new credit evaluation system with the Bank of China that requires financial institutions to include ecological regulation compliance as a factor when assessing requests for loans. Outside the one-party system, he opened up the space for NGOs, advocated greater public participation in environmental policy-making, and encouraged the media to act as watchdog.

14. Yang Dongping, the president of Friends of Nature, called the upgrade a major turning point in China's environmental protection (Yang Dongping, "The Turning Point in China's Environmental Protection Movement," *Biodiversity Matters,* spring 2008).

15. Jonathan Watts, "China Admits Toxic Spill Is Threat to City's Water," *Guardian,* November 24, 2005.

16. The spill and tap cutoff in 2005 were far from unique. In the next eleven months there were 130 other far less widely reported contamination cases on the river, according to Pan Yue (interview in *Newsweek*).

17. The reporting window lasted four days, then the authorities became nervous and it was back to business as usual. The propaganda department ordered the domestic media to cease independent reporting of the scandal. Instead, they were told to reproduce the officially approved version of events distributed by the state-run Xinhua News Agency.

18. Most of the money has been spent near the Russian border to allay the pollution concerns of China's neighbor. The results have been mixed. The tributaries are becoming worse as the main river improves, according to the environmental group Green Longjiang. Li's official position is that the improvements can be observed along the entire waterway. Nonetheless, the river is still foul. Downstream from Harbin, the water quality remains a dismal four on a declining scale of five, which means it is fit only for irrigation and industry. But even this is better than the situation before the 2005 spill, when it was deemed so contaminated as to be of no use anywhere.

19. Several local journalists and officials sympathized with Heilongjiang's government, saying they had to lie because Jilin, the neighboring province, had lied first and the Heilongjiang officials could not contradict them. In real terms, little changed. The maximum penalty for the polluter was just 1 million yuan, an insignificant amount for China National Petroleum Corporation. Most of the officials involved escaped by offering an apology.

20. Li told me that, during the preceding twelve months, 20,000 law-enforcement officials had inspected 8,000 factories and ordered the closure of 250. Heilongjiang had punished seven local authorities who failed to enforce pollution regulations. Their penalty was a denial of all development plans for six months.

21. According to Green Longjiang.

22. He boasted that his office provides information to more than eighty frontpage or prime-time TV news exposés every year, most of them naming and shaming the violators of environmental regulations.

23. Newspapers and television stations played a key role in nurturing green movements in the U.S., Europe, and Japan in the 1970s. But the signs of this happening in China are mixed. Many journalism schools now teach principles that would be more recognizable to their counterparts in Western nations than to their predecessors thirty years ago. Unlike in the past,

the first duty of a reporter is to the public rather than the party. Pioneering media such as the Nanfang Daily newspaper group and *Caijing* magazine, and individual journalists such as Cheng Yizhong, Li Datong, Wang Keqin, Chen Guidi, and Wu Chuntao are pushing back the boundaries of censorship, particularly on environmental issues. And, of course, the Internet has provided a new realm for public discourse and made it far harder for the authorities to cover up scandals.

24. In 2002, there were fewer than fifty registered green NGOs in the country. By 2007, there were almost 3,000 (Jonathan Watts, "The Man Making the World's Worst Polluter Clean Up Its Act," *Observer,* July 8, 2007).

25. Jonathan Watts, "Local Governments Keep Chinese Public in the Dark about Pollution," *Guardian,* September 4, 2009.

26. The 2003 *Practical Manual for Party Propaganda Work,* which includes a foreword by Hu Jintao, notes: "News reporting should hold to the positiveness principle by handling properly the balance of praise and exposing problems. In any case, the reader should be left with feelings of encouragement, trust, courage and hope" (p. 82, trans. *China Digital Times*).

27. Ma Jun, *China's Water Crisis* (Eastbridge, 2004), p. 114.

28. The Taoist-inspired necromantic belief in the importance of balancing strong natural forces, particularly in one's home.

29. The three provinces together cover 793,000 square kilometers. Other definitions of Manchuria and Dongbei (northeast) include parts of Inner Mongolia.

30. He Qiutao (Qing dynasty inspector), "Northern Defense Notes" (1858), cited in Ma, *China's Water Crisis,* p. 113.

31. By the end of the Second World War, Japan had removed an estimated 100 million or more cubic feet of lumber from the northeast (Qu Geping and Li Jinchang, *Population and the Environment in China* [Lynne Rienner, 1994]). Many of the darkest deeds in Japan's militaristic past were perpetrated in this part of the world, which was also a base of chemical and biological weapons experiments on live prisoners.

32. Ma, *China's Water Crisis,* p. 114.

33. Interview with Wang Song, former CITES representative for China.

34. Quoted in Ma, *China's Water Crisis,* p. 115.

35. The whodunnit mystery surrounding the death of China's forests is politically charged. An alternative view, which paints the Communist Party in a far more positive light, is put forward by Qu and Li in *Population and the*

Environment in China. They say most deforestation occurred in the centuries before 1949 as a result of population growth, backward agricultural production, feudal leaders' large-scale construction projects (such as the Great Wall and E'fang Palace), warfare, and the absence of afforestation programs. The latter "path of neglect" was reversed, they say, after the communists took power in 1949, when the government called people to arms with the slogan "Plant trees to cover the country." This quickened steps to reforest barren mountainsides and valleys. But even these defenders of government policy acknowledge the deficit in forested areas continued to rise because of the demand for arable land and timber products. Two huge clearances followed. First, for the dam building and steel smelting of the Great Leap Forward, then during the Cultural Revolution, when the educated students were sent to reclaim land from the wilderness. Over 2,200 years, Qu and Li estimate forest cover in China declined from 42.9 percent to 12 percent (p. 57).

36. The most up-to-date forestry inventory is ten years old; the standing volume of the province's forests is estimated at 1.5 billion square meters, which is 15.4 percent of the total in China (Fredrik Samuelsson, "The Potential for Quality Production in Birch Stands in North-Eastern China Using Different Precommercial Thinning Strategies," MSc thesis, Southern Swedish Forest Research Center, June 2006). Ma estimated that the forests of the northeast, including Heilongjiang, Jilin, and Liaoning, provided a third of China's wood around the turn of the century. Even with the selective cutting of secondary forest that followed, Heilongjiang continued to have the largest annual logging volume in China (Ma, *China's Water Crisis,* p. 116).

37. The figurehead for the conversion was Ma Yongshun, a model worker in the timber industry from the first generation of lumberjacks. In the era before chain saws, he was praised by Mao for a technique that enabled a single person to fell six trees in a day. Ma claimed to have chopped down 36,500 trees before realizing late in his career that his technique was too successful. The forests were disappearing. Alarmed at the consequences of his success, Ma laid down his ax and took up a trowel for planting seedlings. He felt he owed a debt to the mountains. Every year on March 12, national tree-planting day, he would make a very public repayment (Ma, *China's Water Crisis,* p. 116.).

38. Formally known as the "Three-North Shelterbelt," the 50-billion-yuan ($7 billion) project is designed to protect cities and cropland from floods and

the desert. In Heilongjiang, floods are the main concern. This is particularly true since 1998, when the Songhua River system suffered its worst flood in 2,000 years. Desperate to prevent the rising waters from deluging the strategic oil fields of Daqing, the authorities blasted embankments protecting the agricultural plains. The economic damage was estimated at 30 billion yuan. When Premier Zhu Rongji visited the disaster site, he pledged to preserve the forests as a natural barrier against flooding. The eventual aim of the project is to cover 406.9 million hectares or 42 percent of China's landmass with trees (John MacKinnon and Wang Haibin, *The Green Gold of China* [EU-China Biodiversity Programme, 2008], p. 280).

39.	This resolution was passed in 1981 (Liang Chao, "China Now Tops in Most 'Human-Planted' Trees on Earth," *China Daily,* March 12, 2004). Many people did not fulfill their quota, and farmers were later given financial incentives to plant saplings.

40.	Before this, the party organized numerous, but intermittent, mass tree-planting drives (Qu and Li, *Population and the Environment in China,* p. 37).

41.	And perhaps it has. The country is now planting more trees than the rest of the world combined. In Heilongjiang, Provincial Forestry Department figures suggest tree cover has risen to 43.6 percent. Academics in Harbin put the figure at 46 percent.

42.	The State Forestry Administration claims forest cover is increasing by 66 million hectares every year (Jonathan Watts, "China Fights to Hold Back Sands," *Guardian,* February 28, 2006).

43.	Some estimate that up to two-thirds of trees die before reaching maturity because farmers have a financial incentive to plant saplings quickly rather than considering local conditions, the need for diversity, and the effort required to nurture them. Chinese forestry scientists, however, told me the survival rate is about 70 percent.

44.	According to China's Bureau of Statistics, "forest coverage rate" refers to the ratio of area of afforested land to total land area. This indicator shows the forest resources and afforestation progress of a country or a region. In addition to afforested land, the area of bush forest, the area of woodland inside farmland, and the area of trees planted adjacent to farmhouses and along roads, rivers, and fields should also be included in the area of afforested land in the calculation of the forest coverage rate.

45.	Qu and Li, *Population and the Environment in China,* p. 57.

46. Those replanted at the behest of paper and furniture manufacturers often comprise only one or two types of fast-growing tree. Eucalyptus trees dominate the south, poplars the center, and larch and birch the northwest.

47. In 2008, the huge extent of the winter storm damage exposed the quality problem of China's forestation effort. Worst hit were the young and semimature trees which cover about 70 percent of reforested areas. Owing to poor seedling quality and inadequate care, the trees had grown more slowly and were thus weaker and less resilient than if better standards had been maintained. The extensive damage suffered by bamboo forests also illustrates the risks associated with monoculture plantations, since mixed forests could have been expected to withstand better the severity of snow and ice damage. In 2002, for example, larch trees in Heilongjiang suffered such an infestation of pine caterpillars that the Qiqihar Railway Bureau had to halt services while the tracks were cleaned of a 5-centimeter layer of slippery mashed larvae, as recorded by Song Xinzhou of GreenBeijing .net. Song also notes: "Artificial forests are unable to resist natural pests, have poor water retention qualities, do not help prevent soil erosion, and do not support much undergrowth, which leads to more frequent forest fires. Single-species forests, grown to increase coverage alone, not only fail to solve environmental problems, but also create new crises of their own" (Song Xinzhou, "Greening China: Successes and Failures," *China Dialogue,* August 2, 2007).

48. Wang's meetings with Sir Peter Scott, then head of the World Wildlife Fund, led to the creation of a joint project for giant panda conservation at Wolong (see ch. 4). The panda became the symbol of the organization's worldwide conservation in 1981, the same year that China signed up to the Convention on International Trade in Endangered Species, more commonly known as CITES. Wang was the country's representative for most convention negotiations in the years that followed, and he has pressed as hard as anyone in China for the protection of biodiversity.

49. Backed by the environment ministry and tourist agency, this experiment aims to balance protection and development.

50. At this early stage, however, it looks shaky. Local officials appear far more interested in the potential for development than the responsibility of conservation.

51. Tony Whitten, senior biodiversity specialist for the East Asia and Pacific Region at the World Bank, describes the region's forests as "eerily quiet"

after insidious degradation and attrition. He says this is common nationwide and across much of Southeast Asia.

52. As recently as the 1960s, there were more than 200 of these giant beasts in Heilongjiang and Jilin and smaller tigers in more than half the provinces in China. Now there are thought to be only twenty left in the wild (figures provided by the Wildlife Conservation Society). The captive population has increased. Harbin has a giant tiger "conservation" park but, like its counterpart in Xiongsen, this is actually more accurately described as a farm or circus that aims mainly to generate income from tourism and sales of parts for traditional Chinese medicine. Both are under the jurisdiction of the state forestry agency. A healthier wild population of Amur tigers exists in the better-protected forests of Siberia.

53. Each autumn, when the frogs migrate downstream from the mountains, locals trap them with plastic bags snagged on the surface of streams. Others are killed by poisoning or indiscriminate electric fishing. Such tactics are illegal but common. I have seen "fishermen" with batteries strapped to their backs dipping electric rods into ponds and brooks, killing everything that passes between them. Along with pollution and habitat loss, this explains why the population of wild salmon in Heilongjiang has fallen by more than 90 percent (Shapiro, *Mao's War Against Nature*, p. 168).

54. Researchers calculated the benefits of the Changbaishan Nature Reserve were worth 9.3 billion yuan, taking into account its ability to absorb carbon, produce oxygen, conserve water, act as a barrier to wind and desertification, regulate climate, prevent soil erosion, ease the risk of flooding, and assist in pest management by providing a home to birds that eat insects. The cost of building a reservoir with the same water capacity as the reserve has been estimated at 2.8 billion yuan. The Jilin Environmental Protection Research Institute also calculated that a single hectare of forested land conserves 3,000 square meters more water than the same area of nonforested land (Qu and Li, *Population and the Environment in China*, pp. 55–56).

55. *China Youth Daily*, December 31, 2008.

56. One study estimated that 67 percent of the forest was Dahurian larch (*Larix gmelinii*), while 25 percent was white birch (*Betula platyphylla*) (Samuelsson, "The Potential for Quality Production in Birch Stands in North-Eastern China," p. 10).

57. China produces 60 billion pairs of disposable chopsticks every year at the cost of 25 million trees (Ma, *China's Water Crisis,* p. 117).

58. Better known outside China by its Russian name, the Amur.

59. In addition to the logging example cited here, a major cross-border environmental problem is that of water diversion. The Hailaer River (known downstream as Ergun in Chinese and Argun in Russian) is being diverted to replenish the parched Dalai Lake and ease the problems of salination and eutrophication in Inner Mongolia. That means less water in Russia and a loss of habitat for many rare birds in the Daurian wetlands (data from Pacific Environment, www.pacificenvironment.org, and International Rivers, www.internationalrivers.org).

60. From the late 1990s to the early twenty-first century, China's share of exports of round timber from the Russian Far East rose from 10 percent to about 50 percent. About 70 percent is felled illegally. The World Wide Fund for Nature, Friends of Nature, Traffic, Greenpeace, and Pacific Environment have all issued reports showing that the surge in illegal logging in southern Siberia's taiga forests has been predominantly driven by demand from China.

61. Song Weiming, Chen Baodong, Zhang Shengdong, and Meng Xianggang, "Russian Logs in China: The Softwood Commodity Chain and Economic Development in China," Beijing Forestry University, Forest Trends and Rights and Resources, www.forest-trends.org, 2007.

62. Ibid.

63. Some of the wood products are processed and reexported in the form of furniture and flooring to Europe, the U.S., and Japan, but eight out of every ten Siberian logs that come into China are used in the domestic market, mostly for construction (ibid.).

64. Ibid.

65. My thanks to Mary Hennock for this information.

66. Song et al., "Russian Logs in China."

67. China's 2,531 protected areas cover 15.2 percent of the country, well above the international average and more than four times higher than the U.S. wetland reserves cover of 14.5 million hectares (MacKinnon and Wang, *The Green Gold of China,* p. 282).

68. The reserves are usually divided into three zones. The inner core is supposed to be completely off-limits to hunting, logging, building, or any kind of development. The middle ring is for scattered farming and the outer "experimental zone" is for limited economic activity.

69. "At least two to three swans are poisoned every day in Poyang Lake," *Jiangnan Urban News,* January 5, 2009, www.jfdaily.com/news/xwgn/200901/t20090112_505791.htm.

70. Although, as she also pointed out, there are occasional acts of great courage. Confronting poachers can be dangerous because their lives as well as their livelihoods can be at stake. Those caught hunting the rarest animals face a possible death sentence. Shortly before we arrived in Heilongjiang, a People's Liberation Army officer based in the province was awarded a conservation prize for his work in removing traps set by poachers despite death threats and occasional beatings.

71. Mr. Hu and Mr. Wen are by no means the first politburo and government leaders to advocate a sustainable model of growth, but China's modern history does not offer much cause to be optimistic about their policy of "Scientific Development."

72. Cited in Ma, *China's Water Crisis,* p. 124.

73. As the Environment Protection Agency, its representatives could participate in cabinet meetings only as observers. That changed when ministerial status was attained.

74. The ministry has a budget of just over $10 billion per year and just 300 staff at state level, compared with 9,000 who work in the U.S. Environmental Protection Agency in Washington (Elizabeth Economy, *The River Runs Black: The Environmental Challenge to China's Future* [Cornell University Press, 2004]). Many of China's 2,400 regional environmental protection agencies are revenue-generating. In most cases, companies can get away with polluting rivers and the air by paying a fee to the local environmental bureaus. "When the local governments require some new funds, they can go on inspection tours of local companies," he says. "And when they come back, they have their coffers filled." Elizabeth Economy says companies whose emissions have generated complaints are merely charged higher fees.

75. Professor Wang Canfa at China University of Political Science and Law (Xinhua, "China Improves Enforcement of Environmental Laws," June 10, 2005).

76. Local officials frequently divert environmental protection funds and spend them on unrelated or ancillary endeavors. The Chinese Academy for Environmental Planning, which reports to SEPA, disclosed in 2009 that only half of the 1.3 percent of the country's annual GDP dedicated to environmental protection between 2001 and 2005 had found its way to legitimate

projects. According to the study, about 60 percent of the environmental protection funds spent in urban areas during that period went into the creation of, among other things, parks, factory production lines, gas stations, and sewage-treatment plants rather than into waste- or wastewater-treatment facilities (Elizabeth Economy, "The Great Leap Backward?" *Foreign Affairs,* September/October 2007).

77.   The information disclosure law has helped in many regards, but there are still big gaps. The sensitivity of environmental information became evident when the Chinese government asked the World Bank to remove an estimate of the deaths caused by pollution in a joint report ("China Must Come Clean About Its Poisonous Environment," *Financial Times,* July 3, 2007). According to Guo Xiaomin, a former official with the Chinese State Environmental Protection Agency who managed the report's mainland researchers, the information was officially excluded from initial drafts of the report owing to reliability concerns and because of fears that its inclusion would make the report too bulky. However, Guo also admitted that there were concerns that the Chinese public would react badly upon learning about the true extent of pollution-related deaths.

78.   Pan advocated a Chinese form of socialist environmentalism, centered on social justice but borrowing heavily from Western ideas of sustainable development, environmental protection, preservation of resources, and ecological balance. More than technological change, he believed "Scientific Development" was a change of politics, economics, culture, and society. (Pan Yue, "On Socialist Environmentalism," *China Economic Times,* September 26, 2006. Comments also taken from an interview with Zhou Jigang translated and published by *China Dialogue.*)

79.   His replacement in the key post of deputy environment minister was a former member of the Yunnan provincial government, the biggest supporter of a huge hydroelectric scheme due for review (Jonathan Watts, "China's Green Champion Sidelined," *Guardian,* March 12, 2009).

80.   Pan had previously used his power to great effect. In December 2004, the State Environmental Protection Agency suspended the construction of about thirty large projects because they had not undergone the environmental impact assessment required by law. Though some were worth more than a billion dollars, the culprits were named, shamed, and halted. The domestic media described this unprecedented assertion of environmental regulations as "storm" tactics.

81. Offenders are protected by the vast majority of local authorities that defy Beijing and violate state law by refusing to disclose information about pollution. One study found that just 4 out of 113 local governments complied (Jonathan Watts, "Local Governments Keep Chinese Public in the Dark about Pollution," *Guardian,* September 4, 2009).

82. After deadly floods in 1998 were blamed on the deforestation of hillsides, Zhu introduced restrictions of logging in Heilongjiang, Yunnan, and many other areas.

83. The commentator Liang Jiang goes further, suggesting bureaucrats increase waste because it expands their empires (Liang Jiang, "How Is the World to Deal with China's Lack of Fear of Waste?" August 9, 2009 [in Chinese]).

84. The initial Asian Development Bank grant was canceled after government ministries and northeastern provinces fought each other to secure a share of the budget. A new, more focused research and conservation project is now under way, but despite the construction of a smart new headquarters for the reserve staff, the Sanjiang wetlands have been steadily opened up to agricultural development.

85. The national situation is even more worrying. The northern province of Hebei has lost 90 percent of its wetlands over the last fifty years; 80 percent of what is left is polluted. In Shaanxi Province the thirty counties in the Guanzhong area have seen up to 10,000 ponds disappear. Poyang Lake, China's largest freshwater lake, now shrinks to an area as small as 50 square kilometers, down from 4,000 at its peak. The loss of wetlands has meant aridity spreading from the north to the country's fertile south. In 2007, tens of millions of people living around Poyang Lake suffered drinking water shortages. Wetlands in arid and semiarid regions are not faring any better. Alashan, in Inner Mongolia, is seeing wetlands dry up due to water abstraction from the Hei River upstream. Water flowing into this traditionally green area has dropped from 900 million cubic meters to 200 million, leading to the disappearance of hundreds of lakes and ponds. The creation of new farmland around the upper reaches of the Tarim River, in the Xinjiang Autonomous Region, has led to a 350-kilometer stretch of the river drying up, with deserts appearing where lakes once were. (Jiang Gaoming, "China's Evaporating Wetlands," *China Dialogue* website, August 28, 2008). The Haihe, the biggest wetland system in northern (as distinct from northwestern) China, has seen four-fifths of its wetlands disappear

as water is sucked away by megacities such as Beijing and Tianjin (Jonathan Watts, "Wetlands Sucked Dry in China," *Guardian*, February 13, 2006).

86. Rice production is actually far worse for the swampland than corn or wheat because huge amounts of water must be pumped, channeled, and otherwise diverted to flood the fields.

87. Migration accelerates this trend. Old residents of formerly wild areas know what has been lost and often support a limited degree of conservation, but the influx of newcomers means most of the population have no memory of the ecological past. They compare Heilongjiang to the degraded cities and farmlands they left behind and see a land ripe for exploitation. Migrants also tend to be poorer and in a greater hurry to make money. Without a belief in sustainability and no sense of ownership or responsibility, they tear into the black soil, the wetlands, and the forest (Pickles, "Implementing Ecologically Sustainable Development in China").

88. Heilongjiang became the first province in China to move 100 percent to this form of fuel in 2008. The three northeast provinces of Heilongjiang, Jilin, and Liaoning were among the first to use ethanol. The government estimated that, nationwide, half of the fuel sold for cars would be ethanol by 2010 (Xinhua, "China Enlarges Bio-Ethanol Fuel Coverage," April 1, 2008).

89. Remote-sensing surveys show that China's cultivated land area plummeted between 1988 and 2000, from 1,307,400 square kilometers in 1991 to 1,282,400 square kilometers in 2000—or from 1.8 mu (0.0012 square kilometer) per head to 1.5 mu (0.0010 square kilometer) per head. Construction accounted for 56.6 percent of the decrease, 21 percent of land was forested, 16 percent was flooded, and 4 percent became grassland.

Jasper Becker says the shortage of land is used by the government as an excuse for wasteful agricultural practices. "China feeds 20 percent of the world's population on seven percent of the planet's arable land. This fact is often cited by government leaders to excuse rural poverty and the widespread use of chemicals to squeeze more value out of the land. But Japan and South Korea have far higher population densities relative to arable land, yet their economies are considerably stronger and greener than China's" (Becker, *Hungry Ghosts*, p. 262). The former water minister Qian Zhengying has advised Premier Wen to increase food production still further in the area to replace the degraded lands of the northwest.

90. Ma is now going back to the drawing board to try to find a compromise that will allow the area to develop, while minimizing the ecological impact. He is shifting his focus from the top level of government to the local people and local governments—that middle band of China where power now lies. Ironically, to win them over, he once again finds himself advocating the conversion of wetlands to dry field production. It is another turning point, back toward the activity he was doing as a fifteen-year-old pioneer. It is the lesser of two evils. What he helped to do during the Cultural Revolution had a bad impact, but not as bad as what is being done now.

16 Grass Roots: Xanadu

1. He was so impressed with the Taoist monk Qiu Chuji that, after sacking Beijing, he reconstructed the White Cloud Temple in the city in his honor.
2. Scott Mills, *Conservation of Wildlife Populations* (Blackwell, 2007), p. 14.
3. Presentation by Nicholas Stern, former chief economist at the World Bank, based on estimates of CO_2 emissions from energy consumption and cement production using data from the China National Bureau of Statistics, IPCC, the World Bank, and Oak Ridge National Laboratory.
4. See ch. 12.
5. Three aerosol clouds struck Beijing during spring and early summer 2008, dashing hopes that the "Great Green Wall" of poplars and other trees (see ch. 15) might protect the Chinese capital before the Olympics. NASA satellite images showed the worst of them, on March 1, completely obscuring a 150,000-square-kilometer area of land stretching from Beijing down to Xian and halfway across the Bohai Sea. The following day, it hit South Korea, where several schools were closed amid health fears. A day later, Japanese newspapers were warning the year's first *kosa* (yellow sand) had arrived in Okinawa and was heading northeast toward Tokyo, obscuring the sky as it traversed the archipelago. It then made its way toward the Pacific and the western coast of the United States, where millions of tons of dust and other airborne pollutants from China are deposited each year. By one estimate, half the airborne dust in the world comes from China (L. Ochirkhuyag and R. Tsolmon, "Monitoring the Source of Transnational Dust Storms in Northeast Asia," *International Archives of the Photogrammetry, Remote Sensing and Spatial Information Sciences* 37 [2008], Beijing).
6. China has eight distinct gravel desert zones to which the Mongol *gobi* is applied, and four sandy desert zones designated by the Chinese *shadi* or

shamo. (In *gobi* the dunes are more mobile.) The eight gobi regions account for about 42 percent of China's total desert areas (Dee Mack Williams, *Beyond Great Walls: Environment, Identity, and Development on the Chinese Grasslands of Inner Mongolia* [Stanford University Press, 2002]).

7. Ibid.

8. Lester Brown, *The Earth Policy Reader* (Norton, 2002), p. 31.

9. Ibid., pp. 28–31, and personal interview.

10. Cited in Richard B. Harris, *Wildlife Conservation in China: Preserving the Habitat of China's Wild West* (East Gate, 2008), p. 38.

11. Though the extent of the degradation is difficult to assess, because there is no quantifiable definition of "degradation" and hence no accurate statistics.

12. Kerry Brown cites Chinese government figures showing that between 1967 and 1969, 16,222 people died and over 340,000 suffered physical injury during the purge of an alleged Mongolian independence party that later communist leaders admitted had never existed (Kerry Brown, *The Purge of the Inner Mongolian People's Party in the Chinese Cultural Revolution, 1967–69: A Function of Language, Power and Violence* [Global Oriental, 2006]). Judith Shapiro notes that the amount of land cleared in Inner Mongolia was about a twentieth of that in Heilongjiang and a fortieth of that in Xinjiang (Judith Shapiro, *Mao's War Against Nature* [Cambridge University Press, 2001], p. 40).

13. Interview with John MacKinnon, head of the EU-China Biodiversity Programme.

14. By a quirky coincidence, the rodent control headquarters is located next to China's Wildlife Conservation Society.

15. According to Chen, a team of botanists discovered 697 species of plants on the grasslands during a survey in 2005.

16. Speaking more broadly on the entire western and northern grasslands, Harris observes, "It is safe to conclude that many western Chinese rangelands no longer produce the abundance of palatable vegetation they formerly did, have lost soil matter or productivity, and are less efficient at facilitating quick weight gains in domestic livestock" (Harris, *Wildlife Conservation in China*, p. 38).

17. This was seen as a factor in the 2008 milk-contamination scandal. Wholesalers added melamine to watered-down milk to make the protein levels look higher during inspections. At least six infants died after drinking the contaminated milk.

18. See ch. 15, n. 24.

19. South Korea's largest environmental NGO was given funds by the government in Seoul to try to reduce the degradation of the grasslands because the resulting sandstorms are a major problem on the peninsula.

20. According to Dai Qing, on her advice.

21. Among the other leading groups are Global Village of Beijing, whose founder Liao Xiaoyi won the Norwegian Sophie Prize in 2000, and Green Watershed, led by Yu Xiaogang, who won the Goldman Environmental Prize in 2006, the same year that the environmentalist Ma Jun, author of *China's Water Crisis* and founder of another green NGO, the Institute of Public and Environmental Affairs, was named by *Time* as one of 100 people who shape our world (Nick Young, "International Fillip for Chinese Greens," *China Briefing,* May 6, 2006).

22. He added, "When I started out in 1983, there was only one environmental law. It wasn't even a real law. It was a pilot. Now there are twenty-five or more laws and hundreds of regulations. But the environment is still deteriorating."

23. Only 4 out of 113 gave an adequate response, according to a survey carried out by Ma and leading academics (Jonathan Watts, "Local Governments Keep Chinese Public in the Dark about Pollution," *Guardian,* September 4, 2009).

24. Ibid.

25. The NGO newsletter *China Briefing,* published by Briton Nick Young, was banned in 2007, partly because it linked disparate activist groups.

26. Zeng Jinyan (wife of Hu Jia), Xu Jiehua (wife of Wu Lihong), and Yuan Weijing (wife of Chen Guangcheng).

27. Similarly with Tan Zuoren and Chen Guangcheng. Tan won the approval of Premier Wen for his reports on dams and petrochemical plants in Sichuan. But he was arrested after he turned his attention to the shoddy school construction that led to the deaths of thousands of children in the 2008 earthquake. Chen started out by organizing a campaign to get clean drinking water in his home province of Shandong. Later, his exposure of brutal and illegal techniques to enforce the family-planning laws led to his being abducted from the streets of Beijing by plainclothes officials, put under house arrest, and later imprisoned. Others I met who were later locked up include Liu Xiaobo, Gao Zisheng, Sun Xiaodi, and Liu Jie.

28. Music charts in China are even less reliable as a guide to popularity than in the U.S. and Europe, not least because almost all music is pirated and

downloaded for free. At a Climate Change gig at Mao Livehouse, for which he arrived onstage in a white biohazard suit and goggles, Xiao sang to acclaim:

When you're young and
When you're green
Save all the beautiful things
With pride and love we sing
"See we can show you!"

29. It occupied the top spot from December 8 to 14, 2008. Mongolian Cow (Mengniu) Sour Yogurt has a strong association with pop music. *Super Girl* or *Super Voice Girls,* the hugely popular Chinese version of *The X Factor,* is also sponsored by the Inner Mongolia–based firm.

30. This is an unusual but reasonable approach to easing the pressure on the planet. Eating vegetables directly is a far more efficient way to take in energy than consuming meat, which has to be fattened up with grain.

31. Several major NGOs told me they approached Chinese celebrities about fronting wildlife conservation activities, but were turned down so often they gave up.

32. The two are, of course, not mutually exclusive. The challenge is how to rebalance the relationship between man and nature.

33. "Eco-Civilization" research is apparently the new communist orthodoxy. The institute was set up after President Hu made it a key goal.

34. Few lives so vividly illustrated the turbulence that has racked China for the past sixty years. Jiang was born in 1946 in Jiangsu Province to a politically red-blooded family. His parents were former Red Army soldiers, heroes of the war against Japan, but his mother died young and his father was almost beaten to death during the Cultural Revolution as an accused "Black Gang Capitalist Roader." Jiang was nevertheless completely enamored of Mao. He joined the student Red Guard and rose to become deputy head of the revolutionary core group in his college, the Beijing Academy of Fine Arts. He was sent to Inner Mongolia along with the wave of "educated youth" who went to the countryside in 1967, but the air of the steppe failed to soften his rebellious nature. Jiang was jailed for more than three years and narrowly escaped the death penalty for criticizing Communist Party number two Lin Biao in 1970 just before his demise. He founded the "Beijing Spring" reform publication during

the Democracy Wall protests in 1978 and played a prominent role in the Tiananmen Square protests of 1989, for which he spent another eighteen months behind bars.

35. The economy is racing forward at the staggering rate of 38 percent a year. Local authorities expect the size of the economy to triple between 2007 and 2012. If their projections prove correct, Ordos is on course to be a wealthy megacity by 2020 ("Ordos: A Land of Opportunity," *China Daily*, August 25, 2008). According to the Chinese Academy of Social Sciences, the city has the greatest growth potential in China.

36. "The World's Largest Solar Plant Is Planned for the Mongolian Desert of China," United Press International, September 10, 2009.

37. Interview with Sun Lixia, director of the Ordos eco-town project.

38. The pilot eco-town project covered forty-two buildings and fifty-five hectares in one of the city's many new districts.

39. Or so he claimed. Some historians doubt that he ever made it to Kublai Khan's palace.

40. His attempts to invade Japan and Vietnam ended in disaster. His open-minded view of philosophy closed when he turned against Taoism, ordering the burning of three-quarters of the sacred texts.

41. John Man, *Xanadu* (Bantam Press, 2009).

42. Nobody has ever offered a definitive interpretation of "Kubla Khan," which might explain its enduring fascination. The wittiest comment on its inscrutability was offered by the Cambridge University lecturer George Watson, who noted that after millions of words of structural analysis, biographical investigation, and creative interpretation by the world's leading scholars, "We now know almost everything about Coleridge's 'Kubla Khan' except what the poem is about." Coleridge himself dismissed the work as nonsense, a triumph of sound over sense.

43. These are the opening lines. I have reluctantly omitted the rest due to space limitations.

44. Coleridge was an opium addict. The addiction contributed to his death in 1834.

45. Anthropological examinations of successive generations of Mayan skeletons showed declining levels of nourishment as population density grew to a level similar to that of modern China and then collapsed (Donald Hughes, *An Environmental History of the World: Humankind's Changing Role in the Community of Life* [Routledge, 2001], p. 46).

46. Ibid., p. 64.

47. Clive Ponting, *A New Green History of the World* (Penguin, 2007), pp. 3–6.

Afterword: Peaking Man

1. The earth's population is 6.8 billion, average life expectancy is sixty-five years, and humans use or occupy 83 percent of the world's land. The "human footprint" has been defined as "human land uses, human access from roads, railways, or major rivers, electrical infrastructure (indicated by lights detected at night), or direct occupancy by human beings at densities above 1 person per sq. km" ("Last of the Wild Project," Center for International Earth Science Information Network [CIESIN], Earth Institute at Columbia University).

2. Evident during a 2009 visit to Beijing by House Speaker Nancy Pelosi, who refrained from repeating her previous outspoken criticism of China's human rights record to emphasize that Beijing's cooperation on climate change was vital.

3. In researching this book, I came across many suggestions for improving mankind's eco-footprint. The principle of making polluters pay could be expanded to consumers by surcharging goods produced using unsustainable materials. Energy and water should be metered and priced to reflect their pollution costs and scarcity. Conversely, there should be incentives in the form of subsidies and lower taxes for "living lightly." Education should emphasize sustainability, and far more information should be made available about air, water, and soil quality (by adding an environment forecast to the daily weather forecast, for example). Environment insurance companies could be nurtured to offset risk and champion strong precautionary measures. In the political sphere, there should be tighter central government control over regional environmental issues and more rigorous implementation of environmental legislation. More ambitiously, systems of governance could be reshaped to include a politically neutral chamber that represented the long-term interests of the earth rather than the short-term concerns of the electorate.

Bibliography

Books

Ames, Roger. *The Art of Rulership: A Study of Ancient Chinese Political Thought*. University of Hawaii Press, 1983.

Bauer, Joanne R. (ed.). *Forging Environmentalism: Justice, Livelihood, and Contested Environments*. M. E. Sharpe, 2006.

Baum, Richard. *Burying Mao: Chinese Politics in the Age of Deng Xiaoping*. Princeton University Press, 1994.

Becker, Jasper. *The Chinese*. John Murray, 2000.

———. *City of Heavenly Tranquility: Beijing in the History of China*. Penguin, 2008.

———. *Hungry Ghosts: Mao's Secret Famine*. Holt, 1998.

Bell, Daniel. *China's New Confucianism: Politics and Everyday Life in a Changing Society*. Princeton University Press, 2008.

Brandt, Loren, and Thomas Rawski. *China's Great Economic Transformation*. Cambridge University Press, 2008.

Brown, Kerry. *The Purge of the Inner Mongolian People's Party in the Chinese Cultural Revolution, 1967–69: A Function of Language, Power and Violence*. Global Oriental, 2006.

Brown, Lester. *Plan B 3.0: Mobilizing to Save Civilization*. W. W. Norton, 2008.

———. *Who Will Feed China? Wake-up Call for a Small Planet*. Worldwatch Institute, 1995.

Brown, Lester, et al. *The Earth Policy Reader*. W. W. Norton, 2002.

Brown, Paul B. *Global Warming: The Last Chance for Change*. Reader's Digest, 2007.

———. *Notes from a Dying Planet, 2004–2006: One Scientist's Search for Solutions*. iUniverse, 2006.

Buck, Pearl. *The Good Earth.* Washington Square Press, 2004 (first published 1931).

Campanella, Thomas. *The Concrete Dragon: China's Urban Revolution and What It Means for the World.* Princeton Architectural Press, 2008.

Chen, Guidi, and Wu Chuntao. *Will the Boat Sink the Water? The Life of China's Peasants.* Public Affairs, 2006.

Cohen, Joel E. *How Many People Can the Earth Support?* W. W. Norton, 1996.

Coleridge, Samuel Taylor. *Coleridge's Poetry and Prose.* W. W. Norton, 2004.

Collins, Randall. *The Sociology of Philosophies: A Global Theory of Intellectual Change.* Social Science, 2000.

Dai Qing. *The River Dragon Has Come! The Three Gorges Dam and the Fate of China's Yangtze River and Its People.* M. E. Sharpe, 1998.

————. *Yangtze! Yangtze!* Probe International, 1993.

Day, Kristen A. (ed.). *China's Environment and the Challenge of Sustainable Development.* M. E. Sharpe, 2005.

Dharmadhikary, Shripad. *Mountains of Concrete.* International Rivers, 2009.

Diamond, Jared. *Guns, Germs, and Steel: The Fates of Human Societies.* W. W. Norton, 1997.

Du Bin. *The Petitioner: Living Fossil Under Chinese Rule by Law.* Ming Bao, 2007.

Economy, Elizabeth. *The River Runs Black: The Environmental Challenge to China's Future.* Cornell University Press, 2004.

Edmonds, Richard Louis (ed.). *Managing the Chinese Environment.* Oxford University Press, 1998.

Elvin, Mark. *Retreat of the Elephants: An Environmental History of China.* Yale University Press, 2004.

Feng Yongfeng. *Meiyou Dashu de Guajia* (A Country Without Big Trees). China Law Press, 2008.

French, Patrick. *Younghusband: The Last Great Imperial Adventurer.* HarperCollins, 1994.

Friedman, Thomas. *Hot, Flat, and Crowded: Why We Need a Green Revolution— and How It Can Renew America.* Allen Lane, 2008.

Fritz, Jack, et al. National Research Council (US), China Academy of Science. *Urbanization, Energy, and Air Pollution in China: The Challenges Ahead.* National Academies Press, 2004.

Gifford, Rob. *China Road: A Journey into the Future of a Rising Power.* Random House, 2007.

Gittings, John. *The Changing Face of China: From Mao to Market.* Oxford University Press, 2005.

Gore, Al. *The Assault on Reason.* Penguin, 2007.

Guo Kai and Li Ling. *How Tibet's Water Will Save China.* Changan Publishing House, 2005.

Hare, John. *The Lost Camels of Tartary: A Quest into Forbidden China.* Abacus, 1998.

Harney, Alexandra. *The China Price: The True Cost of Chinese Competitive Advantage.* Penguin, 2008.

Harris, Richard B. *Wildlife Conservation in China: Preserving the Habitat of China's Wild West.* East Gate, 2008.

He Jianming. *Jingcai Wu Renbao.* Shandong Wenyi Publishing House, 2007.

He Qinglian. *The Fog of Censorship: Media Control in China.* Human Rights in China, 2008.

Hessler, Peter. *Oracle Bones.* Harper Perennial, 2006.

———. *River Town: Two Years on the Yangtze.* HarperCollins, 2001.

Hewitt, Duncan. *Getting Rich First: Life in a Changing China.* Chatto & Windus, 2007.

Hilton, James. *Lost Horizon.* Macmillan, 1933.

Hughes, Donald. *An Environmental History of the World: Humankind's Changing Role in the Community of Life.* Routledge, 2001.

Hutton, Will. *The Writing on the Wall: China and the West in the 21st Century.* Abacus, 2007

Hyun, In-taek, and Miranda Alice Schreurs (eds.). *The Environmental Dimension of Asian Security.* United States Institute of Peace Press, 2007.

Jiang Rong. *Wolf Totem.* Penguin, 2008.

Kam Wing Chan, Cai Fang, and Du Yang. *The China Population and Labor Yearbook,* vol. 1: *The Approaching Lewis Turning Point and Its Policy Implications.* Brill, 2009.

Kipling, Rudyard. *From Sea to Sea: Letters of Travel.* Cosimo, 2006 (first published 1889).

Kolas, Ashild. *Tourism and Tibetan Culture in Transition: A Place Called Shangrila.* Routledge, 2007.

Kynge, James. *China Shakes the World: A Titan's Rise and Troubled Future—and the Challenge for America.* Houghton Mifflin, 2006.

Lee, James, and Wang Feng. *One Quarter of Humanity: Malthusian Mythology and Chinese Realities, 1700–2000.* Harvard University Press, 2001.

Leonard, Mark. *What Does China Think?* HarperCollins, 2008.

Lewis, Mark Edward. *The Flood Myths of Early China.* SUNY Press, 2006.

Lindert, Peter. *Shifting Ground: The Changing Agricultural Soils of China and Indonesia.* MIT Press, 2000.

Lindesay, William. *Alone on the Great Wall.* Fulcrum, 1991.

Liu, Warren. *KFC in China: Secret Recipe for Success.* Wiley, 2008.

Lonely Planet. *China.* Lonely Planet Travel Guides, various years.

Lynch, Michael. *Mao.* Routledge, 2006.

Lynn, Madeleine. *Yangtze River: The Wildest Wickedest River on Earth.* Oxford University Press, 2007.

Ma Jun. *China's Water Crisis.* Eastbridge, 2004.

MacKinnon, John, and Wang Haibin. *The Green Gold of China.* EU–China Biodiversity Programme, 2008.

MacKinnon, John, et al. *A Biodiversity Review of China.* WWF International, 1996.

Malthus, Thomas. *An Essay on the Principle of Population.* 1798.

Man, John. *The Terracotta Army: China's First Emperor and the Birth of a Nation.* Bantam, 2007.

———. *Xanadu.* Bantam, 2009.

Mars, Neville, and Adrian Hornsby (eds.). *The Chinese Dream: A Society under Construction.* 010 Publishers, 2008.

McNeill, J. R. *Something New Under the Sun: An Environmental History of the Twentieth-Century World.* W. W. Norton, 2001.

McRae, Michael. *The Siege of Shangri-La: The Quest for Tibet's Legendary Hidden Paradise.* Broadway Books, 2002.

Mertha, Andrew. *China's Water Warriors: Citizen Action and Policy Change.* Cornell University Press, 2008.

Mills, Scott. *Conservation of Wildlife Populations.* Blackwell, 2007.

Millward, James. *Eurasian Crossroads: A History of Xinjiang.* Columbia University Press, 2006.

Mitchell, Stephen. *Tao Te Ching, A New English Version.* HarperPerennial, 1988.

Mun Ho and Chris Nielsen. *Clearing the Air: The Health and Economic Damages of Air Pollution in China.* MIT Press, 2007.

National Statistical Yearbook. China National Bureau of Statistics, 2002, 2003, 2004, 2005, 2006, 2007.

Naughton, Barry. *The Chinese Economy: Transitions and Growth.* MIT Press, 2007.

Navarro, Peter. *The Coming China Wars.* FT Press, 2008.

Palmer, Martin, and Elizabeth Breuilly (trans.). *The Book of Chuang Tzu.* Penguin, 1996.

Pan, Philip. *Out of Mao's Shadow: The Struggle for the Soul of a New China*. Picador Asia, 2008.

Patten, Chris. *East and West*. Macmillan, 1998.

———. *What Next? Surviving the Twenty-first Century*. Penguin, 2008.

Pirsig, Robert M. *Zen and the Art of Motorcycle Maintenance: An Inquiry into Values*. Harper, 1999 (first published 1974).

Pomfret, John. *Chinese Lesson: Five Classmates and the Story of the New China*. Henry Holt, 2006.

Ponting, Clive. *A New Green History of the World*. Penguin, 2007.

Qu Geping and Li Jinchang. *Population and the Environment in China*. Lynne Rienner, 1994.

Ramo, Joshua Cooper. *The Beijing Consensus*. The Foreign Policy Centre, 2004.

Rittenberg, Sidney. *The Man Who Stayed Behind*. Simon & Schuster, 1993.

Roberts, J. Timmons, and Bradley C. Parks. *A Climate of Injustice: Global Inequality, North-South Politics, and Climate Policy*. MIT Press, 2006.

Rough Guide to China. Rough Guide Travel Guides. Various years.

Sachs, Jeffrey. *Common Wealth: Economics for a Crowded Planet*. Penguin, 2008.

Sage, Steven. *Ancient Sichuan and the Unification of China*. SUNY Press, 1992.

Said, Edward. *Orientalism*. Vintage Books, 1979.

Shapiro, Judith. *Mao's War Against Nature*. Cambridge University Press, 2001.

Short, Philip. *Mao: A Life*. John Murray, 2004.

Smil, Vaclav. *Global Catastrophes and Trends: The Next Fifty Years*. MIT Press, 2008.

Smith, Adam. *An Inquiry into the Nature and Causes of the Wealth of Nations*. 1776.

Song Ligang and Wing Thye Woo (eds.). *China's Dilemma: Economic Growth, the Environment and Climate Change*. Brookings, 2008.

Spence, Jonathan. *The Memory Palace of Matteo Ricci*. Penguin, 1984.

———. *The Search for Modern China*. W. W. Norton, 1990.

Starr, Frederick. *Xinjiang: China's Muslim Borderland*. M. E. Sharpe, 2004.

Studwell, Joe. *The China Dream: The Quest for the Last Great Untapped Market on Earth*. Atlantic Monthly Press, 2002.

Tang Xiyang and Marcia Marks. *A Green World Tour*. New World Press, 1999.

Theroux, Paul. *Riding the Iron Rooster: By Train Through China*. Houghton Mifflin Harcourt, 2006.

Tibet Information Network. *Mining Tibet: Mineral Exploitation in Tibetan Areas of the PRC*. TIN, 2002.

Tsai, Kellee S. *Capitalism Without Democracy, The Private Sector in Contemporary China*. Cornell University Press, 2007.

Tyler, Christian. *Wild West China: The Untold Story of a Frontier Land.* John Murray, 2003.

Wang Jiawei. *The Historical Status of China's Tibet.* Nationalities Press, 1995.

Wang Sung and Xie Yan. *China Species Red List.* Biodiversity Working Group of China, Council for International Cooperation on Environment and Development, 2004.

Watts, Alan W. *The Joyous Cosmology: Adventures in the Chemistry of Consciousness.* Vintage, 1965.

Wei Yiming et al. *China Energy Report (2008): CO_2 Emissions Research.* Science Press, 2008.

Weller, Robert P. *Discovering Nature: Globalization and Environmental Culture in China and Taiwan.* Cambridge University Press, 2006.

Williams, Dee Mack. *Beyond Great Walls: Environment, Identity, and Development on the Chinese Grasslands of Inner Mongolia.* Stanford University Press, 2002.

Wilson, E. O. *The Diversity of Life.* Harvard University Press, 1992.

Wittfogel, Karl. *Oriental Despotism.* Vintage, 1957.

Wu Xiaoyu. *Coal History Review.* China Coal Industry Publishing House, 2000.

Yan Lianke. *The Dream of Ding Village.* Shanghai Literary Arts, 2006.

———. *Serve the People.* Constable, 2007.

Yang Jisheng. *Mubei: Zhongguo 60 Niandai Dajihuang Jishi* (Tombstone: A History of the Great Leap Forward). Cosmos Books, 2008.

Yang Keming. *Entrepreneurship in China.* Ashgate, 2007.

Younghusband, Francis E. *Among the Celestials.* Elibron Classics, 2005 (first published 1898).

Yu Kongjian and Mary Padua (eds.). *The Art of Survival: Recovering Landscape Architecture.* Images, 2006.

Zhang, Andy. *Hu Jintao: Facing China's Challenges Ahead.* iUniverse, 2002.

Zhang, Lijia. *"Socialism Is Great!" A Worker's Memoir of the New China.* Atlas, 2008.

Zhuangzi, Wang Rongpei (trans.). *Library of Chinese Classics,* vol. 2. Hunan People's Publishing House, 1999.

Reports, presentations, and academic papers

Asia Development Bank, Proposed Loan and Technical Assistance Grant, People's Republic of China: Henan Sustainable Agriculture and Productivity Improvement Project, Project Number 38662. November 2007.

Attané, Isabelle. "China's Family Planning Policy: An Overview of Its Past and Future." *Studies in Family Planning* 33, 1 (2002): 103–13.

Attané, Isabelle, and Christophe Z. Guilmoto (eds.). *Watering the Neighbour's Garden: The Growing Demographic Female Deficit in Asia.* Committee for International Cooperation in National Research in Demography, www .cicred.org, 2007.

Baker, B. B., and R. K. Moseley. "Advancing Treeline and Retreating Glaciers: Implications for Conservation in Yunnan, P.R. China." *Arctic, Antarctic and Alpine Research* 39, 2 (2007): 200–209.

Ball, Philip. "Where Have All the Flowers Gone?" *Nature,* July 24, 2008.

Banister, Judith. "Population, Public Health and the Environment in China," in Richard Louis Edmonds (ed.), *Managing the Chinese Environment.* Oxford University Press, 1998, pp. 262–91.

Bequelin, Nicholas. "Xinjiang in the Nineties." *China Journal* 44 (2000): 65–90.

Bossard, Peter. "China's Role in Financing African Infrastructure," www.international rivers.org, May 14, 2007.

———. "Sichuan Earthquake a Dam-Induced Disaster?" www.internationalrivers .org, February 5, 2009.

Bossen, Laurel. "Missing Girls, Land and Population Controls in Rural China," in Isabelle Attané and Christophe Z. Guilmoto (eds.), *Watering the Neigh-bour's Garden: The Growing Demographic Female Deficit in Asia.* Commit-tee for International Cooperation in National Research in Demography, www.cicred.org, 2007.

Brown, Lester. *Vital Signs 2005.* Worldwatch Institute, 2005.

Butler, Declan. "The Great Contender." *Nature,* July 24, 2008.

Cann, Cynthia W., Michael C. Cann, and Gao Shangquan. "China's Road to Sus-tainable Development: An Overview," in Kristen Day (ed.), *China's Envi-ronment and the Challenge of Sustainable Development.* M. E. Sharpe, 2005, pp. 3–35.

Chenoweth, Jonathan. "Looming Water Crisis Simply a Management Problem." *New Scientist,* August 20, 2008.

Cherry, Chris. *China's Urban Transportation System: Issues and Policies Facing Cit-ies.* Institute of Transportation Studies, University of California, Berkeley, 2005.

Cohen, Joel. "Human Population Grows Up." *Scientific American,* September 2005.

Cyranoski, David. "Putting China's Wetlands on the Map." *Nature,* March 11, 2009.

———. "Visions of China," *Nature,* July 24, 2008.

Dai Qing (ed.). *Beijing's Water Crisis 1949–2008 Olympics*. Probe International, 2008.

Deng Xiangzheng, Huang Jikun, Scott Rozelle, and Emi Uchida. "Cultivated Land Conversion and Potential Agricultural Productivity in China." China Academy of Sciences, July 2005.

Dikotter, Frank. "The Limits of Benevolence: Wang Shiduo (1802–1889) and Population Control." *Bulletin of the School of Oriental and African Studies* 55, 1 (1992).

Economy, Elizabeth. "The Great Leap Backward?" *Foreign Affairs* 86, 5 (September/October 2007).

Elvin, Mark. "The Environmental Legacy of Imperial China," in Richard Louis Edmonds (ed.), *Managing the Chinese Environment*. Oxford University Press, 1998, pp. 9–32.

Figueres, Christiana. "The Ethics of Global Climate Change." Center for Sustainable Development in the Americas, April 2000.

Forest Trends. "China and the Global Market for Forest Products," www.forest-trends.org, March 2006.

Kleinn, Christoph, Yang Yongping, Horst Weyerhäuser, and Marco Stark. "The Sustainable Harvest of Non-Timber Forest Products in China: Strategies to Balance Economic Benefits and Biodiversity Conservation." Sino-German Center for Research Promotion, 2006.

Lee, K. S., M. W. N. Lau, and B. P. L. Chan. *Wild Animal Trade Monitoring at Selected Markets in Guangzhou and Shenzhen, Southern China, 2000–2003*. Kadoorie Farm and Botanic Garden, Hong Kong, 2004.

Leliaert, Frederik, Zhang Xiaowen, et al. "Identity of the Qingdao Algal Bloom." *Phycological Research* 57 (2009): 147–51.

Lewis, Nathan. "Powering the Planet." California Institute of Technology, 2007.

Li Guoying. "Keep Healthy Life of Rivers: A Case Study of the Yellow River." Yellow River Conservancy Commission.

Li Junfeng. "China's Wind Power Development Exceeds Expectations." Worldwatch Institute, www.worldwatch.org, June 2, 2008.

Li Zijun. "Soil Quality Deteriorating in China, Threatening Public Health and Ecosystems." Worldwatch Institute, www.worldwatch.org, July 27 and September 7, 2006.

Lin Erda et al. "Investigating the Impacts of Climate Change on Chinese Agriculture." China-UK Collaborative Project, www.dfid.gov.uk, 2008.

Liu Xiaoyan, Zhou Jianbo, and Yu Songlin. "Practice of Water Regulation on the Yellow River." Yellow River Conservancy Commission Paper.

Logan, Graham A., J. M. Hayes, Glenn B. Hieshima, and Roger E. Summons. "Terminal Proterozoic Reorganization of Biogeochemical Cycles." *Nature,* July 6, 2002.

Ma Jun. "Overexploitation of Southwestern Hydropower Unhelpful to China's Energy Conservation and Pollution Control." Reform and Opening-up Study Series: Poverty Reduction and Sustainable Development in Western China. Social Sciences Academic Press (China), December 2008.

Ma Tianjie. "Environmental Mass Incidents in Rural China," *China Environment Series* 10 (2008–2009). Woodrow Wilson International Center for Scholars.

Mao Yushi, Sheng Hong, and Yang Fuqiang. "True Cost of Coal." Greenpeace, the Energy Foundation, and WWF, October 27, 2008.

Martin, Ronald. "Secular Increase in Nutrient Levels through the Phanerozoic: Implications for Productivity, Biomass, and Diversity of the Marine Biosphere." *Palaios* 11, 3 (1996): 209–19.

McKinsey & Co. "The Coming of Age: China's New Class of Wealthy Consumers." www.mckinsey.com, 2009.

Ministry of Science and Technology, China Meteorology Administration, and the Chinese Academy of Sciences. *First National Climate Change Assessment.* 2006.

Moseley, Robert. "Historical Landscape Change in Northwestern Yunnan, China: Using Repeat Photography to Assess the Perceptions and Realities of Biodiversity Loss." *Mountain Research and Development* 26, 3 (August 2006): 214–19.

Moseley, Robert K., and Tang Ya. "Vegetation Dynamics in the Dry Valleys of Northwestern Yunnan, China During the Last 150 Years: Implications for Ecological Restoration." *Journal of Planet Ecology* 30, 5 (2006): 713–22.

Müller, Benito, Niklas Höhne, and Christian Ellermann. "Differentiating (Historic) Responsibilities for Climate Change." Oxford Institute for Energy Studies. www.oxfordclimatepolicy.org, 2008.

NASA Earth Observatory. "Dust Storm Over East Asia." http://earthobservatory.nasa.gov, March 2008.

Ni Honggang and Eddy Zeng. "Law Enforcement and Global Collaboration Are the Keys to Containing E-Waste Tsunami in China." *Environmental Science and Technology Viewpoint* 43 (2009): 3991–94.

Nickum, James. "Water Management: It's the Economics, Stupid." *China Economic Quarterly,* June 2009.

Ochirkhuyag, L., and R. Tsolmon. "Monitoring the Source of Transnational Dust Storms in Northeast Asia." Wildlife Conservation Society Mongolia Program and National University of Mongolia, School of Physics-Electronics. *International Archives of the Photogrammetry, Remote Sensing and Spatial Information Sciences* (Beijing) 37 (2008).

Oldfield, Philip, and Antony Wood. "2008 a Bumper Year for Skyscrapers, Although the Future Remains Uncertain." Council on Tall Buildings and Urban Habitat. www.ctbuh.org, January 26, 2009.

Olympic press conference transcripts. Wang Sumei (vice director of the Beijing Landscape Forestation Bureau) and Qiang Jian (vice director general of the Beijing Landscape Forestation Bureau). "Landscape and Forestry of Beijing." Official website of the Beijing 2008 Olympic Games. July 7, 2008. http://en.beijing2008.cn.

Organisation for Economic Cooperation and Development. "Integrating Biodiversity Concerns into the Forestry Sector." In *OECD Environmental Performance Reviews: China 2007,* OECD, 2007.

Pew Center on Global Climate Change, with the Asia Society. "Common Challenge, Collaborative Response: A Roadmap for U.S.-China Cooperation on Energy and Climate Change." January 2009. www.pewclimate.org.

Pickles, Michael. "Implementing Ecologically Sustainable Development in China: The Example of Heilongjiang Province." *Georgetown International Environmental Law Review,* April 1, 2002.

Pomeranz, Kenneth. "The Great Himalayan Watershed: Agrarian Crisis, Mega-Dams and the Environment." *New Left Review* 58 (July/August 2009).

Samuelsson, Fredrik. "The Potential for Quality Production in Birch Stands in North-Eastern China Using Different Precommercial Thinning Strategies." MSc thesis, Southern Swedish Forest Research Center, June 2006.

Sayle, Murray. "Overloading Emoh Ruo: The Rise and Rise of Hydrocarbon Civilisation." *Griffith Review* 12: *Hot Air: How Nigh's the End?* Griffith University, 2006.

Sayer, Jeffrey A., and Changjin Sun. "Impacts of Policy Reforms on Forestry Environments and Biodiversity," in William F. Hyde, Brian Belcher, and Jintao Xu (eds.). *China's Forests: Global Lessons from Market Reforms.* Resources for the Future, 2003, pp. 177–94.

Shieh, Shawn. "China's Quiet Activists." *YaleGlobal,* February 25, 2009. http://yaleglobal.yale.edu.

Song Weiming, Chen Baodong, Zhang Shengdong, and Meng Xianggang. "Russian Logs in China: The Softwood Commodity Chain and Economic Development in China." Beijing Forestry University, Forest Trends and Rights and Resources, www.forest-trends.org, 2007

Steinfeld, Edward. "MIT Report Debunks China Energy Myth." *MIT News,* October 7, 2008. web.mit.edu/newsoffice/2008/china-energy-1006.html, 7 October 2008.

Steinfeld, Edward S., Richard K. Lester, and Edward A. Cunningham. "Greener Plants, Grayer Skies? A Report from the Front Lines of China's Energy Sector." China Energy Group, MIT Industrial Performance Center, August 2008.

Taiga Rescue Network and Friends of the Earth Japan. "Plundering Russia's Far Eastern Taiga." 2000. www.taigarescue.org.

United Nations Department of Economic and Social Affairs. "City Dwellers Set to Surpass Rural Inhabitants in 2008." *DESA News* 12, 2 (February 2008).

Wang Tao. "Combating Desertification in the Drylands of China, Key Laboratory of Desert and Desertification." Cold and Arid Regions Environmental and Engineering Research Institute, Chinese Academy of Sciences.

———. "The Development Process of Aeolian Desertification in Typical Areas of Northern China During Last 50 Years." Key Laboratory of Desert and Desertification, Cold and Arid Regions Environmental and Engineering Research Institute, Chinese Academy of Sciences, 2008.

Wang Tao and Lihua Zhou. "Aeolian Desertification in China: Human Activity and State Policy Analysis. Key Laboratory of Desert and Desertification, Cold and Arid Regions Environmental and Engineering Research Institute, Chinese Academy of Sciences, November 6, 2006.

Wei Wanjun. "Current Issues of China's Coal Industry: The Case of Shanxi." Paper presented at the 15th Annual Conference of the Association for Chinese Economic Studies. Melbourne, Australia, October 2–3, 2003.

Winkler, Daniel. "Yartsa Gunbu (*Cordyceps sinensis*) and the Fungal Commodification of the Rural Economy in Tibet AR." *Economic Botany* 62, 3 (2008): 291–305.

World Bank. "Mid-Term Evaluation of China's 11th Five Year Plan." December 18, 2008.

World Bank and State Environmental Protection Agency (PR China). *Cost of Pollution in China: Economic Estimates of Physical Damages.* 2007.

World Wide Fund for Nature. "Living Planet Report 2008." www.panda.org.

————. "China-Africa Timber Trade: The State of Wildlife Trade in China: Information on the Trade in Wild Animals and Plants in China 2007." www.panda.org.

————. "Timber Trade in China: The State of Wildlife Trade in China: Information on the Trade in Wild Animals and Plants in China 2006." www.panda.org.

World Wide Fund for Nature Global Forest and Trade Network. "Illegal Logging in the Southern Part of the Russian Far East 2002." www.wwf.ru/resources/publ/book/eng/13/.

Xiao Jun and Zhu Qiang. "A Bold Attempt to Change Human Behavior to the Environment—Case Study of the China-Sweden Erdos Eco-town Project, Sustainable Sanitation Alliance." www.susana.org/lang-en/publications/publication-database/topic-wg/wg02, 2008.

Xu Jianchu and Jesse Ribot. "Decentralisation and Accountability in Forest Management: A Case from Yunnan, Southwest China." *European Journal of Development Research* 16, 1 (spring 2004): 153–73.

Xu Jianchu and Andreas Wilkes. "Biodiversity Impact Analysis in Northwest Yunnan, Southwest China." *Biodiversity and Conservation* 13, 5 (2004): 959–83.

Yuming Yang, Kun Tian, Jiming Hao, Shengji Pei, and Yongxing Yang. "Biodiversity and Biodiversity Conservation in Yunnan, China." *Biodiversity and Conservation* 13, 4 (2004): 813–26.

Yunnan Provincial Environment Protection Bureau and Project Secretariat. UNEP Regional Resource Center for Asia and the Pacific, Yunnan Province. PR China Case Studies. *Environmental Management in Chengjiang and Jinggu Counties.* March 2006.

Zhao Jianping and David Creedy. "Economically, Socially and Environmentally Sustainable Coal Mining Sector in China." The World Bank, China Coal Information Institute, Energy Sector Management Assistance Program, December 2008.

Index